THE JAMES SPRUNT STUDIES IN HISTORY AND POLITICAL SCIENCE

*Published under the Direction of
the Departments of History and Political Science
of the University of North Carolina*

VOLUME 26
NUMBER 1

Editors

ALBERT RAY NEWSOME
WILLIAM WHATLEY PIERSON
MITCHELL B. GARRETT
FLETCHER M. GREEN
KEENER C. FRAZER

THE PROHIBITION MOVEMENT IN ALABAMA, 1702 TO 1943

By

JAMES BENSON SELLERS, Ph.D.
Department of History
University of Alabama

CHAPEL HILL

THE UNIVERSITY OF NORTH CAROLINA PRESS
1943

ACKNOWLEDGMENTS

I wish to thank all who have assisted me in bringing this study to fruition. To Dr. Fletcher M. Green and Dr. A. R. Newsome of the University of North Carolina I am deeply grateful for reading the manuscript and for their valuable constructive criticisms. Others to whom I am indebted for their assistance are Mrs. M. B. Owen and her staff, especially Miss Frances Hails, of the Alabama Department of Archives and History, for placing much valuable material at my disposal. Messrs. Travis Williams and Allen Morton of the Alabama Supreme Court Library, Montgomery, Alabama, gave me access to the Acts of the Alabama legislature and the Supreme Court reports. The Honorable Edward Goodrich and the Honorable T. S. Woodroof, both of Athens, Alabama, accorded me the use of their law libraries. Birmingham-Southern College Library and the Howard College Library permitted me to use their church records. The Birmingham Public Library granted me the privilege of using its newspaper files. Reverend W. Earl Hotalen, Executive Secretary of the Alabama Temperance Alliance, gave valuable assistance. The Temperance Board of the North Alabama Conference also granted some aid. Reverend F. L. Aldridge of Hartselle, Alabama, allowed me to use his church records. Miss Geneva Hall, former librarian of Athens College, Athens, Alabama, was untiring in her efforts to assemble material. Judge A. M. McConnell and Mr. Roy Malone of the probate office, and Mr. George Sherrill, Register in Chancery, all at the county courthouse, Athens, Alabama, gave me unlimited use of their records. Dr. T. L. Spence, Curator, Montreat, N. C., furnished me with material concerning the Presbyterian Church in Alabama. Honorable John J. Sparkman, M. C. from the Eighth Congressional District of Alabama, obtained data for me from the U. S. Commissioner of Internal Revenue. Mr. Howell Turner, State Auditor, Montgomery, Alabama, provided me with Reports of the State Board of Administration. Mrs. J. S. Hamilton and Mrs. S. T. Slaton, both of Birmingham, Alabama, loaned me Minutes of the Alabama W.C.T.U. Dr. L. L. Gwaltney, editor of the *Alabama Baptist*, let me have access to the files of his paper. Mrs. R. S. Van de Woestyne of Chicago, Illinois, read the manuscript and offered suggestions for condensation. Dr. T. P. Chalker, Dean of Athens College, has read the manuscript and made valuable suggestions. Carrie Autrey Sellers, my wife, has given her assistance in the whole undertaking.

CONTENTS

CHAPTER	PAGE
ACKNOWLEDGMENTS	v
I. Efforts to Regulate the Liquor Traffic in Alabama Prior to Statehood, 1702-1819	1
II. Temperance Movement, 1819-1861	14
III. Legal Restrictions and the Reawakening of the Temperance Forces, 1861-1880	40
IV. Political Aspects of the Temperance Movement, 1880-1898	52
V. The Alabama Dispensary System, 1898-1908	86
VI. Local Option and State-Wide Prohibition, 1904-1909	101
VII. The Constitutional Prohibition Election of 1909	129
VIII. Reaction and Return to County Local Option, 1910-1915	149
IX. Return to State-Wide Prohibition, 1915-1920	176
X. Alabama Under the Eighteenth Amendment, 1920-1933	190
XI. Movement to Repeal the Eighteenth Amendment, 1922-1933	213
XII. Referendum and Return to Local Option	232
XIII. The State Liquor Store System, 1937-1943	260
SUMMARY	290
BIBLIOGRAPHY	294
INDEX	305

THE PROHIBITION MOVEMENT
IN ALABAMA, 1702 TO 1943

CHAPTER I

EFFORTS TO REGULATE THE LIQUOR TRAFFIC IN ALABAMA PRIOR TO STATEHOOD, 1702-1819

When General James Wilkinson, upon the authorization of President James Madison, took Mobile from the Spanish in 1813, the last trace of European control was removed from the area which was to become, in 1817, Alabama Territory and in 1819, the State of Alabama. Prior to that time, France, England, and Spain had controlled parts of that area. And each colonial government had found it necessary to devise ways and means of handling the problem of liquor control. Records of Spanish regulations are meager, but both France and England have left documents which are of great value to the historian, for the roots of the movement which was to become a determined and powerful drive for state prohibition in Alabama, reach back into colonial times and colonial regulations.

That part of Alabama which is known today as Mobile County was settled by the French in 1702 and held by them for sixty-one years.

The French were drinkers of wine. To colonial Mobile they imported from the mother country the beverages which were to them almost necessities of life—red wine, white wine, brandy.[1] Large quantities of wine must have been used by civilian colonists;[2] large quantities were also issued to French soldiers as part of their regular rations. "Not enough brandy has been sent for the wounded and for the sick," wrote Sieur Hubert from Dauphin Island to the superior council of Louisiana on October 26, 1717. And he complained also that "soldiers on detachments during their journeys" and "crews of the flat-boats" needed brandy "instead of wine which spoils in hot weather."[3] An indication of the quantity considered adequate for rations is given in the schedule of prices that officers should pay for various items of subsistence issued by the administrative council on June 21, 1724. Each "captain, lieutenant, second lieutenant, and ensign" was, by that ruling, entitled to "fifty *pots* of brandy per year at the rate of fifty *sous* a *pot*."[4] Inadequacy of supply was often a problem. Jean Baptiste Le Moyne Bienville, writing to Jean Frédéric Phelippeaux Maurepas on May 18, 1733, complained that the price of wine was so high in the province

---

[1] In some instances, cognac and champagne were issued to French army officers, but never in large quantities.

[2] Data covering the number of gallons imported are not available, but from the frequent references to wine in the "Letters of Bienville" and other officials, large quantities of it must have been shipped into Mobile. D. Rowland and A. G. Sanders, *Mississippi Provincial Archives, 1704-1748*, III, 258-259.

[3] *Ibid.*, II, 240.

[4] *Ibid.*, 418-419. *Petit Larousse Illustré:* a *sou* is equal to one cent; a *pot* is equal to one quart.

of Louisiana that three fourths of the officers were obliged to drink water, which, as everyone knew, "impairs the health considerably in hot climates." He suggested that "several hogsheads of wine" be sent over for use of the officers "at an advance of one hundred *per cent* above the price in France."[5]

The Western Company of Louisiana[6] furnished the liquor consumed in French colonial Mobile but the superior council of Louisiana regulated the conditions of its distribution and use. Canteens and dram-shops, through which wine was sold to soldiers and citizens, were directly controlled by the Western Company. "By order of the Commandants Messrs. de Bienville, de Villardeau, and Teague, general directors of the Western Company of Louisiana," a permit was issued in 1719 authorizing "the man named Couturier to keep a canteen at Mobile for the account of the company." This permit fixed prices for brandy, red wine, and white wine. A canteen on Dauphin Island was similarly authorized.[7]

Exorbitant prices were an early concern of the Company. As early as 1706 there was a liquor shop in the province of Louisiana. Bienville was said to be the owner, but the shop was not run under his name.[8] Here wine was sold at 200 *piastres* a cask, and that price held until 1712. Then Governor Antoine de Lamothe Cadillac assured the crown that such enormous profits would not be made under the new regime. His promise bore small fruit, for by the end of 1713 Antoine Crozat's agents in the province were themselves selling wine at 320 *livres* a cask and their prices for small quantities were set at four *reaux* per *pot* for red wine, three for white wine, and four *livres* per *pot* for brandy. In 1714 brandy, red wine, and white wine were selling at retail for three *livres*, thirty *sols*, and twenty *sols* a *pot* respectively.[9] These prices were made the legal rates in the province in 1719, but the trade continued unstable. A turning point came in 1721 when the Company itself reduced the price of wine and brandy at Mobile to 120 *livres* a cask. By the end of 1726 wine was down to twenty *sols* a *pot* and brandy to three *livres* and five *sols*.[10] The evils of excessive drinking also received some attention from the French governors. On October 6, 1726, the superior council enacted a law which provided for the closing of all dram-shops on Sunday during the time of religious services. Other restrictive laws followed. One, enacted March 29, 1727, made it illegal to sell ardent spirits to slaves or even to trust them with intoxicants to be delivered to their masters without the presentation of a written order.[11] An ordinance of December 19, 1733, made it illegal for anyone to sell wine,

[5] Rowland and Sanders, *op. cit.*, III, 260.
[6] The liquor business of Louisiana had many representatives most of whom were doing well, as was the case in many frontier communities.
[7] Rowland and Sanders, *op. cit.*, III, 259-260.
[8] N. M. M. Surrey, *The Commerce of Louisiana During the French Regime, 1699-1783*, p. 273.
[9] Surrey, *op. cit.*, p. 273. *Petit Larousse Illustré:* a *piastre* equals 1 dollar; a cask equals 1,000 kilograms; a *livre* equals 20 cents; a *real* (plural *reaux*) equals 5 cents; a *sol* equals 1 cent.
[10] Surrey, *op. cit.*, pp. 274-275.   [11] Surrey, *op. cit.*, p. 274.

brandy, or other liquors by the pint, *pot*, or cup without first having secured a license from the office of the "ordonnateur."[12] Penalty for violation of this ordinance was set at fifty *livres* and the confiscation of the liquor stock of the offender.[13] On December 7, 1736, the "ordonnateur" declared it illegal to sell to slaves without the direct permission of their masters.[14]

Control of the Mobile area passed from French to British hands in 1763,[15] and the regulation of the liquor traffic there, as well as of other colonial affairs, was assumed by the British West Florida Assembly. This Assembly had its headquarters at Pensacola, but it sometimes held meetings at Mobile.[16] British policy in regard to the sale and consumption of liquors in the colonies under British control was, in general, not very well defined. In British West Florida, however, regulation was used to some rather specific purposes and shows consistent direction.[17]

Like the French, the British in Colonial Mobile were dependent upon imported liquors and required a considerable supply to meet their needs.[18] Some of the higher class colonists had a taste for Portuguese and Spanish wines. The lower classes drank "that bane of health and happiness," New England rum. But the standard drink of the English settler was, according to Bernard Romans, water tempered with a moderate quantity of West Indian rum. Social events and holidays called for special beverages. "Yesterday being New Year's day, the gentlemen of the settlement dined with me and celebrated the day with mirth and good humor," wrote William Dunbar, "our spirits being elevated by the moderate use of good Madeira and Claret."[19]

To the French idea of price regulation and the prevention of the abuses of strong drink, the British added one new and important principle, that of licensing for revenue. The first act placing a duty on intoxicants was passed in 1766.[20] Its purpose was to supplement "the Sum Granted by

---

[12] An official who gives orders.   [13] Surrey, *op. cit.*, pp. 274-275.
[14] *Ibid.*, p. 276. Lack of enforcement defeated this law.
[15] In this new political division, Mobile was in Charlotte County.
[16] Governor Peter Chester wrote to Lord George Germain "that the Gentlemen of influence at Mobile did not want an assembly for fear that it would pass an act regulating the Indian trade,—such an act would restrain their traders from taking profuse quantities of rum into the Indian nation." P. J. Hamilton, *Colonial Mobile*, p. 245.
[17] John Allen Krout says: "If there is any basic element present, it is a confused idea, perhaps a by-product of the existing mercantile theory, that some sort of regulation is better than none." J. A. Krout, *The Origins of Prohibition*, pp. 16-17.
[18] Data concerning the number of gallons imported are not available, but since rum was an important commodity in the economic life of the colonies, large quantities were probably shipped into Mobile. D. A. Wells, "Influence of Rum and Whiskey on the Commercial Life of the Colonies," *Princeton Review*, March, 1884.
[19] B. Romans, *Concise Natural History of East and West Florida*, p. 116; D. Rowland, *Life, Letters, and Papers of William Dunbar*, pp. 56-57.
[20] According to this act, a duty of three pence per gallon was imposed on rum, brandy, and any other distilled liquors imported into the province. Masters of vessels importing distilled liquors into the province of West Florida were required to

Parliament for supporting the Civil Government of the Province."[21] Similar acts were passed in 1768 and 1770, and the practice of imposing liquor duties for revenue to meet contingent government expenses was quite well established.[22]

To the British also belongs the credit for the first use of the license as a check upon liquor consumption. In 1764 the Council resolved that not more than three retailers should be licensed to sell spirituous liquors in Pensacola, and not more than four in Mobile.[23] Two years later, the Assembly of West Florida enacted a law to regulate the sale of alcoholic liquors at taverns, public houses, and tippling houses.[24] In that same year the provisions of 1764 regarding the limiting of licenses were extended. Applicants for retail licenses must bring to the governor "a Recommendation from the justices at the Quarter Session of the Peace for the District where such Person or Persons may reside." A limit of three licenses for Mobile was set. Moreover, no tradesman able to pursue his trade was eligible for a license; skilled workers were too scarce in West Florida.

A fine of "Ten Pounds Sterling" was set for violations of this law, and the license fee was put at the same figure. This fee was to be "paid into the Hands of the Church Wardens," who were required to give security to the amount of two hundred pounds sterling, and "to be accountable to the Justices and Vestry of the District where they reside for all such moneys as they shall receive by virtue of this Act." The Justices in Quarter Session were to determine the disposition of this money.[25]

Provisions of this law were repeated and strengthened in 1771, when the Assembly passed "An Act for the better regulation of Taverns and Public Houses." By this act licenses were required for the sale of liquors

---

report to the Receiver General's office within forty-eight hours after their arrival and obtain permission to land the said liquors. For violating this provision of the law, a fine of two pounds sterling was imposed upon the offender.

[21] "Transcript Records of the British West Florida Assembly," December 22, 1766. (Alabama Department of Archives and History.)

[22] In addition to the use for contingent government expenses, the liquor tax went for the purpose of building and maintaining roads. Pursuant to an act of December 10, 1766, providing revenue for such purposes, the rates were fixed as follows: for one puncheon (2 barrels or 72 gallons) of rum or pipe (141 gallons) of wine, two ryals (one ryal was $5.17); for one hogshead (63 gallons) of wine, one ryal. "Transcript of Records of British West Florida Assembly," December 22, 1766. For later laws, see ibid., December 30, 1768; May 19, 1770.

[23] "Minutes of the Council," November 25, 1764; C. O. 5:632. (Alabama Department of Archives and History.)

[24] No distinction seems to have been made between a tavern and a public house. A tippling house proper was a place where liquors only were sold. They were operated independently of other businesses, and they were very much like a modern saloon. Taverns and public houses were also frequently called tippling houses through confusion.

[25] "Transcript Records of the British West Florida Assembly," November 24, 1766. Another stipulation in the law forbade gaming in public houses and violation of this provision was punishable by a fine of forty shillings.

in quantities of less than two gallons and responsibility for investigating the fitness of applicants for licenses was placed upon the Justices of the Quarter Session. Only after the judges had considered and approved the claims of an applicant could he apply to the governor or commander-in-chief of the province for the license. The license, when granted, specified the tavern or public house for which the permission was given. As in the act of 1766, no "Carpenter, Bricklayer, Shipwright, Smith, Tanner, Cooper, or any other trade whatsoever" was eligible for such license. Upon the granting of the license, the successful applicant was required to furnish bond in the amount of "Twenty Pounds" to guarantee the faithful performance of the provisions of the law. License fees were to be used, the law stated, to pay for the building of a road and bridges between Pensacola and the village on the east side of Mobile Bay.[26]

"Drunkenness and Debauchery" claimed the special attention of the Assembly in 1766, when a law was passed to the effect that no person "hired to work by the day" was entitled to pay for days when he was "Deemed Drunk." The preamble of this "Act to Restrain Drunkenness and Promote Industry" gives clear indication of the attitude of the legislators toward excessive drinking, at least on the part of workers. It reads as follows:

> Whereas Drunkenness and Debauchery in every community tend very much to enervate the Constitution of such unhappy persons as are addicted to these Vices and when added to the extremities of heat and cold peculiar to this climate destroy many subjects that would otherwise be useful to the Society in general and their own Family in particular and whereas the promoting of Industry and good order among Tradesmen and Labourers ought to be one of the first Institutions in an Infant Colony....[27]

Slaves and sailors also came under the special scrutiny of the lawmakers. By a law of December 24, 1766, retailers were forbidden to "Give, sell, utter, or deliver to any Slave or Slaves any Beer, Ale, Cyder, Wine, Rum, Brandy, or other spirituous liquors whatsoever without the leave or consent of the Owner or Other Person having charge of such slave or slaves."[28] This law was made even more drastic the following year by an act which forbade retailers to allow slaves to meet or drink on their premises, under penalty of a forty shilling fine, and which held the liquor dealer responsible for disorders committed by Negroes and slaves in their shops. This act of 1767, however, was disallowed by His Majesty in Council on January 15, 1772.[29]

Retailers were, by the law of 1766, forbidden to sell spirituous liquors to common laborers; and they must not "Trust or give Credit to any

---

[26] "Transcript Records of the British West Florida Assembly," July 12, 1771. The license fee for all places outside of Mobile and Pensacola was fixed at two pounds sterling.
[27] "Transcript Records of the British West Florida Assembly," December 15, 1766.
[28] Ibid., December 24, 1766.
[29] Ibid., June 2, 1767.

Sailor above the sum of five shillings sterling." For the rest of the inhabitants and settlers in the province the debt limit was five pounds sterling.[30]

No single problem troubled the British governors more than that of the red man and liquor. The exchange of rum for furs was a profitable business for the white man, and as such was difficult to curb and control in spite of the fact that drunken Indians could, and frequently did, start disturbances destructive not only to themselves and their property but to the white men as well.

As early as February 28, 1765, the Council of West Florida ruled that only "His Majesty's Superintendent for Indian Affairs," or one of his deputies might "for the space of one Month . . . sell, exchange or give any spirituous Liquors to Indians." Violation of this law was to be punished by a fine of five pounds sterling and a month's imprisonment in the common gaol.[31] The Council further provided that no trader might have in his possession at any time more than eighteen gallons of rum or other strong drink. Under no circumstances was it legal to use such liquor in barter with the Indians.[32]

Further legislation to protect both Indians and whites had the backing, not only of the English governors but also of some of the leading Indian chiefs. Chief Mattaha of the Chickasaws, the most powerful chief present at the congress of Choctaws and Chickasaws held in Mobile December 1, 1771 to January 6, 1772, complained that his people were getting too much rum. "It flows in upon all plantations and settlements roundabouts."[33] Similar complaints were registered by the Choctaws who in 1777 appealed to the British superintendent for protection against the losses and injuries to their race caused by too free access to rum.[34]

Such protests helped to bring, in 1778, a proclamation from the governor which made stringent restrictions upon the liquor trade with Indians. Unlicensed persons were forbidden to carry rum into any Indian town, to sell, give away, or otherwise dispose of rum to Indians in any part of the province. Merchants and traders must report to the superintendents the quantity of rum then held in their possession, and those who in the future received imported rum, particularly at the ports of Pensacola and Mobile,

---

[30] *Ibid.*, November 24, 1766. In 1771, Mary Offut petitioned the Council of West Florida for relief for having sold "a Single quart of Spirits to a common laborer," through error. The records do not show whether she got her relief. *Ibid.*, October 1, 1771.

[31] "Minutes of the Council," February 28, 1765.

[32] *C. O.*, 5:623, pp. 220-226. (Library of Congress.)

[33] Chester to Hillsborough, February 20, 1772, *C. O.*, 5:589, pp. 23-26; see also "Minutes of Congress," *C. O.*, 5:589, pp. 125-162.

[34] A letter from Lord Germain, dated White Hall, October 11, 1777, and presented at a council meeting in Pensacola, called attention to the complaints. Lord Germain conveyed the King's commands: the Council and Assembly should pass such acts as would give the superintendent power effectively to check that evil. "Minutes of the West Florida Council," held in the Council Chamber at Pensacola.

must immediately store the supply and not dispose of it without proper license. Those who disobeyed or evaded this proclamation were liable to seizure and imprisonment as enemies of the district.[85]

The Spanish authorities took cognizance of the bad effects of intoxicants upon the health of Indians, and the Council of the Indies ordained laws in 1637 and 1640 to prohibit the sale of wine to Indians in Spanish colonies. Since Florida was a province of New Spain, these laws applied to that territory. The chief justices and magistrates were not to permit any persons to sell wine on account of the great harm which resulted to the health and preservation of Indians. The viceroys and courts were required to punish parties guilty of violating these laws.

The Indians in New Spain used a drink called pulque which they distilled from the juice of maguey plants. Under the pretext of preserving this stimulant it was corrupted by adding certain roots, boiling water, and lime which made it injurious to health. The Council of the Indies forbade the adulteration of pulque by appropriate legislation in 1529, 1545 and 1672. The authorities in New Spain, therefore, ordained and commanded that no ingredients should be added to this simple native juice of the maguey to make it stronger, hotter, or more biting by mixture, distillation, or infusion. They also ordained that the viceroys and magistrates of Mexico observe with particular care the execution of this law and not allow any other shops to operate except those given legal permission, and that appropriate penalties be imposed when violations occur. On July 23, 1671, the viceroy and tribunal of the Royal Court of Mexico issued some ordinances on the use of this drink and approved of the pulque shops on condition that the number should not exceed thirty-six, of which twenty-four should be for men and twelve for women. The sites of all these shops should be separated by districts and watched over by the various justices and inferior ministers. The high authorities charged and commanded the viceroy and court to pay close attention to the correction of these abuses and to observe exactly and punctiliously the provisions of these said ordinances, punishing with all severity any violator in order that the example might serve as a warning to others and cause them to desist from entering into the liquor traffic.[86]

Subsequent records show that the provisions of these laws did not meet the approval of some of the high officials. For example, Bernardo De Galvez favored selling strong beverages to the Indians. "When Viceroy Galvez assumed control over Provincias Internas, he introduced some important changes of policy, as fully set forth in his elaborate instructions of August 26, 1786, to General Ugarte y Loyola." Galvez advised this general to encourage the Indians to drink intoxicating liquors in order to

[85] "Minutes of the West Florida Council," January 1778-1779. The exact date of the proclamation is not given.
[86] *Recopilación de Leyes de los Reinos de las Indias*, Tomo Segundo, Leyes XXXVI and XXXVII.

bring profit to the traders, to gain the good will of the Indians, to lower their efficiency as fighters, and to increase their dependence upon the Spanish.[37]

The Spanish government had an excellent legal system for the protection of the Indians. The trouble with the relations of the Spanish in America and the Indians was that the men who controlled the governmental policy were materialists while the makers of the laws were idealists.[38] The fact remains, however, that the laws were better than their execution, that is, the laws for the protection of the Indians.

In 1783 the British ceded both East and West Florida to Spain, and in the same year, by the Peace of Paris, the United States came into possession of formerly British territory north of the thirty-first parallel between the Mississippi and the Chattahoochee rivers, a tract which included all of the present state of Alabama except that part of Mobile and Baldwin counties south of the above-mentioned line. On April 7, 1798, an act of Congress created the Mississippi Territory and the American rule in the future Alabama began.[39]

In drinking habits the American settlers in the territory did not differ greatly from the British and others who preceded them. New England and West Indian rum were probably imported and consumed in considerable quantities, but necessity tended gradually to replace the imported beverages with the home-distilled corn whiskey. If a backwoods farmer made a good crop of corn, he could not transport it to market as corn; but he could and did distill it into whiskey, carry it by horse or mule to the nearest trading post, and receive in exchange the foods and goods which he needed.[40]

In the problems met and the means taken to meet them there is little break between the English and the United States regimes. The problems created by the sale of liquor to Indians was one of the first to concern the

---

[37] Elizabeth H. West, "The Indian Policy of Bernardo De Galvez," *The Proceedings of the Mississippi Valley Historical Association*, VIII (1915); *Broadside* (Texas State Library, Austin, Texas).

[38] Dr. Elizabeth H. West to the author, May 15, 1941.

[39] *United States Statutes at Large*, I, 549. This political division was bounded on the west by the Mississippi, on the east by the Chattahoochee, on the north by a line drawn due east from the mouth of the Yazoo to the Chattahoochee rivers, on the south by the thirty-first degree of north latitude. By a second act, approved March 7, 1804, the Mississippi Territory was enlarged through the addition of the tract of country lying north of the territory and south of the state of Tennessee and bounded on the east by Georgia and on the west by the Mississippi. *Ibid.*, II, 303. In 1811, Congress authorized the President to take charge of Florida, including the territory west of the Perdido River.

[40] Data concerning the amount of liquor imported, manufactured, and consumed are not available, but from frequent references to liquor in the letters of officials of the Territory, it seems that large quantities must have been manufactured and consumed. The first statement found concerning distilleries in the Territory occurs in the *American State Papers*. This report is incomplete, as it fails to give the amount of whiskey manufactured, but it states that six distilleries were operating in 1810. *American State Papers*, Finance, II, 630.

new American government. Within six months of the organization of the Mississippi Territory, Governor Winthrop Sargent issued, October 18, 1798, a proclamation which prohibited the "giving or vending to any Indian or Indians at or within three miles of any settlement of white people, any Whiskey, Rum, Brandy, or other Ardent Spirits, upon penalty of being punished with the utmost rigour."[41] In the following April he reported to Timothy Pickering, Secretary of State, that the Territory had by law prohibited the Indians from "receiving intoxicating liquors, but by permission of the superintendent."[42]

Nevertheless, the governor was alarmed over the liquor traffic among the Indians a year later. The laws to prevent sales to them had not proved sufficient, he wrote to the judges of the Mississippi Territory in April, 1800, and he warned that

unless we may apply an immediate remedy, it is more than probable this Country will very soon be involved in an Indian War, for the frequent affrays which happen and the Violence thereof are Matters of Notoriety.[43]

Such "affrays" continued to be "Matters of Notoriety" and governor after governor struggled with the problem they created. With them struggled also the best of the Indian chiefs and the Indian agents. "It is impossible for me to prevent my bad people from selling liquor to the Indians," wrote Governor William C. C. Claiborne on June 3, 1803, to Silas Dinsmore, agent to the Choctaw Nation, "and the consequence is that disputes often arise between the White and Red men and sometimes mischief is done."[44]

"I beg you would stop Whiskey Trade," Chief Puchshannubbia wrote to Governor Sargent in 1808, "it would be a Grate Good for us and I should be glad to hear from you on the Subject as I have hear vearious Reports. . . ."[45]

The problem continued unsolved. On May 26, 1810, Judge Harry Toulman wrote from Fort Stoddard to Governor David Holmes to tell him of a double murder which had occurred among Indians encamped near the fort who had obtained, "from some of our citizens, spirituous liquors." In a drunken spree one Indian had killed his brother-in-law. "The wife, fearing that she would fall a sacrifice to the vengeance of her husband's family, if her brother should escape unpunished, directed her

---

[41] H. Toulman, *A Digest of the Laws of the State of Alabama, 1823*, pp. 727-730.
[42] D. Rowland, *The Mississippi Territorial Archives, 1798-1803*, I, 69, 139.
[43] D. Rowland, *The Mississippi Territorial Archives, 1798-1803*, I, 231.
[44] *Ibid.* On May 17, 1804, Claiborne again wrote that he did all he could to keep whiskey from the Indians, "but some of my bad men will sell liquor to them." *Ibid.*
[45] "Transcripts of Mississippi Territorial Records," September 4, 1808. (Montgomery: Alabama Department of Archives and History.) John Pitchlyn, agent to the Choctaw Nation, wrote to Governor Sargent on September 14, 1808: "Its a request of the Chiefs to prevent the trade of Whiskey Which is the greatest Enemy a red man has altho he will give all he has for it—by the Whites Selling So Much Spirits it has been the Cause of the Deaths of Ten of our men in the Course of a few months." *Ibid.*, September 15, 1808.

son, a young man eighteen or twenty years old, to take satisfaction for the murder of his step-father."[46]

Three years later, Governor Holmes wrote to T. Brashears asking him to "inform the Chief" that he was using his "best exertions" to check the traffic in whiskey. "I find it very difficult," he said, "to detect the people who are engaged in this unlawful and mischievous trade."[47] And, as late as 1816, the same governor received from a public blacksmith at the Choctaw agency, a complaint that liquor sold by white people had caused the death of eight or ten fine young warriors during the past year and that Indians, under the influence of liquor, were burning and destroying each others' property.[48]

Even provisions for the confiscation of the goods of surreptitious traders apparently could not check the illicit traffic. Such regulations are on record as early as 1804. "You will be pleased to allow John Lewis six dollars for compensation for the whiskey which he says was taken from him by Captain Rudy," wrote Governor Claiborne to Samuel Mitchell, agent of the Choctaw Nation in August of that year. And he added:

Lewis acted very improperly in selling whiskey to the soldiers and deserves to have lost it, but since he has assured you that he did not act wrong intentionally, it may be advisable to make him some remuneration.[49]

An "Act to regulate Taverns and restrain Tippling Houses," apparently the first licensing law in the Territory, was passed in 1803. Applicants for license under this act had to be endorsed by six or more reputable freeholders and had to submit their application to the county court. If this court saw fit to grant the license, the applicant had to pay to the clerk of court a fee of $20.00 for county use. Keepers of taverns or tippling houses were also required to furnish bond to the amount of $300 to guarantee their faithful observance of the law's provisions.[50]

A unique provision of this law, and one which was to continue in subsequent laws of the Territory, was price fixing. A "fair table of rates" was to be drawn up by the clerk of the county court, who was authorized to charge the tavern keeper a fee of twenty-five cents for this service. This table had to be posted in the "entertaining room" of each tavern. Any deviation from the established rates was liable to a fine of $10.00. The fine for selling intoxicants without license was $20.00.[51]

[46] "Transcripts of Mississippi Territorial Records," May 26, 1810.
[47] "Executive Journal of Governor Holmes," Book 2, p. 333.
[48] "Transcripts of Mississippi Territorial Records," October 13, 1816.
[49] "Transcripts of Mississippi Territorial Records," August 17, 1804. An Indian trader named John Kincaid petitioned Governor Claiborne to release him from a fine of $500 placed on him by Silas Dinsmore, agent to the Choctaw Nation. The Governor agreed to have the case reconsidered. *Ibid.*, January 17, 1805.
[50] *Statutes of the Mississippi Territory* (1807), pp. 357-361.
[51] *Statutes of the Mississippi Territory* (1807), pp. 357-361. The law provided that the "justice of the county courts shall fix the rates and prices to be paid at all taverns in their respective counties, once a year at least, for liquors."

A second license law, passed in 1812, was designed especially to meet the increasing practice of selling ardent spirits without license. It made the clerks of county courts responsible for furnishing each year to the "superior courts" lists of persons licensed to sell liquor during the preceding year. Clerks neglecting to prepare such lists were fined $50.00. The superior court delivered these lists to the grand jury and on the basis of the information in them the jury was required to "present" all persons guilty of violating the act. Those found guilty after trial by jury were to be fined $100.00.[52]

That grand juries in subsequent years acted upon such violations of the license laws is evidenced in the records of the Superior Court of Law and Equity of Madison County. Some twenty-three cases involving the retailing of "spirituous liquors" "contrary to the law" were heard by that court in the session of November, 1814. One or two defendants admitted guilt, but in practically all cases presentments were quashed, or the accused acquitted. Fewer cases are recorded in the years following. In only one instance is there indication that a man who had been retailing spirituous liquors "without first obtaining a license . . . to the evil example of society and contrary to the statute of this Territory" was actually convicted and fined. Clayton Talbot was the offender and the court ruled in 1816 that he pay a fine of $10.00 and costs.[53]

Tavernkeepers, particularly those outside the centers of population, complained that license fees were too high, and some relief was granted them in the "Act reducing the Tavern Licenses . . ." passed in 1814. By this law, persons living outside town or village limits might secure a license for $10.00 instead of $20.00. At the same time, provisions for law enforcement were made more stringent. Every tax assessor, collector, and sheriff was required to report to the attorney-general every violation of law that came to his knowledge. Clerks of county courts who failed to furnish the courts with lists of persons purchasing tavern licenses were to be fined $100.00.[54]

Like the French and the English before them the American territorial governors found it advisable to curb the use of strong drink by Negroes. It is interesting to note that the law of 1803, by which retailers were

[52] Toulman, *op. cit.*, p. 731.
[53] "Minutes of the Superior Court of Law and Equity of Madison County, Mississippi Territory, 1811-1816," *passim*. Other evidences of law enforcement appear in the Superior Court Minutes of Washington County which contain a case of seizure of 165 gallons of liquor by the Collector of Customs for the District of Mobile at the Port of Fort Stoddard. Robert R. Montgomery, the owner, produced vouchers showing that duties had been properly paid and the goods were released to him. Other cases came to similar ends; goods were released to the proper parties on receipt of certificates of payment of duties.
[54] Toulman, *op. cit.*, p. 731. In 1816 merchants and shopkeepers were authorized to sell intoxicants by the quart without license from the county court, but liquors could not be drunk without their consent in their stores or on their premises. *Ibid.*, pp. 732-733.

forbidden to sell intoxicants to slaves without the consent of their masters, also forbade such sales to soldiers without permission of their commanding officers.[55]

This is no indication, however, that the territorial government expected soldiers to stay away from drink. Whiskey was part of the regular rations issued by the subsistence department in the Mississippi Territory.[56] On August 7, 1813, Major Daniel Beasley wrote from Mims Block House to General F. L. Claiborne at Mount Vernon Cantonment as follows:

We have a number of men on fatigue now, and will have for some time. Could we be furnished with whiskey to give them an extra gill in such case as has been usual, they expect it; and I allowed it to them yesterday, out of the whiskey composing a part of the rations drawn and brought here, in expectation that it may be replaced. If you think it right to allow the extra gill to fatigued men, an opportunity offers to send it up by Dr. Osborne.[57]

A few days later, August 13, the Major noted that "Ensign Swann arrived today, and brought two barrels of flour and a bbl. of whiskey, instead of one of flour, pork and whiskey, each, as you wrote me."[58] "Corn meal and pork I suppose can be easily procured, and occasionally whiskey," Governor David Holmes said to Lieutenant Colonel Stoddard on April 14, 1814, in a letter discussing food for the troops. "Subsistence must be secured at the point of rendezvous."[59]

To deprive a soldier of his whiskey rations was indeed a severe form of discipline. One Private John Waters of the Fourth Infantry was found guilty by a military court in 1819 of desertion from his post at Montpelier. Part of his sentence was to "have his head shaved on the right side at the end of every month and to have his rations of whiskey stopped during the term of his enlistment."[60]

[55] The fine imposed for drunkenness was not very burdensome. "Every person convicted of drunkenness . . . shall . . . for every such offense forfeit and pay one dollar." *Statutes of Mississippi Territory* (1816), p. 237. Toulman, *op. cit.*, p. 729. Anyone selling liquor to slaves was fined $10 for the first offense and $20 for succeeding offenses; those who sold to soldiers were fined $20. Restrictions on sales to slaves were made much more stringent by a law of 1805 which made it illegal to sell to them, without the consent of their masters, "any commodity whatsoever." *Ibid.*, p. 729.

[56] During the territorial period ardent spirits were generally thought of as food. Consequently, in 1815, the Mississippi Territorial Assembly passed an act which declared that if any butcher, baker, brewer, distiller, tavern-keeper, retailer of wines or spirituous liquors, or other person or persons should sell, offer, or expose for sale any adulterous food or liquors, such persons should forfeit and pay a fine of five dollars, with costs. *Ibid.*, p. 690.

[57] "Transcripts of Mississippi Territorial Records," August 7, 1813.

[58] "Transcripts of Mississippi Territorial Records," August 12, 1813.

[59] "Executive Journal of Governor Holmes," Book 2, pp. 443-445.

[60] "Transcript Records of the Mississippi Territory," July 19, 1819. "In this that the said John Waters did desert from his company stationed at Montpelier on or about the 12th of March 1819. The prisoner pleaded not Guilty; found guilty by the Court and sentenced to be Branded with the letter 'D' in the forehead, to reimburse the United States the sum of thirty dollars and amount paid for his apprehension, to make good the time lost by desertion and to serve the balance of

One of the most interesting of the regulations made by the Mississippi Territorial Assembly was an act passed in 1812 which provided "that any person elected to serve in the House of Representatives of this territory, who shall, either directly or indirectly, give or agree to give to any elector, money, meat, or drink, or other reward, in order to be elected, or for having been elected for any county, shall be expelled."[61] Thus early did the problem of political "treating" which was to vex later generations of reformers come to the attention of Alabama lawmakers.

When Congress on March 8, 1817, created Alabama Territory, it provided that laws in force in the old Mississippi Territory should continue effective until repealed or altered by the new Alabama Assembly.[62] Records of that Assembly for the two years before statehood came, show no changes in existing liquor laws and add nothing to the story of the early efforts to control the traffic.

French, English, and American governments in colonial and territorial Alabama acted on the premise that the moderate use of liquor was natural and good. They had no qualms about the "right" or "wrong" of drinking. They had recognized that control of prices was sometimes advisable lest citizens be imposed upon. They had seen possibilities for public revenue in government control of the liquor traffic. They had abundant evidence in the rough, pioneer country around them that certain men and certain groups of men were not to be safely trusted with a strong drink and that the community, to protect itself from violence, must control and limit the sale of intoxicants to soldiers, to slaves, and especially to Indians. Licensing had been found a practical means of regulating the traffic and obtaining revenue from it. Year by year the restrictions had grown more numerous and more detailed.

Alabama became a state on December 14, 1819.[63] The foundations were already laid by that time for the temperance and prohibition movements which were to be an important part in the history of the state.

---

his term of enlistment with a Ball & Chain attached to his Leg: to have his head shaved on the right side at the end of every month and to have his rations of whiskey stopped during the term of his enlistment. . . ."

[61] Toulman, *op. cit.*, pp. 675-928.
[62] *United States Statutes at Large*, III, 371.
[63] *United States Statutes at Large*, III, 608.

CHAPTER II
TEMPERANCE MOVEMENT, 1819-1861

The moral issue of temperance was added to the practical question of liquor control very soon after Alabama's entrance into statehood, and throughout the period which preceded the Civil War this issue grew in importance in the public mind. Educational, religious, moral, social, and political forces took up the cause. Socially minded men and women everywhere began seriously to consider their personal responsibility for the solution of the problem of drink. Clergymen thundered in their pulpits against the evils of alcohol; editors and businessmen were stirred to take sides in the fight; politicians learned the magic of the temperance banner; and schoolmasters found material for temperance teaching in the textbooks of the day.

Behind the movement lay the eighteenth-century philosophy of the perfectibility of man. Man is a rational creature, said the temperance reformers. Let him once understand the evil of strong drink, let him realize its harmful effects upon himself and upon society, let him reason out the beauties and blessings of self-control and temperance, and his free will must inevitably lead him to abstinence. Sin was, to the minds of these philosophers and reformers, merely the product of ignorance. In education lay the panacea for all the ills of society.[1]

For such education organization was essential. To some extent existing institutions—the church, the press, the school—could be used. But, in addition to these, an organization directly consecrated to the single object of temperance reform was clearly needed. Therefore the temperance society came into being and became the outstanding phenomenon of the liquor control movement in the ante-bellum period.

Fundamental to all the temperance societies of the day was the voluntary pledge of their members to abstain from all use of intoxicants except for mdicinal purposes.[2] Usually the societies were men and women not naturally given to the excessive use of alcohol, but the Washingtonians owed their dramatic appeal and power to the fact that they were, for the most part, reformed drunkards. Following the usual pattern of organizations of the day, the temperance groups adopted constitutions, elected officers, and held weekly meetings for their members and for the purpose of enlisting new recruits to the cause. These meetings, well advertised and open to the general public, served more than an educational and reform

[1] J. A. Krout, *The Origins of Prohibition*, p. 125. For a fuller discussion see Chapter V of *Rousseau and Education According to Nature*, by T. Davidson.
[2] Pledges varied. Some societies pledged to abstain from wines and cider, as well as intoxicating liquors.

purpose in those days of limited opportunity. They were important avenues of social intercourse for many people. Sometimes the program of such meetings consisted of a debate; more often a speaker "orated" on the evils of intemperance. Picnic dinners were a common feature and the succulent barbecued meat went far to help the members endure long hours of poor speaking. Sometimes temperance organizations formally celebrated the Fourth of July in gay uniforms.[3]

Records of these societies, except in the religious and secular press of the time, are meager. The men and women who formed the backbone of the movement were sturdy folk, but they shared the common carelessness for the preservation of documents which is the despair of the historian. Enough remains, however, to tell an interesting human story.

Quite naturally the churches took the lead in the early temperance movement and the first temperance societies were formed within their memberships. Their unflagging zeal in keeping temperance propaganda ever before the younger generation was ultimately the most powerful single fact in bringing about the swing of public opinion to favor statewide prohibition. It is not known when the first temperance society was organized in Alabama, but there is evidence to show that one was operating as early as 1828 in connection with the Valley Creek Presbyterian Church in Dallas County.[4]

Not all the churches were enlisted in the cause. The Episcopalians and the Primitive Baptists[5] stood aloof. The Catholic Church never took a definite stand on temperance, and, though some individual Catholics became ardent temperance workers, temperance societies were never found among Catholic churches. Father Theobald Mathew, affectionately known as the "Apostle of Temperance," was one of the best known of the Catholic reformers. He did not come to Alabama until 1850, when the temperance activity there was well advanced, but he gave in that year a series of stirring lectures on the evils of intoxicants, administered the total abstinence pledge, and presented "medals to hundreds of the citizens" of Montgomery.[6]

Even in the most enthusiastic of the temperance churches, differences marked the early years of the movement.[7] The feeling that the church

[3] *Williams' Directory of Huntsville*, (1858), p. 26. *Southern Advocate*, 1858-1859, *passim*. A firm in Huntsville specialized in supplies for temperance societies. *Southern Advocate*, March 2, 1849.

[4] "Minutes of the South Alabama Presbytery," (April 3, 1828), II, 17. In 1820 the Round Island Baptist Church tried for drunkenness a member who "came forward and confessed his sins and asked to be forgiven." "Minutes of the Round Island Baptist Church," Limestone County, (April, 1820), p. 44.

[5] Some members of the Primitive Baptist Church took pride in "never having voted a temperance ticket."

[6] M. P. Blue, *History of Montgomery, Alabama*, p. 47. Father Theobald was a native of Ireland.

[7] The resolution adopted by the Bethlehem Baptist Association in 1836 was typical of the resolutions of the early years of the temperance movement. It reads as follows:

Resolved, That in accordance with the holy principles of the Bible, it is plainly

ought not to "mix politics with religion" was strong and most churches limited themselves to advocating moral suasion in dealing with habitual drunkards.

The three denominations which led in temperance work were the Baptist,[8] the Methodist, and the Presbyterian. Their ministers soon began to preach regularly against intemperance, and their members were more and more severely censured and disciplined for using, making, or vending ardent spirits.[9]

The rules of the Methodist Church were formulated in the *Discipline* of 1832, which classified intemperance as an immorality and dealt with offenders accordingly.[10] District conferences grappled with the problems

---

the duty of all men, and especially members of churches, to abstain entirely from the trafficking in ardent spirits, as we believe the use of intoxicating liquors to be immoral in the highest degree, injurious to the souls and bodies of men, destroying health, prosperity, mental faculties, moral feelings and character, disqualifying men for the enjoyment of heaven, and preparing them for eternal misery. We most affectionately advise all members of churches to abstain from the use of intoxicating liquors as a common drink, and to use their influence to induce others to do so, likewise. Hosea Holcombe, *A History of the Rise and Progress of the Baptists in Alabama*, p. 113.

[8] The first reports on temperance are found in the records of the Baptist churches.

[9] Among outstanding temperance Methodist ministers of this period were Reverend James McFerrin, a pioneer preacher, and Bishop James O. Andrew.

In 1826 the Bethlehem Baptist Association sent out a *circular letter* strongly urging all church members to refrain from trafficking in or using ardent spirits. W. B. Crumpton, *A Book of Memories*, p. 188.

In 1825 the North Alabama Presbytery unanimously answered *yes* to the question: "Ought a member of the church who does not keep a house of entertainment to be censured for retailing spirituous liquors?" "Minutes of the North Alabama Presbytery," (October 3, 1825), I 12.

In 1828 the same Presbytery resolved that its members would abstain personally from use of ardent spirits and prohibit use of them in their families except for medicinal purposes, and would work to discountenance vice by actively promoting those organizations which had in special view the suppression of liquor abuses. *Ibid.*, (September 11, 1828), p. 65.

Also in 1828 the Valley Creek Church of the South Alabama Presbytery reported that "the Temperance Society was introduced and the views of the members having been expressed on its approbation—Resolved to adopt the resolution of the Synod on this subject." "Minutes of the South Alabama Presbytery," (April 3, 1828), II, 17. In 1829 this Presbyterian church approved the formation of "A State Temperance Society," and promised to support such a project. *Ibid.*, (November 19, 1829), pp. 52-53.

The Methodists of northern Alabama were a part of the Tennessee Conference when the General Conference took high ground on temperance in 1828.

In 1829 the Cahaba Baptist Association sent out a *circular letter* on temperance, "which was greatly needed; there were many drunkards in the churches. It was needed not only in the Cahaba Association, but also in the associations generally throughout the state." Holcombe, *op. cit.*, pp. 142-143.

[10] The rule concerning the sale and use of liquors reads as follows: "If any member of the church retail or give spirituous liquors, and anything disorderly be transacted under his roof on this account, the preacher who has the oversight of the circuit shall proceed against him as in the case of other immoralities; and the person accused shall be cleared, censured, suspended, or excluded, according to his conduct as in other charges of immoralities." *Doctrine and Discipline of the Methodist Episcopal Church*, (1832), pp. 91-92.

of disciplining members and ministers, usually trying persuasion first, but resorting, in case of need, to severe measures. One preacher, tried by a quarterly conference at Shiloh Church of the Jasper District, April 3, 1837, was found guilty of selling intoxicants and forthwith expelled from the church.[11] In that same year a complaint was made against D. H. Norwood, a lay member of the Centerville Circuit, for retailing spirits. Norwood acknowledged his guilt, promised not to sell any more after his stock on hand was gone, and the conference thereupon acquitted him.[12] In 1850 the Montgomery Station revoked the license of Richard Jones, local preacher, for trafficking in spirituous liquors.[13]

An attempt to alter the rules of the *Discipline* so that lay members as well as ministers who sold ardent spirits were liable to expulsion was made in 1853. The Alabama Conference passed a resolution requesting the General Conference to make such a change. Apparently the General Conference was unwilling to enact additional legislation on this matter, for in 1858, upon consideration of memorials presented,[14] the Committee on Temperance, through its chairman, T. Madden, reported a resolution that "offenders should be dealt with as in other cases of immorality."[15]

Similar reluctance to take too drastic action on temperance rulings was found in other denominations. In 1853 the Rechab Baptist Church was seeking admission to the East Liberty Baptist Association. The Rechab Church had in its *Decorum* a pledge that its members would of their own free will agree to forfeit membership in the church if they used liquor except for medicinal reasons, frequented places where it was sold and drunk, or sold it themselves.[16] After warm debate and the rejection of the first report of the committee appointed to consider the matter,[17] the East Liberty Association adopted the following resolution:

Resolved, That we think it improper under the present aspect of affairs to receive the Rechab Church as a component member of this body, in as much

[11] Anson West, *History of Methodism in Alabama*, p. 550.
[12] "Minutes of the Centerville Circuit," (May 13, 1827).
[13] "Minutes of the Montgomery Station," (November 4, 1850). A station is a Methodist Church to which a minister devotes his full time.
[14] E. H. H. Mitchell presented the memorial. *Journals of the General Conference of the Methodist Church, South*, (1846-1858), p. 385. A similar memorial was presented from the Quarterly Conference of the Selma Station. It was referred to the Committee on Temperance. *Journals*, (1846-1858), p. 436.
[15] *Ibid.*, p. 486. This attitude is an echo of the approach which the Methodists maintained in the 1830's. In 1832, for instance, the members of the Blount County Circuit resolved that they would abstain from the use of intoxicants, except medicinally, and would use their influence to "put down the abominable practice." "Minutes of Blount County Circuit," (March 10, 1832). In 1833 the members of the Tennessee Conference declared that they would neither take, buy, use nor sell ardent spirits and that they would discourage the use of them. J. B. McFerrin, *History of Methodism in Tennessee*, III, 424-425. Such mild resolutions were typical; as late as 1858 the same cautiousness is evident.
[16] W. C. Bledsoe, *History of the East Liberty Baptist Association of Alabama*, pp. 63-64.
[17] Members of the committee were Elder John R. Humphries, K. L. Haralson, and Levi White.

as it shows by its letter to us that it has set up a new test of fellowship in its decorum. The Association hereby declares her intention not to set up or countenance in others any new test of fellowship in our denomination. While we are in favor of temperance, we are opposed to connecting the reformation with the churches, but advise the churches composing this body to leave their members to act according to their discretion outside of the church in such a manner as they may think proper.[18]

Possibly this does not place the East Liberty Association on high temperance ground, but no doubt the resolution embodied the feelings of the majority of the Baptists of the day.[19]

Presbyterian societies had first organized as early as 1828. In 1829 plans of that denomination for a state temperance society had failed, but some of the individual churches made total abstinence a requirement for communion and ministers were urged to preach on temperance and to discipline their colleagues for the excessive use of ardent spirits.[20]

The South Alabama Presbytery seems to have been the first organization to take official action on the temperance problem. In 1832 it adopted a moderate resolution against the sale of liquor by members,[21]

[18] Bledsoe, *op. cit.*, p. 63-64.
[19] Hosea Holcombe gives a notable instance of expulsion of Elder Henry Petty, a Baptist minister, from the Pilgrim's Rest Church. Brothers "Barnes, Sanders, and Stout of Mobile, and W. R. Stansel, G. Williams, and G. Gardner of Pickens" testified against him. Holcombe, *op. cit.*, p. 240. See also *ibid.*, pp. 344-345.
[20] In 1829 the South Alabama Presbytery unanimously adopted resolutions to exhort church members to abstinence and to membership in temperance societies. The report also contained the suggestion that abstinence should be made a requirement for communion. Pursuant to the resolution regarding the communion, four churches, Valley Creek, Mount Pleasant, Marion, and Euchee Valley reported "at the next fall meeting of Presbytery" that they had done so. The Fairview Church opposed the suggestion. "Minutes of South Alabama Presbytery," (February 27, 1834), III, 97-98.

The Synod of Alabama adopted in 1843 another hortatory resolution urging all Presbyterian ministers and licentiates under its jurisdiction to preach one or more discourses within their respective churches or neighborhoods, as soon as convenient to each, in support of the cause of temperance. The Synod further recommended that the ministers and members cooperate in organizing temperance societies in places where they did not exist. "Minutes of the Synod of Alabama," (January 19, 1843), I, 80-81.

[21] "Minutes of the South Alabama Presbytery," (March 8, 1832), II, 148-150. The resolution was as follows:

1. Resolved, that every minister be required to preach or deliver an address on the subject of Temperance; and endeavor to organize Temperance Societies, whenever practicable.

2. That the Presbytery do solemnly and earnestly recommend to all the Ministers, Elders, and members of our church to join Temperance Societies, and that they do all in their power to promote this cause, a cause so well calculated to advance the Redeemer's Kingdom.

3. That Church Sessions be directed to take into consideration the propriety of making total abstinence from ardent spirits a term of communion and report at the next fall meeting of Presbytery.

4. That every member of Presbytery be required to report at the next fall meeting, the number of Elders, and private members that refuse to unite with Temperance Societies, and whether any are engaged in the traffic of ardent spirits.

5. That this Presbytery regard the traffic in ardent spirits as highly injurious to

and a year later amended this resolution to include manufacture as well as sale. The Tuscaloosa Presbytery in 1837 declared that "to distil or vend ardent spirits or to furnish materials for making them is an immorality which in a church member demands the discipline of the church."[22]

In 1847 the Reverend W. K. Patton voluntarily came before the East Alabama Presbytery and confessed to a self-instigated partnership between himself and another man in an establishment where liquors were sold. Patton had entered the business on behalf of his son, a minor. He was convinced that his business was greatly injuring his Christian and ministerial character, and he had given it up. The Presbytery resolved "that they regarded the conduct of brother Patton . . . with unqualified grief."[23] James Donaldson, a member of the Hebron Church of the Tuscaloosa Presbytery, appealed to that Presbytery in 1841 after having been convicted of drunkenness. The decision in his case was reversed after investigation.[24] The Reverend N. A. Penland, in 1853, was refused a dismission to the Presbytery of Memphis because the Tuscumbia Presbytery under which he was serving found him guilty of the intemperate use of ardent spirits and opium.[25] This decision was later reversed, after a long trial, and Penland was authorized to "connect himself with the Presbytery of Brazos, Texas, as a minister in good and regular Standing."[26]

Typical of the early temperance organizations endorsed by the Baptist, Methodist and Presbyterian churches was the Huntsville Temperance Society, founded in 1829. It was a branch of the American Temperance Society and, according to its constitution adopted October 2, 1829, was required to make "an annual report to the parent society." Members agreed to abstain from the use of distilled spirits except as medicine; to prohibit the use of drink by their families; to provide no drink for their friends or for persons in their employ; and to discountenance the use of intoxicants in their community.[27] Greeting this new society with enthusiasm, the *Southern Advocate* declared:

> By the thinking part of our community, Intemperance is regarded as an awful and desolating torrent . . . more destroying than the sullen and poisonous waves of Asphalititis. . . . This evil may and must be arrested . . . we wish

the cause of Christ; and recommend the members of the churches under their care to abstain from it. Also see, *ibid.*, (October 25, 1833), p. 44.

[22] "Minutes of the Tuscaloosa Presbytery," (October 3, 1837), I, 70.
[23] "Minutes of the East Alabama Presbytery," (April 14, 1847), II, 65.
[24] "Minutes of the Tuscaloosa Presbytery," (October 14, 1841), I, 201.
[25] "Minutes of the Tuscumbia Presbytery," (April 22, 1853), I, 64; (September 8, 1855), I, 78-79.
[26] Penland had moved to Texas during the trial.
[27] The officers provided for were president, vice-president, secretary, and treasurer. According to Article V, these officers, all elected annually, formed the nucleus of an executive committee; other members of the committee were to be appointed from the members of the society in such number as circumstances might require. This committee could call special meetings, but a general meeting was held annually on the third Monday in September. No provision was made for amending the constitution. *Southern Advocate*, October 2, 1829.

them success; and . . . earnestly recommend a general attendance at the Masonic Hall, this evening.[28]

The Huntsville Temperance Society, according to data available in the local press, appears to have continued active until 1845.[29] The records, however, which would have given the strength of its membership and its proceedings, have been lost.

The first society founded in the Blackbelt was supported by the Pleasant Valley Presbyterian Church. It was organized at Selma, April 3, 1828, and its stated purpose was "to guard the temperate against the dangerous allurements of a fashionable but destructive vice, to preserve our youth against its fatal snares."[30] The Tuscaloosa Temperance Society, founded on April 24, 1829, also had the backing of the Presbyterians.

Although the church was an important ally of the temperance forces, it was by no means the only root of temperance organizations in Alabama. As the question became more and more pressing and interest became more general, county and state organizations grew up. These were sometimes affiliated with local churches; sometimes they had only secular affiliation with the national societies.

The American Temperance Society was founded in Boston, Massachusetts, in 1826.[31] The year 1828 marked the beginning of Alabama's first temperance society in Dallas County. Five years later, Alabama sent her first representative to the convention of this national organization.[32] Contact with the national organization helped intensify a sentiment already strong in Alabama. By the end of 1829 the American Temperance Society had sponsored the formation of eight units in Alabama,[33] and these units became formally affiliated with the parent associations in 1831.[34] Curiously enough no new affiliations seemed to have been recorded after the convention of 1833.

The local societies were widely distributed throughout the state. The majority of them were located in the Tennessee Valley and in the Blackbelt,[35] at that time the most populous sections of the state.

One of the most important early non-denominational societies was the "Union Temperance Society of North Alabama," organized at the Camp

---

[28] *Ibid.*, September 25, 1829.

[29] In 1845 this organization came actively to notice for the last time when it tried to get the Council of Huntsville to raise the retail liquor license to $2,500.

[30] *Selma Courier*, January 29, 1829.

[31] By 1831 the American Temperance Society had established branch organizations in nineteen states. *Permanent Temperance Documents of the American Temperance Society*, pp. 1-15; D. L. Colvin, *Prohibition in the United States*, p. 15. At the National Convention in Philadelphia in 1833, almost five thousand local societies from various parts of the United States were represented.

[32] The representative was W. T. Brantley. *Permanent Temperance Documents of the American Temperance Society, Sixth Annual Report*, pp. 96-97.

[33] *Permanent Temperance Documents of the American Temperance Society, Fourth Annual Report* (1831), p. 28.

[34] *Ibid.*, p. 38.

[35] Krout, *op. cit.*, p. 130.

Ground near LaGrange. In addition to the usual pledge of personal abstinence, the members promised to circulate publications which should encourage temperance. The Union was designated as a federation of temperance societies, and any society might join upon presentation of an authenticated copy of its constitution.[86] Whether this society was effective in its chosen work one may only guess from newspaper references; its formal records were not preserved.

An early county temperance group was the Madison County Temperance Society. The *Southern Advocate* of September 25, 1830, records an annual meeting of this organization held in the Huntsville Presbyterian Church and attended by "a numerous assemblage of citizens." Arthur F. Hopkins, Esq., President of the Society, delivered "an appropriate and interesting address," and representatives were appointed for the meeting of the State Society to be held in Tuscaloosa in December.[87]

Other county units took up the work in other localities.[88] Closely bound to each other and to other temperance units, they helped to complete the network of organization which was gradually covering the state of Alabama.

The Alabama State Temperance Society was organized in 1834,[89] but little is known of its work during the first eight years of its existence. This organization was directed by a president, vice-president, secretary, and treasurer. The chief burden of administration fell upon the secretary and the special committees appointed from time to time to arrange for the holding of state temperance conventions. The objectives of this society, stated in the *Jacksonville Republican,* are both concrete and idealistic:

> To devise ways and means to arrest Drunkenness . . . and thereby expel from our State a vast amount of crime and misery.
> To meet together face to face, from all parts of the State, and compare notes in this grand enterprise.
> To adopt some means for the advancement of temperance through the influence of the Press, thereby sending "glad tidings" to remote and obscure places of degradation and vice, where the voice of the Temperance Orator is never heard.
> To form a band of co-laborers in the cause of true patriotism and philanthropy, erecting a beacon light, that those who are afar off, may see, and be guided. . . .

---

[86] *Southern Advocate,* September 4, 1829. A member of the Union might withdraw by notifying the secretary of his intention.

[87] Officers elected were Arthur F. Hopkins, president; Hon. John M. Taylor, vice-president; Harry I. Thornton, treasurer; John Martin, secretary; Dr. Thomas Fearn, Dr. D. M. Wharton, Beverly Crawford, James G. Birney, and Dr. Edward Pickett, executive committee.

[88] Another county unit was the Pickens County Temperance Society, which held a meeting at Bridgeville in August, 1842. The *Pickensville Register* was "pleased to witness the progress" of temperance in the county.

[89] *Permanent Temperance Documents of the American Temperance Society, Seventh Report* (1834), I, 12.

To form some systematic and efficient organization calculated to advance the Temperance Reformation in Alabama.[40]

Another type of temperance organization destined to play an important part in the history of the movement in Alabama was the fraternal order.

In this group one may perhaps place the Washingtonians, although in Alabama this organization was never an independent unit, but was attached to temperance societies already functioning. This unique order was founded on April 2, 1840, by six inebriated blades, who met for gaming and drinking at Chase's Tavern in Baltimore. For a lark, the revelers sent a committee to a near-by church where a temperance orator was holding forth. Apparently the orator was unusually gifted, for the delegation sent to scoff, returned repentant and immediately set about converting their dissipated friends to total abstinence. The Washingtonian pledge, drawn up by William K. Mitchell, was directed primarily toward the reform of habitual drunkards. It reads:

We, whose names are annexed, desirous of forming a society for our mutual benefit, and to safeguard against a pernicious practice which is injurious to our health, standing, and families, do pledge ourselves as gentlemen, that we will not drink any spirituous or malt liquors, wine, or cider.[41]

No other society ever had the initial success that this order had. Hundreds of thousands of men addicted to drink turned from their evil ways and flocked to the new standard.[42] Alabama took up the cause very early. In the year following the organization of the Washingtonians, Mobile reported 2,000 signers of the pledge. But the novelty wore off and the old temperance societies were soon functioning again according to their old principles.[43]

Of much more importance in Alabama was the order known as the Sons of Temperance, which was introduced into the state in 1847 and became the most powerful and thriving of all Alabama's temperance organizations, the parent of other vigorous groups.[44]

The order, national in scope, had been projected by a group of Washingtonians in New York as early as 1842. It represented the attempt of these reformers to solve the problem of holding the interest of recruits to the temperance cause after the initial excitement of conversion had worn off. To the customary objectives of liquor reform and temperance the new

[40] *Jacksonville Republican*, November 15, 1843.
[41] Krout, *op. cit.*, pp. 182-183.
[42] D. L. Colvin, *Prohibition in the United States*, p. 23.
[43] E. H. Cherrington, *The Evolution of Prohibition in the United States of America*, p. 123.
[44] The Daughters of Temperance was introduced into Alabama in 1849. By the end of 1852 a number of unions had been organized. Another organization for women was the Matrons and Maidens of Temperance, or Selma Division No. 91, Sons of Temperance. *Crystal Fount*, April 2, 1852.
The Cadets of Temperance, an order of adolescent boys, was introduced into the state in 1849. By 1852 enthusiasm for the order had cooled. *Ibid.*, February 27, 1852.

organization added sickness and death benefits to members, aid to needy brothers, and much of the ceremony and secrecy of ritual belonging to a masonic lodge.[45]

The features of secrecy—the grip, signs, and symbols—had little reality. The organization had few secrets and its constitution was open to all. But its use of the devices common to secret orders brought the opposition of many citizens who did not believe in such procedures, including the members of the Primitive Baptist Church. Some thought also that the order was entirely too democratic.[46] As the poorer classes flocked to its banner, the richer and better trained men more and more held aloof.

Organization of the order was hierarchical. At the base were the local divisions with their individual members. Representatives from these divisions had a voice in the affairs of the Grand Division whch controlled the work in the state. The final authority was the National Division made up of the State Grand Divisions.

When organization began in Alabama, the Sons of Temperance were fortunate in enlisting John Finn, Most Worthy Patriarch of Tennessee. This ardent worker traveled over the state delivering temperance addresses and organizing local divisions of the order.[47] He, with other zealous helpers, worked to such good effect that by 1849 the state had more than 300 local divisions and the Sons of Temperance had superseded all other societies in effectiveness.[48] The Sons of Temperance admitted as much quite smugly, declaring at their state convention that "all other organizations have served their day." Formal records of the 1849 convention were not preserved, and it is impossible to state with accuracy the number of individuals enrolled in the movement, but estimates from 15,000 to 20,000 are given. Such figures would represent at least one fourth of the male population of the state.[49] A very large proportion of the Sons of Temperance were members of the Baptist church.[50]

Other fraternal temperance orders followed the example of the Sons of Temperance and organized for reform and for mutual benefit. One of these was the Grand Temple of Honor incorporated in 1853.[51] Another,

[45] *Southern Advocate*, October 2, 1847. The objectives of the Alabama organization were: (1) to prevent the manufacture, sale and use of liquor; (2) to furnish pecuniary assistance to indigent members and families in event of sickness or death; (3) to establish a universal brotherhood in love, purity, and fidelity; (4) to elevate the characters of its members; and (5) to give united effort, discipline, and permanence to the cause of temperance. [46] *Ibid.*
[47] T. H. Hobbs, "Diary, 1844-1862," September 16, 1847; S. Ellis, *The History of the Order of the Sons of Temperance, 1842-1848*, pp. 205-207.
[48] *Minutes of the Alabama Baptist State Convention* (1849), p. K.
[49] *Ibid.*
[50] *Crystal Fount*, November 28, 1851. This paper gave the estimate that there were 20,000 members in 1849.
[51] *Acts of the Fourth Biennial Session of the General Assembly of Alabama* (1853), pp. 320-321. The Grand Temple or either of its subordinates might sue or be sued, might hold real estate to the value of $10,000, might adopt regulations not in conflict with state laws, had no banking privileges. No newspaper references were found concerning this organization.

more widespread, was the Independent Order of Good Templars, founded in central New York in 1851 and introduced into Alabama in 1859.[52] The Grand Lodge of Alabama, organized in May of that year, had a nucleus of eleven lodges. By the next annual meeting twenty-four new lodges had been formed. They were concentrated in the counties bordering on the Tennessee River.[53]

The school and the press, as well as the pulpit and the lecture rostrum, were enlisted in the temperance struggle. Temperance teaching in the schools came largely through the use of such textbooks as Noah Webster's *The American Spelling Book* and McGuffey's readers. The speller contained many passages which preached temperance sermons with the ostensible purpose of enlarging vocabulary.[54] McGuffey's *Reader* printed "Beware of the First Drink"[55] among other less convincing temperance stories. The temperance propagandists were not unconscious of the value of thus beginning their work upon the younger generation, and that work unquestionably bore its fruit half a century later.

The movement began to develop its own newspapers in the 1840's, probably as a result of the Washingtonian activities and the increasing interests in the local societies. *The Alabama Temperance Advocate,* published by B. D. Harrison & Company, at Wetumpka, in 1844, was the pioneer in this field. Its publisher declared: "No pains will be spared nor attention refused to render the *Advocate* a useful instrument in promoting the cause which it will espouse. . . . Kind treatment and moral suasion are the means we shall recommend to effect the desired object."[56] After a brief career this paper was discontinued.

The Sons of Temperance inspired several publications. First came the *Orion,* published at Montgomery in 1848 by James M. Norment. It was semi-monthly and in its two years of life changed hands twice and

[52] *Cyclopedia of Temperance and Prohibition,* p. 241. Wine and cider were included in the abstinence pledge of this order, and they were pledged to "discountenance" the manufacture, sale, and use of liquor.

[53] *Proceedings of the Grand Lodge of the Independent Order of Good Templars of Alabama, (1860, April 18-19),* p. 4. Lawrence County had erected ten temples in less than ten months; Madison began with eight lodges, three had been discontinued; Morgan had three lodges; Limestone had lost two of its three chapter lodges; Franklin came in for the first time with three lodges; Marshall, Lauderdale, and Jackson reported active lodges.

[54] Noah Webster, *The American Spelling Book Containing the Rudiments of the English Language* (1826), p. 154. For example, "The practice of drinking spirits gives a man red eyes, a bloated face, and an empty purse. It injures the liver, and produces dropsy, occasions the trembling of the joints and limbs, and closes life with slow decay or palsy. . . . Spirituous liquors shorten more lives than famine, pestilence, and the sword."

[55] The story ends: "Ah, my dear boys, when old Uncle Philip is gone, remember that he told you the story of Tom Smith, and said to you, 'Beware of the first drink!' The man who does this will never be a drunkard." W. H. McGuffey, *Third Eclectic Reader* (1st ed. 1857), p. 113.

[56] *Jacksonville Republican,* February 14, 1844. No copies of the *Alabama Temperance Advocate* were found.

altered its name to *Sons of Temperance*.⁵⁷ *The Crystal Fount*, the state organ of the Sons of Temperance, was begun in 1849 by John F. Warren at Tuscaloosa. Its masthead declared it to be: "Devoted to temperance, morality, literature and general intelligence; and neutral in politics and religion." Following the general trend of the movement it represented, it ran up an unprecedented circulation, then gradually declined. It died in 1852.⁵⁸

Another advocate of the temperance cause appeared in Montgomery the year of the demise of the *Crystal Fount*. It bore the name of the *Times* and was edited by R. C. Holifield, Jr. Lack of financial success soon forced this paper to abandon its exclusively temperance object and join the ranks of the Democratic party papers in 1853. In 1855 it was renamed the *Southern Times* with Holifield, A. A. Lipscomb, and W. P. Hilliard as editors and proprietors.⁵⁹ It was discontinued in 1856.

The political papers of the state were usually sympathetic to the temperance cause so long as it was divorced from politics. They emphasized the importance of temperate living, but they generally opposed candidates for political office who ran on a temperance ticket. Among the important papers which took this stand were the *Southern Advocate* (Huntsville); the *Democrat* (Huntsville); *Daily State Guard* (Wetumpka); the *Dallas Gazette* (Cahaba); *Alabama State Intelligencer* (Tuscaloosa); the *Independent* (Gainesville); and the *Jacksonville Republican*.

It was inevitable that the rising tide of temperance sentiment and propaganda should correspondingly strengthen opposition to the cause. Some of this opposition grew out of the nature of the people and their long established habits and traditions. Most gentlemen of the Old South were accustomed to use intoxicants. They prided themselves on knowing when to quit, but they regarded whiskey as a food and considered ardent spirits an important concomitant of hospitality.⁶⁰

---

[57] R. L. James bought it in 1848 and, with M. P. Blue, ran it for a short time. Then it was sold to W. W. Thompson, who moved to Hayneville and published it as the *Sons of Temperance* until November, 1849. W. W. Screws, "Alabama Journalism," in *Memorial Records of Alabama*, II, 189-190. No copies of the *Orion* were found.   [58] Screws, *op. cit.*, p. 177.

[59] *Ibid.*, pp. 189-190. No copies of the *Times* were found. Dr. Lipscomb had a wide reputation as a scholar and writer. The intention was to make the *Times* a first-class literary paper, but apparently public support for the project was lacking.

[60] The inventories of various estates, to be found on record in the office of the Probate Judge of Madison County, seem to bear out this fact. For example, in the property of William Lewis, listed December 21, 1832, there were thirty-six barrels of whiskey; in that of Robert Graham, listed January 18, 1850, fifty gallons of whiskey and sixty gallons of brandy. Decanters, stills, and worms, were also part of some inventories. "Probate Record Book," No. 6, pp. 27-28; 176; 180; 612; No. 10, p. 31.

The will of Thomas Fearn, dated March 30, 1860, provides "that all groceries and liquors of every kind and all provender ... may be kept on hand for use free of charge of such of my children as may be living with me or of those who may care to visit my home." *Ibid.*, No. 1, p. 305.

The Lafayette entertainment committees spent more than $3,000 for wines and

At dinner parties, says William Birney, cut-glass decanters glittered on the sideboard and wine glasses of varied hue and thickness were placed before each guest. To refuse a drink proffered by one's host was an affront.[61] The introduction of a moral issue into the matter received scant sympathy from these men.

Professional men followed the example of high society. When a traveler familiar with Alabama in the ante-bellum days returned to the state in 1899, he noted with surprise that, in the courts of law, the sheriff, the jurors, the judge, and the lawyers were all sober. He felt as though he were in church, and remembered the days when courts were disturbed by brawls and public meetings made riotous with intoxication.[62] Even the clergy quite commonly followed Paul's admonition to Timothy and carried in their saddle bags "a little wine for the stomach's sake."[63]

And among the rank and file, convivial drinking was a matter of course. "Found a wretched inn, with no possibility of procuring anything save liquor," Tryone Power noted in his travel diary in 1834; he went on to describe the scene aboard the steamboat which took him from Montgomery to Mobile and which carried also rough but merry hard-drinking planters who carried their liquor very well, but did complain of dyspepsia.[64]

R. C. Holifield, editor of the *Temperance Times,* described conditions he saw in Cahaba in 1854, giving a picture which, with some allowance for the bias of the writer, may be taken as typical of the day. He wrote:

> Men drink here as a matter of course publicly and privately, young and old, rich and poor, christian and sinner. If every village in Alabama presented such an array of drunken sinners, nothing but the power of God could hold society to-gether for ten days. We understood from some citizens that its present aspect was somewhat uncommon and uncharacteristic, owing to the large number of strangers in attendance upon the Land Office, a greater portion of whom were a "sweet set." The few sober men of Cahaba have a great work to accomplish, and must commence . . . by pulling down those three doggeries that infest the place.[65]

Some unregenerate drunkards were proud of their prowess. About eight miles from Moulton, in the Old Town Cemetery, can still be seen the whiskey jug crowning the tombstone of one Alexander Bowling. It was put there at Alexander's request, in memory of a man who lived and died in a pleasant state of intoxication.[66] There were also, of course,

---

liquors when Lafayette visited America in 1825. See the Original Vouchers of the Lafayette Entertainment Committees of Montgomery, Cahaba, and Mobile.

[61] *James G. Birney and His Times,* p. 48.
[62] J. E. Saunders, *Early Settlers of Alabama,* p. 45.
[63] B. F. Riley, *A Memorial History of the Baptists in Alabama,* p. 115.
[64] T. Power, *Impressions of America,* I, 100-101.
[65] *Dallas Gazette,* October 13, 1854.
[66] Information obtained from Wayne Young, Landersville, Alabama. Of another man, William Fancher, jeweler of Cahaba, the obituary notice stated: "When sober, he was a hard-working man, and an excellent workman." *Dallas Gazette* (Cahaba), November 21, 1856.

natural enemies to the cause—those whose business was the manufacture and distribution of liquor and who viewed with alarm any move to curtail its use.

The manufacture of liquor in Alabama prior to 1860 was confined largely to corn whiskey.[67] Nearly every well-regulated plantation and farm had its own distillery and a considerable quantity must have been produced though official records, taking account only of the larger stills, do not show a great volume of production.[68] Most of the distilleries recorded by the census of 1840 were located in the Northern District of Alabama. Of a total of 195 plants listed, 168 were in this region. Madison County led in quantity of production—28,950 gallons from eleven stills. Jackson, with twenty-nine plants, led in number of distilleries. Two northern counties, Randolph and Franklin, reported no distilleries; they were exceptions to the rule.[69]

Records concerning the number of retailed dealers are also incomplete. Alabama had about two hundred retailers scattered unevenly through the state in 1827.[70] By 1845 that number had increased to 448.[71] The influence of temperance societies may have checked the increase of saloons in centers of population; it did not cause the saloons to disappear.

In fact, by 1840, temperance advocates were mourning over a decline in temperance sentiment. Perhaps the elections of that year, with their

[67] Some farmers operated fruit distilleries for short intervals during the year to make brandy for home consumption.

[68] In 1820, according to available records, only eight distilleries were operating. These were producing whiskey valued at $4,650. *Digest of Accounts of Manufacturing Establishments in the United States and of Their Manufactures* (1820), p. 23. In 1840, first date of the next reliable data, 188 stills producing 127,230 gallons were reported. The same report showed seven breweries producing only 200 gallons. In the stills and the breweries 230 men were employed and $34,212 invested. *Sixth Census of the United States* (1840). *Compendium of the Inhabitants and Statistics of the United States*, p. 222.

The census reports for the number of distilleries operated in 1850 and 1860 are incomplete and of little value in computing the amount of whiskey produced before 1860. Statistics show that there was only one distillery in Alabama in 1850, its product was valued at $2,500. In 1860 only three distilleries were reported; their product valued at $11,700. *Senate Documents*, 35 Congress, 2nd Sess. No. 39, p. 47. *Manufactures in the United States in 1860, Compiled from the Original Returns of the Eighth Census* (1860), p. 14.

From the report for 1860, it is evident that many small plants were omitted from consideration in number three, especially since the report for 1840 showed 195 establishments operating in that year.

[69] *Sixth Census of the United States* (1840). *Compendium of the Inhabitants and Statistics of the United States*, p. 222.

[70] Mobile County had 68; Conecuh 36. More than three fourths of the distilleries were in the Northern District, but most of the retail establishments were in the Southern. Better transportation facilities in the South probably help to explain this fact. "Reports of Probate Judges."

[71] *Ibid.* In 1830 the population of Alabama was 309,527; in 1850, 771,623. *U. S. Census Reports*. Greatest increase in number of liquor retailers had come in the less populous counties. They were growing faster, perhaps, and they did not feel so much the influence of temperance societies and the high license taxes as did the urban centers. One city in this period had a license fee of $2,500, another of $1,000 per annum.

political treating, had helped to distract men's minds from high and sober things. "It is with deep regret we view a decline of energy on the subject," declared the Baptist State Convention, ". . . it is a lamentable fact, that in many parts of our country, there is an increase in the odious sin of intemperance, arising from the increase of tippling shops."[72] "The cause of temperance is rapidly retrograding," asserted the Baptist Convention of 1844.[73] In 1846 the same body was moved to lament that the blighting, withering influence of intemperance was "causing disturbances in our churches, distractions in the social circle, and disarming its victims of all moral, social and virtuous feelings."[74] The same note was sounded in the Convention of 1847: "your committee regard Temperance Societies as good, but have reason to fear that the churches have depended too much upon these societies to carry on temperance reform; hence decline has ensued."[75]

Natural antagonisms and self-interests, made conscious and aggressive by the consciousness and aggressiveness of the temperance drive, would account for some of this "decline." The difficulty of sustaining revival enthusiasm in a consistent long-time effort must have entered into it. As the tension between North and South increased, distrust of the national organizations as one more instance of Yankee meddling, helped to weaken their influence.

But unquestionably one thing which raised obstacles in the smooth path of the temperance reformers in this period was their initial excursion into the field of politics.[76] When the temperance advocate realized that moral suasion was not enough to accomplish his ends and turned for help to the lawmaking machinery of the state, he ceased to be a harmless fanatic and became a menace to powerful interests. It was inevitable that the battle lines should be more sharply drawn. But the story of the first political activities of the temperance forces in Alabama deserves a section to itself.

[72] *Minutes of the Seventeenth Anniversary of the Baptist State Convention of Alabama* (1840), pp. 6-7. The committee on temperance recommended adoption of a petition to the legislature asking for a law to suppress liquor. *Ibid.*
[73] *Journal of the Proceedings of the Baptist State Convention* (1844), p. 9. Similar "painful interest" was shown in the 1845 convention. *Ibid.*, 1845, p. 17.
[74] *Minutes of the Twenty-second Anniversary of the Alabama Baptist State Convention* (1848), pp. 17-18. Moderate drinkers were just as bad as the "inebriate himself."
[75] *Minutes of the Alabama Baptist State Convention; and the Baptist Bible Society* (1847), pp. 9-10. The church was urged to renew with increased vigor the fight against liquor, and ministers were admonished to preach and members to abstain. The Baptist State Convention of 1842 had stressed the desirability of organizing temperance societies and was very sanguine about their success where they were in operation. *Journal of the Proceedings of the Baptist State Convention in Alabama* (1842), p. 7. The Pine Barren Baptist Association adopted a pessimistic report on temperance in 1858. It complained of desertions and said that the liquor forces were "bidding defiance to the few remaining troops of the temperance army." *Minutes of the Pine Barren Association* (1858), pp. 8-9.
[76] L. Dorman, *Party Politics in Alabama from 1850 Through 1860*, pp. 108-110.

THE PROHIBITION MOVEMENT IN ALABAMA 29

Liquor regulation in the young state of Alabama followed the precedents set in colonial and territorial days. The legislators were primarily occupied in preventing the sale of intoxicants to and by persons unable to handle them wisely and in making the traffic provide revenues for public use.

Fear and distrust of the free Negro was responsible in 1822 for an Alabama law making it illegal for "any free Negro or mulatto, either directly or indirectly, to retail any kind of spirituous liquors within this state."[77] The penalty for the first violation of this act was a $10.00 fine. The penalty for a second offense was a whipping on the bare back up to a maximum of twenty-five stripes in addition to the fine. Provisions of this law were made more stringent and the fine doubled in 1852. Free persons of color who, by treaty between the United States and Spain, had become citizens of the United States were exempted.[78]

The sale of liquor to slaves without the permission of owner or overseer was prohibited in 1838 and violators of this law were made "subject to all the pains and penalties of wilful and corrupt perjury" and in addition lost their licenses. In 1857 captains of boats were forbidden to sell or give liquor to slaves in their employ.[79] The first law specifically forbidding the sale of intoxicants by slaves was passed in 1850.[80]

Students were included among those who needed protection from liquor sellers and the General Assembly in 1848 passed a law forbidding the sale of intoxicants to students of the University of Alabama or of any academy or school in the state. The courts were required to make vigorous efforts to enforce this law and fines ranging from $50 to $500 might be imposed for its violation. Circuit judges were required "to give this act specifically in charge to the grand jury at each term of the circuit court over which they respectively presided."[81]

Whiskey continued to be regarded by the lawmakers as a food throughout this period. In 1858 they decided upon a fine of not less than $100 with possible imprisonment for six months for anyone who "shall woefully use tobacco, strychnine, or any other poisonous or unwholesome substance" in the manufacture of spirituous or malt liquor.[82]

Effort was made also to bar the sale of intoxicants from certain areas, and many acts were passed before 1861 forbidding liquor sales in terri-

---

[77] *Acts Passed at the Fourth Annual Session of the General Assembly of Alabama* (1822), p. 61.
[78] *Code of Alabama* (1852), p. 341. No free person of color might retail, or assist in retailing liquors. The fine was increased to $20.
[79] *Acts, Annual Session* (1838), p. 75; *Acts, Sixth Biennial Session* (1857), pp. 290-291.
[80] *Acts, Annual Session* (1850), p. 15.
[81] *Acts, First Biennial Session* (1847), p. 63. Fines were to be assessed by the jury.
[82] *Acts, Sixth Biennial Session* (1857), pp. 290-291. The fine was increased to $500 and the term of imprisonment made from six to twelve months two years later. *Acts, Seventh Biennial Session* (1859), p. 70.

tory around schools, churches, and even towns. The first definitely dry territory in Alabama was created in 1835 when a special act provided that no spirituous liquors could be sold in the town of LaGrange or within three miles thereof.[83] Seven years later the town of Auburn in Lee County and the territory within a radius of three miles was similarly made prohibition area.[84]

The first Alabama state license law, passed in November, 1820, set a tax of $25.00 on every retailer in a city or town and $10.00 on each retailer in the country or on the highways. Tavernkeepers were required to pay an extra $10.00 for the privilege of selling liquor.[85] Four years later country and highway retailers had their fees reduced to $5.00.[86]

After 1824 license fees gradually increased. Urban dealers were paying $15.00 and rural dealers $10.00 in 1827.[87] Ten years later a new law required retail dealers to procure the "recommendation of six reputable freeholders . . . and enter bond and security, to be approved by the Court, and to pay the sum of twenty dollars in open court, for the use of the county."[88]

Rates continued to stiffen. In 1849 the retail fee on steamboats or other water craft was $60.00; at a single location in a city, $75.00; in towns or villages of 500 inhabitants, $37.50; in smaller towns and villages, $25.00; in the country, $15.00.[89] In 1852 the fee was raised to $40.00 in towns of more than 500 and less than 1,000 inhabitants; to $30.00 in smaller towns and villages; and to $20.00 in the country.[90]

Under such circumstances, it is small wonder that a vigorous attack against the license system developed. The protest included practical complaint against the gouging fees, but the loudest protest was the voice of the temperance agitator proclaiming that, in licensing liquor, the state was licensing sin. "If the constitution be so construed as to afford protection to this trade," declared John F. Warren, editor of the *Crystal Fount,* "it will require no greater stretching to afford succor to the burglar and the highway robber—this traffic must be done away with."[91] His paper, the official organ of the Sons of Temperance, began a caustic campaign against the license system in 1852, and received some support from other papers, both secular and religious. The *South Western Baptist* declared that the

[83] *Acts, General Session* (1835), p. 62.
[84] *Acts, General Session* (1842), p. 105.
[85] *Acts, Second Session* (1820), p. 11. The act was called "An Act to Raise Revenue for the Support of the Government, for the year one thousand eight hundred and twenty one." The tax was to be paid to the clerk issuing the license.
[86] *Acts, Sixth Annual Session* (1826), p. 13.
[87] *Acts, Eighth Annual Session* (1828), p. 13.
[88] *Acts, Called Session* (1837), p. 37.
[89] *Acts, Second Biennial Session* (1849), p. 8.
[90] *Code of Alabama* (1852), p. 134.
[91] *Crystal Fount,* May 21, 1852. See also, March 25, 1852. The editor considered license a relic of the Dark Ages, similar to the sale of indulgences by the Catholic Church.

license law sanctioned vice and should be repealed.[92] The Macon County Temperance Society resolved "That the licensing of houses for retail of spirits, by our own town, county, or state authorities, otherwise than for medicinal and mechanical purposes, is detrimental to the highest and best interests of society, fraught with untold evils, and should be opposed and discountenanced by every lover of his species."[93]

License fees were an increasing source of irritation, but there was another sore spot which in the years between 1820 and 1850 troubled some reformers even more. The disorder resulting when candidates followed the custom of treating the electorate with liquor was obvious to the law-abiding citizen. Agitation on this began long before the license law caused trouble.

Commenting on the election of 1825, the *Southern Advocate and Huntsville Advertiser* declared:

... it is a matter of regret that they cannot exercise the elective franchise without the aid of barbecue and whiskey. Are they, because they are well drenched with ardent spirits, any better able to appreciate the worth, or scan the motives of the several candidates? Can they, when in that situation, more readily discover that one may be a fool, or another a demagogue, than when sober?[94]

Answering his own rhetorical queries, the editor declared that the custom of treating tended to befuddle the judgment of the voters and make them easy prey to the unprincipled politician. He wished the practice could be done away with, but he was not optimistic about this possibility.

Never in our lives before did we witness such a profusion of treating on any public occasion, & it is the first time that we have ever seen bottles paraded in rows in different parts of the public square, with labels containing the names of the several candidates, which a stranger who did not know the custom, would have taken for the name of the liquor the bottle contained, and not the person who furnished it.[95]

In addition to demoralizing the voters, said the *Advocate* editor, the practice put heavy expense upon the candidates. This complaint was echoed, either silently or outspokenly, by more than one aspirant for office. One such candidate wrote in protest to the *Advocate* in 1828. It went sorely against his better judgment, he said, to be forced to eat raw shoat and sip liquid fire with his fellow aspirants for honor.[96]

By 1829 citizens of Dallas County were circulating anti-treating subscription papers, pledging themselves to unite to do away with this pernicious practice.[97] In the same year an association was formed at Tuscaloosa for the suppression of abuses of electioneering; its members

[92] *South Western Baptist*, March 2, 1852.
[93] *Macon County Republican*, October 14, 1852.
[94] *Southern Advocate*, August 5, 1825.
[95] *Southern Advocate*, August 5, 1825.
[96] *Ibid.*, May 2, 1828.   [97] *Selma Courier*, May 21, 1829.

agreed to vote for no office-seeker who electioneered by treating with whiskey.[98] A similar pledge was included in the constitution of the Tuscaloosa Temperance Society in that year;[99] politicians who were intemperate in their personal habits were also banned by this society. In 1846 the Tuscaloosa County Baptist Association resolved to support no man for public office who was known "to resort to treating with ardent spirits to secure his election."[100]

Active in all phases of the temperance movement, the churches were among the first groups to look to the law as a means of securing desired reform. It was a Baptist minister, Hosea Holcombe, who in 1838 presented to the Alabama legislature the first of the memorials of that year asking reform.[101] He had to defend his memorials against the usual charge that they were in violation of public liberty, unconstitutional, and did not have the support of public opinion. Two years later, when the Baptist State Convention petitioned the General Assembly to "pass such a law as they, in their wisdom, may deem expedient to suppress the retail of intoxicating liquors," they declared that ten thousand citizens joined in their request that liquor establishments be banished from the state.[102]

Such petitions seem to have met little response. The practice of election treating continued unabated and temperance leaders could not see that sheriffs and grand juries made any effort to correct it. License fees continued troublesome both to consciences and to pocketbook. Then, in 1851, Maine passed her state-wide prohibition law. This law influenced public sentiment in Alabama as it did all over the United States.[103] Here was clear indication that reform was possible and clear direction as to the means of securing it. By 1853 a movement for a strong "Alabama Liquor Law" was under way. And since, as the *Macon Republican* remarked, in order to secure the passage of legislation modeled upon the Maine Law it would be necessary to elect men favorable to its enactment,[104] the temperance organizations boldly took their first step into the political arena.

The Sons of Temperance took the lead in the movement. They sponsored a specially called convention at Selma, November 24, 1852, which considered temperance reformation and decided to memorialize the legislature of 1853, requesting a local option law. The bill, drawn up by an especially appointed committee, was entitled: "An Act to enable the in-

---

[98] *Niles' Weekly Register*, XXXVI (1829), 166.
[99] *Alabama State Intelligencer*, May 8, 1829. This paper thought such a requirement eccentric; the state constitution was the only instrument that should define the qualifications of the candidates for office.
[100] H. B. Foster, *History of the Tuscaloosa County Baptist Association, 1834-1934*, p. 49.
[101] *House Journal of the State of Alabama* (1838), pp. 19, 20, 24, 25, 28, 62, 80, 86.
[102] *Minutes of the Seventeenth Anniversary of the Baptist State Convention*, p. 6.
[103] Krout, *op. cit.*, pp. 294-296. The following states passed such laws: 1852, Minnesota, Rhode Island, Massachusetts, and Vermont; 1853, Michigan; 1854, Connecticut; 1855, Iowa, Indiana, Delaware, Nebraska, New York, and New Hampshire.
[104] *Macon County Republican*, October 14, 1852.

habitants of every county, city, town, and village, and election precinct within the State of Alabama, to protect themselves from the evils arising from the sale of intoxicating liquors."[105]

Meeting in May, 1853, the Friends of Temperance carried the campaign further by drawing up a memorial to be signed by citizens and used to influence the legislature favorably toward the local option bill. The memorial reads:

> The undersigned citizens of ———— believing the traffic in ardent spirits productive of incalculable injury, and demoralizing in its tendency, respectfully memorialize your Honorable Body to enact a law similar in its provisions to the "Bill" recommended by the Convention of the Friends of Temperance, held in the city of Selma, on the 24th and 25th of November, 1852. And in duty bound your petitioners will ever pray, &c.[106]

Local temperance organizations bent their effort to secure signatures for this document, and, by the time it reached the General Assembly in January, 1854, it carried the endorsement of "at least one hundred thousand souls."[107]

One more step was needed to round out campaign plans. The Friends of Temperance Convention took that step at the May, 1853, meeting. They decided to make a determined drive that the men who composed the General Assembly of 1854-1855 should be men willing to listen to their petition. County committees were instructed to find out how the candidates for the General Assembly stood on local option. A committee of five was appointed to investigate the stand taken on temperance by the gubernatorial candidates. This committee was instructed to ask each aspirant for the governor's chair whether he would approve the passage of a law "giving the people the right, by majority vote, to protect themselves from the evils arising from the sale of intoxicating drinks, if such a law be passed by the legislature."[108] If no regular party candidates took the proper stand in this matter, the members of the convention were urged to set up independent candidates who could be counted on.

Finally the convention, through resolutions drawn up by John Wilmer and unanimously adopted, provided for a thorough canvass of opinion in the state on the matter of temperance. Committees were appointed to "obtain the opinions of the eminent jurists of the State as to the Constitutionality of the Alabama Law"; to "obtain an expression on Temperance" from such groups as "the Medical Faculty in each county"; the

---

[105] "Proceedings of the Alabama State Temperance Convention," held at Selma, (November 24-25, 1852). The impulse for this convention had come when the Grand Division of the Sons of Temperance met in Decatur and appointed a committee to issue the call.
[106] "Proceedings of the Convention of the Friends of Temperance," held in Selma, (May 19, 1853).
[107] "Journals of the House of Representatives," (January 30, 1854). Journals of the Senate and House of Representatives, 1845 to 1855, have not been published.
[108] "Proceedings of the Convention of the Friends of Temperance," held in Selma, (May 19, 1853).

"Reverend Clergy of all denominations"; "all instructors of Youth"; "the Bench, the Bar, and officers of the Court." Aid of the ladies was specifically requested. And a special committee of three was commissioned to "ascertain from the Convicts in our State Penitentiary how many of their number committed the crimes for which they are convicted, while under the influence of intoxicating drinks."[109]

For the next six months temperance workers followed the lines laid down by this convention. The Order of the Sons of Temperance, having instigated the whole movement a year before, naturally took a leading part in the effort to make temperance an election issue. They sent a questionnaire to the three gubernatorial candidates, John A. Winston, A. Q. Nicks, and William S. Earnest, requesting them to state their views on the proposed local option law. Winston and Nicks refused to commit themselves. They said they would sanction any law passed by the General Assembly upon that matter. Earnest, however, stated that he favored local option with precincts as election units. The Sons of Temperance forthwith held a state convention and declared Earnest to be their candidate.[110]

This was perhaps the first time the Sons of Temperance had gone quite as frankly into the political arena, but apparently it was not the first time they had attempted to use political influence. As early as 1849 J. J. Hooper of Chambers County wrote the *Alabama Journal* that the Whigs had lost a member of the General Assembly in the election because three of their candidates were "Sons of Temperance." Many of the Whigs in Chambers County were Primitive Baptists who would vote for no member of this order.[111]

The first excursion of the Sons of Temperance into governor-making was equally unfortunate. Winston was elected by a vote of 30,116, while Earnest received only 10,127 votes and Nicks 3,763.[112]

Temperance forces, in some counties at least, worked hard to elect legislators favorable to their cause. "We will boldly meet the enemy at the ballot box," resolved a convention in Tuskegee in April of election year.[113] The Lee County temperance forces, convening in May at Auburn, resolved to require all candidates to make unequivocal statement of their position and to support no one who would not endorse local option.[114] Records of the General Assembly do not show how many of the members elected in 1853 carried the stamp of approval of the temperance organizations. From the performance of these legislators it would seem reasonably certain that the temperance advocates among them were few.

[109] *Ibid.* A. B. Cliterall, A. B. Phister, and B. Holt were designated as the committee to present memorials and petitions to the next legislature.
[110] *Southern Advocate*, July 13, 1853.
[111] *Alabama Journal*, August 15, 1849.
[112] L. Dorman, *op. cit.*, p. 86.
[113] *Macon Republican*, April 28, 1853.
[114] *Ibid.*, May 5, 1853. If all candidates were opposed, the temperance forces proposed to bring out their own men.

The Biennial Session of the General Assembly of Alabama of 1853-1854 convened on November 14, 1853. The time had come for the presentation of the resolutions and petitions prepared by the Friends of Temperance and for the introduction of the local option bill. The Select Committee on Temperance of the house of representatives brought in an unfavorable report on January 30. R. B. Lindsay, speaking for the committee, said that he and his colleagues deemed it "inexpedient to pass such a bill." True religion and morality, they felt, advanced more securely if left to the free acceptance of the people; "the blessings of Temperance will be more successfully and more properly disseminated by admonitions of its disciples, and the persuasion of its advocates than by penal enactments or prohibiting statutes."[115]

Meanwhile the senate had, since January 10, been considering the resolutions of the State Temperance Convention of May, 1853. It had referred these resolutions to its Committee on Temperance[116] and on February 11, this committee, through J. H. Clanton brought in its report. The committee believed, said its spokesman, that the petitioners were right in considering the trade in ardent spirits a curse, but it differed with them regarding the legislation needed to suppress this evil. It was their opinion that "this trade should in a great degree belong to those who have charge of the internal policy in the several counties in this state." It should be "committed to the Courts of Commissioners of Revenue and Roads." In this way decisions on the question of license or no license could "be made in the election of those officials" and the whole matter "divorced from all political elections."[117] Undaunted by failure the temperance forces went on with their campaign. They immediately called a state convention, which met in Montgomery on May 31, and began to plan for the election of 1855.[118] Dr. Thomas Herndon at this meeting urged that the Sons of Temperance resolve to support no man for governor or for the legislature who did not favor prohibition. Only in that way could a repetition of the unfortunate happenings of a few months previous be avoided. Dr. A. A. Lipscomb outlined in his report the course of action which became the program of the Friends of Temperance during the ensuing months. The heart of his proposal was local option. He pledged the members of the convention to use their influence to procure the election of legislators who would favor the passage of such laws as would place the retail of alcoholic liquors within the control of the people in the cities, towns, villages, wards, or election precincts in the state. A clear and unequivocal statement of position in this matter was to be required of all candidates.[119]

The State Temperance Convention in the following year carried for-

[115] House Journal, (February 20, 1854).
[116] The Senate Journal, Biennial Session (1853-1854), January 10, 1854.
[117] Ibid., February 11, 1854.
[118] Alabama Weekly Journal, June 3, 1854.
[119] Alabama Weekly Journal, June 3, 1854.

ward this program. It resolved that the legal voters of each election precinct or municipality should be permitted to decide for themselves the question of license or no license to retail ardent spirits, instead of leaving the decision to the probate judge and six freeholders of the county.[120]

George R. Shortridge of Montevallo was selected by the temperance forces to oppose Governor John A. Winston, Democrat, for reelection. On May 19 the Democratic county convention at Livingston had endorsed the administration of Governor Winston and urged his reelection. In the present governor, it resolved, the people had a tried and faithful friend, and one who for his ability and faithfulness merited their entire confidence and support.[121]

Temperance was not the only issue of the campaign. Education, state aid, and "Knownothingism" all entered into it. Shortridge, with a platform which contained a plank on each of these issues, was dubbed the *"Fusionist"* candidate. The *Macon County Republican* pilloried him as "an old Hunker Union Democrat steeped to the eyes in submission," and charged that he had sworn by Democracy all his life, until he found a prospect of higher wages in the employ of "Sam."[122] The *Independent* said that Shortridge was an advocate of sumptuary laws, which would gag the people of Alabama. The editor declared:

> A drinking majority in Alabama, has the same right to decree that a temperance minority shall swallow a pint of whiskey per day, as a temperance majority would have to declare that a drinking minority should confine themselves to cold water. It is a subject, we believe, entirely *dehors* the scope of legislative duties.[123]

Strongly against Shortridge and for Winston were the Primitive Baptists, who "took pride in the fact that temperance and other reforms of the fifties did not have any support from their church," and the *Sag Nichts*, an organization composed largely of Germans, with headquarters in Mobile. The balance of power in the gubernatorial election that year lay with these two groups.[124]

Winston defeated Shortridge by a vote of 42,238 to 30,639. Shortridge carried fifteen counties, twelve in the Blackbelt, Mobile and Baldwin in the southwest, and Lawrence in the Tennessee Valley. Winston carried the eighteen North Alabama counties where the temperance vote was strong by a majority of about 10,000. North Alabama voted largely on party lines.[125]

Similar discouragement came in the legislative elections. The temper-

---
[120] *Democrat*, June 14, 1855. On December 8, 1854, the Baptist State Convention resolved, "That we would see with great pleasure the manufacture and sale of ardent spirits as a beverage suppressed by legal enactment." *Minutes* (1854), p. 23.
[121] *Independent*, May 19, 1855.
[122] *Macon County Republican*, July 19, 1855.
[123] *Independent*, January 13, 1855.   [124] Dorman, *op. cit.*, pp. 111, 115.
[125] Senate Journal (1855-1856), p. 29. There is little evidence to show that the temperance vote was of any great value to Shortridge. Dorman, *op. cit.*, pp. 116, 118.

THE PROHIBITION MOVEMENT IN ALABAMA 37

ance forces had put out candidates in several counties and failed to elect them. The legislature which assembled in November, 1855, was composed of sixty-one Democrats and thirty Americans in the house, and twenty Democrats and thirteen Americans in the senate.[126] The records do not show how many members of this General Assembly were friendly to the cause of temperance, but again their actions showed little bias in that direction. With the support of the *Southern Advocate*[127] the proponents of a local option law urged the General Assembly to act. The Select Committee on Temperance in the house brought in an adverse report and the bill got no further.[128]

Failures of this kind did no good to the cause of temperance in the state. The Sons of Temperance, leaders in the excursion into politics, suffered perhaps the most. The order's close affiliation with the Know Nothing Party probably caused many to desert the ranks. When J. F. Dowdell, a member of the Sons of Temperance elected to Congress from the Montgomery district in 1855, stated that temperance was dead as a political issue and that he was now advocating education as a means of removing intemperance instead of trying to remove it through legislation, he practically sounded the death knell of the Sons of Temperance in Alabama.[129] The order was rarely mentioned in the newspapers of the state after the election of 1855.

The campaign of the temperance forces was not entirely without effect upon the General Assembly of 1855-1856, and upon the legislatures which succeeded it. Governor Winston effectively blocked most of the temperance legislation of the 1855-1856 session. He vetoed, on the grounds that it created a monopoly, a bill which would have put the sale of liquor into the hands of the druggists.[130] He vetoed also several bills to prohibit the sale of liquor near educational institutions. One such bill prohibited the sale of ardent spirits within three miles of Athens Female Institute. It was an unjust aspersion upon the youth of the state, declared Governor Winston to imply that education could not be attained where liquor was sold. Then, with some sarcasm, he added: "Perhaps the protection was designed to protect the professors and teachers employed." If so, he recommended choosing teachers "raised and educated at the South and not those who come from a land where prohibitory measures are deemed necessary to keep them sober." He went on to admonish parents:

> But, so long as parents and others only teach temperance and lecture on the ruinous effects and horrors of liquor, with a side-board or closet full of the best brands—so long as many, who are so fierce in their demands for legislation on the subject, have only to go or send to the drug store to do what Paul recommends to Timothy—to take a little wine for the stomach's sake—and so

[126] *Montgomery Advertiser*, August 21, 1855.
[127] *Southern Advocate*, May 23, 1855.
[128] House Journal (1855-1856), February 11, 1856.
[129] *Montgomery Mail*, August 2, 1855.
[130] *Montgomery Advertiser*, February 27, 1856.

long as the champions of legislative temperance are most eloquent under the inspiring influence of alcohol, little or nothing can or ought to be hoped for from legislation to advance the cause of temperance.[131]

Vetoing a similar bill in reference to the newly incorporated Cheunnenuggee Female College in Macon County, Governor Winston said that, while it was true that boys might sometimes buy liquor if it were on sale near their school or college, such was certainly not true of young women in Alabama. "I stood pledged," he concluded, ". . . not to approve such bills. My course heretofore on that question was discussed at length and endorsed by the people."[132]

Petitions to subsequent General Assemblies began to have the effect of increasing dry areas. In 1857 the selling of spirits within two miles of Athens Academy in Montgomery County was forbidden under penalty of $200 to $500 fine; Burnt Corn Academy, in Monroe County, was made the center of a dry area with a radius of a mile and a half. The sale of liquor within the corporate limits of the town of New Market and within a radius of three miles of that town was also forbidden, and a two-mile area around the Baptist Church near Pine Level in Montgomery County also became dry.[133]

Dry territory increased by the enactments of the 1859 General Assembly. Six towns—most of them in North Alabama—three academies, two churches, and one beat were made prohibition territory. Twelve counties now had prohibition somewhere within their limits.[134]

Certain laws with local option features received favorable attention in the General Assembly of that year. One directed the sheriff of St. Clair County, upon petition of fifteen householders residing within the township in which the village of Springville was located, to advertise and to hold an election at Springville, for the purpose of ascertaining the opinion of the people as to the prohibition of ardent spirits within one mile of Springville Academy.[135] Another provided that persons who desired to retail spirituous liquors in precinct No. 5, in Shelby County, must file with the probate judge the written consent of the majority of the voters of that precinct.[136]

The General Assembly of 1861 carried the idea further. One of its special acts provided that no one could obtain a license in any town or pre-

---

[131] *Journal of the Senate of Alabama* (1855-1856), pp. 237-239. Apparently the governor somewhat misjudged the habits of the young ladies in Alabama schools. One of them, Mollie Johnston, student of the conservative Athens Female Institute, wrote on Christmas Day, 1866, to relatives in Dardanell, Arkansas: "Christmas Gift, Dear Ones: . . . Between two and three o'clock this evening our long talked of Christmas dinner came, black berry wine came first. Madam [Childs] honored my glass with this wish, 'May you drink wine with your Ma at many happy Christmas dinners in the future.' Affectionately from your Mollie." Private letter.
[132] House Journal (1855-1856), February 1, 1856.
[133] *Acts, Sixth Biennial Session* (1857), pp. 290, 292, 293, 344.
[134] *Ibid.*, pp. 314, and *passim.*
[135] *Acts, Seventh Biennial Session* (1859), p. 585.
[136] *Ibid.*, p. 583.

cinct in Walker County without the recommendation of a majority of the taxpayers.[137] Another made written consent of a majority of the voters requisite before a license to retail liquor in quantities less than a gallon could be obtained in the Danville election precinct in Morgan County.[138] Branchville, in St. Clair County, asked and secured a special law prohibiting the granting of a license if a majority of the voters in the precinct cast a "Prohibition" vote.[139]

The pre-war days of Alabama's statehood thus saw the question of liquor control transformed from a matter of expediency into one with strong moral aspect, one which could form the basis of a crusade within the churches and which engendered its own complex organization. In those years a patient faith in the power of education slowly gave way before an urgent desire to press action directly through political channels. Following that desire for political action, the temperance organizations and even the cause of temperance in the state were not conspicuously successful. They may have weakened temporarily their own effectiveness and power. Yet the fact remains that when the temperance forces began to ask why the General Assembly of the state should not pass an act which would regulate the liquor traffic in the entire state, the liquor question was in politics to stay. They had sown a seed which would bear fruit in years to come.

[137] *Acts, General Assembly* (1861), p. 229.
[138] *Ibid.*, p. 175.
[139] *Ibid.*, p. 177. Sixteen communities were made dry by special acts at this session. *Ibid., passim.*

CHAPTER III

LEGAL RESTRICTIONS AND THE REAWAKENING OF THE TEMPERANCE FORCES, 1861-1880

The Civil War served both to accelerate and to retard the temperance movement in Alabama. On the one hand, the stringent control exercised by the government as an emergency measure gave to the prohibition forces a telling demonstration of the practical possibility of such government regulation in normal times. On the other hand, the hates and fears generated in the conflict left the temperance organizations with internal problems which curtailed their usefulness and in some cases actually terminated their existence.

Whiskey, a necessary part of the soldier's ration in colonial and territorial times,[1] became in the war years of 1861 to 1865 a luxury for soldiers and civilians alike. The grain from which it was distilled was needed for food, and the government assumed control of liquor manufacture with a strong hand. Distillation of grain in the state of Alabama "except under the direction and authority of the Governor" was forbidden by the General Assembly in 1862. Fines of from $500 to $20,000 were to be levied upon offenders.[2] The use of peas, potatoes, molasses and sugar in the manufacture of distilled liquor was forbidden by similar and more stringent legislation in 1863.[3]

A slight relaxation in the laws came the following year, when the General Assembly repealed the legislation of 1862 and 1863 and authorized the distillation of certain products. The distillation of corn and wheat, however, remained under legislative ban and fines for the violation of the law were raised to $5,000 minimum and $50,000 maximum. Violation of the law also made the offender liable to imprisonment for one to twelve months, the imprisonment to be substituted for or added to the payment of the fine. Distillers of cane, molasses, or fruit might once more operate, but they must pay license fees of $100 per 40-gallon still, and must also pay taxes on their product. Liquor distilled from cane was taxed $10 a gallon; that from fruit, $5 a gallon. The penalty of distilling without license was from $5,000 to $50,000 for the first offense with a discretionary imprisonment of from one to three years.[4]

[1] "Mississippi Territorial Transcripts," *passim*.
[2] *Acts, Second Regular Annual Session* (1862), p. 43. Governor John G. Shorter approved the act on December 8, 1862, and it went into effect ten days later. On April 2, 1863, Governor Shorter issued an order to prohibit the distillation of liquor. "Original Letters of Governor John G. Shorter."
[3] *Acts, General Session* (1863), *passim*.
[4] *Ibid.* (1864), pp. 95-101.

Whiskey for use in the Confederate army hospitals was growing scarce by June, 1864. To meet the emergency a law of the Confederacy, approved June 14, 1864, authorized the Surgeon General and the Commissary General "to make all necessary contracts for the manufacture and distillation of whiskey, brandy, and other alcoholic and spirituous liquors" for the use of the government. They might, if they saw fit, establish "manufactories or distilleries."⁵ After careful study of the raw materials available, the Surgeon General ordered the erection of a distillery in Wilcox County, Alabama.⁶

War-time measures of this kind served to fix in men's minds the fact that government could, if it would, control and regulate the liquor traffic. They also helped to emphasize an idea new since colonial days—the idea that whiskey and other strong drinks were a luxury, not a necessity.

The war ended, and Alabama came once more under control of a Federal Government which had itself during the war years been exercising control of liquor manufacture. More government regulation became a fact, if not always a palatable one.

The United States Congress had enacted a law in July, 1862, which laid a tax of twenty cents a gallon on ardent spirits.⁷ This tax was three times increased in 1864, as the need for revenue for war purposes became more pressing; it rose to 60c, to $1.50, and to $2.00. Taxes began to recede when the war ended,⁸ but they were still high enough in the minds of Alabama distillers. Many of them took the short and practical way of expressing their opposition; they did not purchase the federal licenses which were required for distillers and for wholesale and retail dealers. Ten years after the reestablishment of the federal revenue system in the state the total number of Alabama grain and fruit distilleries licensed was only forty-four.⁹

The situation was somewhat improved after the government offered amnesty for violators of the revenue law in 1876. By 1881 the number of grain and fruit distilleries operating under federal license had increased to eighty-three.¹⁰

United States revenue collections in the state increased from $30,145.86 in 1869 to $69,468.87 in 1881. These figures indicate 1,206 licensed retailers in the former year; 2,078 in the latter.¹¹

⁵ *Public Laws of the Confederate States of America*, II, 271.
⁶ W. M. Robinson, "Prohibition in the Confederacy," *American Historical Review*, XXXVII, 54-56.
⁷ W. E. Johnson, *The Federal Government and the Liquor Traffic*, p. 102.
⁸ *Ibid.*, p. 107. The rate in 1875 was 90c a gallon. This rate remained unchanged until 1898 when it was raised to $1.10 per gallon. *Ibid.* Malt liquors were taxed in 1862 at $1.00 a barrel; the rate was reduced to 60c in 1863, but restored to its former level in 1864. A. F. Fehlandt, *A Century of Drink Reform in the United States*, p. 140.
⁹ *House Executive Documents*, 44th Cong. 2d sess. No. 4, p. iv.
¹⁰ *Ibid.*, 47th Cong. 1st sess. No. 4, p. xl.
¹¹ *Ibid.*, 41st Cong. 2d sess. No. 4, p. 209; *ibid.*, 47th Cong. 1st sess. No. 4, p. xxxviii. Forty-nine wholesalers were licensed in 1878. *Ibid.*, 45th Cong. 3d sess.

Enforcing the internal revenue laws was not easy. The collection of the taxes was largely in the hands of the hated Republicans, and this patronage helped keep the party alive in the state. There is abundant evidence, however, that distillers who operated without federal license did not do so with impunity. In 1876-1877 fifty-two illicit stills were seized and seventy persons arrested.[12] Between 1876 and 1881, 268 illicit stills were seized, 949 persons arrested, one officer killed, and four wounded.[13]

The state legislature as well as the national government continued, after the war ended, its policy of taxing liquor for contingent government expenses. In 1865 an "Act to establish Revenue Laws of the State of Alabama" set license rates for liquor dealers which ranged from $100 to $300 according to the size of the communities in which they operated. Some relief from these rates was given in the revenue act of 1874, under which licenses for retailers ranged from $75 to $125, and those for wholesalers from $30 to $75.[14]

Records of the city of Huntsville give an interesting and typical example of the trend and fluctuation of license fees during the sixties. After years of grumbling, the saloonkeepers of the city petitioned the mayor and board of aldermen in 1867 "for a reduction of their licenses, as the time will now admit it, the state and county having reduced theirs one hundred per cent."[15] They obtained the reduction. Fees which had been $600 dropped to $200.[16] Three months later the rates were slightly raised again, to $300 per annum for retail dealers, and at that level they remained until 1891 when they dropped to $200.[17]

Following well-established precedent, the General Assembly of the sixties and seventies continued to use the license system, not only for revenue, but also for regulating the character of the traffic. An act passed in March, 1876, stipulated that an applicant for a license must present to the judge of probate the recommendation of ten respectable freeholders and householders who lived within ten miles of him and who were willing to

---

No. 4, p. xxxviii. The total revenue collected in 1878 by revenue officers was $53,130.14. *Ibid.*, 44th Cong. 2d sess., p. 52. For total collections in 1881, see *ibid.*, 47th Cong. 1st sess. No. 4, p. xl.

[13] *House Executive Documents*, 45th Cong. 3d sess. No. 4, p. viii.

[13] *Ibid.*, 46th Cong. 2d sess. No. 4, p. xiii; *ibid.*, 46th Cong. 3d sess. No. 4, p. xxiii; *ibid.*, 47th Cong. 1st sess. No. 4, p. xxii.

[14] *Acts, General Session* (1865-1866), pp. 9-10. The rates imposed were: on steamboats or water crafts, $150; in the country and in villages with less than 500 people, $100; in cities, 500 to 1,000, $150; in cities, 1,000 to 5,000, $200; in cities of more than 5,000, $300. The 1874 reductions were as follows: on steamboats, $100; in places of less than 1,000 people, $75; in cities between 1,000 and 5,000, $100; in larger cities, $125. A retail dealer was one who sold in quantities of less than a quart. *Ibid.* (1874-1875), pp. 37-38. Wholesalers under this 1874 law were charged the following fees: in places of less than 1,000, $30; in places between 1,000 and 3,000, $50; in cities with more than 3,000 people, $75.

[15] "Minutes Book D. of the City of Huntsville," June 1867, p. 63.

[16] *Ibid.*, July 2, 1867, pp. 171-172.

[17] *Code of Huntsville* (1871), p. 65; *ibid.* (1891), pp. 73, 75.

vouch for his moral character. He must also subscribe to an affidavit that he would faithfully obey the law. Among his promises was a solemn pledge that he would not "knowingly sell or give away any vinous or spirituous liquor to any minor or person of unsound mind without the permission of his or her parent or guardian."[18]

This ban on the sale of liquor to "persons of unsound mind" had been enacted by the General Assembly of 1872-1873. It had been extended in the next session to include minors and persons of known intemperate habits.[19] Other laws were passed in this period designed, as were these, to prevent the misuse of liquor. The legislature of 1872-1873 seems to have been particularly active in this matter. It frowned upon the excessive drinking of its own members in the state capitol building cloak rooms and offices and ruled that no intoxicating liquors might be sold within "the enclosure of the capitol buildings, in the city of Montgomery."[20] It took cognizance also of the old problem of election treating and forbade candidates to treat voters with liquor on the day before election or on election day.[21] And finally, it prohibited the selling or giving away of liquor within one mile of a church on any day when religious services were being held. Incorporated cities and towns were excepted from this regulation. Violators of the law were subject to fines of from $20 to $50 and might also be imprisoned in the county jail and set to hard labor.[22]

New dry spots appeared on the map of Alabama as the lawmakers continued, after 1866, the practice of prohibiting by special enactment, the sale of liquor within specified distances of towns, churches, schools, and other such places. Between 1866 and 1880 dry territory had been established around 146 churches, 35 schools, 37 towns, 15 coal mines, and 13 factories. The radius of the protected districts ranged from one to six miles. During this period only 19 laws of this nature were repealed and only 4 amended.[23]

---

[18] *Acts, General Session* (1875-1876), p. 227. The act was called "an Act to regulate the granting of licenses to retail vinous or spirituous liquors in this State." The affidavit which the dealer had to make was as follows:
"I do solemnly swear that I will not knowingly sell or give away any vinous or spirituous liquor to any minor or person of unsound mind without the permission of his or her parent or guardian; that I will not violate the act approved February 20, 1875, 'to prohibit the disposing of agricultural products between the hours of sunset and sunrise' nor will I suffer the same to be done, knowingly, by any partner, clerk, agent, or any other person on or about my premises, if in my power to prevent the same, and that I will not allow any gaming of any kind on or about my premises." This affidavit had to be administered by some officer authorized by law to administer oaths, and had to be filed in the office of the judge of probate. *Ibid.*

[19] *Ibid.* (1872-1873), p. 137; (1874-1875), p. 280.

[20] *Ibid.* (1872-1873), p. 534. Dexter Avenue, near the entrance of the capitol grounds, had developed into a favorite resort for those who wished to stroll and drink liquor.

[21] *Ibid.*, p. 76.

[22] *Acts, General Session* (1872-1873), p. 81.

[23] *Ibid.* (1866-1870), *passim*. Seventeen such acts were passed in 1870; thirty-two in 1872; forty-one in 1873; and seventy in 1874.

Most of the petitions for such legislation came from rural districts. Of the 210 requests considered by the General Assembly of 1874-1875, about 60 per cent came from country areas.[24] Those presented in 1880-1881 were overwhelmingly from such communities.[25] This continued to be true throughout the time when the practice of petitioning for special legislation continued in the state.

The first law granting the people the privilege of prohibiting or legalizing the sale of liquor was passed in 1874. By it the probate judges in twenty-two counties were required, upon petition of any freeholder in their respective counties, to order an election "forthwith" to determine whether the qualified voters desired "to prevent the sale or giving, or other disposition of spirituous liquors" within the prescribed distance of "any city, town, village, church, schoolhouse or any other place that he may petition."[26] If the majority of votes polled in such an election were for "prohibition," it would then be "unlawful" for the probate judge to issue licenses to any one in the area prescribed. The managers, who were appointed by the probate judge and notified by the sheriff, held the elections in the usual manner and reported the results of the elections to the probate judge.[27]

Moderate legislation of this kind did not, of course, satisfy the temperance societies. But they found themselves in the years just following the war faced with such grave dissensions in their own ranks that they were for some years powerless to exert any great influence. The heart of their difficulties was the race question. Later the need to control the sale of liquor to irresponsible black men would be a rallying point for a concerted attack upon the saloon and its evils in which temperance societies, churches, and citizens would join. But in the post-war confusion more than one strong temperance organization was wrecked on this rock of race antagonism.

The Sons of Temperance were the first to suffer. They had been inactive during the war years, but they reorganized as soon as the war was over and took up the fight they had begun in the forties. The Athens Division No. 3 was organized in July 1869, and began to hold monthly meetings in September of that year. According to a notice of one of its meetings in a local papers, the worthy patron desired "a full attendance that none of us be called laggards in the holy cause of temperance."[28] In August of the same year a division was organized at Mooresville.[29] By

---

[24] *Senate and House Journals* (1838-1909), *passim*.
[25] *Ibid.* (1880-1881), *passim*.
[26] *Acts, General Session* (1872-1873), pp. 81, 274-279. The counties were Jackson, Clarke, Shelby, Randolph, Coosa, Winston, Fayette, Cleburne, Tuscaloosa, Monroe, Marion, DeKalb, St. Clair, Calhoun, Sanford, Jefferson, Baldwin, Cherokee, Clay, Lauderdale, Morgan, and Blount.
[27] *Ibid.* (1874-1875), pp. 276-277.
[28] *Athens Weekly Post*, September 24, 1869.
[29] *Ibid.*, August 13, 1869.

1876 the order had one grand division in Alabama.[30] But the taint of Northern origin was strong, and men had not forgotten the ill-starred political activities of the order in the fifties. The Sons of Temperance never regained even a fraction of their former influence.

For a time it looked as though the mantle of the Sons of Temperance had fallen upon the Independent Order of Good Templars. This order also had ceased functioning in the sixties. It was reorganized on April 12, 1870, at Huntsville. Twenty-one lodges were represented, and the reports showed an aggregate membership of 1,049. The members adopted a resolution "deprecating the introduction of politics into the order," and declared that "the cause of Temperance was onward and upward."[31] The Reverend R. A. Wilson of Fort Hampton, Limestone County, came to the fore as the most prominent leader and organizer of this Order.[32]

At the second annual meeting of the Grand Lodge of Alabama, held at Madison, October 4, 5, 1871, fifty lodges were represented and forty-six of these reported an aggregate membership of 1,150.[33] M. L. Whitten, Grand Worthy Christian Templar, said in his report at this meeting, however, that the Order had not met the success he desired. Some of the lodges, once flourishing, had ceased to function, but new ones were fast taking their places. It appeared that honest effort on the part of intelligent friends of temperance was needed for the "building up of our noble institution," said the secretary, and he suggested the importance of spreading more information about the Order and its purposes.[34] The Order resolved, under the direction of Alonzo S. Elliott, to adopt the *Good Templar's Advocate* as its official organ.[35]

Between 1870 and 1875 the Order grew rapidly, adding some 13,783 members.[36] Then the race question raised its head to confuse and disrupt the organization. In 1876 the Grand Lodge of Alabama had only 10,977 members[37] and by the following year confidence was entirely broken and the Good Templars were superseded in the leadership of the temperance movement by a new organization.

The editor of the *Athens Post* analyzed the trend of events and the reasons behind them. He said:

The remembrance of the Sons of Temperance is all of that order that now remains in the South—at one time it was largely in the lead, but as soon as

[30] *Centennial Temperance Volume* (1876), p. 651.
[31] *Moulton Advertiser*, April 29, 1870.
[32] *Alabama Beacon*, January 8, 1870.
[33] *Proceedings of the Second Annual Session of the Grand Lodge of Alabama, I.O.G.T.*, (October 4-5, 1871), Appendix.
[34] *Ibid.*, p. 3.
[35] *Ibid.*, p. 14. The resolution also commended the paper to the subordinate lodges and friends of temperance in the state, and instructed the Executive Committee to try to increase the circulation of the periodical.
[36] *Proceedings of the Sixth Annual Session of the Grand Lodge of Alabama* (1875), p. 12. At the fourth annual session, 177 lodges were represented, with a membership of 6,336. *Ibid., Fourth Annual Session* (1873), pp. 32-38.
[37] *Centennial Temperance Volume* (1876), pp. 241-242.

the negro became an integral part, the South could no longer continue; hence its speedy dissolution in the Southern States. The Good Templars having taken their place, rapidly rose in public favor until it was whispered that the negro was entitled to that order as a matter of right.[38]

The trouble had begun as early as 1866. The Grand Lodge of America, central body of the Good Templars, had decided in that year that the "order had taken into consideration no more the color of a man's skin than the color of his hair or eyes."[39] This was good Northern doctrine, but far from acceptable to a South struggling with the post-war problems of the freed Negro. Following the letter of the decision, the Good Templars of Alabama attempted to set up separate lodges for Negroes. But the white Templars refused to give the quarterly password to the Negro members and the arrangement served only to stir antagonisms. In 1873 the Grand Lodge of Alabama expressed, in no uncertain terms, their determination to manage their own affairs in their own way. They resolved:

1st ... that we will submit to no action by any parties, whether individuals or Lodges, which interferes with, or disturbs the social relations of the white and colored races.
2nd. That, as by the fundamental law of our Order, each Grand Lodge is invested with sole jurisdiction over its own territory and all Subordinate Lodges therein, this Grand Lodge will jealously guard and defend this right, and our Lodges and people need fear no alarm from anything the R. W. Grand Lodge either has done or may do.

Committees were appointed to help put these resolutions into effect.[40]

Dissatisfaction was increased when the Right Worthy Grand Lodge reaffirmed the decision of 1866 at Louisville, Kentucky, in 1876, and repeated the affirmation the following year at Portland, Maine. At this latter convention, a petition signed by fifty delegates urged the Grand Lodge "to require the Southern States to admit Negroes under the penalty of having the South declared unoccupied territory and being organized by missionaries of the Right Worthy Grand Lodge."[41] This was going altogether too far. It is small wonder that the Good Templars of Alabama found it impossible to swallow so dictorial a pronouncement. They would go forward in the temperance cause with zeal, regardless of sectional disputes and differences, but they would do so through an organization whose policies were theirs to shape and direct. The establishment of the new order of Templars of Temperance was their answer to what appeared a Northern challenge.

This organization was formed in the city of Huntsville on June 6 and 7, 1877. Its movers were, for the most part, men who were veterans in

---

[38] *Athens Post*, June 29, 1877.   [39] *Ibid.*
[40] *Proceedings of the Fourth Annual Session of the Grand Lodge of Alabama, I.O.G.T.* (October 1-3, 1873), p. 25.
[41] *Athens Post*, June 29, 1877.

the temperance cause. C. M. Haynes of Athens was made the Grand Templar and A. S. Elliott of Huntsville the Grand Secretary. With forty Temples and a membership of about 1,400, the new order started out to develop a vehicle for temperance effort "entirely free from fanaticism and puritanical ideas; liberal enough to strike the reason and appeal to the judgment." It was a strictly Alabama organization; the Grand Temple was supreme. Such an organization, its founders confidently believed, was much better suited to the needs of its people than a national order which claimed to be a "mythical chain of love encircling the world."[42]

Disgruntled Good Templar lodges formed the backbone of the new order. The fee for the transfer of a lodge was $5.00; for the enrollment of a new Temple $10.00.

The Templars of Temperance limited membership to whites; but no devotees of temperance could ignore the Negro. They decided to work with the Negro community through the medium of an organization known as the "True Reformers" which had been set up for the colored people by the Grand Lodge I.O.G.T. of Kentucky. The Grand Secretary was instructed to take steps necessary for the introduction of this organization into the state.

For the better education of the public, the Templars of the new order began to publish within a month after their organization, an official organ, the *Friend of Temperance.* It was printed in Gainesville and edited by Dr. A. D. Hill and Alonzo S. Elliott.[43]

While leadership among temperance organizations passed during these years from the Sons of Temperance to the Good Templars and finally to the Templars of Temperance, other organizations played important, if minor, roles. The Murphy Club was active between 1873 and 1880. It

---

[42] *Athens Post,* June 29, 1877. The principal and more prominent features of the order were total abstinence from all intoxicants; the formation of societies to encourage such abstinence; an exclusively white membership; a local self-government; and a state organization.

The pledge was: "No member shall make, buy, sell, use, furnish or cause to be furnished to others, as a beverage, any spirituous, vinous, malt, or other intoxicating liquors, and every member shall discountenance the manufacture, sale, and use thereof in all proper ways."

There was a first degree, in which the business of the order was conducted, with a temporary pledge which was binding during membership. The second degree was a life-long pledge which was optional for all members. There were open meetings and the "Murphy Pledge" for public meetings.

A mutual benefit department secured to members insurance on their lives, without expensive machinery or large salaries to officers. This was not compulsory.

The officers of the Grand and Subordinate Lodges and all temperance orders uniting with this body were entitled to honors corresponding to those previously acquired. Members whose lodges or organizations united, as a body, were exempt from initiation fees, but were required to pay for the new books and charter furnished them.

[43] *Huntsville Advocate,* July 28, 1877. The first temperance paper established in Alabama after the Civil War was the *Good Templar and Crystal Fount. Journal of Proceedings of the Fourth Annual Session of the Grand Lodge of Alabama, I.O.G.T.* (October 1-3, 1873), pp. 6-7.

held a state convention in Montgomery in 1878 which lasted three weeks and which drew about 800 delegates who "having signed the pledge now wear the blue."[44]

All temperance organizations were included in a call to a convention in Montgomery in 1878 held for the purpose of making plans to correct the evils of the liquor traffic.[45] Another state-wide convention was held in Montgomery in 1881.[46] It should be noted, however, that influence of this type of organization was on the wane. The men who had led the temperance societies and worked earnestly in their ranks were more and more turning to direct political action to secure their ends. The women would shortly develop a powerful organization of their own.

When the Murphy Club met for its 1878 Convention, W. P. Tanner complained bitterly of the lukewarm attitude of the church toward the temperance cause. He said:

> The work would have been a great success here had the Christian people given their influence and presence to the meetings, but with a few noble exceptions, they drew about them their robe of self-righteousness, saying, O, we are Christians, members of Christ's church; what is the use of our joining the temperance movement? The church is good enough temperance society for us.[47]

He was probably not the only temperance enthusiast who made such criticism. Temperance voices had been largely silent in the Alabama churches during the decade of the sixties. And when, after the strain of war was lifted, the religious organizations of the state took up again with vigor the cause of temperance, they tended to regard the curbing of intemperance as merely an aspect of church discipline.

The Baptists seem to have been an exception in the matter of sustained interest in temperance even during the war years; for although the state conventions of the period ignored the matter, individual associations kept the issue before their people. In 1862 the Canaan Baptist Association urged ministers to preach once a year on temperance and to exercise strict discipline in dealing with members guilty of "drinking intoxicating liquors except as medicine."[48] The reading of the Scriptures as a remedy for intemperance was recommended by this same association in 1864.[49] By 1873 it was ready to recommend that its member churches "advise our people to avoid the use as a beverage of ardent spirits and also not to make or vend the same."[50] Similar action on the part of other Baptist churches is on record for these years.[51]

The Methodist Episcopal Church, South, renewed its opposition to the

---

[44] *Athens Post*, June 21, 1878. In the same year Rogersville reported a Murphy Club with 110 members. *Ibid.*, May 17, 1878.
[45] *Montgomery Advertiser*, June 21, 22, 1878.
[46] *Bibb Blade*, August 25, 1881.   [47] *Athens Post*, June 21, 1878.
[48] *Minutes of Canaan Baptist Association* (October 4-6, 1862), p. 7.
[49] *Ibid.*, (October 1, 1864).   [50] *Ibid.*, (October 4-7, 1873).
[51] For example see *Minutes of the Bigbee Association* (October 10-12 1868), pp. 6-7.

liquor traffic about 1870. Its conference that year unanimously adopted a report on temperance which declared that intemperance, given a "lamentable impulse" by the war, was rapidly increasing throughout the state; deplored the fact that the "warnings of the pulpit have been feeble, compared with what they might have been" and that "not a few of the official members" had "gone into the traffic in ardent spirits"; and recommended the following resolutions:

Resolved, That this Conference pledge itself to renewed and increased efforts in opposing the wide-spread evils of intemperance.
Resolved, That the traffic in ardent spirits *for gain,* is inconsistent with the profession and vows of church membership, or welfare of society.
Resolved, That the use of intoxicating liquors, as a beverage, or the drinking of drams, is contrary to both the "spirit and letter" of the general rules of the Methodist Church.[52]

Two years later the Conference urged more frequent temperance sermons and stricter discipline, and endorsed the efforts of the temperance organizations.[53] A resolution urging the General Conference to insert in the *Book of Discipline,* "a special rule against the sale of intoxicating liquors except for medicinal purposes" was adopted by the Alabama Conference in 1873.[54]

The Presbyterians took up the temperance fight, in some areas at least, as soon as the war was over. "The sin of intemperance has prevailed to an alarming degree; young men are making shipwrecks of themselves, and those whom God has mercifully spared from the missiles of war, are now falling under the hands of a more deadly foe," declared the Tuscaloosa Presbytery in 1866.[55] Similar pronouncements marked the deliberations of this group during the next decade.[56]

By the seventies the churches of this denomination were in full cry over the evils of drink. In 1870 the South Alabama Presbytery declared that "The demoralizing influence of the war is still manifest in the Sabbath breaking, *intemperance,* violence, & over-reaching which are but too common in the land."[57] "There is a complaint in some of our churches," said the East Alabama Presbytery in 1876, "of the evils of intoxicating liquors, and dancing being practiced by some members to the injury and scandal of the churches. So that we still have reason to cry aloud and spare not, warning even members of their pernicious ways."[58] "We hear complaints

[52] *Minutes of the Alabama Conference of the Methodist Episcopal Church, South* (1870), pp. 3, 25-26.
[53] *Ibid.* (1872), p. 13.   [54] *Ibid.* (1873), p. 11.
[55] "Minutes of Tuscaloosa Presbytery," (April 26, 1866).
[56] "In some parts of our bounds intemperance is sadly on the increase," said the meeting in 1867. *Ibid.,* (April 11, 1867), p. 289. In 1874 they were still complaining of "the deadly ravages of intemperance in a few places." *Ibid.,* (October 29, 1874), p. 245.
[57] "Minutes of the South Alabama Presbytery," (April 21, 1870), p. 372. In 1879 the same body complained of "excessive drinking of intoxicating liquors, among some even of our church members." *Ibid.,* (October 25, 1879), p. 335.
[58] "Minutes of the East Alabama Presbytery," (April 12, 1876), IV, 397.

of intemperance," declared the Associate Reformed Presbyterian Synod of the South in 1871, "which we know are well founded. We are alarmed at its progress. The evil deserves the most serious consideration, and demands a vigorous effort for its suppression."[59]

The Congregational churches of the state of Alabama in 1877 laid careful plans for the fight on intemperance. Each church was urged to undertake some definite and systematic work for the cause; each minister was exhorted to preach frequently on the subject. Special emphasis was to be given to education. Tracts were to be distributed; pledges circulated; and the teaching of children and young people was to be emphasized. Moderate drinking was especially condemned as the starting point for drunkenness and the source of crime. Reports from individual churches on the progress of temperance work were to be called for in the conference of 1878.[60] In 1879 the conference report on temperance exhorted all church members to total abstinence.[61]

The religious periodicals read by churchmen of the state were naturally ardent supporters of the prohibition movement. They varied, however, in the strength and direction of their support. The *Alabama Baptist* advocated rigid regulation of the liquor traffic as well as personal abstinence. Methodist papers coming into the state from Tennessee, Mississippi, and Georgia, were active in the general cause of temperance.[62] The *Christian Observer,* published in Louisville, Kentucky, and the official organ of the Presbyterian Church, was friendly toward the temperance cause but not aggressive in its crusade for action.

The secular press, meanwhile, maintained in general a friendly attitude toward temperance, coupled with a conviction that the way to attain this goal was through moral suasion. Among the newspapers most friendly toward the temperance cause were: *Alabama Beacon* (Greensboro), *Union Springs Herald, Selma Times, Eutaw Whig, Athens Post, West Alabamian* (Carrollton), *Tuscaloosa Blade,* and *Southern Advocate* (Huntsville).

Since practically all of the newspapers of the state were Democratic, prohibition could scarcely be a party issue. It is significant, however, that the strongest voices for temperance in the public press came from the counties where Negroes formed a large part of the population.

The years of Reconstruction in the South meant reconstruction for the temperance forces as well as for other institutions of the section. But the war and the aftermath of the war had not permanently weakened the

[59] *Minutes of the Associate Reformed Presbyterian Synod of the South,* (September 14-18, 1871), pp. 37-38.
[60] *Minutes of the Second Annual Meeting of the General Conference of the Congregational Churches of the State of Alabama* (1877), p. 7.
[61] *Ibid.* (1879), p. 9.
[62] Prior to 1880, the Methodist Church did not have a newspaper published in the state. The members of the church subscribed to Methodist papers published in Tennessee, Mississippi, and Georgia, all of which actively supported temperance. The members of the Presbyterian Church also were without a state publication in this period.

movement. They had in fact given it new strength. For in the lesson of the war days men glimpsed new possibilities of government action and control. And in the social upheaval caused by the sudden freeing of the Negroes a greater urgency than ever before was added to the cause. Fear of the drunken black man spurred the temperance people to take more vigorous measures to promote prohibition. Here was a problem which must be solved for public safety as well as for public morality. The saloon, where blacks and whites mingled and where crime was bred, must go.[63]

By 1880 the temperance forces of Alabama were ready for the next phase of their fight.

[63] *The South in the Building of the Nation*, X, 574-575. No saloon was complete unless it was peculiarly constructed and arranged with a view to facilitating violation of the law and encouraging clandestine habits. Back and side doors, operators and "family entrances," were designed solely for admitting and serving patrons on Sunday and during prohibited hours, or for furnishing individuals, including women and minors, who had to be screened from the public gaze. It was a common thing, also, for the saloon to make merchandise of prostitutes, gambling, and other forms of vice. *Cyclopedia of Temperance and Prohibition*, p. 606.

The saloon was singled out as a peculiar dangerous, and objectionable institution by men of affairs. Even fire insurance companies pronounced it an "unsafe risk.". Intense opposition was displayed by every person interested whenever it was proposed to place a saloon in the neighborhood of a church or school. In many instances the staunchest anti-prohibitionists were quick to resent attempts to locate saloons near their residences or places of business. Property owners and real estate agents frequently refused to lease premises to retail liquor dealers unless enormous rents were paid.

CHAPTER IV

POLITICAL ASPECTS OF THE TEMPERANCE MOVEMENT, 1880-1898

Political action was to mark the development of the temperance movement in the decades of the eighties and nineties. And in this action the temperance societies of Alabama were more and more to assume the role of educators of public opinion rather than generals of active battle. In that role, however, old and new organizations played an important and necessary part. Their emphasis was placed on developing leaders rather than enrolling large numbers of rank and file members.

The abating of sectional hatred, as the Civil War receded into the past, lessened the need for sectional organizations. The Templars of Temperance, having served the purpose of a troubled day, ceased to function. The Independent Order of Good Templars came out of eclipse and enjoyed a final period of prosperity and influence before it finally disbanded about 1895.

M. M. Sweat, editor of the *Temperance Herald* and R. H. Powell, editor of the *Union Springs Journal*, were important leaders in this order which, by 1883, had taken a new lease of life. At the thirteenth annual convention of the Grand Lodge held at Montgomery, April 10, 11, 1883, with thirty lodges from all parts of the state represented, Sweat, Grand Worthy Chief Templar, alluded briefly to past difficulties and stated that a large number of new workers had been put into the field. One of these was T. B. Demaree of Louisville, Kentucky. The Grand Chief Templar himself had, during the preceding year, delivered thirty-two lectures, organized thirteen lodges, and added 365 members to the Order. The Grand Worthy Secretary, Dionysius A. Clements, reported a membership in the state of 1,883. Thirty-six new lodges had been organized and four reorganized, while eleven had forfeited their charters. The receipts of the Grand Lodge were $834.26.[1]

There was every reason to believe that this progress would continue, said these leaders. The convention adopted the *Temperance Herald*, published by D. A. Clements, as its official organ and started an aggressive campaign for temperance reform which was to continue for the next dozen years. Commenting on the meeting the *Advertiser* declared:

> The Grand Lodge of Good Templars in this State which met in this city Tuesday, attracted quite a number of gentlemen who are prominent in the order. The heavy rains of Sunday night and Monday no doubt hindered a great many who otherwise would have been present, but the gathering was respectable as

[1] *Montgomery Daily Advertiser*, April 11, 1883.

to number and eminently so as to personnel. Their deliberations were in the highest degree conservative and will no doubt result in great good.²

The Catholic Total Abstinence Union developed considerable strength in this period. The fifth annual convention of the Diocesan Union of Mobile was held in Birmingham in July, 1882, with representatives from four societies present. The Reverend J. J. Browne, president of the Union, delivered the principal address, and the Reverend Father Roche of Birmingham, speaking at the evening meeting, exhorted the delegates and their friends to fight steadfastly against "the greatest curse that is visited on mankind."³

A new kind of temperance organization, and one which for zeal and influence was to exceed most of its predecessors, came into Alabama in 1881, when the first local union of the Woman's Christian Temperance Union was founded at Tuscaloosa. The new society immediately caught the imagination of Alabama women. Mrs. Thomas La Crade became the president of the Tuscaloosa Union and, when the second unit was formed at Gadsden in 1884, the ministers as well as the leading women of the community sponsored its organization.⁴

This militant organization of women had been formed at Hillsboro, Ohio, on December 23, 1873, and by 1883 had organized unions in every state except North Carolina and Mississippi. The Alabama unions of Selma, Gadsden, and Tuscaloosa assembled delegates in January, 1884, for the formation of a state Union and for affiliation with the national W.C.T.U.⁵ Mrs. L. C. Woodcliffe was chosen president of the state Union, Mrs. Charles Sibert, corresponding secretary, and Mrs. M. A. Branch, treasurer.⁶

A pledge of total abstinence and dues of fifty cents were required by the constitution adopted at this meeting. The members pledged themselves to support prohibitory measures to abolish the liquor traffic and to engage in active effort to organize new unions throughout the state. Men

---

² *Ibid.*, April 12, 1883. The next annual meeting was held at Cross Plains in Calhoun County, April, 1884. The society continued to hold annual meetings and to agitate for temperance reform until about 1895, but it had ceased to exert much influence several years before it ended.

³ *Montgomery Daily Advertiser*, July 13, 1882. The officers elected were: Reverend J. J. Browne, Birmingham, president; Reverend D. Savage, Montgomery, vice-president; J. B. Sampson, Montgomery, secretary; M. Murphy, Birmingham, treasurer; Hugh Hatton, Warrington, Florida, sergeant-at-arms.

⁴ M. T. Jeffries, "Sketch of Alabama W.C.T.U."

⁵ T. M. Owens, *History of Alabama and Directory of Alabama, Biography*, II, 1411-1412.

⁶ Jeffries, *op. cit.* The Woman's Christian Temperance Union of Alabama was incorporated at Tuscaloosa, January 13, 1887. The incorporators were M. S. Searcy, A. R. Searcy, Jennie Donoho, Mary Moody, Ella M. Leland. "Records of Domestic Corporations of Alabama," I, p. 446. At the second meeting of the state convention held at Selma, 24 auxiliaries with a membership of 550 were reported. In 1904 there were 34 auxiliaries with a membership of 619. This number grew to 43 Unions with 945 members in 1908. *W.C.T.U. Minutes*, (November 13, 14, 1884), pp. 8, 9; (November 9-11, 1904), pp. 33-34; (November 17-19, 1908), pp. 21-22.

were to be allowed to become honorary members if they paid the annual dues of fifty cents.[7]

With the sweeping zeal that was to characterize the movement everywhere, the convention set up ten departments of work and appointed a superintendent for each. These departments covered: juvenile work, Sunday school work, temperance literature, scientific investigation and legislation, work among young women, state and county fairs, temperance Bible reading or evangelistic work, the press, unfermented wine, and work among the colored people.[8]

The scattering of energy implied in this wide and varied program was undeniably a source of weakness. With a fine lack of discrimination the ladies took up arms against everything they considered untrue, unjust, and unchristian. By 1904 they had added departments of work among railroad employees, flower missions, prison and jail work, work among lumbermen, purity, a medal contest, red-letter days, etc. to an already crowded program of action.[9] In the field of education, however, especially the education of children and young people, they performed work the effects of which were deep and far-reaching, work which laid foundations for wider public concern with temperance in the minds of a generation just coming into maturity.

Printed matter formed a large part of their ammunition. The state corresponding secretary reported that 2,000 pieces of literature had been distributed in 1890.[10] And the local unions helped to swell this volume. In 1890 the Attalla Union with only twelve members distributed 700 pieces of literature "in various departments of work." The Union at Birmingham gave out 1,000 tracts that year, as well as many newspapers.[11] Though the official state organ of the Union, the *White Ribbon,* did not begin publication until 1903, the W.C.T.U. members found plenty of temperance newspapers to which they might subscribe for their own edification and for distribution to the public. Among these were the *Union Signal,* the *World's W.C.T.U., A Knot of White Ribbon, New Crusade,* and *Telegrams.*

Children were always a chief concern of the W.C.T.U., and children in the Sunday schools very early claimed special attention. In the late seventies the National W.C.T.U., following the lead of the National Temperance Society, began to exert pressure on the International Sunday School Committee to adopt regular temperance lessons in the quarterlies

[7] *W.C.T.U. Minutes,* (January 22, 1884), pp. 12-13.
[8] *Ibid.,* p. 2.
[9] *W.C.T.U. Minutes,* (November 9-11, 1904). There were 17 departments with a superintendent for each.
[10] *Ibid.,* (April 17, 1890), pp. 46-51. In 1903 the superintendent of work among railroad workers reported that 65 letters had been written and 41,573 pieces of literature and 76 magazines had been furnished to bridge trains, railroad families, and depots by that department alone. *Ibid.,* (January, 1903), p. 44.
[11] *Ibid.,* (April 16-17, 1890), p. 38. In 1905 the Gadsden Union distributed 5,000 pieces of temperance literature. *Ibid.,* (December 5-7, 1905), p. 25.

THE PROHIBITION MOVEMENT IN ALABAMA 55

provided for the use of young people. The committee appointed to urge this measure was also to look into the teaching of temperance in the schools and colleges.[12] In 1880 a Sunday school department was organized with Miss Lucie E. G. Kimball of Illinois as superintendent.[13] The International Sunday School Committee was not easily persuaded. It paid little attention to the petition signed by several thousand people which, in 1881, requested quarterly temperance lessons.[14] It took no action in 1884, when hundreds of similar petitions flooded in upon its meeting at Louisville, Kentucky.[15] But in 1887 it yielded to pressure, and temperance lessons became a regular part of the Sunday school curriculum.[16]

This move for temperance Sunday school lessons received early support in Alabama, not only from the W.C.T.U. itself, but also from the churches. The Baptist State Convention of 1885, at which were represented 249 Sunday schools with an enrollment of 8,927 young people, resolved "that we endorse the movement of the W.C.T.U. toward the procurement of quarterly temperance lessons in the International Lesson Series."[17] On March 27, 1887, the first temperance lesson appeared in the quarterlies of the Southern Baptist Church. Such lessons were to be a quarterly feature from that time on.[18]

The General Conference of the Methodist Episcopal Church had endorsed temperance lessons in 1880.[19] The Methodist Episcopal Church, South, followed suit. The General Conference of that body in 1886 adopted a report which recommended "that our Sunday School Editor shall occasionally provide for a Scripture lesson on Temperance, to be taught in our Sunday schools during quarterly periods in which the regular course of lessons shall fail to provide therefor."[20] In 1885 the North Alabama Conference resolved "that we will teach temperance from the pulpit, in the Sunday-school, and from house to house until public opinion is properly educated."[21] Schools of this denomination began to have temperance lessons in their quarterlies June 26, 1887. During the next ten years such lessons appeared, not with absolute regularity, but with a fair

[12] Cherrington, *op. cit.*, pp. 200-201.
[13] *Ibid.*, p. 206.
[14] *Ibid.*, p. 209.
[15] *Ibid.*, p. 222.
[16] *Ibid.*, pp. 229-230.
[17] *Proceedings of the Sixty-fourth Annual Session of the Baptist State Convention of Alabama*, (July 17-21, 1885), p. 38.
[18] J. R. Sampey, *The International Lesson System*, p. 217. Another temperance lesson was provided on June 26, and such lessons were outlined for each quarter thereafter. *Ibid.*, p. 218.
[19] *Journal of the General Conference of the Methodist Episcopal Church* (1880), pp. 246-247. The Alabama Conference included "the Lebanon, Birmingham, West Alabama, and South Alabama Districts, embracing also the Sand Mountain and Scottsboro Charges, and also that portion of the state of Florida lying west of the Appalachicola River."
[20] *Ibid.* (1886), pp. 197-198. In 1898 the Conference endorsed the work of the W.C.T.U. in "educating the children as to the effects of alcohol on their bodies," through Sunday School lessons. *Ibid.* (1898), pp. 125-126.
[21] *Minutes of the North Alabama Conference of the Methodist Episcopal Church, South* (1885), p. 23.

degree of persistence.[22] Since the Alabama Conference and the North Alabama Conference of this Church claimed a Sunday school enrollment in 1887 of some 50,737 boys and girls, the field of temperance education here was wide indeed.[23]

The Presbyterian Church in the state, with an enrollment of 3,936 Sunday school scholars in 1885,[24] was somewhat less inclined to follow the lead of the W.C.T.U. The Alabama Sunday schools used lesson material prepared by the General Assembly's Publication Committee and that Assembly had taken no action on the inclusion of temperance lessons and had in fact refused to commit itself on the point when petitioned by the W.C.T.U.[25] But the Church had adopted the International Sunday School System of lessons and, therefore, took notice of the plans formed by the committee.

The *Earnest Worker,* an official organ of the Presbyterians, announced in 1886 that during the following year a "Temperance Lesson" would be included in the schedule for each quarter.[26] The first Temperance Lesson with full text and comments to be published in this magazine, however, did not appear until May 21, 1893. Other lessons followed on October 29 of that year and in March, 1894. They were entitled: "Against Intemperance"; "Abstinence for the Sake of Others"; "Wine a Mocker."[27]

While thus directing considerable energy toward the education of the approximately 63,500 boys and girls enrolled in Sunday schools,[28] the W.C.T.U. by no means neglected secular education nor forgot the child outside the school. Loyal Temperance Legions, Bands of Hope, Kindergarten Schools banded the children together to learn the bad effects of intoxicating liquor. Declamation contests, frequently events of considerable importance with medals for the winners, helped to stir young imaginations.[29]

As early as 1884 the society began an active campaign for temperance teaching in the public schools which was to mark its most significant achievement in the Alabama liquor control movement. In that year the W.C.T.U. petitioned the legislature to enact a law requiring scientific

[22] *Senior Sunday School Quarterly of the Methodist Episcopal Church, South,* June 27, 1887. A similar lesson also appeared in the next quarterly on September 25. Most of the quarterlies in the years that followed contained such lessons.
[23] *Minutes of the Alabama Conference of the Methodist Episcopal Church, South* (1887), Statistical Report. Records for 1885 for the Alabama Conference were not available. See also *Minutes of the North Alabama Conference of the Methodist Episcopal Church, South* (1887), p. 42.
[24] *Minutes of the General Assembly,* (1885).
[25] Letter from Dr. S. M. Tenney, Curator, Montreat, N. C.
[26] *Earnest Worker,* December, 1886, pp. 277-278. This article contained a detailed announcement of all lessons for the year 1887, and provided for a "Temperance Lesson" at the end of each quarter: March 27, June 26, September 25, December 24.
[27] *Ibid.,* May 21, October 29, 1893; March, 1894.
[28] By 1887 the combined enrollment of Baptist, Methodist, and Presbyterian Sunday schools had reached this total.
[29] *Minutes of the W.C.T.U.,* (December 1, 2, 1893), p. 63; (December 5-7, 1905), p. 22.

instruction in the public schools on temperance and the evil effects of alcohol on the various organs of the body.[80] The General Assembly failed to pass such legislation and similarly ignored a second petition framed by the Selma convention in November of that year.[81] The lawmakers did, however, on February 10, 1885, but physiology and hygiene on the list of subjects in which applicants for teachers' certificates were required to pass an examination.[82] And in 1891 the continued agitation of the W.C.T.U., reinforced by the demands of the churches, brought success. The General Assembly directed teachers to give instruction on the evil effects of alcohol on the body and mind.[83] The significance of this legislation is apparent when one realizes that, during 1908, when the temperance effort reached its climax in Alabama, there were in the schools of the state 258,998 white and 127,480 colored children all being fully taught the dangers of intemperance.[84]

In addition to the generous support given by most churches to the educational efforts of the W.C.T.U. in their Sunday schools, religious aid to the temperance cause continued strong during the last years of the nineteenth century. Most denominations actively sought, through petitions to the General Assembly, to ban the sale of liquor near their houses of worship,[85] and such petitions generally received favorable attention by the lawmakers, so that dry areas were created around an increasing number of churches in the state. Churchmen and preachers took active part in the work for temperance, and the deliberative bodies of the various denominations continued to exhort members to abstinence and in some cases to record their willingness to take aggressive action to suppress the hated traffic.

The Baptist State Convention heard and adopted reports on temperance and resolutions against the liquor traffic at every annual session from 1880 to 1900. As early as 1881 they were on record as favoring all movements which looked to the suppression of the sale and drinking of intoxicating liquors;[36] and in 1883 they were ready to launch a vigorous attack

[80] *Minutes of the W.C.T.U.*, (January 24, 1884), p. 9.
[81] *Ibid.*, (November 13-14, 1884), p. 19.
[82] *Acts, General Session* (1884-1885), p. 113.
[83] *Ibid.*, (1890-1891), pp. 350-351. Some of the textbooks used were: J. C. Cutter, *Anatomy, Physiology and Hygiene*, 1887; J. H. Kellog, *Physiology and Hygiene*, 1894; D. F. Lincoln, *Hygienic Physiology*, 1892; R. S. Tracy, *The Essentials of Anatomy, Physiology, and Hygiene*, 1886. *The Elementary Spelling Book*, by Noah Webster, 1866, taught temperance indirectly by the use of terse statements, such as: "The man who drinks rum may soon want a loaf of bread," p. 40. McGuffey's *Readers*, containing lessons on temperance, were used until 1903.
[84] *Biennial Report of the State Department of Education* (1906-1908), p. 129. The General Conference of the Methodist Episcopal Church was on record as favoring "the introduction of a temperance text book in the public schools" as early as 1880. *Journals of the General Conference of the Methodist Episcopal Church* (1880), p. 246.
[85] *Senate and House Journals* (1880-1899), p. 138, *passim*. See also, *Acts* (1880-1899), *passim*.
[86] *Proceedings of the Baptist State Convention* (1881), p. 25.

from which they did not withdraw until prohibition in Alabama was an accomplished fact. The 1883 Report on Temperance was very definite. It declared:

> This Convention, as a body of Christian men who are citizens of the State of Alabama, ought to commit themselves to labor for Constitutional Prohibition as a *final* aim, and to labor for anything which may be best in our respective sections, and which looks to state and United States Constitutional Prohibition.[37]

"The Baptist Church is no home for a drunkard or a liquor vendor," resolved the Convention of the following year. It recorded its support of "sober men for office," local option, legislative petitions for the creation of special dry areas; and it declared

> that every good citizen should feel responsibility for the enforcement of the prohibition laws; that the public should be educated on ill effects of intoxicating liquor; that the weak points in the existing liquor laws should be strengthened; that constitutional prohibition be their final aim.[38]

A committee of five, whose duty was to work for temperance publicity in the secular press, was appointed by the Convention of 1885.[39] In 1886 the Convention pointed with pride to the part the Baptists were playing in the extension of dry territory and the advance of temperance. Some fifty-seven associations, said the Committee on Temperance, had in the past year adopted reports on temperance, ranging in length from three lines to three and one-half pages.[40]

A decade later the fight was still being waged by this church. The 1896 Report gave specific advice to church members on the ways in which they could make their influence felt in the temperance cause. They were to do this:

> By abstaining from the use of alcoholic liquors as a beverage, themselves; by refusing to sign whiskey petitions; by refusing to rent their houses for liquor shops; by refusing to vote for any man for office who is an habitual dram-drinker or drunkard and who patronizes the saloon.[41]

To these suggestions, the convention two years later added the recommendation that members vote for national or local prohibition if the opportunity should be presented.[42]

The lead of the Baptist State Convention was followed by most of the local associations of that denomination, and a vigorous campaign to out-

---

[37] *Proceedings of the Baptist State Convention* (1883), p. 23.
[38] *Ibid.* (1884), p. 19.   [39] *Ibid.* (1886), pp. 36-37.
[40] *Ibid.* Lowndes, Wilcox, and Dallas (except the city of Selma) were contiguous counties having prohibitory laws. Randolph, Bibb, Monroe, nearly all of Chambers, Sumter, Choctaw, Clarke, Washington, Escambia, Lee, Fayette were dry, and there were other dry areas around churches, schools, and mines. Baptists felt justified in taking a good deal of credit for such results.
[41] *Proceedings of the Baptist State Convention* (1896), pp. 42-43.
[42] *Ibid.* (1898), p. 33.

law whiskey developed. As early as 1884 the Coosa River Association resolved to do all in its power to banish liquor from the land.[43] The Eufaula Association adopted a report in 1887 which recommended that "Hygiene Physiology with special reference to the use of alcoholic drinks be taught in our public schools."[44] The Pine Barren Association resolved in 1895 that its member churches would set aside at least one Sunday in each year for the discussion of temperance.[45] The Calhoun County Association recorded in 1898 its opposition to the use of strong drink and urged its members to total abstinence.[46]

The early stand of the Baptists may have helped stir other churches to action. In 1882 the Alabama Conference of the Methodist Episcopal Church, South, declared that its membership could not "consent to take a less advanced position on this question than other religious denominations and the various scientific and medical associations of the country." Therefore, it resolved to

do all in our power to enlighten the public mind and educate public sentiment to a higher appreciation of the fact that the use of intoxicating liquors as a beverage is not only a great public evil, but a grievous sin, damaging to the church and ruinous to the individual, and we pledge ourselves and will urge our members to the support of all proper measures and movements for its suppression.[47]

The Methodists had joined the Baptists to lead an all-out battle against the demon rum. Steadily, year by year, the committees on temperance brought in their reports.[48] The report of 1888 declared that the cause of prohibition was identical with the cause of temperance, but added that Methodists could not endorse the National Prohibition party because it advocated woman suffrage which the church considered degrading to womanhood. The delegates of that year were reminded that the consumption of liquor appeared to be declining; the campaign of education in the dangers of alcohol was opening men's eyes. Methodists, declared the report, should not go on the bond of any man who had been indicted under the temperance laws, or render any assistance in his defense unless he was believed to be innocent. The Conference then resolved neither to slacken its efforts nor to stifle its plans until the prohibition of the manufacture, sale, and consumption of alcoholic liquors should be written into both state and federal constitutions.[49]

Four years later the Alabama Conference took special cognizance of a bill before the house of representatives which called for the repeal of the prohibitory law in Macon County. The Alabama Conference Female

[43] "Minutes of the Coosa River Baptist Association" (1884), p. 10.
[44] "Minutes of the Eufaula Baptist Association" (1887), pp. 8-9.
[45] "Minutes of the Pine Barren Baptist Association" (1895), p. 9.
[46] "Minutes of Calhoun County Baptist Association" (1898), p. 13.
[47] *Minutes of the Alabama Conference* (1882), p. 18.
[48] *Ibid.* (1882-1898), *passim.*
[49] *Minutes of the Alabama Conference* (1888), pp. 26-27.

College was located at Tuskegee and the Conference was, therefore, the largest property holder in the county. A memorial went to the legislature protesting the passage of that bill or any other measure which would legalize liquor sales in this area.[50] The prohibitory law remained untouched.

A vigorous declaration that the saloon and brewery had joined hands to destroy the home marked the Conference of 1898. The canker had penetrated to the halls of legislation, and controlled the utterances of the secular press. Lawmakers, elected largely by church members, continued to legalize and protect the traffic. "Resolutions accomplish nothing unless reduced to action," the report stated. "Our ministry and membership should not only preach and pray against it, but we should vote against it, and use every legitimate means, individually and collectively, to drive alcoholism from our fair State."[51]

The North Alabama Conference of the Methodists followed a similar line of action. In 1887 this body sweepingly resolved that rum should be banished from the earth; that the power of the saloon should be broken; that the manufacture of ardent spirits should be prohibited, except for medicinal purposes; that moral suasion should be used for the drinker and prohibition for the seller; that the discipline of the church should be strictly enforced; and that the work of the W.C.T.U. should be endorsed.[52] The Conference of 1893 declared itself in "full and hearty sympathy with the utterances of our Discipline in reference to the manufacture, sale, and use of alcoholic liquors," and pledged more conscientious observance of these rules. Its members also promised to work for temperance legislation and for the enforcement of temperance laws "without committing ourselves to any partisan political measure."[53] In 1896 this Conference requested the presiding bishop to appoint Reverend L. F. Whitten and T. C. Banks as delegates to the Anti-Saloon League Convention to be held in Cleveland.[54]

Considerably less aggressive was the stand of the Presbyterians. The Synod of Alabama in 1884 complacently adopted a report that "the evils of worldly amusements and intemperance are represented as being either on the decline or entirely wanting, a fact which should be highly gratifying to every pious heart."[55] Subsequent reports kept this mild, unwor-

[50] *Ibid.* (1892), p. 17. [51] *Ibid.* (1898), p. H-I.
[52] *Minutes of the North Alabama Conference* (1887), pp. 200-230.
[53] *Ibid.* (1893), p. 58. The provisions of the Discipline were: "Let all our preachers and members faithfully observe the General Rule which forbids 'drunkenness, or drinking spirituous liquors, unless in cases of necessity.' ...
"Let all our preachers and members abstain from the manufacture or sale of intoxicating liquors to be used as a beverage, from signing petitions for such sale, from becoming bondsmen for any person as a condition for obtaining a license, and from renting property to be used for such sale. If any member shall violate any of the provisions of this paragraph, he shall be deemed guilty of immorality; ..." *The Doctrines and Discipline of the Methodist Episcopal Church, South* (1890), Chapter V.
[54] *Minutes of the North Alabama Conference* (1898), p. 48.
[55] *Minutes of the Synod of Alabama* (October 29, 1884), p. 163.

ried tone.[56] The individual Presbyteries adopted temperance reports. They varied in strength from that of the North Alabama Presbytery, in 1888, that "this Presbytery condemns most heartily the practice of patronizing saloons & the drinking of strong drinks as a beverage or in any way aiding or abetting the liquor traffic";[57] to that of the Tuscaloosa Presbytery in 1891, that "Intemperance in the use of intoxicants does not prevail among our people."[58]

When the Anti-Saloon League of America, in 1896, requested the Associate Reformed Presbyterian Synod of the South to send delegates to the Washington Convention, the Synod expressed sympathy with the object of the League but did not "think it advisable to ally the Synod as an ecclesiastical body with the Anti-Saloon League."[59] The same body in the following year noticed the temperance problem sufficiently to recommend that "ministers, elders, deacons, and members do all they can by word, life, and act to abolish the evil,"[60] and in 1898 they acted favorably on the W.C.T.U.'s request for a temperance Sunday in the Sunday School.[61] But an aggressive tone is missing from their records as from those of other Presbyterian bodies of the day.

The Congregational Church, not strong in numbers, continued consistent support to temperance with strong emphasis on education. Its pastors were urged to speak out against intemperance. The distribution of tracts was encouraged. Subscriptions to good temperance papers, such as the *Temperance Banner*, were strongly recommended to church members.[62] In 1887 the Congregational Association of Alabama declared that some of the churches had given up the use of fermented wine in the communion service and that some had written the temperance pledge into their creed. Bands of Hope were being organized among the children and the older people were joining W.C.T.U. groups. This convention again implored pastors and delegates to fight for temperance in their home communities.[63] In 1890 the Committee on Temperance recommended the distribution of temperance literature, the preaching of sermons, and redoubled effort toward the enforcement of prohibitory laws.[64] In 1898 the Committee on Temperance recommended the organization of a temperance society in the churches.[65]

The Disciples of Christ were latecomers in the fight, but the strength

[56] The last one declared that "intemperance and worldly amusements do not prevail among our members." *Ibid.* (November 5, 1895), p. 215.
[57] *Minutes of the North Alabama Presbytery* (November 2, 1888), III, 49.
[58] *Minutes of the Tuscaloosa Presbytery* (April 21, 1891), p. 144.
[59] *Minutes of the Associate Reformed Presbyterian Synod of the South* (October 22-26, 1896), p. 843.
[60] *Ibid.* (October 21-25, 1897), p. 37.
[61] *Minutes of the Associate Reformed Presbyterian Synod of the South* (November 10-14, 1898), p. 1,854.
[62] *Minutes of the Congregational Association of Alabama* (1884), pp. 18-19.
[63] *Ibid.* (1887), p. 17.
[64] *Ibid.* (1890), pp. 22-23.
[65] *Ibid.* (1898), p. 13.

of their efforts far exceeded their numerical importance in Alabama church circles. Organized in 1887, the Christian Missionary Convention of this denomination recorded as early as 1891 flat opposition to "the manufacture, sale, and use as a beverage, of intoxicating drinks."[66]

The displacement of wine with grape juice in the observance of the Lord's Supper was for the protection of reformed inebriates. Such individuals could not commune without being tempted to resort to intoxicants to allay their thirst. Some individuals would refuse to take part in this religious rite because they could not resist the "demon rum." It was also shown that the children of the Bands of Hope who were pledged to abstain from all intoxicants could not partake of sacrament when fermented wine was used without feeling that they had at least approached the point of violating their trust.

The first article found setting forth reasons why churches should change from the use of fermented to unfermented wine for communion was written in 1848. In that year M. Stuart wrote *Scriptural View of the Wine Question* in which he said:

> I regard it as all but absolutely certain, that unfermented wine was used at the original celebration of the Lord's Supper, which followed the celebration of the Passover. Any other wine was inadmissible on that occasion.[67]

Stuart thought that Christians should be enlightened in regard to this subject and that sober and judicious efforts should be made to bring the churches back to the ancient practice. This should be done since it was then in the power of the churches to procure unfermented wine.[68]

Since fermented wine was a temptation to persons addicted to strong drink, the national W.C.T.U. began a strong agitation in 1874 to abandon wine for communion. At the first meeting of this organization Frances E. Willard presented a "plan of work" which was adopted. Section V of this plan, SACRAMENTAL WINE, reads in part as follows:

> We strongly recommend our Unions everywhere to appoint a committee of ladies in each church who shall seek to enlist the pastor and church officials in offering only unfermented wine at the Communion table.[69]

In 1879 Frances E. Willard, President of the National W.C.T.U., stated in an address that it was clearly the first duty of the church, by positive legislation on the part of the highest ecclesiastical conventions, "to cleanse the church and to expel this enemy from the pulpit and the pew." The use of fermented or alcoholic wine for sacrament had been so sharply criticized by the W.C.T.U. that general attention has been called to the subject, she said, and as a result thousands of churches had abandoned its use.[70]

[66] *Minutes of the Alabama Christian Missionary Convention* (1884), pp. 18-19.
[67] *Ibid.*, pp. 56-57. [68] Stuart, *op. cit.*, pp. 56-57.
[69] *Minutes of the First Convention of the National W.C.T.U.* (1874), pp. 22, 26 and 34.
[70] *Minutes of the Sixth Annual Convention* (1879), pp. 15-16.

The Committee on Unfermented Wine in 1880 reported that it had petitioned the governing bodies of the national religious agencies to use their influence in favor of unfermented wine at communion in all churches represented by them. Such petitions were addressed to the General Assembly of the Presbyterian Church, U.S.A., and the General Conference of the Methodist Episcopal Church. The latter responded favorably by the passage of a resolution favoring the exclusive use of unfermented wine at communion. The Methodist Episcopal Church in 1880 also embodied the following statement in its *Discipline:* "Let the pure, unfermented juice of the grape be used in administering the Lord's Supper."[71] This provision has been repeated in all the subsequent *Disciplines* of the Methodist Episcopal Church.

In 1883 the report of the National W.C.T.U. on Unfermented Wine stated that an appeal had been made to the Presbyterian Church, U.S.A., and of the South "to take such action as in your wisdom seems best; to secure the use of the pure, unfermented juice of the grape—in Christ's own words, 'the fruit of the vine,'—as a memorial of his blood shed for the remission of sins."[72] In 1895 the Presbyterian Church, U.S.A., adopted a report on communion wine as follows: "It is the sense of this Assembly that unfermented fruit of the vine fulfills every condition in the celebration of the Sacrament."[73] In 1892 the General Assembly of the Southern Presbyterian Church declared that in its judgment "the Scriptural elements to be used in the Lord's Supper is the fermented grape juice" but it had no serious objection to the use of unfermented grape juice for this ordinance.[74] In 1893 the General Assembly declined to rescind the action of the previous year.[75] In 1916 the General Assembly adopted a report which leaves the matter of the use of wine or grape juice to the discretion of the session of each church.

The Alabama W.C.T.U. was organized in May, 1884; and Mrs. Rosa Parker of Gadsden, corresponding secretary, reported at the second meeting held in November of that year that she had "circulated literature on unfermented wine for sacramental purposes."[76] In 1886 the Collinsville Union reported[77] that steps had been taken to secure the use of unfermented wine for communion, and the Fort Payne Union reported that one church was using the unfermented wine.[78]

In 1887 Mrs. Marietta Sibert, Superintendent of Unfermented Wine, said that she had corresponded with a number of ministers in the state. About a dozen of them had endorsed this department of the W.C.T.U. and expressed their willingness to use the pure grape juice, when they

[71] P. 87.
[72] *Minutes of the Tenth Annual Meeting* (1883), Appendix lxxvi.
[73] *Minutes* (1895).
[74] *Minutes*, pp. 450-451. [75] *Minutes* (1893), p. 47.
[76] *Minutes of Alabama W.C.T.U., Second Report* (1884), p. 11.
[77] *Fourth Annual Report* (1886), p. 27.
[78] *Ibid.,* p. 29.

could get it, for sacrament. Mrs. Sibert stated that she wrote a paragraph for the *Alabama Christian Advocate* and requested the editor to call attention of ministers to the subject of introducing "unfermented wine at the Lord's table." In response to her paragraph she said that two articles appeared in the *Advocate* calling on all ministers to aid in this important work. At the North Alabama Conference which met in Tuscaloosa in November, 1887, she had the following resolution offered: "*Resolved*, That we recommend the use of unfermented wine at the Lord's table." Mrs. Sibert stated that both her pastor and presiding elder assured her that the resolution would have passed had it not been for the disapproval of Bishop J. C. Keener. She said she had received reports from sixteen different places concerning the use of unfermented wine. Athens reported no union, but the pastor of the Methodist Episcopal Church, South, had expressed the desire to use wine for sacrament and asked her if he would be able to get it. The Attalla union reported that the Methodist Church was using unfermented wine, and that the pastor was willing to use it in all the churches in his circuit. The Collinsville union reported that much literature on this subject had been distributed and the movement had met with more encouragement than was expected. The president of the W.C.T.U. prepared the grape juice and the Baptist and Methodist churches were using it. About a half-dozen other churches in the county were also using it. The Uniontown union reported "the subject as one they dare not speak of, and their ministers are of the opinion they should not speak of this department of W.C.T.U. work."[79]

The Alabama W.C.T.U. continued annually to appoint a superintendent of unfermented wine. Although neither of the Methodist Conferences nor the Baptist State Convention ever adopted any rules on the subject, their churches had practically abandoned the use of wine for communion by 1910. Mrs. N. F. Sorrell, superintendent of this department in that year stated that "Very few churches reported that do not use grape juice."[80] The *Doctrines and Discipline of the Methodist Church* as adopted by the unified church in 1939 confirmed what many members of the Methodist Episcopal Church, South, had been doing for a number of years. The new *Discipline* requires that "the pure unfermented juice of the grape be used" for communion.[81]

Dr. L. L. Gwaltney, editor of the *Alabama Baptist,* said that each Baptist church chooses the elements used for communion throughout the state and that, so far as he knew, all of them were using grape juice. He thought that the agitation of the W.C.T.U. had been the driving force behind the transition. The African Baptist church of Alabama adopted a report on temperance in 1888 and embodied the following statement concerning the Lord's Supper: "We recommend, further, the use of unfer-

[79] *Minutes of the Alabama W.C.T.U.* (1888), pp. 57-59.
[80] *W.C.T.U. Minutes* (1910), p. 32.   [81] P. 518.

mented wine for Communion purposes, in as much as the least temptation may lead one astray."[82]

Dr. J. S. Chadwick, former editor of the *Alabama Christian Advocate* and an outstanding minister in the North Alabama Conference, said that the change from wine to grape juice for communion was a "by-product of the prohibition movement" and that the W.C.T.U. supplied the initial impulse for the adoption.

Few and rather short-lived were the temperance newspapers in Alabama during these years. The *Alabama Good Templar,* begun at Talladega in 1876, never gained extensive circulation. It struggled for five years and was discontinued.[83] The *Friend of Temperance* had an equally short span of life, from 1877[84] to 1882. The *Temperance Herald,* which the rejuvenated Independent Order of Good Templars adopted as their organ in 1880, seemed in good enough condition in 1883 to warrant continuation by vote of the Grand Lodge.[85] A brief sally into the political arena was made by the *Alabama Prohibitionist,* established at Union Springs in 1884 to plead the cause of the National Prohibition party, just introduced into Alabama.[86] Its editors were Frank and Edward Leslie, and they launched a campaign of caustic criticism of the Democratic party for its failure to endorse local option.[87] The unwillingness of conservative temperance leaders to support the new party led to early discontinuance of the journal of that party.[88]

The church newspapers, taking their cue from the official bodies which sponsored them, were favorable to the cause of prohibition to the degree prescribed by these bodies. They were generally in favor of keeping out of politics. Even the *Alabama Baptist,* aggressively favoring prohibition, took that attitude.[89] The *Alabama Christian Advocate,* official organ of the Methodists, reflected that denomination's distrust of the Prohibition party. It took the position that "the thoughtful men of the church, the men of cool heads whose judgment is sound enough not to be warped and misled by something that under the guise of reform conceals grave dangers, are solid against any third party movement."[90] The Prohibition party's endorsement of high protective tariff was one of the dangers which, in the *Advocate* editor's mind, made thoughtful men distrust and shun it.[91] As was to be expected, the stand of the *Alabama Presbyterian,* published in Birmingham, was friendly but conservative.[92]

[82] *Minutes,* p. 18.
[83] *Our Mountain Home,* September 10, 1881.
[84] *Huntsville Advocate,* July 28, 1877.   [85] *W.C.T.U. Minutes,* 1884.
[86] *Ibid.*   [87] *Ibid.*
[88] *Union Springs Herald,* December 1, 1888.
[89] *Alabama Baptist,* March 11, 1886.
[90] *Alabama Christian Advocate,* August 2, 1888.
[91] *Ibid.,* August 9, 1888.
[92] *Alabama Presbyterian,* August 1896, IV, No. 8. The *Y.M.C.A. Monthly Magazine* also supported the cause of prohibition. *Y.M.C.A. Monthly Magazine,* November 1886.

Temperance through moral suasion continued to be the slogan of the secular press. Even the editors most favorable to the cause were willing to fight to keep it out of politics. The *Montgomery Daily Advertiser* threw its considerable political influence to the side of those working for local option,[93] but it could not stomach the Prohibition party. The Democratic party, said this editor, had done much for prohibition in the state; the new party could only weaken its influence for good.[94] The *Selma Times* took substantially the same position.[95]

The weeklies in the counties reflected the same opinion. One or two of them were willing to support specific pieces of legislation. The *Bibb Blade* came out in favor of a law to prohibit the sale of liquor in Bibb County in 1881.[96] The *Conecuh Star,* published at Evergreen, was enthusiastic over the success of prohibition in that county in 1885-1887. The editor declared that the people would not have barrooms back under any circumstances and predicted that within five years there would not be a still or barroom within the state.[97]

But the Prohibition party found, as a rule, only bitter opposition from the county newspapers. Said the *Clarke County Democrat,* one of the staunchest friends of temperance:

> The cause has already suffered incalculable injury from the impatience and imprudence of its leaders.... We repeat: The Democratic Party is the only power in Alabama capable of aiding the cause of prohibition, and hence the man or set of men who would weaken or injure the party, in the same measure, would weaken or injure the cause of prohibition.[98]

The editor of this paper also felt that defeat of the constitutional amendment proposed in 1887 was a good thing; the state had been saved thereby from a demoralizing and humiliating experience.[99] The *Bibb Blade* editor was righteously indignant when he received "a package of National Prohibition tickets" for distribution through his office. He made his position clear:

> Bibb is a prohibition county as far as temperance is concerned; she is something else in politics, and that something else means Democracy, full-fledged and square to the line.[100]

Other weeklies scattered through the state which favored a non-political brand of temperance effort were: *Our Mountain Home* (Talladega); *Alabama Beacon* (Greensboro); *Alabama Courier* (Athens); *Daily Times* (Eufaula); *Greenville Advocate; Limestone Democrat* (Athens); *Pine Belt News* (Brewton); *Shelby Sentinel* (Columbiana); and *Union Springs Herald.*

[93] *Montgomery Daily Advertiser,* February 5, 1881.
[94] *Montgomery Daily Advertiser,* 1881-1899, *passim.*
[95] *Selma Times,* 1880-1899, *passim.*
[96] *Bibb Blade,* 1880-1881, *passim.*   [97] *Conecuh Star,* May 15, 1887.
[98] *Clarke County Democrat,* December 8, 1887.
[99] *Clarke County Democrat,* December 8, 1887.
[100] *Bibb Blade,* November 5, 1884.

The appearance of the definitely anti-prohibition newspaper was a new development of this period. One of the most important dailies of the state, the *Mobile Register,* published in the largest urban center and reaching many subscribers throughout southern Alabama, took such an aggressive stand against the reformers that it was willing to declare saloons preferable to prohibition.[101] The *Tuskegee News* asserted in 1882 that the prohibition laws had proved failures wherever they were tried. "Whiskey is bought and sold and used just as it used to be," said the editor, adding his conviction that "the use of ardent spirits cannot be regulated by law."[102]

These new dissenting voices were evidence of the increasing importance which the prohibition fight was assuming in the political arena. As churches, temperance societies, and the religious press continued to stir the public conscience and educate the public mind toward active expression of conviction, it was quite natural that opposition to the reforms now looming very near should consolidate itself and find its own expression. The political battle for temperance was swinging into new intensity in these years from 1880 to 1899.

The legislature which convened late in 1880 found itself faced with a veritable flood of bills relating to temperance and prohibition. Stirred by the new scientific revelations regarding the effects of alcohol upon the body, and irritated by the license system and by the growing political influence of the liquor interests, the friends of temperance were launching a new phase of their campaign which, for determination and aggressiveness, was not to be matched until the climax of the battle in 1907.

Most of the bills proposed and considered followed precedents already established. They dealt with license laws, the creation of prohibition areas, local option and similar measures which had been considered in one way or another by the preceding legislatures. It is significant, however, that in this legislative session of 1880-1881 the distilleries of the state, for the first time in history, found the hands of the lawmakers raised to limit the field of their activity. The temperance forces, long directing attention solely to the restriction of the sale and use of alcohol, were, perhaps a bit belatedly, beginning to realize the part played by the maker of intoxicating drinks. The "Act to prohibit the manufacture, or sale, or other disposition of vinous, spirituous, or malt, or other intoxicating liquors within the limits of the counties of Limestone and Clarke in this State"[103] passed in 1881, had some successors in the years which followed.[104] The

[101] *Mobile Register,* March 20, 1886; *Clarke County Democrat,* March 25, 1886, "The Spread of Prohibition."
[102] *Tuskegee News,* March 1, 1882.
[103] *Acts of Alabama* (1880-1881), p. 170.
[104] The 1884-1885 Session of the General Assembly passed three acts which prohibited the manufacture of liquor in Sylacauga, precinct No. 11; in Electic; and within a specified radius of the M. E. Church in Elmore. The 1896-1897 Session also passed three acts against distilling ardent spirits within specified distances of certain

number of such acts was small compared to the number directed at the distribution of liquor.

Possibly this indifference of the General Assembly and the friends of temperance may have had something to do with the great increase in the business of liquor manufacture during this period. Corn whiskey distilled in the state increased from 11,669 gallons in 1880 to 116,108 gallons in 1899. This increase was not steady. It fluctuated from year to year, with the low of 1,215 gallons reached in 1888. Distilleries increased in number also—from four registered plants in 1880 to thirty-seven in 1899[105]—and at the same time increased in capacity. In 1880 only two distilleries were capable of handling twenty bushels of grain a day; by 1900 one plant had reached a daily capacity of one hundred bushels.[106]

Fruit distilleries outnumbered the distilleries of grain. They increased from 23 registered distilleries in 1880 to 234 in 1896, and then dropped to 129 in 1899.[107]

The United States government records on such registrations obviously do not include the illicit stills, of which there were many.[108] Evasion of law, particularly in the mountains of northeast Alabama, became so flagrant that at one time the United States government sent a company of soldiers into Cleburne County to break up the illegal business.[109] Between 1880 and 1899, 8,580 criminal prosecutions were instituted by the Internal Revenue Department, most of them having to do with liquor law violations.[110]

Meanwhile, registrations of retail and wholesale liquor dealers showed decrease. In 1881, 2,076 retailers were licensed by the United States government; in 1899, only 1,096.[111] Registrations of wholesale dealers dropped from 51 to 30 in the corresponding years.[112] The average number of retail dealers licensed in these years was 60; of wholesalers, 30. Malt liquor dealers found better opportunities as the dry areas increased—there

---

places. Two similar acts were passed in 1898-1899, which forbade the manufacture of liquor within six miles of Union Hill Baptist Church in precinct 17, Henry County, and within three miles of Pleasant Point schoolhouse in Limestone County.

[105] *Annual Report of the Commissioner of Internal Revenue* (1907), p. 72. The fluctuations were great. In 1882, 4,291 gallons of corn whiskey were produced; in 1892, 9,964. After 1899 the number of plants decreased. There were only 18 in 1907.

[106] *House Executive Documents*, 56th Cong. 2d sess. No. 11, p. 99.

[107] *Ibid.*, 54th Cong. 2d sess. No. 11, p. 55; 56th Cong. 1st sess. No. 11, p. 96. Usually the fruit establishments outnumbered the grain by from four to six times.

[108] *United States Internal Revenue Reports* (1880-1899), *passim*.

[109] *Ibid.*

[110] *Ibid.* In 1880 there were 438 criminal indictments; the lowest number in any one year was 116 in 1882. There were also 354 civil and *in rem* cases in this period.

[111] *House Executive Documents*, 47th Cong. 1st sess. No. 4, p. xxxiii; 56th Cong. 1st sess. No. 11, p. 70. The saloon was a persistent institution. When a county became dry, the incorporated towns were usually exempted from the provisions of the law. Retail dealers continued to purchase licenses from the United States government even after Alabama became dry by statutory enactment.

[112] *House Executive Documents*, 47th Cong. 1st sess. No. 4, p. xxxiii; 50th Cong. 1st sess. No. 4, p. xxxiii; 46th Cong. 3d sess. No. 4, p. xcv.

were 186 of them registered in 1899[113]—but breweries were never numerous, the average number registered by the federal government yearly from 1880 to 1899 being only three.[114]

Considerable revenue came from the liquor interests. In one typical year, 1888, 528 retail dealers paid taxes amounting to $90,962.50, and 78 wholesale dealers added an amount of $14,500. Dealers and distillers together paid taxes amounting to $105,832.50.[115]

The control of this large industry was carried on mainly through the license system with only scattered territory under local option. It is not surprising, therefore, that the temperance forces were moved to attack the license system itself.

Under the license law of 1875 the endorsement of ten freeholders was sufficient for a man who wished to set up business as a retail dealer in intoxicants.[116] By 1880 the public was finding this liberality of the law far from satisfactory. Revision of the law was demanded by citizens, one of whom declared in a communication published in the *Montgomery Advertiser* that the law as it stood put "the source from which comes three-fourths of the crimes . . . in the hands of corrupt men."[117] This accusation was echoed by many others in the columns of the *Advertiser* and other papers.

Some relief was granted in 1886-1887, when the General Assembly stiffened the requirements and made it necessary for license applicants to secure the endorsement of twenty respectable householders and freeholders residing in the applicant's town, city, or precinct, who were willing to state that the applicant was of good moral character. In districts where there were fewer than twenty householders and freeholders, a majority of the number therein was acceptable. Applicants were required to take and file an oath not to sell to minors or persons of unsound mind without the permission of parents or guardians, or to any person of known intemperate habits, and not to keep their places of business open on Sunday.[118]

Once in a while a probate judge refused to grant a license. And once in a while the refused applicant sought to overturn the judge's decision by mandamus proceedings. The most notable case was that of Dunbar *vs.* Frazer. Probate Judge T. L. Frazer had refused to issue a license to Dunbar. Dunbar sought an order from the judge of the third circuit to force Frazer to act. The issue which developed was whether Frazer's action was *judicial*, following the intention of the Session Acts of 1884-1885 to free authority to grant licenses from previous ambiguity, or merely

---

[113] *Ibid.*, 56th Cong. 1st sess. No. 11, p. 70.
[114] *Ibid.*, 1880-1899, *passim.*
[115] *Biennial Report of the State Auditor of Alabama for the Fiscal Year Ending September 30, 1887,* ed., September 30, 1888. One distillery and two breweries were operating at that time. Only one license to retail liquor on steamboats was issued in 1888. [116] *Acts* (1875-1876), pp. 227-228.
[117] *Montgomery Daily Advertiser*, November 12, 1880.
[118] *Acts* (1886-1887), pp. 24-35.

ministerial as Dunbar claimed. The circuit court sustained Frazer and the Supreme Court, to which Dunbar appealed, similarly held that the judge's duty was at least quasi-judicial. It declared that

> provision is made for contesting this application for license, by a denial under oath that the applicant is a person of good moral character and a proper person to be licensed; and witnesses may be produced and examined as to this issue, the determination of which by the judge of probate is declared by the statute to be final.[119]

Frazer and the constitutionality of the act were both sustained, since Dunbar got no license.

Dissatisfaction continued and many persons were inclined to believe that raising license fees would at least ameliorate the nuisance. They argued that the fees should be so high that only a few dealers could afford to pay them—"the fewer the better." Under such public pressure the legislature in 1887 acted to increase fees. Persons engaged in the business of retailing liquor on water craft, railroad cars, etc., were required to pay $250, and the state had a lien upon such craft or cars for this fee. License fees in towns and cities ranged from $125 in towns of less than 1,000 inhabitants to $300 in places numbering a population of more than 10,000. Dealers in lager beer paid fees at one-fourth the rates set for other dealers. The wholesale fee was $200 and applied to any dealer selling a quart or more at a time. Compounders and rectifiers paid $200; distillers, except distillers of fruit, $200; and brewers, $15. To these license fees county commissioners might add taxes for county purposes not to exceed fifty per cent of the state levy.[120]

License fees for retail dealers in towns and cities were somewhat increased in 1894. The new rate ranged from $150 to $325. Other rates, including those for vendors on boats and trains, distillers, wholesale dealers, compounders, and rectifiers remained unchanged.[121]

---

[119] *78 Alabama*, 538, December, 1885.
[120] *Acts* (1886-1887), pp. 34-35.
[121] *Ibid.* (1894-1895), pp. 1192, 1216-17. Rates remained the same as in 1887 for retailers on boats and trains; retail dealers in towns of less than 1,000 paid $150; those in places with 1,000 to 3,000 inhabitants, $200; those in places with 3,000 to 10,000 inhabitants, $325; dealers in lager beer paid one fourth of these rates. There apparently was much drinking under the license system. The following paragraph illustrates this fact. The *Mobile Register* declared: "Christmas day has been distorted to the vilest of purposes and to gratify the lowest appetites.... All day long from morning to night young men and mere boys might be seen along the most public streets, screaming in drunken delight at their own insanity. Negroes, females as well as males, staggered and shouted in idiotic drunkenness. The stench from the sidewalks, filthy and slippery with human beastliness, was not more disgusting than the maudlin speech and vacant features of these Bacchanalians. Lascivious glances and brutal curses, were necessarily followed by open violence. It was a common thing to see knots of men surrounding a drunken companion who flourished a knife or pistol. When night closed in the unearthly yells of wandering drunkards broke into the peace and quiet of homes where children were being taught to reverence the name of Him who came to bring peace and good will to men." (Copied by the *Jacksonville Republican*, January 20, 1883.)

Far from correcting the evils of the liquor traffic, the high license fees aggravated them. Enlisting the cupidity of misguided taxpayers, the system made the whole people financially interested partners in the ruin wrought by the liquor traffic. It engendered moral torpor and blindness among the voters. It deepened the entrenchment of the liquor interests and made the enforcement of regulatory statutes more difficult. It provided the liquor traffic with a bulwark against a change in government policy which might derange public revenues. It gave the liquor interests more and more political power. It helped to perpetuate in Alabama the greatest evil of the age.[122]

Statutory license laws were necessarily of legislative origin, but their application and enforcement were in the hands of local authority. Naturally the people learned to look to the local rather than to the state authorities as the distributors of the license prerogative. Hence they came to consider these local license-dispensing bodies as the proper agencies to refuse licenses and to prohibit the traffic in ardent spirits. The relation between local license and local option is very close.

The local option advocates directed their big guns on the General Assembly of 1880-1881. Petitions demanded for the people the privilege of protecting themselves against the abuses of the liquor traffic. License laws had failed to give such protection. "If the Legislature should deny us this privilege," declared "Eufindor" in a communication to the *Montgomery Advertiser*, "although it cannot be positively reached as a body, yet the moral, human Christian people of the state will hold every man who votes against it responsible before the Bar of Public Opinion, and before God."[123]

Editorially, the press of the state took up the cause. The *Montgomery Advertiser* approved the appointment of a joint committee to consider local option and believed that this move would result in the introduction of a bill which would respond to the earnest calls for relief then crowding upon the attention of the legislators.[124] "The people are tired of special legislation, and a law alike benefiting the entire state would be a wholesome change," said the editor of the *Alabama Courier*.[125] The editor of the *Troy Messenger* saw in the local option measure the solution of the difficult liquor problem. "There is much opposition to absolute prohibition," he said. "Local option is far more popular, and eminently more democratic."[126] He very early recognized that the chances for the passage

---

[122] Opposition to the liquor traffic sometimes led to violence. The Reverend Lamar, of Greenville, made some declarations in a sermon against barrooms of that place and thereby incurred the ill will of some of his hearers who went to his home and bespattered it with eggs. The home of J. B. Stanley, editor of the *Greenville Advocate*, and the drug store of R. A. Payne also had eggs broken on them because these men endorsed the preacher's remarks. *Eufaula Weekly Times and News*, July 21, 1885.
[123] *Montgomery Advertiser*, December 24, 1880.
[124] *Ibid.*, February 5, 1881.
[125] *Alabama Courier*, January 20, 1881.
[126] *Troy Messenger*, February 10, 1881.

of a general law were very slight. The *Alabama Christian Advocate,* even after the fight had been lost in 1880-1881, continued to hope that the next legislature would "give the people an opportunity to prohibit the manufacture and sale of intoxicating liquors in the State."[127]

Already on the books of the state were laws allowing to certain counties the privilege of local option. Twenty-two counties had been given such right in the Local Option Act of 1874, but there is little evidence that any of them had used the right until new agitation drew attention to it.[128] The first county local option election was held in Randolph County in November, 1880, and that county was the first in the state to abolish the saloon by popular vote.

The victory was not won without a fight. The liquor interests were well organized in Randolph County and they fought stubbornly to retain their vested interests. Local option, they pleaded, would take away "the rights of American citizens." That phrase, repeated with vehemence and profanity, became the slogan of the "wets." The prohibition forces countered with records of crime and the burden of taxes for the maintenance of courts and jails.[129] The southern part of the county, including the towns of Rock Mills, Roanoke, and Luina, proudly claimed that they had had prohibition for years and pointed out its blessings to the rest of the state. Population had increased, and real estate values had risen from 25 to 100 per cent. The drunken rowdy and the fighting "bully" had disappeared; in their place were sober, peaceful, law-abiding citizens. Nearly every community had its churches and schools, and some of these schools were the equal of any in east Alabama. Trade had more than doubled. The election of November 15, 1880, brought victory to the prohibition forces by a vote of 628 to 453.[130]

The General Assemblies of 1880 to 1890 showed themselves quite willing to pass special local option laws, providing for elections called in designated areas upon petition to the probate judge of the county. In 1882-1883 Calhoun, Dale, Henry, Pickens, Tallapoosa, Bullock, Chilton, Lee, and Covington received such legislative permission.[131] The next session passed acts for Colbert, Talladega, Conecuh, Chambers, Etowah, and Jackson counties and special acts for Oakville and Moulton in Lawrence County.[132] Talladega and Cleburne were added to the list in the following session and precinct 12 in Butler County and precinct 1 in Lee County were also included.[133] In 1889 legislation was passed for Geneva County and for several precincts in Walker County.[134] Eden precinct of St. Clair County got its local option bill in 1893.[135]

[127] *Alabama Christian Advocate,* August 3, 1881.
[128] *Supra,* p. 82, Ch. IV.
[129] *Montgomery Advertiser,* November 20, 1880.
[130] *Montgomery Advertiser,* November 20, 1880.
[131] *Acts* (1882-1883), *passim.* All local option acts required elections.
[132] *Ibid.* (1884-1885), *passim.* [133] *Ibid.* (1886-1887), *passim.*
[134] *Ibid.* (1888-1889), *passim.* The precincts in Walker County were: precinct 1, Day's Gap, Carbon Hill, and Jasper. [135] *Acts* (1892-1893), *passim.*

A number of counties and towns availed themselves of the privileges granted by such acts. In general, the counties voted against prohibition; the towns for it. Few elections, if any, were held in the most populous counties and in the cities. The following table tells part of the story.[136]

COUNTIES VOTING FOR PROHIBITION

Year	County	Vote
1883	Calhoun	a majority of 1,300 votes
1887	Jackson	a majority of 884 votes

COUNTIES VOTING AGAINST PROHIBITION

1883	Dale	a majority of 600 votes
1883	Henry	a majority of 700 votes
1883	Talladega	a majority of 570 votes
1883	Tallapoosa	a majority against
1885	Colbert	a majority of 540 votes
1885	Pickens	a majority of 700 votes

TOWNS VOTING FOR PROHIBITION

1883	Trenton	a majority of 76 votes
1883	Thompson	vote not listed
1885	Florence	vote not listed
1885	Troy	vote not listed
1886	Anniston	a majority of 339 votes
1889	Moulton	vote not listed
1893	Andalusia	a majority of 29 votes

TOWNS VOTING AGAINST PROHIBITION

1885	Athens	a majority of 38 votes
1886	Greenville	a majority of 116 votes
1891	Carbon Hill	a majority of 58 votes
1891	Jasper	a majority of 21 votes

The General Assemblies from 1880 to 1890 were similarly friendly toward petitions from rural areas for the prohibition of liquor sales in certain specified districts.[137] Approximately 467 churches, 78 schools, 2 factories, 99 precincts, 37 towns, 11 townships, 27 coal mines, 5 post offices, 9 railroad stations, 2 parks, and 30 counties received such protection in the period. Only 25 such acts were repealed.[138]

[136] The total vote for and against prohibition was not given.

[137] Notices were placed in the local papers before the applications were taken to the legislature. The following from the *Bibb Blade,* October 28, 1880, is typical: "TAKE NOTICE. An application will be made to the next Legislature of Alabama to enact a law to prohibit the sale or giving away or disposition in any other way, of intoxicating liquors within five miles of the Court House at Centerville, Bibb County, Ala."

[138] *Local Acts* (1880-1899), *passim.* The following table shows the number of local acts passed by years:

Places	1880	'82	'84	'86	'88	'90	'92	'94	'96	'98	Total
Churches	86	34	68	67	61	58	20	16	46	11	467
Schools	8	8		8	5	8	3	2	31	5	78
Factories							1	1			2

But a general state-wide local option law was another matter. From 1880 until the administration of Governor B. B. Comer, prohibition forces repeatedly tried to secure such a law. The General Assembly of 1880-1881 turned a deaf ear to such appeals and subsequent General Assemblies followed suit.

Advocates of local option urged that this solution of the liquor problem required no new statement of position, no confession of faith as to tariff, silver coinage, race problems, suffrage, or similar vexing questions. Essentially non-political and non-partisan, it would avoid party antagonism and enable the people themselves gradually to eliminate a traffic detrimental to their welfare. State-wide prohibition would follow naturally as the local option system spread.

But local option as a temperance measure had many radical defects. Its tacit recognition that the liquor traffic was not criminal in itself increased the difficulty of enforcing all liquor regulations. Special statutes were needed to give authority to courts and officials to deal with and punish violators. Legislators willing to enact, maintain, and enforce such laws had to be chosen, and the election of such men was, of course, bitterly opposed by the liquor interests. A non-partisan petition sometimes brought on elections so non-partisan that neither the Democratic nor the Republican party would endorse the measures; yet these parties and their politicians were responsible for the enforcement of the statute if the election carried. Local option, like license, made revenue local but drew funds from a large area. It was always a compromise measure or a temporary expedient. Its greatest danger was that it proclaimed an armistice which held the prohibition forces inactive but left the liquor forces free.

The rebuff received at the hands of the General Assembly of 1880-1881, when the petitions for state-wide local option failed to produce action, convinced the prohibitionists of the need of stronger state-wide organization. They moved to strengthen themselves.

The question of calling a state temperance convention came up at the eleventh session of the Grand Lodge of the Independent Order of Good Templars, held at Union Springs, in April, 1881. R. H. Powell, Grand Worthy Christian Templar, presented the proposition and the Lodge received it with enthusiasm. The executive committee was instructed to look into the matter, to confer with friends of temperance, and was given authority to call a general state convention if it found enough response to

Precincts		15	25	17	8	7	10	2	11	4	99
Towns		5		3	5	6	6		9	3	37
Townships		2		5	1		1		2		11
Coal mines		5	15		7						27
Post Offices		1		1	2	1					5
R. R. Stations		3	3		2	1					9
Parks					1	1					2
Counties	8	4		4	3	2	3	1	2	3	30
Repeals			16		3	1	2			3	25

justify such action.[139] The committee lost no time in following these instructions. August 9, 1881, was set as the date for the meeting; Montgomery was designated as the convention city. Delegates and representatives from every lodge of Good Templars, Division of Sons of Temperance, Temple of Woman's Christian Temperance Union, from all churches, Sunday schools, Young Men's Christian Associations, Bible Societies, and all other organizations interested in the cause of temperance were urged to attend, with properly attested credentials. According to the committee, a full representation was much desired

that we may confer together as to the best method of advancing the interests of the cause of Temperance, securing the enforcement of such prohibition Legislation as has already been enacted, and the entire and absolute prohibition of the liquor traffic, which are measures of paramount importance, and demand the attention of every patriotic citizen.[140]

The State Temperance Convention assembled on the appointed day in the hall of the house of representatives. W. P. Tanner of Montgomery was made its president; C. R. Rencher of the same city, J. E. Lee of Morgan County, Hon. A. J. Robinson of Conecuh County, Reverend B. F. Riley of Lee County, Reverend L. R. Gwaltney, D.D., of Perry County, vice-presidents; and M. M. Sweat of Montgomery, secretary.

Nineteen counties were represented by some eighty-nine delegates. Montgomery County furnished thirty-six of these. In the assembly, taking active part in its deliberations, were twenty colored delegates. Their presence added a note to the meetings which had not been heard in earlier conventions. "If the Anglo-Saxon and the Hebrew will stop selling whiskey, I will guarantee that the Ethiopian stops drinking it," declared one of these Negro brethren. A paper expressing Negro views and written by two Negro pastors in Marion was read by Dr. Gwaltney and, by vote of the convention, ordered preserved among the records.[141]

Two main questions engaged the thought of the convention: (1) Is prohibition of the sale of ardent spirits consistent with a republican form of government and a legitimate subject of legislation? (2) How may the prohibition of the traffic in spirituous liquors be effectually secured in Alabama?[142] The Committee on Ways and Means of Temperance Work recommended tackling these problems by state-wide temperance organization and the convention accepted this report. It provided for the establishment of a State Executive Committee with three members from each Congressional district, and with five more in the district in and around Montgomery. The calling of conventions, election of officers, and general supervision of temperance work rested in the hands of this committee.

[139] *Montgomery Advertiser*, July 1, 1881.
[140] *Ibid.*
[141] *Bibb Blade*, August 25, 1881.
[142] *Alabama Courier*, August 18, 1881.

Operating under such direction, county executive committees would carry the work into every corner of the state.[143]

Resolutions declaring the close relation of the temperance question to the family and the church, the right of the people to make the laws which governed them, and the determination of the delegates to work for the prohibition of the manufacture and sale of liquor throughout the state by general or special enactments were enthusiastically passed. The convention was careful to emphasize its complete non-partisan nature. It resolved

> That the temperance question ought not to enter into politics, for there is no need whatever of affecting the political affiliations of any friends of the temperance cause, but eminent propriety in enlisting in its behalf the organization of political parties and their presses, without reference to party issues, feeling that it is the bounden duty of the party in power to do what is best for all people.[144]

Final resolutions commended the prohibition movement to the sympathy of the people of the state and authorized the preparation, by a specially appointed committee of five, of an address to the people on temperance and the purposes of the convention.

Provided thus with a close-knit organization to coordinate their activities and stirred to new enthusiasm by the spirit generated in the convention hall, Alabama friends of temperance went into energetic battle. Once again, in some counties, prohibition candidates for the legislature appeared and some of them were elected.

Strong and sometimes sincere opposition to their efforts came from a group of people who were convinced that prohibitory laws had proved themselves failures.[145] They pointed to the many infractions of these laws in counties which had become dry territory by special legislation. Grand jury reports on crime in dry counties gave them their best ammunition. "At the spring term of the St. Clair County Circuit Court of 1882, there were 120 cases on the State Docket, most of which were whiskey cases," reads a typical item in the *Troy Messenger*.[146] The declaration of the Cleburne County Grand Jury that it found crime to be on the increase and that the improper use of liquor was the fruitful source of a large portion of such crime did not escape their attention.[147]

The editor of the *Tuskegee News* aligned himself with this group. Prohibition in Macon County was a fiasco, he declared.

[143] *Alabama Courier*, August 18, 1881. The county committees were to have one member in each beat or precinct. The courthouse beat was to have three additional members who would constitute the County Central Executive Committee, with authority to call meetings and supervise the work. The county committees were to elect their own chairmen and to report, when requested, to the State Executive Committee.
[144] *Ibid.*
[145] The prohibitory laws were frequently violated.
[146] *Troy Messenger*, April 6, 1882. St. Clair was a prohibition county.
[147] *Ibid.*, October 12, 1882.

We do not know that the law has checked drinking of whiskey at all, but it does deprive the State and county of several thousand dollars for license. The object of such a law, we take it, was to check the use of intoxicating liquors, and if we are right in our construction, the law is already a failure, not only in this county, but everywhere in the state. . . .[148]

Even the *Alabama Christian Advocate* was inclined to admit the failure of prohibition. It attributed this failure to the "Whiskey power" in the state, the ignorant colored vote, and the scheming politicians. In Tuscaloosa County, said the editors, prohibition had been defeated "through the money of saloonkeepers" and the influence of unscrupulous politicians.[149]

The friends of temperance met assertions with counter-assertions, and statistics with statistics. They, too, used reports of grand juries, but used them to prove the decrease of crime in dry territories. They made capital, for instance, of the report of the grand jury at the spring term of the Pike County Circuit Court in 1882, that few serious violations of the law had been found and that crime was generally on the decline.[150] A similar report of the Randolph County grand jury also supported their contentions.[151] The *Clarke County Democrat* said that the prohibitory laws were working well and giving general satisfaction to whites and Negroes alike. The editor thought people were taking a more sensible view of the matter, and beginning to appreciate the motives of lawmakers in passing such laws. Some of them, he said, had been the most unremitting drinkers in the county; they ought to know the evils of drink if anyone did. In Wilcox and Monroe counties, made dry by special acts in the session of 1880-1881, the liquor traffic had not been absolutely stopped, but the laws were working well and a new peace and order about town was a great improvement over conditions existing under the old law.[152]

Increase of dry territory through special enactments was encouraging to the prohibition forces. But they were by no means satisfied to continue this piecemeal progress. Since only a state-wide prohibition law would satisfy them, they prepared for another convention.

The call for this convention, sent out October, 1882, was signed by a committee of ten men who called themselves "Temperance Workers and friends of the cause in Alabama." This committee, the call asserted, conscious of the need for organized effort in the cause of temperance if the goal of prohibitory legislation was to be reached, had consulted and corresponded with friends of temperance all over the state and were convinced that a state convention should be called. All temperance organizations, associations, and societies, ministers of the Gospel, and church members of every faith, and friends of temperance, regardless of party

---

[148] *Tuskegee News*, March 10, 1882.
[149] *Alabama Christian Advocate*, November 23, 1882.
[150] *Ibid.*, April 27, 1882.
[151] *Alabama Progress*, October 12, 1882.
[152] *Clarke County Democrat*, March 30, May 17, 1882. Wilcox and Monroe counties were made dry by special acts during 1880-1881.

predilections, or color, in every county were accordingly urged to send delegates to meet in Montgomery on November 21, 1882.[153]

When the convention met at McDonald's Opera House, John T. Tanner, Mayor of Athens, was made temporary chairman, and George P. Keys, editor of the *Alabama Progress,* was elected secretary. Introduced by R. H. Powell, editor of the *Union Springs Herald,* Tanner struck the keynote of the meeting by declaring its object to be the elimination of intoxicating spirits in Alabama and eventually in the United States.[154]

At the outset of the convention, the non-partisan character of the gathering was affirmed in a resolution which earnestly invited "the cooperation of all parties in the state to put away the dreadful monster intemperance from our midst."[155]

The delegates were not inclined to look with favor on local option; they thought the public not yet sufficiently educated on the subject to take wise action under such opportunity. They opposed repeal of any prohibitory laws then in force. They endorsed the proposition that instruction regarding the effect of alcohol upon the human body be made a part of the school curriculum.

The chief effort of the convention was directed toward an attempt to get indirectly from the General Assembly what earlier conventions had failed to get directly. They recommended a bill requiring that a would-be retailer of liquors procure, for his application for license, the recommendation of a *majority* of freeholders who were real estate owners in the precinct in which he proposed to set up a shop. This *majority* would be required to make the guarantees of moral character which, under the existing law, were provided by ten householders and freeholders. Notice of hearings on license applications was to be published by the probate judge in the local newspapers and all sons of recommenders were required to present themselves at the county seat on the day appointed, when recommenders would be examined under oath.

One can hardly fail to admire the ingenuity of this proposed legislation. Had it been enacted into law the prohibition forces would have secured prohibition throughout the state, except in certain rural precincts where the freeholders were few in number, dead bent on a dram shop, and all close to the probate judge's office.

Needless to say, it was not so enacted. The temperance forces welcomed the addition of twelve more dry counties to the list in 1882. But they seemed to make little progress toward the goal of state-wide prohibition. They had a little flurry of hope in 1883, when a prohibition bill was introduced in the senate and received a favorable report from the committee on temperance. But action on the bill was indefinitely post-

[153] *Ibid.,* October 19, 1882.
[154] *Montgomery Daily Advertiser,* November 24, 1882.
[155] *Ibid.*

poned.[156] Another convention, looking toward more effective pressure on the legislature of 1884-1885, was obviously needed.

W. H. Barnes, president of the Alabama State Temperance Association, sent out the call and the new convention assembled in Tuscaloosa on January 22, 1884, and elected R. H. Powell president, and John T. Tanner secretary.

Exciting debate developed around the question of high license versus total prohibition. The latter was the goal of the Temperance Alliance, but the convention finally agreed, as a temporary measure, to memorialize the General Assembly to pass a license law similar to that in force in Florida. Unanimously the delegates voted that Alabama senators and representatives be urged to oppose a bill pending in Congress to extend the time for paying the tax on bonded whiskey.[157] At this point in the heated discussion an old gentleman rose to say: "I am opposed to trying to stop the sale of whiskey as long as it is made. You had as well try to dip the Atlantic dry with a coffee pot, or try to put out hell by pouring water on it with a teaspoon."[158] Roars of laughter drowned out the rest of his speech.

Progress reports from various parts of the state occupied the greater part of the afternoon session. Great enthusiasm greeted these evidences of rapid and steady growth of prohibition sentiment. Among the prominent men who participated in the reports and the discussion on them were President A. S. Andrews of the Southern University at Greensboro; Dr. Peter Bryce, Superintendent of the Alabama Insane Hospital; and Colonel R. A. Hardway of the University of Alabama. Once more Negro delegates had their place in convention proceedings.[159]

The three temperance conventions of 1881-1884 had demonstrated the enthusiasm that could be generated and the influence that could be wielded by a state-wide alliance. But results, in terms of legislation, had not been very satisfactory. In alliance with the National Prohibition party, leaders of the temperance cause thought they saw an opportunity to increase the power of the movement. They began to consider the formation of such a party in Alabama.

The National Prohibition party had been organized in 1869, largely by the Independent Order of Good Templars. It had held its first national convention at Columbus, Ohio, February 22, 1872, and had then put into the field candidates for the offices of president and vice-president of the United States.[160]

In 1884 John T. Tanner, president of the Alabama Temperance Alli-

[156] *Senate Journal* (1882-1883), pp. 359, 536. The twelve counties were Escambia, Monroe, Clarke, Wilcox, Crenshaw, Tallapoosa, Bibb, Pickens, Etowah, Cherokee, DeKalb, and Limestone.
[157] *Montgomery Advertiser*, January 25, 1884.
[158] *Moulton Advertiser*, February 21, 1884.
[159] *Montgomery Advertiser*, January 25, 1884.
[160] Colvin, *op. cit.*, pp. 68, 88.

ance, attempted to introduce the party into his state. The attempt proved abortive; St. John, prohibition candidate for president, polled only 610 votes in Alabama.[161]

When the next state temperance convention, called by Z. S. Parker, secretary of the State Temperance Alliance, met in Athens the following July, the delegates considered but voted down a proposition that they put into the field a state prohibition ticket. They believed that such action would not be "the nearest way to what is most wanted—positive prohibition."[162] Instead, they turned to the dominant party in the state and appointed a committee to request the next State Democratic Convention to endorse local option. They would demand of the General Assembly a local option law and later a vote of the people on the question of prohibition.

Both before and after the meeting of the Democratic Convention the question of the formation of a Prohibition party in Alabama was aired in the public press. In general the newspapers, most of them Democratic in their affiliation, were vigorous in their opposition. The organization of such a party, said the *Clarke County Democrat,* would be a deadly blow to the temperance cause, for it would so "weaken the Democratic party as to endanger its success in the future administration of the State Government," and the Democratic party was the staunchest friend the temperance advocates had. The formation of a Prohibition party "can only work mischief for prohibition and may prove injurious to the Democratic party," said *Our Mountain Home,* adding that few prohibitionists in the state would be guilty of supporting third party candidates against the regular ticket.[163] The *Montgomery Advertiser* also saw "havoc to the prohibition cause" in such a move, and was somewhat conscious, too, of the chuckles with which the Republicans were watching this possible split in the Democratic ranks.[164]

Even some of the clergy came out vigorously against the new party. Reverend B. F. Riley, well-known Baptist minister, summed up his reasons for his stand as follows:

(1) Local option would not be practical in the Blackbelt of the state where the large ignorant Negro vote would always support liquor.
(2) Such an organization would cause the opposition to the prohibition movement to stiffen.
(3) It was sheer folly to try to build up a party of opposition to the Democratic party in the state.
(4) It appealed to those who had already committed themselves "to the present state ticket."
(5) The Prohibition party of the United States had committed itself either directly or indirectly to woman suffrage.[165]

[161] *One Hundred Years of Temperance,* p. 555.
[162] *Clarke County Democrat,* April 1, 1886.
[163] *Our Mountain Home,* June 30, 1886.
[164] *Montgomery Advertiser,* July 1, 1886.
[165] *Montgomery Advertiser,* June 25, 1886.

In June, 1886, the Democratic Convention assembled. It considered and flatly refused the cooperation asked by the temperance forces. Local option, it believed, would be impractical in the Blackbelt because of the large Negro vote which would always favor whiskey.[166]

The editor of the *Alabama Prohibitionist* voiced the bitter disappointment of the temperance forces in an editorial.[167] He took a fling at the personnel of the convention. There were Christians and patriots there, he admitted, but there was also

> the red nosed old fogy, who classes whiskey and poker among the "cardinal principles" of democracy. . . .

Every temperance man in the state had hoped that the convention would declare for "Home Rule" in Alabama, but

> Modern democracy acknowledges no interest in the home. . . . It was a convention totally lacking in politeness, because when the local option resolution was offered by Hon. Samuel Blackwell of Morgan County, an old red-nosed whiskeyite moved to adjourn, and all the other old red-nosed whiskeyites seconded the motion and the thing dissolved in the wildest confusion—just because this little question of temperance came so near getting "into politics" as to thrust itself up in the form of a mild resolution in the great convention. "The wicked flee when no one pursueth," and they fled . . . in a manner clearly intended to insult the men who framed it and to bring a shout of applause from the villainous crew who conduct the rum traffic in Alabama.

He characterized the party platform as "the same old stereotyped harangue" and supposed that the endorsement of Governor O'Neal's administration included "his numerous drunks while in office." The choice of Thomas Seay as candidate for governor, he admitted, was a good one, but he doubted whether he would dare actively to support the effort of the prohibitionists to let the people decide whether "a murderous, robbing, damning, God-defying, home-destroying traffic shall exist in this state." The rest of the slate were out-and-out "whiskey men" and the editor of the *Prohibitionist* finished his polemic by declaring:

> We will not support such a party until liquor ceases to ruin and pillage and destroy and its sale thereby becomes an honest calling.

Only one course seemed open to the friends of prohibition. And an immediate call for a convention to organize a Prohibition party went out. It declared that "many of the patriotic and Christian voters of Alabama were

---

[166] *Greenville Advocate*, December 15, 1886, ascribed the defeat of a prohibition election by 116 votes to the colored vote in favor of whiskey. "The colored vote was against us," the article said. "Let us pity not blame them. It is a deplorable state of affairs in which they can be bought by whiskey. They are not responsible for their acts under the influence that was brought to bear upon them. A few were brave and firm and true to the end. . . . Deserving of special mention is Clarence Underwood who, when an order was given to put out the lights of the Baptist Church in order to stop the Temperance meeting, stood up with a courage worthy of record and said: 'These lights shall not be put out unless it be done over my dead body.'"

[167] Copied from the *Alabama Prohibitionist* by the *Eufaula Weekly Times and News*, June 17, 1886.

'tired of supporting parties which . . . refused even to admit the rights of the people to determine by ballot whether the ruinous liquor traffic shall be legally continued.'" It invited all "sincere friends of the cause of prohibition" to meet at Birmingham on July 6.[168]

Unfortunately the convention which assembled on the appointed day at the skating rink got off to a very bad start. There were plenty of curious onlookers, but only seventy-five delegates and of these more than one third were residents of Birmingham. Even this small group found it impossible to work together. The convention had hardly begun before it split in two.

Frank Leslie, editor of the *Prohibitionist* and secretary of the convention, precipitated the fight by deliberately asking Chairman John T. Tanner who should be enrolled as members of the convention. The chair ruled that none should be enrolled who could not come in under the printed call, and the fight over "party or no party" was on. Some of the leaders present, among them Reverend D. I. Percer, L. S. Handley and Major George Brooks of Birmingham; Reverend W. C. Oliver of Calera, and Judge L. C. Coulson of Jackson, conservatively contended that the call did not clearly show the intention of the convention to organize a third party. Frank and Ed Leslie contended flatly that it did.

The result was that the left wing withdrew to the McMeekin Hotel and organized a separate convention with J. C. Orr of Hartselle as chairman and R. J. Barry of Birmingham as secretary. Judge Coulson "made a red hot" speech on the delusive hopes so long held out by the old parties. A committee was appointed to draft a platform, and this platform was adopted the following day.[169] It declared that

the liquor traffic is the gigantic crime of crimes—the source of poverty, crime and insanity; the arch enemy of labor, the foe of industry, the destroyer of private and public virtue, the fountain of political corruption, the parent of sedition, anarchy, vice, and social industrial disorder. . . .

It asserted that the suppression of this traffic had become "the supreme political as well as moral issue of the day," and that the Prohibition party is "the only political organization which favors such suppression." It resolved upon the formation of a new party allied to the national Prohibition party and pledged support to that party in its efforts to secure "both State and National Constitutional Prohibition of importation, manufacture, and sale of all alcoholic beverages."

Planks were adopted which endorsed the efforts of the W.C.T.U. to secure a law making scientific temperance instruction obligatory. They declared the Christian Sabbath to be "a boon so valuable to humanity that the

---

[168] *Montgomery Advertiser*, July 1, 1886. Among the members of the committee were John T. Tanner, J. C. Orr, A. S. Narrell, L. F. Whitten, G. L. Thomas, E. Leslie, R. G. Barry, and W. A. Wall.

[169] *Montgomery Advertiser*, July 8, 1886.

THE PROHIBITION MOVEMENT IN ALABAMA 83

State cannot but lie in its trust which neglects to guard it from destruction," and acknowledged the "supreme authority of Almighty God."

On the subject of liquor control the platform favored prohibition of the manufacture, importation, transportation, and sale of intoxicants. It declared that

> To aid, abet, or in any other way assist the drink traffic, either by granting license, signing petitions for license, leasing property for saloon purposes, is to become accessory to the whiskey business.

It asserted that inasmuch as "three-fourths of the criminals are products of the liquor traffic" prohibition would "solve the problem of convict labor and the management of penal institutions." It demanded for the people of Alabama the right to vote on the question of a constitutional prohibitory amendment.

Planks on free public education, fair ballot counting in elections, railroad and highway improvement, and the rights of free *versus* convict labor completed the platform on which the new party prepared to stand.

As their candidates they chose John T. Tanner of Limestone County for governor; General George L. Thomas of Jefferson for secretary of state; M. S. Stephens of Elmore for treasurer; C. J. L. Cunningham of Walker for attorney general; Reverend L. F. Whitten of Birmingham for auditor; and L. C. Coulson of Jackson for superintendent of education.

It was a fusionist ticket. Tanner was well known as a prohibition leader. Coulson had been for years a leading Republican and J. C. L. Cunningham was also a member of that party. Whitten was a Methodist preacher with high standing in the North Alabama Conference. Stephens and Thomas were little known outside their own communities.

The Republicans on the ticket were evidently put there to catch the votes of members of that party. And there is some reason to believe that the Republican party, holding its convention simultaneously with the Prohibitionists, might have stayed out of the field had General Thomas or some other acceptable man headed the Prohibition ticket. The Republican executive committee, however, did not like Tanner; he had said too much about the Democratic party. They went ahead with their own slate. Meanwhile both Thomas and Whitten withdrew from the Prohibition slate, declaring themselves unwilling to run against Democratic nominees as long as the Republicans were in the field.[170] Even if the Republicans had wholeheartedly joined with the Prohibition party, they could not, in all probability, have given them the strength they needed; the Republicans had polled a scant thirty per cent of the votes in the elections of 1884. The presence of Republicans on the Prohibition ticket helped to drive off some Democrats who otherwise might have given their support.

A storm of ridicule and abuse in the public press greeted the birth of the new party. The *Montgomery Advertiser* declared it "A Roaring

---

[170] *Montgomery Advertiser*, July 8, 1886.

Farce" which would "serve to amuse" but could have no other effect.[171] The Democratic nominee, Thomas Seay, said: "I hold the question to be a moral as distinguished from a political one, and I believe its injection into politics is opposed by every consideration or propriety of the moral law."[172]

Undaunted, the Prohibition party laid plans for a vigorous campaign. Tanner stumped the state, rallies were held in various counties, and temperance orators assumed the role of crusaders. The Democrats watched the campaign with very little concern. The Prohibitionists had unwisely chosen to play into their hands by basing their compaign on local option. Here was no new and unknown danger, but an issue satisfactory alike to the Democrats and to the liquor forces who were quite confident that they could keep their vested interests under local option in practically every large city in the state. Newspapers all over the state began to come out for local option but said, "by all means keep prohibition out of politics." Both Democrats and Republicans were quite willing to tolerate local option if in so doing they could freeze out the new party.

When the election returns were in, it was discovered that Tanner had polled 636 votes.[173] The old parties had polled approximately the same number of votes as they had in 1884.

But the fight went on. The Temperance Alliance of Alabama convened at Montgomery on November 16 and memorialized the General Assembly for more stringent license provisions, for a general local option law, and for a popular referendum on a prohibition amendment. Resolutions were passed inviting the cooperation of the W.C.T.U. and urging the Negroes to organize state and county alliances. More intensive organization in support of the Prohibition party was planned.[174]

Under such pressure, together with that directly exerted by the Prohibition party, a state-wide prohibition bill was introduced into the house in 1886, but it was adversely reported by the temperance committee.[175] In 1887 the senate, lacking one vote of being unanimous, resolved to submit the question of prohibition to the voters of Alabama; but the motion was permitted to die in the house without a vote.[176]

The presidential election of 1888 found the Prohibition party in Alabama still in the field and still under heavy fire. Church papers, agitated by certain commitments of the national party, led the attack. Said the *Alabama Christian Advocate:*

[171] *Montgomery Advertiser,* July 8, 1886; see also July 15, 1886.
[172] *Clarke County Democrat,* July 29, 1886.
[173] *Alabama Courier,* September 2, 1886.
[174] *Our Mountain Home,* November 24, 1886. The executive committee proposed to organize the counties into Alliances all over the state and to use these Alliances to build up the power of the Prohibition party.
[175] *House Journal* (1886-1887), pp. 358, 1302.
[176] *Our Mountain Home,* February 16, 1887.

The conservative and thoughtful temperance men of this country have not and will not identify themselves with this party, because it has incorporated into its platform *woman suffrage* and other *silly things* which have not the remotest bearing upon the great temperance issues now before the public. Therefore, we think it mighty proper for the real temperance workers of this state to come together at an early day and organize as temperance workers under our local option laws, ignoring politics and political parties and presenting to the public the temperance cause on its own merits.[177]

It was folly to make prohibition a political question, said the *Alabama Baptist*.[178] The *Montgomery Advertiser* declared that the Democratic party had adopted the only fair and just rule on the subject, that of "allowing each community to control the sale of liquor for itself."[179]

The Prohibition party polled only 583 votes for Clinton B. Fiske, candidate for president on the Prohibition ticket.[180] The party was barely holding its own in Alabama.

It continued to struggle, however, until 1904. It obtained only 239 votes for its state ticket in 1892;[181] but in the presidential campaign of 1896, it rolled up the slightly encouraging total of 2,147. Two years later W. B. Witherspoon, Prohibition candidate for governor, was confident of success. He informed the *Eufaula Times and News* that he expected "to be one real red-headed Governor in a few months."[182] He was wrong; he got only a few votes. Reverend W. B. Crumpton, Baptist minister and candidate in 1900, also received scant consideration.[183]

Old party affiliations were too strong. The Prohibition party in Alabama never had a chance of breaking these ties. But it performed a service to the cause of prohibition by its continual agitation. It kept the prohibition question before the people and caused many local elections to be held. Its leaders gained valuable experience in the techniques of the temperance fight; they could use them effectively in the final phases of that fight which began as the new century opened. Thwarted and limited, the temperance group was nevertheless growing in strength.

[177] *Alabama Christian Advocate*, August 9, 1888.
[178] *Alabama Baptist*, August 7, 1888.
[179] *Montgomery Advertiser*, October 13, 1888.
[180] *World Almanac* (1889), p. 251.
[181] W. P. F. Ferguson, "Prohibition Party," *New Encyclopedia of Social Reform*, p. 974.
[182] *Eufaula Times and News*, April 21, 1898.
[183] Ferguson, *op. cit.*, p. 974. The Prohibition vote was 2,173 in 1900 and 612 in 1904.

CHAPTER V

THE ALABAMA DISPENSARY SYSTEM, 1898-1908

Experiments with a new type of liquor control in South Carolina caught the attention of Alabama reformers in the middle nineties. The South Carolina Dispensary Law had been enacted in 1893. It was based largely on the Gothenburg system of private monopoly in Sweden and it had been introduced into South Carolina by Governor Benjamin Tillman, probably as an ingenious means of blocking the enactment of state-wide prohibition—a measure which had seemed about to pass in South Carolina since 1889—without winning the enmity of the drys.[1]

The South Carolina law provided for a complete state monopoly of the liquor trade, both wholesale and retail, and forbade private citizens to sell liquor. It was administered by a state board of control, whose five members were elected by the General Assembly. This board appointed the central commissioners and subordinate officers and fixed their salaries. It also appointed county boards of three members each who were responsible for the choice of local dispensers.

The immediate closing of over 600 licensed saloons gave South Carolina temperance forces reason for rejoicing. The rejoicing was short-lived; for the liquor forces began a campaign of bribery and general malpractice which was, within a dozen years, to undermine the effectiveness of the law and result in its repeal. As Colvin states:

The state board, together with the county boards, and local dispensers and clerks, formed a network of office-holders, appointed through political influence who were engaged in a debauching traffic. The system attracted a low class of unscrupulous politicians and naturally there was much corruption, graft, malfeasance, and defalcation. Nearly every man connected with it was besmirched by the corruption.[2]

The defects of the law were less apparent than the virtues when Senator Frank S. Moody of Tuscaloosa began to study its operation. He was convinced that South Carolina had solved the problem so vexing to

[1] In 1889 a prohibitory bill was defeated in the house of representatives by eight votes. At the next session it passed the house but was defeated in the senate. In 1892 popular vote showed a majority of approximately 10,000 out of a vote of 68,000 in favor of prohibition. In 1893 the prohibition measure seemed sure of passage. It had been approved 57 to 37 in the house, and was about to pass the senate. Then Governor Tillman stepped in. He had been recently elected as the representative of the radical or reform faction of the Democratic party and many thought that he did not wish to alienate his supporters by depriving them of their whiskey. For the prohibition bill he had substituted the dispensary bill, letting it be known that the prohibition advocates must take this or nothing. The bill passed and the law took effect July 1, 1893. Colvin, *op. cit.*, pp. 293-294.

[2] In consequence of this corruption, the legislature abolished the dispensary in 1906 and the matter of maintaining local dispensaries was left to the counties.

his own state. He began to write articles and make speeches advocating similar legislation in Alabama, and in 1897 introduced a state dispensary bill into the senate.[3]

Temperance forces in Alabama at that time were feeling a good deal of discouragement. The license system, the oldest form of liquor regulation, was far from satisfactory. High license fees, though they reduced the number of dealers, had the unfortunate effect also of concentrating control of the traffic in the hands of a few politically powerful men. Territories made dry by legislative enactment were constantly flooded by liquor from adjacent wet areas. Local option, so widely hailed as the great solution, was a disappointment; most of the counties had voted wet in the local option elections. The dispensary system was recognized by the temperance advocates as a compromise with evil, but it seemed almost a necessary compromise. The dispensary would be better than the open saloon. Some of the leading ministers, politicians, and the W.C.T.U. endorsed Senator Moody's proposal.

His first bill, stubbornly opposed by the liquor interests, was adversely reported by the senate temperance committee,[4] but in 1898 an act establishing a dispensary at Clayton in Barbour County, followed almost at once by acts establishing two other dispensaries, one at Columbia and the other at Dothan in Henry County, inaugurated Alabama's experiment with the new type of liquor regulation.[5]

The Clayton act provided that the intendant and board of the councilmen then in office and their successors constitute "The Dispensary Commissioners of Clayton, Alabama," and maintain a "dispensary, in the said town, for the sale of spirituous, vinous, malt liquors, ciders and other intoxicants." A dispensary manager, serving for one year and removable at any time for neglect of duty or violation of law, was to be appointed by the commissioners. The commissioners were authorized to make all necessary rules, such as setting the amount of liquor to be sold to any one customer at any one time, and providing for periodical analysis of the liquor for chemical purity. The manager was required to take an oath that he would faithfully perform his duties and to give bond of $500. He was to sell for cash only and turn over weekly to the commissioners all money he received.[6]

The statute forbade the sale of liquor except in sealed packages ranging from one-half pint to four gallons. The dispensary could not open before 6:00 a.m. and must close by 6:00 p.m. On Sunday, election day, and the day before election, it could not open at all. Loitering and loafing about the establishment were forbidden.[7]

To inaugurate the dispensary, the commissioners were authorized to

[3] *Senate Journal* (1896-1897), pp. 220, 238.
[4] *Senate Journal* (1896-1897), pp. 229, 238.
[5] *Local Acts* (1898-1899), pp. 105-109, 670-675, 131-135.
[6] *Local Acts*, pp. 105-106.   [7] *Ibid.*, p. 107.

borrow money or pledge the credit of the board and pay the obligation out of the first sales and profits. After the initial costs had been met, profits were to be paid by the commission to the Clayton town treasurer, who would place it in the general fund to be disbursed by the town council. The dispensary commissioners were to receive $25 a year for their services; the secretary and treasurer of the board were to get $150.[8]

On January 1, 1899, the Clayton dispensary opened and friends of temperance watched it with hopeful eyes. In August the *Clayton Record* declared it was "no longer an experiment." The editor thought it was "working admirably in all respects, morally and financially." He added:

> If prohibition would prohibit, if it could be made universal in its application, the *Record* would favor it, but for practical purposes . . . a dispensary is the thing.[9]

At Dothan also first reports were encouraging. Early in July the *Dothan Siftings* pointed to the record of net profits of $1,593.02 for the first six months of the dispensary's existence, and also to the great decrease in cases on the mayor's docket. There had been 200 cases during the last six months of the barroom system; only 72 in the first half-year of the dispensary system. Fines which had been $607 in the former period had dropped to $224.50. Here was a showing, said the editor, which must make "all unprejudiced people" admit "that the dispensary is the thing to solve the long troublesome liquor question." A number of Dothan's prominent citizens who had at first opposed the measure were now ready to admit that fact.[10]

Meanwhile, Senator Moody was pressing for an early enactment of a more inclusive dispensary law. At Birmingham during the Christmas holidays of 1898, a large meeting at Seals Hall backed by prominent citizens and the Pastors' Union heard Moody declare his intention of introducing such a bill as soon as the legislature reconvened.[11] He made good his promise and, on January 19, 1899, the new bill was before the senate. The fight was on in earnest, with most of the temperance leaders and many of the newspapers on one side, and the liquor interests and some of the largest dailies of the state on the other.[12]

The *Alabama Christian Advocate* came out for the bill on the date of its introduction, and urged "immediate and vigorous action in its support" upon all "friends of temperance and good order."[13] Methodist ministers in the Birmingham District had already pledged their full endorsement in formal resolutions which contemplated canvass of church members and

[8] *Ibid.*, p. 108. Salaries were to be paid out of the proceeds of the dispensary.
[9] *Clayton Record*, August 17, 1899.
[10] *Dothan Siftings*, July 9, 1899. Only nine of the seventy-two cases in the first six months of 1899 had been charged with drunkenness.
[11] *Birmingham News*, January 8, 1899.
[12] *Mobile Register*, January 20, 1899.
[13] *Alabama Christian Advocate*, January 19, 1899.

circulation of petitions, and which urged local legislators to support the bill. They expressed to Senator Moody "appreciation of his efforts in behalf of the welfare of our state."[14]

Other ministerial bodies took up the cause. The Jefferson County Presbyterian Ministers' Union unanimously pledged support.[15] The Pastors' Union of Birmingham, composed of all ministers of the city, appointed a committee to get up a monster petition; planned a canvass of every precinct in Jefferson County; and sent lobbyists to Montgomery. One member of the petition committee declared that the only persons who refused to sign the document were politicians, saloon keepers, and those who rented property for saloons.[16]

Most of the secular newspapers favored the Moody bill. The editor of the *Alabama Courier* (Athens) thought the dispensary system would pay any city out of debt. Athens with a dispensary would be able to become "one of the most progressive towns in the State."[17] Taxes could be reduced, the bonded indebtedness paid, and the town beautified.[18]

The editor of the *Tuscaloosa Gazette* said that the whiskey interests might just as well recognize the fact that the idea of the dispensary had come to stay. If the Moody bill failed of passage this time, it would be the main issue of the 1900 election. It would take more than the $46,000 which the liquor interests were reported to be spending to defeat the measure. Thousands of votes could not be bought with money or whiskey; and the movement of the people which was being led, not by fanatics but by representative men and women in each community, would surely prevail.[19]

The *Gazette's* neighbor, the *Tuscaloosa News,* took the opposite side. It argued that such a law would place Tuscaloosa at a disadvantage in competition with neighboring cities.[20] The *Birmingham Ledger* and the *Mobile Register* admitted that the dispensary plan might work in small towns but were sure that it would not work in cities as large as Birmingham and Mobile. Moreover, it would deprive some people of property and others of employment.[21]

The Moody bill passed. It received a vote of 16 to 2 in the senate, and 57 to 11 in the house.[22] By executive approval it became a law on February 18, 1899, to go into effect on January 1, 1900.[23]

[14] *Ibid.*
[15] *Ibid.*
[16] *Montgomery Advertiser,* January 27, 31, 1899.
[17] *Alabama Courier,* February 2, 1899.
[18] *Montgomery Advertiser,* January 31, 1899.
[19] *Tuscaloosa Gazette,* February 2, 1899. Two years previously when such a bill was talked of in the legislature, the press of the state "laughed it out of court," said the editor. The *Montgomery Journal,* the *Selma Times,* and the *Opelika News* supported the Moody bill. Many of the weeklies took the same stand.
[20] *Tuscaloosa Gazette,* January 12, February 28, 1899. Tuscaloosa was Moody's home community.
[21] *Birmingham Ledger,* January 11, 1899; *Mobile Register,* January 29, 1899.
[22] *Acts* (1898-1899), pp. 108-115; *Senate Journal* (1898-1899), p. 881; *House Journal* (1898-1899), p. 643.
[23] *Senate Journal* (1898-1899), p. 108.

Under this law each incorporated town or city in which the sale of liquor was not prohibited by law had authority to set up a dispensary and to carry on the business of buying and selling liquor. Incorporated towns or cities having a population of 10,000 or less were limited to one dispensary; larger communities might add another distributing center for each additional 10,000 inhabitants. Dispensaries must be within the corporate limits of the towns and cities. The municipalities must invest not less than $300 and not more than $2,500 in each establishment, and the liquor provided must be "of the purest and best quality."[24]

The dispensary manager was to be nominated by the board of county commissioners and elected by, and responsible to, the legislative body of the town or city involved. The operator, chosen for two years, was required to take oath that he would obey the laws and local regulations, to furnish bond, and to make weekly reports to the local legislative bodies.[25] The salaries of such managers were to be fixed before election by the legislative bodies of the communities. They were not to be less than $100 nor more than $3,000 a year. They could not be made dependent upon the amount of the sales of the dispensary.[26]

Liquor could not be sold in quantities less than one-half pint; it must be put up in sealed packages. Only one sale a day to any one customer was allowed. No sales could be made between 6:00 p.m. and 6:00 a.m. Dispensers must not drink, consume, or give away liquor on their premises, nor permit anyone else to do so. They must buy their supplies for cash and sell for cash. Daily and weekly accounts must be carefully kept and reported. On the first day of each year towns or cities having dispensaries must pay to the state treasurer an amount of money equivalent to that required of liquor dealers in their communities in 1898. At the same time, payments equivalent to county taxes on liquor dealers in 1898 must be made to the county treasurer.[27]

Unlawful sales were made misdemeanors, punishable by a fine of from $50 to $100. Manufacturers were allowed to sell their products wholesale in sealed packages to authorized dispensers.[28]

A county with no incorporated town or city could operate one dispensary through its court of county commissioners or board of public revenue. A board of county commissioners could also conduct dispensaries outside of the incorporated towns and cities under its jurisdiction, but could do this only after a petition for such a dispensary signed by twenty freeholders and householders had been filed with the probate judge.[29]

[24] *Acts* (1898-1899), p. 108.
[25] *Acts* (1898-1899), p. 110.
[26] *Ibid.*, pp. 110-111.
[27] *Ibid.*, p. 111.
[28] *Acts* (1898-1899), p. 112.
[29] *Ibid.*, pp. 112, 113, 114, 115. Such dispensaries were under the same regulations as those operated by towns and cities. The county had to pay into the state treasury on the first day of each year the same amount of money that was paid by such county into the state treasury in 1898 as a license tax for the sale of liquors.

Seventeen counties[30] were included under the provisions of the Moody bill. Several counties and cities were specifically exempted, and in two counties the act was not applicable to the sale of domestic wines made from locally-grown grapes.[31] Some counties had become dry by local option elections or by special legislation and were therefore, at their own wish, not included in the operation of the new law. The act did not affect the status of prohibition in twenty counties.[32]

Jefferson County was one of those exempted. The liquor interests and the saloon keepers had worked hard to secure this exemption. Protests voiced the disappointment of many citizens, among them the editor of the *Alabama Christian Advocate,* who declared that friends of temperance in the county would not give up the fight until their county was included under the new legislation. He noted that four out of six of the county's representatives had voted for the bill. Much had been accomplished in a short time, he said, and he predicted that as soon as the advantages of the dispensary system were allowed to prove themselves the measure would "sweep the state like a prairie fire." "The days of the saloon are numbered," he added. "Let all the people work and pray for its end."[33]

He was unquestionably too optimistic. Blind tigers and private whiskey jugs bore witness to public complacency regarding the liquor traffic. But the new law was hailed as a hope by citizens of some counties where prohibition laws had resulted in lower public revenue without noticeably lower liquor consumption. A letter signed "York" in the *Southern Home* in the summer of 1899 spoke of these men as follows:

We are very tired of seeing thousands of dollars going out of Sumter County to aid the schools and treasuries of other counties when we need this revenue. When the wholesomeness of the dispensary law as it is now in those

---

[30] *Alabama Courier,* February 23, 1899; *Standard Gage,* February 23, 1899. Counties included under the act were Bullock, Chambers, Cleburne, Colbert except the town of Cherokee, Coffee, Dale, Elmore, Etowah, Geneva, Henry, Jackson, Limestone, Pike, Russell except Girard, Butler except Greenville, Perry except Uniontown, and Randolph except Roanoke.

[31] *Acts* (1898-1899), p. 114. Exempted were Dallas, Walker, Cullman, Winston, Madison, Montgomery, Lawrence, Morgan, Blount, Mobile, Pickens, Lee, Tallapoosa, Coosa, Talladega, Barbour, Shelby, Lauderdale, Marengo, Crenshaw, Covington, Tuscaloosa, Fayette, Macon, Calhoun, Marshall, Jefferson, Baldwin, Greenville in Butler, Roanoke in Randolph, Uniontown in Perry, and Cherokee in Colbert. The two counties where the law was not applicable to domestic wines were Cleburne and Marion.

[32] *Standard Gage,* February 23, 1899; *Alabama Courier,* February 23, 1899. These counties were Autauga, Bibb, Cherokee, Chilton, Choctaw, Clarke, Clay, Conecuh, Covington, De Kalb, Escambia, Franklin, Greene, Hale, Lamar, Marion, Monroe, St. Clair, Sumter, Washington, and Wilcox.

[33] *Alabama Christian Advocate,* February 23, 1899. The largest places where dispensaries were operated under this bill were Union Springs, LaFayette, Tuscumbia, Sheffield, Wetumpka, Gadsden, Geneva, Dothan, Columbia, Athens, Troy, Clanton, and Ozark. There were a number of smaller towns with dispensaries.

counties, . . . is made apparent to other counties, they will come to our rescue and every one will rejoice in the overthrow of the unbridled demon. . . .[34]

A considerable decrease in "social drinking" and "drinking among the younger class" had been brought about by the dispensary law in Limestone County, said the *Alabama Courier* soon after the law was effective.[35] Some people who had had small accounts formerly with local saloons did not care to drink from a bottle. About two years later the same paper declared that the Athens dispensary had "beyond question solved . . . the question of selling whiskey. The records of the city court . . . will prove that."[36]

The dispensary idea spread rapidly. Eight new dispensaries were authorized by the legislature in 1900-1901,[37] in spite of bitter opposition from the liquor dealers who used not only petitions but the ablest lobbyists they could find to block their establishment.[38]

The activity of the anti-dispensary forces was not limited to the halls of the legislature. In Athens, within a year after the establishment of the Athens dispensary, they had stirred up enough public sentiment to demand an election to determine whether or not the system should be continued in that town. Probably the city authorities were responsible for allowing the opposition to gain such headway. Their records clearly showed drunkenness to be on the decline and the dispensary to be operating at a profit, but they were very slow in giving this information to the public. To the editor of the *Alabama Courier* it looked as if they were trying "to keep everybody in the dark." "This is the wrong idea," he protested, ". . . Let the facts be known. Turn on the lights."[39]

The fight thus precipitated was bitter. "Men were forgotten, and the friends of the dispensary threw themselves into the fight." They "saved the dispensary with a great victory" when the matter came to a vote in June, 1902. Small majorities in a handful of beats were the only returns favorable to the opposition. It looked as though the liquor question in Limestone County was settled for a while.[40]

[34] *Southern Home*, cited in the *Tuscaloosa Gazette*, August 24, 1899.
[35] *Alabama Courier*, November 22, 1900.
[36] *Ibid.*, March 6, 1902.
[37] *Acts* (1900-1901), pp. 610, 837, 1412, 1827, 2205. These dispensaries were for Roanoke in Randolph County; Wedowee, Randolph County; Camden, Wilcox County; Marion, Perry County; Pike County; Oneonta, Blount County; Thomaston, Marengo County; and Tuscaloosa, Tuscaloosa County. By the Constitution of 1901 the name of the lawmaking body was changed from General Assembly to legislature.
[38] Crumpton, *How Alabama Became Dry*, pp. 14-15. The exponents of the dispensary also used lobbyists, often so imbued with the cause that they paid their own expenses. Petitions for and against dispensary bills were sometimes presented to the legislature from the same communities. *House and Senate Journals* (1900-1901), *passim*. [39] *Alabama Courier*, March 6, 1902.
[40] *Alabama Courier*, June 19, 1902. In Athens it won by a majority of 270; at Elkmont, 102; and at Pettusville, 83. The official count showed that the dispensary had been sustained by a majority of approximately 500 votes. The paper did not give the exact number of votes cast.

THE PROHIBITION MOVEMENT IN ALABAMA 93

Encouraging financial reports from various dispensaries marked the year 1902.[41] The Lauderdale County dispensary at Florence reported a first year's business of $21,555.35, and a profit of something over $4,000.[42] Profits at Roanoke for the year were reported at $6,500.[43] Union Springs made $7,500 in its first year of operation.[44] On July 1, 1902, the LaFayette dispensary declared an annual dividend of $5,400.[45] Tuscaloosa, which established its dispensary on January 1, 1902, was able to report six months later that it looked as though profits for the first year would run to $25,000.[46]

Community improvements boomed as the dispensary proved its success. More money was available for schools, roads, and other community interests. One town abolished city taxation and used half the dispensary proceeds to put in a sewerage system and a waterworks.[47]

Such records and accomplishments helped to make the dispensary attractive to new towns and counties. Petitions to the legislature in 1903 led to acts establishing dispensaries in eight new locations.[48]

A special act of this legislature provided that on August 4, 1903, the citizens of Talladega should vote whether to change from the saloon to the dispensary. Both friends and foes of the dispensary threw their best efforts into the fight which ensued. The advocates of change used newspaper publicity and called on Frank S. Moody, father of the dispensary law, to help their cause along. Their arguments, summarized in *Our Mountain Home*, ran along these lines:

1st. The dispensary system places the liquor traffic under the control of a reputable citizen whose salary is the same whether he sells much or little and therefore he is under no temptation to induce people to trade with him.

2nd. It closes up the barroom, that central point of idleness and crime, and limits ... the purchaser to one package a day.

3rd. It prevents drinking on the premises and suppresses "treating," that most prolific source of debauchery.

4th. It applies the profits of the traffic to the public schools and to that extent sanctifies whatever there is of immorality in the sale or use of intoxicating liquors.

[41] J. E. Timmons, "The Dispensary System in the State of Alabama," *Outlook*, LXXI (1902), pp. 454-455. Of the profits the county got $1,320.83, the town of Florence $2,839.00; and salaries accounted for $1,020.78.
[42] *Alabama Courier*, April 17, 1902.   [43] Timmons, *op. cit.*
[44] *Ibid.*   [45] *Ibid.*
[46] *Ibid.* No dispensary was ever located in Mobile, Montgomery, or Birmingham, the three largest cities of the state. The largest towns in which they were operated were Tuscaloosa and Florence.
[47] *Ibid.* The report did not give the name of this town.
[48] *Local Acts* (1903), pp. 87, 316, 385, 453, 529, 603, 642, 647, 667, 706. Dispensaries were provided for Cottonwood, Houston County; Abbeville, Henry County; Centerville, Bibb County; Georgiana, Butler County; Enterprise, Coffee County; Goodwater Beat No. 4, Coosa County; Brantley, Crenshaw County; and Ozark, Dale County. At this session the Moody Law was repealed in so far as it had to do with Coffee County; but the special act, approved February 12, 1901, to establish a dispensary in Beat 14, Crenshaw, was amended to enlarge the powers of the Dispensary Commissioners.

5th. It lightens the burden of taxation and tends to decrease crime. . . .

6th. It limits the opportunity of the dram drinker and tends to prevent his becoming a drunkard.

7th. It is . . . a movement away from vice and lawlessness and in the direction of morality and prosperity.[49]

Against such argument the saloon keepers quoted Silena Moore Nolman, President of the W.C.T.U., who had said:

The dispensary is the most complete contrivance ever invented to fasten the liquor traffic on any people. Its effects are far worse than the saloon; the dispensary has set back the cause of temperance indefinitely in Alabama; the saloon is not half as bad as the dispensary; fight it from your state at any cost.[50]

A vote for the dispensary was a vote for drunkenness, said the virtuous saloon men. A vote for the dispensary was a vote for bad liquor, they urged, since dispensary managers, pressed by the necessity of showing a profit, would buy and sell cheap liquor and inferior liquor. A vote for the dispensary was a vote for transferring drunkenness from the saloon to the home. And moreover, they added, six good business houses in Talladega would have to be vacated and a number of people would lose their jobs if the dispensary came in.[51]

J. H. Hicks headed the campaign organization of the friends of the dispensary; D. R. Van Pelt was the manager of the opposition forces. Apparently Van Pelt's cohorts were better organized. The vote showed 918 against the dispensary and 699 for it.[52] Talladega kept its saloons.

A similar election in Walker County[53] on the same day, however, had the opposite result. The editor of the *Mountain Eagle* (Jasper) noting the vote of 955 to 842 in favor of the dispensary, said, "*The Eagle* feels that in advocating the adoption of dispensaries it did nothing but its duty—that which it conceived to be the best for our county and its people."[54]

Between 1903 and 1907 existing dispensaries developed in comparative peace. They gained new friends among the stern moralists who approved the cold, crude, repellent atmosphere which made these distributing centers anything but a poor man's club. The dispensary, they noted with approval, stripped the tinsel and glamor from the buying and selling of whiskey. There were no mirrors, no shining counters, no brass rods, no tables, and no chairs filled with "good fellows." Nothing in the set-up encouraged treating since the purchaser might not drink his liquor on the premises.

[49] *Our Mountain Home,* July 29, 1903.
[50] *Ibid.,* July 7, 1903.   [51] *Ibid.,* July 29, 1903.
[52] *Ibid.,* August 12, 1903. The opponents of the dispensary had two committeemen in each beat in the county.
[53] The election had been authorized by special act of the legislature. *Local Acts* (1903), pp. 137-138.
[54] *The Mountain Eagle,* August 5, 1903. Opposed to the *Eagle's* view were the *Oakman News* (see July 31, 1903), and the *Carbon Hill Enterprise.* The editor of the latter said that he had "been offered a big sum of money to advocate the dispensary cause," but he declined the bribe. See issues of July 24, 31, 1903.

Nothing tempted a young man to take a drink when he did not want it. If the dispensary had done no more than destroy the treating habit, they asserted, it had proved its worth.[55]

Then there was the financial aspect of the thing which was also gratifying. The small rent of an inconspicuous building and the dispenser's salary of perhaps $50 a month were the principal expenses; beyond these, the proceeds went directly to the public. "I might say that perhaps the dispensary contributed more to the success of our public schools than any other single thing," wrote one observer of the Dothan situation. "If it had not been for our dispensary, our schools could not be absolutely free schools as they are now."[56]

But opposition to the dispensary gathered strength in the years between 1903 and 1907. The system had never satisfied some people who thought it a shameful compromise with the devil. It had been criticized by others because rural sections got too little of the benefits. Neglect of managers to give out reports and financial statistics resulted in public distrust and dissatisfaction.[57] Opponents of the system began to point out that the dispensary manager was not free from the pressure of the profit motive; his salary could probably not be increased unless he did a good business. His temptation to push sales was almost as great as was that of the private dealer. Moreover, under the new system, the public, who could contemplate with equanimity the success or failure of a saloon keeper, had a stake in the success of the liquor trade. The cupidity of the taxpayer was appealed to by the dispensary.[58]

Accusations that dispensaries sold impure liquor became more frequent. "No Wonder It Sets Them Crazy . . . ," exclaimed one editor, charging that chemical analysis of the liquor drunk in the county showed that people were drinking "alcohol, arsenic, alum, aloes, bitter almonds, blood, chalk, cherry laurel, coculus, indicus, copperas, gypsum, henbane, isinglass, lime, lead, logwood, nux vomica, opium, oil of juniper, oil of turpentine, tobacco, sugar of lead, resin, etc."[59]

Senator Benjamin Tillman of South Carolina, father of the dispensary, did not conclusively dispose of this accusation—though he thought he did —when he told a Buffalo audience in 1901 about a man who was in the habit of going to town regularly to buy a quart of whiskey and "stopping on the way home to share it with a couple of cronies." In the old days

[55] *Montgomery Advertiser*, February 25, 1905. The management of the dispensaries never failed to praise its financial success.
[56] *Montgomery Advertiser*, February 25, 1905.
[57] *Supra*, note 39.
[58] *Tuscaloosa Gazette*, January 19, 1899; *Alabama Courier*, February 18, 1899.
[59] *Wilcox Banner* (Camden), March 29, 1906. Quoted from *S. S. Journal*. See also *Luverne Journal*, August 10, 1905: "The Louis 66 sold by the dispensary today is not the quality of whiskey sold by the dispensary 3 years ago. . . . We serve notice that the law must be carried out and the people protected against poisonous drugs." The law had placed emphasis on the purity of the liquor to be sold. *Acts* (1898-1899), pp. 108-115.

he had reached his home "straight as a line without a drop left in the bottle." Then the dispensary came to town. The man was able to buy "a bigger quart of whiskey than he ever bought before and a better quart." However, when he stopped for his usual convivial drink, "he knew nothing until two o'clock in the morning when he woke in a cornfield and found the bottle was only half empty."[60] To the good Senator, the worse the kick, the better the whiskey.[61]

Graft and malfeasance in office was also charged against dispensary managers. "The Luverne Dispensary is knowingly run in open violation of the law," asserted the *Luverne Journal* in August, 1905. It added the warning that "unless a change is made, some one in authority will be indicted by the grand jury." Five months later the same editor declared: "The Dispensary school money has been recklessly . . . appropriated by both the school board and the Dispensary Commissioners. That it has been visited by graft, cannot be denied."[62] Lax administration of the law left plenty of room for the "blind tiger."

Far from discouraging drunkenness the dispensary helped to promote it, its enemies complained. In the good old days a man bought a small drink and drank it quietly in the saloon. Now, according to law, he must buy at least a half pint at a time. He took his bottle outside and often treated his friends on the streets and highways. Negroes and whites gathered in alleys and passed around the bottle in the worst kind of drinking parties. Drunkenness had become so bad along the highways of the Blackbelt that ladies did not dare to venture out on Saturday afternoons. On Saturday nights, said the editor of the *Wilcox Banner*, the roads leading from Camden were "filled with drunken Negroes, cursing, racing and shooting in all directions." Vigilance of the town officials, he added, kept them from disorder in the vicinity of Courthouse Square, but "the public road becomes a race track and the flash of the hip-pocket gun lights the darkness. . . ."[63]

The same newspaper told of a minister who, having watched young men drinking and swearing in a barber shop of a dispensary town, had warned his congregation from the pulpit, "you may build up your town, but it will be at the expense of the manhood of your youth." The editor advised the "good old fathers who still believe that the dispensary is the best solution of the liquor question" to "step down town some Saturday night and have their eyes opened." To this editor as to many others, per-

[60] Colvin, *op. cit.*, p. 296.
[61] According to Colvin this was in harmony with what had long been recognized; namely, that alcohol was the outstanding deleterious factor in liquor and, no matter how pure it was, it was a habit-forming, narcotic poison.
[62] *Luverne Journal*, August 10, 1905; January 25, 1906.
[63] *Wilcox Banner*, January 25, 1906. See also, *ibid.*, January 28, 1904; ". . . Public drunkenness in the country towns is almost of daily occurrence, but public sentiment would condemn the locking up of a citizen for a simple spree; and when murder or assaults to murder follow these indulgences, the only palliation of the offense heard is, 'Oh, he was drunk.'"

haps the worst thing about the whole system was that it took the social stigma from drinking. He cited in support of this view an article from the *Linden Reporter* which declared that the "dishonor" of the new system lay in its association with the best men of the community.

Good men, church men, endorsing the sale of a thing that their very natures, their religion, condemn![64]

It must have been early apparent to temperance leaders that the spread of dispensaries was leaving untouched large and important areas. On October 1, 1907, fifty-six dispensaries were in operation. They were scattered through twenty-five counties, but eighteen of them were in seven counties which constituted the dispensary stronghold of the state.[65] Large cities were entirely untouched. Obviously, the dispensary was not the panacea its friends had hoped it would be. Perhaps local option was better after all. Certainly the need for reform still existed and state-wide prohibition was still the desirable goal.

Legislation along the more traditional lines was still necessary in the years when the dispensary experiment was being tried. Towns and schools and churches continued to petition for special acts creating dry territory around them, and the legislatures continued to receive such petitions favorably. A few laws authorizing wine manufacture, and even encouraging the use of home-grown grapes, were enacted.[66] License fees

[64] *Ibid.*, February 1, 8, 1906.
[65] *Annual Report State Auditor* (1907), pp. 732-735.

County	Population*	Registered Voters**	Dispensaries**
Houston	38,000†	2,757	3
Tuscaloosa	36,147	4,318	2
Pike	29,172	3,151	2
Walker	25,162	4,895	6
Limestone	22,387	2,750	1
Crenshaw	19,668	2,980	2
Bibb	18,498	2,784	2
Total	189,034	23,638	18

* *United States Census Reports*, 1900.
** *Reports of the State Auditor of Alabama*, 1906.
† Houston County was constituted in 1903 and the figures as to its population in 1906 are only an approximation.

[66] *Acts* (1900-1901), p. 335, and *passim*. Prohibition was given at this session to Jackson; Marshall; Chambers, except as provided for in the act approved February 18, 1899; Macon, except for the town of Tuskegee; and Russell, except the city of Girard. Prohibition was also given to one high school, Owenton College, and the locality within the boundaries of Warren School district in Coffee County. The Dexter Avenue Methodist Church of Montgomery got prohibition for its immediate neighborhood. The region near the Alabama Consolidated Coal Company in Etowah County was made dry, and two towns, Courtland and Altoona, got prohibition. Ensley received permission to sell malt, vinous and spirituous liquors within its borders. An act was passed to "encourage the growth and regulate the disposition of pure wines made from grapes and wine-berries grown in Alabama," and an act authorized the manufacture and sale of such wine in Colbert, Madison, Baldwin, Shelby, Henry, Mobile, and Marion counties.

continued to claim the attention of lawmakers both as regulatory devices and, especially as sources of revenue.

In 1900 license fees were considerably raised. They ranged now from $200 for retailers in small towns to $350 paid by dealers in large communities and by those who sold liquor on steamboats and railway trains. Dispensary managers were subject to the same license requirements as any other retailers. Dealers in lager beer and dealers in wines paid much reduced rates. Wholesalers paid a fee of $300. They could not sell liquor in quantities of less than one quart or allow the liquor to be drunk on their premises without forfeiting their classification as wholesalers. Retailers, however, could do a wholesale business on the side and retain their classification.[67]

City licenses also went up. The scale which Decatur adopted in 1902 ranged from $50 to $500, and even that did not seem enough to the city fathers who, the following year, raised the fee for retail dealers to $1,000, and in 1907 put a still heavier burden on these same venders, setting their license cost at $1,250.[68] Huntsville in 1905 raised the license fee for retail liquor dealers from $250 to $500, largely to satisfy the prohibitionists in the community. Fees for other dealers were correspondingly advanced.[69]

Meanwhile, in spite of the dispensary, in spite of the creation of new dry territory, and in spite of advancing license fees the manufacture of liquor in Alabama steadily advanced. In 1900 there were 116,094 gallons of whiskey distilled. Four years later revenue was paid on 157,194 gallons and by 1907 the total output had risen to 214,255 gallons.[70]

Local Acts, Regular Session (1907), p. 158, and *passim*. The seven counties gaining prohibition at this session were Dale, Franklin, Henry, Houston, Lamar, Macon, and Sumter. Special elections were provided for Fayette, Perry, and Tuscaloosa counties. The area around twelve churches was made dry, and also the area near three schools in rural districts. A special act prohibited the manufacture of liquors in Cherokee County. Four prohibitory laws were amended, and five repealed. Park Hotel at Montrose, Baldwin County, and the town of Florala were authorized to sell liquor. A special act prohibited the sale of liquor in Etowah County except Gadsden and Attalla; and another special act authorized the sheriff of Lawrence County to procure and publish annually a list of persons, firms, and corporations procuring United States internal revenue licenses for the sale of liquor.

[67] *Acts* (1900-1901), pp. 236-237. Others paid fees as follows: dealers in towns of 1,000 to 3,000 population, $250; 3,000 to 5,000, $275; 5,000 to 10,000, $300. Rates for dealers in lager beer were one fourth of these rates; for dealers in wine, one tenth. Any person engaged in the business of selling cider at retail, where he was not the manufacturer of it, was required to pay a license tax of $10.

[68] "Minute Book of the City of Decatur," December 16, 1902, p. 237. The license for retail dealers was $500; wholesale, $100; retail dealers in malt liquors, $50. *Ibid.*, pp. 634-635. The 1903 fees for wholesalers remained unchanged. *Ibid.*, p. 307. Other fees remained unchanged.

[69] "Minute Book of the City of Huntsville," September 19, 1905, p. 168. The fee for retailers of malt liquors was raised from $150 to $200; for wholesalers in spirituous liquors, from $50 to $300; and for wholesale dealers in malt liquors, from $50 to $100.

[70] *United States Internal Revenue Reports* (1900), p. 439; *ibid.* (1904), p. 239;

THE PROHIBITION MOVEMENT IN ALABAMA 99

This increased production did not mean more distilleries. On the contrary, the 33 plants licensed by the United States government in 1900 had shrunk to 14 by 1908.[71] Fruit distilleries, which prior to 1900 had outnumbered those of grain, were in that year exactly on a par—there were 33 of those also.[72] The records of 1908 show no fruit distilleries paying revenue to the federal government.[73] There were approximately five breweries operating annually between 1900 and 1908.

Illicit distilleries continued to operate, but there is no way of estimating their number or the quantity of their production. One hundred and forty such stills were destroyed and 12 removed in 1900; 153 were destroyed in 1908. The destruction of 1,076 stills and 1,301 arrests for law-breaking are recorded in the *United States Internal Revenue Reports* from 1900 to 1908.[74]

Some 1,192 retailers purchased licenses from the federal government in 1900; 1,779 in 1906.[75] Though the number then decreased to 1,319 as prohibition spread in 1907, there were more registered retail liquor dealers licensed by the United States government in 1908 than in 1900. There were more wholesale liquor dealers, too; 71 in 1908 as against 46 in 1900.[76] Retail dealers in malt liquor had nearly doubled their number in the period. There had been 219 of them in 1900; there were 434 in 1908. Even greater proportion of increase was shown by the wholesalers of malt liquor. From 28 in 1900 they had increased to 89 by 1908.[77]

It is interesting to note the discrepancies between national and state records. From July 1, 1906, to June 30, 1907, the federal reports show issuance of licenses to 1,748 persons and firms in Alabama.[78] State records show only 754 saloons and 56 dispensaries in operation during the fiscal year of 1907. Apparently 938 federal license holders did not bother to

---

ibid. (1907), p. 176. There was a considerable decline in 1908, the amount manufactured being only 122,266 gallons.

[71] *House Executive Documents*, 56th Cong. 2d sess. No. 11, p. 96; *Annual Report of the Commissioner of Internal Revenue* (June 30, 1908), p. 74.

[72] *House Executive Documents*, 56th Cong. 2d sess. No. 11, p. 96.

[73] *Annual Report of the Commissioner of Internal Revenue* (June 30, 1908), p. 74.

[74] *United States Internal Revenue Reports* (1900-1908), *passim; House Executive Documents*, 56th Cong. 2d sess. No. 11, p. 271; *Annual Report of the Commissioner of Internal Revenue* (June 30, 1908).

[75] *United States Internal Revenue Report*, 56th Cong. 2d sess. No. 11, p. 68. All local saloons and retail dealers had to purchase licenses from the United States government. A saloon was a place of business in which liquor was sold by the drink and in bottles. It was usually made as attractive as possible. A retail establishment might be a place in which liquors were sold in bottles and usually lacked the attractive features of the saloon. *Ibid.*, 59th Cong. 2d sess. No. 20, p. 51; *Annual Report of the Commissioner of Internal Revenue* (June 30, 1907), p. 95.

[76] *Annual Report of the Commissioner of Internal Revenue* (June 30, 1907), p. 85; *House Executive Documents*, 56th Cong. 2d sess. No. 11, p. 68. In 1906 the high point of 90 was reached.

[77] *Reports of Internal Revenue Department* (1900-1908), *passim; House Executive Documents*, 56th Cong. 2d sess. No. 11, p. 68; *Annual Report of the Commissioner of Internal Revenue* (June 30, 1908), p. 97.

[78] *Annual Report of the Commissioner of Internal Revenue* (1907), p. 95.

obtain either state or county license. Did they fail to open the businesses for which they had asked license? Did they operate in violation of the laws of the state?

On October 1, 1907, twenty-one Alabama counties were under prohibition;[79] twenty-one under license;[80] sixteen had the dispensary only;[81] and nine had both dispensary and saloon.[82] Of the state's 754 saloons,[83] Mobile County licensed 165; Jefferson, 198; and Montgomery, 130.[84] The rest were scattered through 27 counties, but 106 of them were in another 7 of the state's counties. Ten counties, then, with 599 of the 754 saloons,[85] and another seven in which were concentrated the dispensaries of the state, made up the liquor stronghold of Alabama. The ten strong license counties were moreover the dominant political, industrial, and financial centers of the state. Political leaders from them determined the politics and policies of Alabama, and these leaders had effectively strangled any attempt to injure seriously the liquor interests in their populous and growing home territories. In the seventeen dominant liquor counties of the state lived 39 per cent of the people of Alabama, 707,822 of the state's 1,828,697. About the same proportion of the registered voters, 80,615 out of 208,932, was concentrated in this area. Obviously the reformers who wanted more stringent restrictions upon the liquor traffic and those who would be content only with state-wide prohibition had heavy odds against them.

[79] Prohibition counties were Autauga, Cherokee, Choctaw, Clarke, Clay, Conecuh, De Kalb, Escambia, Franklin, Greene, Hale, Jackson, Lamar, Lauderdale, Lawrence, Marion, Marshall, Monroe, St. Clair, Sumter, Washington.
[80] Counties under license were Baldwin, Coosa, Covington, Cullman, Colbert, Calhoun, Dale, Dallas, Elmore, Etowah, Fayette, Jefferson, Lee, Madison, Morgan, Mobile, Montgomery, Pickens, Russell, Tallapoosa, Winston.
[81] Counties having dispensaries only were Bibb, Bullock, Chambers, Cleburne, Geneva, Henry, Houston, Macon, Perry, Pike, Randolph, Tuscaloosa, Coffee, Walker, Wilcox, Chilton.
[82] Counties having both the dispensary and the saloon were Barbour, Blount, Butler, Crenshaw, Limestone, Lowndes, Marengo, Shelby, Talladega.
[83] *Anual Report of the State Auditor* (1907), pp. 736-739.
[84] *Annual Report of the State Auditor* (1907), pp. 736-739.
[85] *Ibid.*, pp. 732-735.

CHAPTER VI

LOCAL OPTION AND STATE-WIDE PROHIBITION, 1904-1909

While the dispensary experiment was in full swing, two things happened to encourage the temperance forces in Alabama. The first was the removal of the Negro from the ballot box. A. B. Moore wrote that "By the elimination of the ignorant Negro vote, which was a source of corruption, the constitution [of 1901] contributed a great deal to the improvement of elections in Alabama."[1] "The stronghold of the whiskey power in the state has been eliminated, by the disfranchisement of the Negro, and others like him," declared the *Alabama Baptist* in 1908, and the editor voiced a general spirit of optimism when he added, "now with a fair count we can carry the state."[2] Now that people's attention could be drawn away from the power of the black man's vote, they could with greater patience work upon the solution of the real problem. The Negro could no longer vote on liquor, but he could drink it. And whites and Negroes could now join hands to protect the ignorant black man from the evils of intemperance, and to safeguard the white man and white woman from the violence of the liquor-crazed black. In 1903 Professor Councill, head of the Negro school at Huntsville, spoke for the best people of his race when he pleaded for the salvation of his people from the white man's saloon as the first step toward the social and moral regeneration of the black race.[3] Restraint of the Negro and protection of the white population became a powerful double motive which drove the forces of prohibition toward greater effort. For black men and for white men, the saloon must go! J. F. Clark wrote in 1906 that

> The saloon is a place of rendezvous for all classes of the low and vulgar, a resort for degraded whites and their more degraded negro associates, the lounging place for adulterers, lewd women, the favorite haunt of gamblers, drunkards and criminals. Both blacks and whites mix and mingle together as a mass of degraded humanity in this cess-pool of iniquity. Here we have the worst form of social equality, but I am glad to know that it is altogether among the more worthless of both races.[4]

[1] A. B. Moore, *The History of Alabama*, p. 909. Dr. Crumpton stated that "The most faithful and dependent servant when sober, the Negro becomes dangerous when crazed with drink. The fine women of the Blackbelt and their gallant, brave husbands breathed more freely when prohibition came, because of the change for the better with the Negro." *How Alabama Became Dry*, p. 13.
[2] *Alabama Baptist*, April 23, 1902.
[3] *Alabama Christian Advocate*, September 3, 1907. The editor predicted that the growth of prohibition in the state was destined to be more and more accelerated as its vital bearing upon the issue was brought to light.
[4] *Ibid.*, January 4, 1906. Clark's article was entitled "The Saloon and Racial Equality."

The second spur to the temperance workers was the introduction into the state of the aggressive and powerful Anti-Saloon League. Characteristically the Baptists took the lead in this movement—took it, in fact, before the rest of the churches were quite ready for action. At the Baptist State Convention of 1903 a committee including O. F. Gregory, C. S. Rabb, Wm. M. Blackwelder, W. D. Dunn, and John V. Dickinson, was appointed "to confer with the general religious bodies of the state looking to the organization of an inter-denominational anti-liquor league."[5] Chairman Gregory was obliged to report to the 1904 Convention that while the committee had "addressed communication to each of the several bodies of the Presbyterian, Methodist, Cumberland Presbyterian, and Christian denominations" any effective action on the committee's part had been "thwarted by the failure [of these bodies] to send any official reply."[6]

Within a few months of the Convention Dr. R. A. Baker and Dr. G. W. Young, superintendent and assistant superintendent of the Anti-Saloon League of America, had authorized S. E. Wasson, pastor of the First Methodist Church of Florence, and W. B. Crumpton, secretary and treasurer of the Baptist State Board of Missions, to invite churches, Sunday schools, young people's societies, educational institutions, and temperance societies to send representatives to Birmingham on October 17, to organize a state Anti-Saloon League. Preparations for this meeting were going forward with enthusiasm.[7] Wasson and Crumpton mailed over three thousand personal letters to preachers, lawyers, doctors, teachers, merchants, and farmers all over the state asking their cooperation. The *Alabama Christian Advocate,* the *Alabama Baptist,* all of the daily papers in the state, and about forty of the leading weeklies published the call for the meeting.[8] Railroad companies made excursion rates for delegates.[9]

Seasoned temperance leaders answered the call with enthusiasm. Among them were Reverend Frank Willis Barnett, editor of the *Alabama Baptist,* who presided at the meeting; Reverend Henry Trawick, editor of the *Alabama Christian Advocate;* Reverend E. E. Folk of Nashville, editor of the *Baptist and Reflector;* Reverend J. H. McCoy; W. P. Brewer; and Frank Leslie, former co-editor of the *Alabama Prohibitionist.* With such men to back it and with Reverend W. B. Crumpton, active temperance leader for twenty-five years, as its president, the Alabama Anti-Saloon League got off to an auspicious start. Reverend S. E. Wasson was elected vice-president and Reverend I. D. Steele, secretary and treas-

[5] *Minutes of the Alabama Baptist State Convention* (July 22, 1903), pp. 32-33.
[6] *Alabama Baptist State Convention* (July 20, 1904), pp. 24-26.
[7] *Alabama Christian Advocate,* September 15, 1904.
[8] *Alabama Baptist,* October 6, 1904.
[9] The Southeastern Passenger Association granted a rate of one and one-third fares for round trips to those attending the meeting in Birmingham.

urer. This board of directors was an impressive collection of strong and devoted temperance veterans.[10]

The new League stated its purpose as the creation of "a hearty sentiment in favor of temperance and work for the nomination and election of men to the legislature who were in sympathy with the movement to restrict the liquor traffic." Vice-President Wasson tried to make it clear that the movement was non-political, that it would work within the framework of existing parties.[11]

United action by churches, Sunday schools and temperance societies was to be directed firmly, persistently—but conservatively—against the saloon. Local option was the immediate goal and steps were to be taken at once to elect legislators committed to this measure for the next General Assembly.[12] A membership open to all who would subscribe to the League's purposes was declared to be the final authority on all matters of League action.[13]

The Board of Trustees carried forward the action of the organization after the initial meeting had adjourned. They strengthened the organization by appointing a state superintendent who could work full time to secure the affiliation of other temperance societies with the new League and to organize subsidiary leagues throughout the state.[14]

The Alabama Anti-Saloon League was hailed with enthusiasm by many of the religious bodies. "It is a matter for encouragement and thanksgiving that marked progress is being made in putting this evil down," read a report on temperance adopted by the Baptist State Convention in 1905.[15] Thirty-eight Baptist associations that year endorsed the work of the Alabama Anti-Saloon League and the proposed general local option law.[16] At its annual meeting in 1905 the North Alabama Conference of the Methodist Episcopal Church, South, noted "with approval the growing sentiment in favor of temperance" and endorsed "most heartily the efforts of the Anti-Saloon League to secure the passage of a general local option law. . . ."[17]

Real and rapid progress for the Alabama League began with the coming of Reverend Brooks Lawrence as superintendent, in June, 1906. He came from Ohio, where he had been successfully fighting against the liquor traffic in a district composed of twenty-five of the most populous counties

[10] *Birmingham News*, October 18, 1904. Trustees elected were J. W. Stagg, P. D. Ratcliff, J. H. McCoy, I. D. Steele, E. H. Cabiness, A. H. Carmichael, S. E. Wasson, J. R. McMullen, R. E. Patton, D. C. Cooper, W. B. Crumpton, S. M. Hosmer, James D. Norman, and Millard M. Sweat.
[11] *Alabama Baptist*, October 26, 1904.
[12] *Ibid.*, January 18, 1905.   [13] *Birmingham News*, October 18, 1904.
[14] *Alabama Baptist*, October 26, 1904. The W.C.T.U. and local church temperance organizations affiliated with the Anti-Saloon League.
[15] *Alabama Baptist State Convention* (July 21, 1905), p. 32.
[16] The majority of the Baptist associations also endorsed local option at their annual conventions in 1906. *Minutes of the Baptist Associations, passim*.
[17] *Minutes of the North Alabama Conference* (November 22-27, 1905), p. 56.

of the state. He was, his friends declared, a Presbyterian minister of pleasing address, unblemished character, and indomitable energy. "The affairs of the Anti-Saloon League will be entirely safe in his hands," declared President Crumpton. "He will call to his assistance good men of all denominations and of every political party."[18] Brooks Lawrence did exactly that, and did it effectively. Within two months he was editing the *Alabama Citizen,* the new official organ of the Alabama Anti-Saloon League published at Birmingham. He gave to it an aggressive and positive tone, venturing quite boldly into the field of politics, but declaring always that his paper was non-partisan. News of the temperance movement throughout the nation found its place in the *Citizen's* columns.[19]

When the State Democratic Convention met on September 19, 1906, pressure had become so strong that the politicians found it advisable to adopt a platform plank endorsing county local option.[20] B. B. Comer, the Democratic nominee for governor, went before the voters on this plank and was elected.[21] Even before the election was held, the Sipsey Baptist Association was able to declare: "The Anti-Saloon League of Alabama is . . . making itself felt. . . . A majority of the candidates for the legislature . . . have committed themselves in favor of the much needed temperance legislation."[22] The government officials endorsed by the voters on election day were strongly bound by pre-election commitments. The friends of temperance could look forward confidently to a local option law.

In his first message to the legislature Governor Comer declared that there was an almost universal demand for a well-defined and equitable local option law. "I will simply suggest that it is one of the essential features of our great democracy that the great majority shall rule," he said.[23]

The leaders of the Anti-Saloon League had the bill ready before the legislature met on January 9, 1907. R. F. Lovelady, an enthusiastic temperance leader of Jefferson County, introduced it in the house of representatives on January 15.[24] The Lovelady bill provided that if one fourth of the voters of any county should apply to the probate judge, he must order an election on the question of prohibition of the sale of liquor in saloons. Dispensary areas were exempted from the provisions of the act for a two-year period.[25] The bill was turned over to the committee on temperance and the battle for its acceptance was on. Said the *Birmingham Ledger's* Montgomery correspondent on January 20:

Chairman Ballard of the Temperance Committee of the House, will hold a public meeting Tuesday afternoon at 5 oclock, when the local option bill will

[18] *Alabama Christian Advocate,* June 21, 1906.
[19] *Alabama Citizen,* October, 1906.
[20] *State Democratic Platform,* 1906; *Alabama Citizen,* September, 1906.
[21] *Birmingham News,* November 6, 1907.
[22] *Minutes of the Sipsey Baptist Association* (October 24-25, 1906), p. 11.
[23] *Senate Journal, General Session* (1907), p. 121.
[24] *House Journal* (1907), p. 210.   [25] *Acts* (1907), p. 200.

be taken up and discussed. This is a bill which will cause much debate, and those opposed to it will use all their power to defeat it. The bill was drawn up by the Anti-Saloon League of Alabama, and it is said the members of the league are anxious for it to pass as it is without any amendments, but that is hardly probable. It is understood that the saloon interests are opposing the bill with much energy.[26]

The *Ledger* was right. The liquor dealers, fully aware of their precarious situation, were using the ablest politicians and the shrewdest lawyers to represent them before the temperance committees, before the legislature, and in the lobbies.[27]

Ranged against this liquor lobby was the best talent the prohibition forces could command. Dr. W. B. Crumpton, president of the Alabama Anti-Saloon League, was one of the leaders. He found the lobbying practice of the liquor forces in sharp contrast to the frugal methods of his own friends, whose advocates at the capitol were wont to pay their own expenses at some cheap Montgomery hotel, whereas the liquor dealers

had one of the shrewdest Jews who could be found from Mobile, who boarded at the chief hotel, where he dined and wined at his convenience the members of the Legislature and guests of his liking. *He was on the job all the time.* I was often called away, or my money gave out. The Jew and I got right chummy. I depended on him to post me when I returned, about what had been done.[28]

The Reverend G. W. Young, assistant superintendent of the American Anti-Saloon League, was another lobbyist for the bill. The *Alabama Citizen* in January carried his picture and announced that during January and February he had been assigned to the state of Alabama, "with headquarters at Montgomery during the session of the Legislature."[29] Brooks Lawrence, who had worked so valiantly to pave the way for the bill, supplemented his efforts as a lobbyist by using the columns of the *Citizen* to urge the people of the state to make their wishes known by letters to legislators. As early as September, 1906, he wrote:

We give below the most complete list yet published of members of the House and the Senate. We want to urge upon our friends the importance of writing at once to members from your county and senatorial district.

Urge them to support this proposed local option law. Point out to them the importance of selecting a speaker of the House and the President Pro Tem of the Senate who will give the moral elements a square deal in appointing the temperance committees in both bodies, men who are not saloon controlled.[30]

[26] *Birmingham Ledger*, January 20, 1907. The correspondent's name was not given.
[27] *Montgomery Advertiser*, February 16, 1907. In some cases the liquor dealers themselves appeared before the temperance committees to defend their business.
[28] Crumpton, *op. cit.*, pp. 14-15. "I have been a lobbyist whenever the legislature was in session," said Dr. Crumpton.
[29] January, 1907.
[30] *Alabama Citizen*, September 1906, January and February, 1907.

The newspapers, especially the county papers which had been advocating local option for the past two years, were generally friendly to the bill. "The Alabama newspapers are all right," declared the editor of the *Citizen,* "and when we say they are all right, it comes nearer the truth than some might think, for the vast majority of the newspapers and editors of Alabama are with us in this fight against the liquor traffic."[31]

There were exceptions, however. The *Birmingham Ledger* was lukewarm. "Local option is better than some forms of prohibition," the editor remarked, "but a man doesn't like a county where one side of a branch is prohibition and the other is not. If possible Alabama ought to have one law for all her people."[32] The *Montgomery Advertiser* thought the larger cities might suffer from the operation of the bill. It would hardly be fair, the editor thought, for one fourth of the voters of Montgomery County, perhaps nearly all of them from the county precincts, to decide that the citizens of a city should have an election on the liquor question. Mobile, Birmingham, Selma, or Anniston might feel the effects of such inequitable legislation.[33] The editor of the *Mobile Register* agreed with him.[34]

The churches came out strongly for the proposed law. Gone was the apathy and diffidence which had often in past years kept religious leaders from taking an active part in the political fight for temperance. They had, it may be supposed, at last come to the conclusion that the liquor traffic could not be overthrown by moral suasion alone. They were ready to act and act vigorously.

With all galleries filled with eager spectators, the temperance committees of House and Senate held a joint meeting on the Lovelady bill on January 22. W. B. Crumpton, G. W. Young, Brooks Lawrence, and W. A. Davis of Anniston spoke eloquently in its favor.[35] The next day the adjourned session heard from the opposition in the person of Thomas Clarke, an able lawyer. He cautioned his hearers about the harm to be done to the cause of temperance through ill-advised and drastic legislation. He cited the failure of the anti-canteen law in the army. He urged the legislators to examine the bill most carefully for possible defects. The chief bone of contention, he declared, was whether the county or the precinct should be made the unit; the present bill ignored a majority of the citizens in a precinct or municipality—that was not fair. Clarke was supported in his argument by Felix Blackburn.

Since the temperance forces had the last word, Dr. G. W. Young brought the discussion to a close, maintaining that "local option is the best solution that has ever been suggested to regulate the whiskey traffic." He answered his opponents by saying that it was quite impractical to make the

[31] August, 1906.
[32] February 14, 1907.
[33] *Mobile Register,* February 11, 1907.
[33] February 16, 1907.
[34] February 12, 1907.

town the unit in such legislation; the county seats were centers of the counties and might well be assumed to represent the sentiment of the whole people. When Young finished speaking the committee went into executive session.[36]

By a vote of 11 to 8 the house temperance committee voted on January 25, to report the Lovelady bill favorably. But they added certain amendments. The provision that a county which had once voted in prohibition might not reconsider its vote while a county voting wet might call another election after two years did not seem fair to the committee. They favored an amendment giving all counties the right to reconsider a vote after the two-year period.[37]

The fight was now transferred to the House. It got off to a good start with "the gallery filled to overflowing with ladies and gentlemen." The legislators who, according to the *Advertiser*, spent two hours and a half in "repeating campaign speeches and telling in general of the terrible effects of the liquor traffic," were fully conscious of their audience.

Several of the speakers directed their glances to that same gallery during their speeches, flung their arms upward in declaiming what they had done and what they would do in the future to king alcohol, and called on all to witness them cast their votes for the right—as they saw the right.[38]

Only one point of controversy marked the discussion. All the legislators declared themselves in favor of temperance and local option. They disagreed merely as to whether the county, as proposed by the bill, or the city and precinct, as advocated by the liquor interests, be made the unit for local option.[39]

Eugene Ballard of Autauga, chairman of the temperance committee, reported for his committee favoring the county unit plan. He was supported by Jere C. King of Jefferson, Jerome T. Fuller of Bibb, Fleetwood Rice of Tuscaloosa, and N. M. Rowe and A. D. Kirby of Madison. R. T. Goodwyn of Montgomery led the forces of the precinct unit supporters, and W. L. Pitts of Perry and F. O. Hoffman of Mobile also spoke for that side.

Dr. Lovelady of Jefferson, author of the bill, questioned the candor of those opposing the measure when they seemed to argue that there would be nothing but crime under the county unit system and no crime at all under the beat unit system. Probably the advocates of the minority report were sincere, he admitted, but the whiskey interests of the state were also on that side.[40]

The argument ended with an earnest speech by A. H. Carmichael of Colbert. The greatest benefit of the constitution of 1901, he said, was the

[36] *Mobile Register*, January 25, 1907.
[37] *Montgomery Advertiser*, January 27, 1907.
[38] *Montgomery Advertiser*, February 7, 1907.
[39] *Ibid.*
[40] *Montgomery Advertiser*, February 7, 1907.

liberation of the people from the domination of the saloon. Now the people demanded that their legislators make that liberation secure by supporting the majority report. To settle that point he called for the vote on the minority substitute. The vote, taken by roll call, was 26 to 70 against that substitute.[41]

Chairman Ballard then offered, as a substitute to the original bill, a new version jointly acceptable to his committee and to the senate committee.[42] When this revised bill came to a vote, it was passed 81 to 2; only J. A. Coleman of Lowndes and Alexander D. Pitts of Dallas voted "No."[43]

The battle in the senate developed more heat. Senator Robert Elias Spragins denounced the bill as "a sham, a pretense, a measure which pretends to be a local option bill, and which in fact is a prohibition bill." The governor, he declared, must certainly veto such a bill; he had asked for an equitable local option bill, not such a bill as this. Senator Elias Perry Thomas of Eufaula declared that "faith had been broken by the gentlemen who led in this movement." They had assured him that where dispensaries were established, the bill would provide that no elections might be held for four years; they had not made good this promise. Senator H. P. Merritt of Tuskegee also feared the effect of "another whiskey election" on a county where a dispensary was in operation. He said:

> Blind tigers have flourished in the prohibition districts of my county in the past. We have just cleared out those blind tigers after a vigorous campaign. During the last term of court of my county, between $6,000 and $7,000 in fines were collected from the keepers of blind tigers. If we are precipitated into a fight of dispensary or no dispensary, those who had been interested in blind tigers would unite with the prohibition people to destroy the dispensary.[44]

Senator John F. Wilson of Oneonta answered such complaints by saying that efforts to defer the time when the bill should become effective were only attempts "to postpone the day of judgment." A great wave of temperance reform had started and nothing could stop it. The people of Alabama demanded that the bill pass. Senator Norman Gunn of Thomasville admitted that in his district they had both prohibition and blind tigers, but he favored the bill just the same as part of a great reform movement. The passage of the bill would make history for the state of Alabama declared Senator G. T. McWhorter, chairman of the committee reporting the bill. His committee had carefully considered all amend-

---

[41] *House Journal* (1907), p. 1127.

[42] O. C. Maner, who had supported the city and precinct unit measure, declared in favor of local option and pleaded for unanimous passage. *Montgomery Advertiser*, February 8, 1907.

[43] W. L. Pitts of Perry offered an amendment to provide that no election to displace a dispensary should be held within four years of the passage of the local option law; his motion was tabled. *House Journal* (1907), p. 1134.

[44] *Montgomery Advertiser*, February 21, 1907.

ments offered and they knew that the bill they had reported "represented the best in the temperance movement."[45]

The Senate, however, added some amendments before passing the bill. These amendments provided for holding of elections to establish dispensaries, postponed for two years the application of the bill to dispensaries, provided for a uniform system of ballots, and ruled that elections might be held every two years.[46] The bill thus amended was approved by the House, returned to the Senate, and there passed on February 21, 1907, by a vote of 22 to 0.[47]

The Lovelady Local Option Bill, chief storm center of the 1907 legislature, became a law when Governor Comer affixed his signature to it on February 26.[48]

"I consider the passage of the county local option law the greatest victory for temperance reform in the history of the state of Alabama," declared Brooks Lawrence. The two-year exemption for dispensaries did not bother him much. He considered it "a hollow tooth that decays and drops out at the end of that period when our law will have full application to all liquor counties of the state."[49]

In the newspapers only a few voices expressed disapproval of the measure or doubt of its success. The *Montgomery Advertiser* and the *Mobile Register,* skeptical throughout the fight, continued to find the law impractical and unfair to the large cities. The *Birmingham Age-Herald* predicted that the legislature had stirred up a good deal of trouble when it passed the bill. "Hot campaigns over the liquor question may not be altogether desirable," said the editor, "but the legislature is about to make them inevitable, and we will, therefore, be compelled to accept the situation."[50] Many large cities, said the *Montgomery Journal,* would now be "forced to give up the sale of liquor by being voted down by the counties...."[51]

Meanwhile the advocates of the dispensary system had been working to perfect that method of liquor control. Just ten days after the passage of the Lovelady bill, Senator Moody brought to the senate a bill which applied the principle of local option to dispensaries, and provided for county elections on the question of establishing dispensaries upon petition to the probate judge of one fifth of the qualified voters of the county.[52] The committee on temperance, to whom the bill was referred, brought in a favorable report.

Not much opposition developed in the Senate. A proposition to except cities of over 20,000 from the county unit plan was tabled. An amend-

[45] *Montgomery Advertiser,* February 21, 1907.
[46] *Acts* (1907), pp. 200-205.
[47] *Senate Journal* (1907), pp. 1031-1063.
[48] *Acts* (1907), p. 205.
[49] *Alabama Baptist,* February 27, 1907.
[50] March 1, 1907.   [51] February 27, 1907.
[52] *Senate Journal* (1907), p. 283.

ment offered by Elias Perry Thomas imposed a penalty upon any dispensary purchasing agent who should receive rebates was accepted. The bill passed by a vote of 20 to 0.[53]

Stronger disagreement in the House, where the temperance committee brought in a favorable report on the bill on February 22, resulted in a motion to postpone action upon it indefinitely. The motion was lost, and the bill finally received the House approval by a vote of 57 to 14.[54]

The two local option laws were the principal accomplishments of the legislature of 1907. The lawmakers enacted certain other measures designed to aid enforcement of these laws or to curb and control the liquor traffic.

In spite of strong opposition led by Jake Weiss, head of the liquor lobby, the temperance forces skillfully guided by Lee McMillan of Wilcox County managed to pass the Merritt bill that repealed the two-year exemption for old dispensaries.[55]

To counteract the complaint that dispensary profits all went to the city or town while a large part of dispensary income was paid in by county people, the legislature authorized dispensary cities to contract to give the county fifty per cent of the net revenue of the dispensary.[56]

"On a recent Sunday in Birmingham," said Dr. Lovelady to his fellow legislators, "no less than fifty prescriptions calling for whiskey were filled by one Birmingham druggist."[57] The legislators agreed that this was excessive and passed an act limiting druggists' prescriptions to one fourth of a pint each.[58]

Almost as important in its implications as the local option law, was the Anti-Shipping law also passed in 1907.[59] It prohibited the shipment, transportation, or solicitation of orders for liquor in any prohibition district in the state. The Senate passed the measure by a vote of 26 to 3.[60] The House gave it a vote of 65 to 3, in spite of efforts made by Representative Hoffman of Mobile, to hold up the action of the law until Congress should have similarly restricted interstate shipments of intoxicants.[61] The legislature recognized the weight of Hoffman's argument sufficiently to address to Alabama Congressmen a resolution urging them to

do all in their power to secure the passage of a federal law prohibiting the interstate shipment of intoxicating liquors or beverages into prohibition districts of the various states.[62]

[53] *Senate Journal* (1907), p. 283.
[54] *Birmingham Ledger*, March 2, 1907. Rice of Tuscaloosa led the fight for the bill and John L. Hughston of Lauderdale, and F. O. Hoffman of Mobile, led the opposition to it. *House Journal* (1907), p. 218.
[55] *Acts* (1907), p. 626. *Alabama Baptist*, August 28, 1907.
[56] *Acts* (1907), p. 626. The payment was to be made to create a sinking fund for the redemption of bonds issued by the county in constructing public roads.
[57] *Montgomery Advertiser*, February 21, 1907.
[58] *Acts* (1907), p. 727.
[59] *Ibid.*, p. 488.
[60] *Senate Journal* (1907), p. 1939.
[61] *House Journal* (1907), p. 2116.
[62] *Acts* (1907), p. 784.

The legislature of 1907 had made very clear the views of the people, and the liquor dealers saw the handwriting on the wall. Hitherto they had ignored, insofar as they could, the laws which displeased them. They had paid little attention to complaints that they were disregarding and violating the laws of the land.[63] Now they launched their own reform movement. The dealers in Mobile and Montgomery led the crusade. It was, of course, a protective move. The liquor dealers recognized that the editor of the *Mobile Register* was telling the truth when he said:

> It is the *Register's* opinion that the matter of license or prohibition rests almost wholly in the hands of the men who sell the liquor. . . . Prohibition in a city with Mobile's attitude toward liquor, would not give relief. It would mean unlicensed sale; underhand sale; instead of open sale; bad whiskey sold for good whiskey; and a weakening of the moral status of the community. Nevertheless, the people will take prohibition in preference to a continuance of existing conditions.[64]

The Retail Liquor Dealers' Association of Mobile moved first to secure from the city council a stiffening of license rates. Licenses which had been from $75 to $150 were increased to $200, and licenses for the sale of malt liquors, formerly from $30 to $50, were set at $75. Variations in fees according to districts were eliminated. All dealers in the city were obliged to pay the same rate.[65]

The Mobile dealers held a mass meeting to declare themselves solidly in favor of strict enforcement of the Sunday laws. Fifty-nine of them signed a pledge not to sell liquor on Sunday. They admitted rigid observance of the law was their only safeguard against the rising tide of public opinion, and observe it they would, even if it meant the employment of private detectives.[66]

Such action seemed to Major Jake Weiss of Mobile, wholesale liquor dealer and senator from Mobile County, to promise speedy solution of the liquor problem. He declared that

> every responsible retail and wholesale whiskey dealer wants to see the dive eliminated. . . . I feel sure that the conscientious saloon men will not stand in the way of a raise [of license fees] providing it will cut out the irresponsible dealer and put the traffic on the highest possible plane.[67]

The "conscientious saloon men" of Montgomery also moved to put their business on "the highest possible plane." They sent a committee to the judge of the criminal division of the city court and to the mayor to urge stricter law enforcement. They were out to show the people, they declared, that the liquor business conducted in accordance with the letter

---

[63] The Reverend W. J. E. Cox said: "The Sunday law has been utterly disregarded by the saloon keepers in general. When some great crime has been committed and the community has been aroused, there has been some effort to close the saloons on Sunday for a week or two. The 'lid' has not been put on effectively if reports are true." *Alabama Baptist*, April 3, 1907.
[64] March 2, 1907.
[65] *Mobile Register*, March 15, 1907.
[66] *Ibid.*, March 15, 16, 1907.
[67] *Birmingham Ledger*, June 10, 1907.

of the law could solve the liquor problem without recourse to prohibition. Saloon owners pledged themselves, by affixing their signatures to a petition, to inform the authorities of all violations of law. They made plans to form a Saloon Men's Protective Association.[68]

All this, thought the editor of the *Montgomery Advertiser*, was just plain good business. He said he was no sentimentalist but he knew that the best interests of the city required stricter regulation of the retail liquor business.

> Under a higher license system, many neighborhoods will be relieved of the nuisance and trouble that come from the corner liquor shops. There will be fewer meeting places for those who are disposed to be lawless and that class will be more under the eye of the law. It will greatly reduce the criminality that burdens our police records and lessen the expense of governing our city.[69]

The editor of the *Birmingham News* correctly interpreted this movement and the reasons for it. The increasing power of prohibition sentiment, the growing strength of the anti-saloon movement all over the South, was, he felt, much more an expression of public resentment against the political activities of the liquor interests than it was of public will to do away with the liquor traffic. The arrogance of the liquor dealers who had disobeyed laws with impunity and pointed their effort toward control of the polls, had at last "struck a snag." Perhaps the liquor interests were aware now of their mistakes. One thing was certain, the editorial concluded:

> They may as well reconcile themselves to one of two things: to observe the laws and stay out of politics as an organization, or else be forced to close their grog shops and go out of business.[70]

It looked as though the liquor interests had chosen the first alternative. Had they awakened too late to save themselves?

Coosa County was the first to try out the operation of the new local option law. Most of the county was already under prohibition in 1907, but three saloons at Goodwater were a thorn in the flesh to the temperance advocates of the town.[71] They determined to get rid of them. A mass meeting in the Goodwater Presbyterian Church on May 13 launched the movement. The Goodwater Anti-Whiskey and Anti-Saloon League was organized and drew up resolutions declaring that prohibition in Coosa County was necessary for the good of the community "morally, financially, intellectually, and religiously." The League pledged itself "in the name of humanity" to work for an election which would banish the evil from the neighborhood and asked the aid of all citizens toward this end. Copies of the resolutions were sent to "our Senator and Representative personally," and the legislature was warned that "we are opposed

[68] *Montgomery Advertiser*, May 25, 1907.
[69] *Ibid.*, June 20, 1907.
[70] March 20, 1907. [71] *Alabama Citizen*, July, 1907.

to the sale or other disposition of . . . intoxicants . . . and not to pass any special law enforcing the same on us. . . ."[72]

Between the date of that meeting and July 6, when the question came up for vote, a vigorous campaign was waged in the county. Speakers from the Anti-Saloon League harangued the people, temperance tracts were distributed, and the saloon forces worked steadily and quietly emphasizing a direct canvass of voters. The result was an overwhelming victory for the temperance forces. The vote was 696 to 138, and only one precinct showed a majority against prohibition.[73] The three saloons of Goodwater prepared to go out of business.

Four more counties swung into the temperance column in September elections: Butler, Pickens, Talladega, and Tuscaloosa. All four were the scenes of hot battles.

Butler, which held its election on September 21, was considered one of the strongest liquor counties in the state. Though liquor was sold only in Greenville, it was thought that the county seat would control the election. Greenville, however, upset all predictions by turning in a majority of twenty-six against the sale of liquor. Of the total 1,213 votes, 716 favored prohibition.[74]

Two days later a well-prepared and hard-fought campaign in Pickens County came to its close. The movement had started there when, in response to one hundred personal letters sent by Reverend E. P. Smith of the Carrollton Baptist Church and Reverend S. N. Barnes of the Carrollton Methodist Episcopal Church, South, ninety-five citizens agreed to sponsor a mass meeting on May 17 at the Reform Baptist Church. A campaign committee of six prominent men was organized and, upon the advice of Brooks Lawrence, it set out to enlist in the cause every pastor in the county. Sermons from a score of pulpits carried the message to the people. In each precinct three workers were assigned the job of circulating petitions and overseeing activities. An accurate mailing list of voters, indicating each voter's view on prohibition, gave the campaign committee much basic information. A flood of temperance literature flowed through the county and many voters received free copies of the *Alabama Citizen*. Every known argument for the saloon was answered in the thousands of tracts prepared and circulated by the campaign committee. Special effort, crowned with considerable success, was directed toward the businessmen and largest taxpayers, who were appealed to in the name of self-interest as well as community welfare. As the campaign drew to its close, contracts with local newspapers insured generous space for prohibition publicity, 2,500 personal letters went out from headquarters, a W.C.T.U. organizer came down to work with the women and children, and speakers stumped the countryside. The effort continued until election day. Not even the

[72] *Birmingham Ledger*, May 13, 1907. [73] *Alabama Citizen*, August, 1907.
[74] *Greenville Advocate*, September 28, 1907.

barrage of letters and literature sent out from the Wholesale Liquor Dealers' Association in New York could counteract such well-organized and thorough work. The whiskey interests carried one beat in the county by a majority of twelve. They polled a total of 157 votes; the prohibition vote was 1,060.[75]

Talladega and Tuscaloosa both voted on September 30. In the former county 235 votes for liquor out of a total of 1,273 gave clear indication of the public will. Talladega itself voted 304 to 77 in favor of prohibition and nine Talladega saloons thereby were forced out of business when the year ended.[76] The Tuscaloosa election aroused special interest because it was directed against the dispensary. Friends of the dispensary thought success of the prohibition forces would mean a death blow to the dispensary system in the state.[77] Senator Moody, who lived in Tuscaloosa, did all he could to protect the institution he had fathered, but Fleetwood Rice led the temperance forces to final victory. The vote was 783 for the sale of liquor and 1,330 against it.

Alabama had only twenty-one prohibition counties on July 1, 1907. Now, with five successful local option elections and with six other counties made dry by special enactment, she had thirty-two. The total was rolling up to landslide proportions. Seven counties voted overwhelmingly for prohibition in October and six more in the early weeks of November.[78]

Among these later elections the one in Jefferson County is especially significant. Jefferson was the most populous county in the state and held a strategic place in the movement for local option. The campaign there originated with the Baptist pastors, who on August 12 resolved in favor of a local option election, pledged themselves to work for it and preach for it, and appointed a committee whose duty was to organize public meetings. At about the same time the Pastors' Union of Birmingham launched a similar effort, and organized a similar committee "with plenary powers." R. F. Lovelady was made chairman of this committee and representatives of the Christian, Methodist, Baptist, and Presbyterian churches worked with him.[79]

---

[75] E. P. Smith, "How Pickens County Was Carried for Prohibition," *Alabama Citizen*, October, 1907.

[76] *Alabama Citizen*, October, 1907. Five saloons at Sylacauga were also affected:

[77] *Ibid.*

[78] *Tuscaloosa News*, October 2, 1907; *Alabama Citizen*, October, November, 1907. Six of these counties had gone dry by special acts: Randolph, Houston, Chilton, St. Clair, Dale, Henry. Dry by local option were Coosa, Butler, Pickens, Talladega, Tuscaloosa. Elections were ordered for Lowndes on October 11; Lee, October 14; Calhoun, October 15; Wilcox and Bullock, October 26; Jefferson, October 28; Etowah, October 29. Every county holding an election between October 1 and November 15, 1907, had a landslide vote for prohibition. By the time these elections were over the prohibition counties of the state numbered forty-five. Campaigns were carefully organized under local Anti-Saloon Leagues led by ministers and church members.

[79] *Alabama Baptist*, August 14, 1907. In addition to Chairman Lovelady, the committee of the Pastors' Union included Reverend A. R. Moore, pastor of the First

Signatures for the needed petition for the election were vigorously solicited during August. By September 19 some 4,650 voters, most of them church members, had affixed their names to the document, which was forthwith presented to Probate Judge S. E. Green. The managers of the campaign declared that they had really secured about 7,000 names, but some lists had been mislaid and others were late coming in. However, even with the withdrawal of fifty-two names after the petition reached the judge's office, the number was well over the required twenty-five per cent of the estimated 9,330 voters in the county, and the judge ordered the election for October 28.[80]

The drys set aside Sunday, September 22, as a day for special sermons and speeches. "At almost every Protestant church in the county some mention was made of prohibition, or a whole service was given over to the subject . . . several pulpits had a visiting minister and in several instances mass meetings were held in churches." Judge W. A. Covington of Georgia, delivered an address before a large crowd at the Jefferson Theatre. W. L. Sessions, chairman of the prohibition campaign committee, presided, and among the guests was Governor Comer. "No political campaign in recent years," declared the *Advertiser* the next day, ". . . will compare to the one now on. . . . It will take a great effort to stop the wave that is sweeping over the county; money alone will not cut off the tour of the moral elements."[81]

The whiskey forces, until now conducting a sort of anonymous campaign, recognized that the time had indeed come for "great effort." A gigantic "defense fund" had been raised by the big distillers and brewers at their Cincinnati conference, and Alabama prepared to make use of its share. Two weeks before the election the anti-prohibitionists met at Birmingham. They recorded their concern with the "momentous economic and social questions" involved in the campaign, their belief that the open saloon stood "as a guard against . . . illicit retailing," their horror of the blind tiger which "like the midnight assassin, plies its avocation under cover of darkness, enticing the young and weak" and recognized "no law of God nor of man." They said they would "view with alarm the establishment of blind tigers in such communities as East Lake, Woodlawn, Avondale, East Birmingham, Owenton, and the many other highly moral communities of the county." They pledged their best efforts toward the proper exercise of the police power in the regulation of saloons, and

---

Christian Church; Reverend H. M. Dobbs, pastor of the Five Points Methodist Episcopal Church, South; P. C. Ratliff, Baptist layman; and Reverend S. J. Foster, of the South Highlands Presbyterian Church. The committee was empowered to decide on the date for the election after consultation with the laymen and businessmen of the county.

[80] *Birmingham News*, September 20, 1907. 9,330 votes had been cast for sheriff in the last general election, which had drawn an especially full vote.

[81] September 23, 1907.

declared that they would vote for no candidate "who does not agree to enforce laws for the perfect regulation of the liquor traffic."[82]

The newspapers of Birmingham took sides in the campaign. The *Birmingham Ledger* declared itself "squarely for prohibition," predicting that it would decrease crime in the county by fifty per cent.[83] The *Birmingham News* took the same stand. The editor insisted that public safety was jeopardized by the saloon and that businessmen were coming more and more to favor sober men for positions of responsibility. Even the liquor dealers refused to employ drunkards as bartenders. Conditions in Jefferson County had been scandalous for years, said the *News*. The saloon had played too large a part in politics.

Seldom is an election held in this county without unmistakable evidence of a big corruption fund raised and distributed by the liquor interests to control the ballot box.[84]

The time had now come, said the editor, when the people might, by an overwhelming vote against the saloon, register their will to end such conditions and at the same time warn any who might contemplate engaging in illicit liquor traffic.[85]

On the other side was the *Birmingham Age-Herald* which contended that prohibition would be the ruin of Jefferson County. Skilled labor would at once move to other parts of the state. The experiment was foredoomed to failure. "If prohibition prohibited," said the editor, "then it might be largely a moral question." But he did not think it did. The campaign had "stirred up more rancor than any city, county, or state contest within the past ten years." If the prohibitionists were to win, "business would have a serious backset, while suffering and crime would be more in evidence than ever."[86]

Wishes colored pre-election forecasts. The *Birmingham News* faced the day "serenely confident of victory"; only the size of the majority was in question, the editor thought.[87] The *Age-Herald* was equally sure that the prohibition party was "losing ground steadily"; a prohibition defeat by a "very decisive majority" was as good as settled.[88] The editor of the *Montgomery Journal*, watching the progress of the campaign, predicted victory for the prohibition forces. Everywhere in Alabama, not alone in Jefferson County, said the editor, there was "a tidal wave that seems to

---

[82] *Birmingham News*, October 14, 1907; see also *ibid.*, September 20.
[83] September 30, 1907. The editor also thought that prohibition would not, as its opponents claimed, hurt business. He maintained that a large conservative group favored prohibition in the belief that it would help business.
[84] *Birmingham News*, October 1, 1907; see also *ibid.*, October 3, 1907; September 28, 1907. The editor deplored the fact that the streets of Birmingham were often overcrowded with more or less dangerous Negroes, idlers who spent a large part of their time in the liquor joints and dives in the process of becoming criminals. He said, "It is hard to realize a more threatening condition than that of numbers of Negroes under the constant influence of the saloon."
[85] *Ibid.*, October 18, 1907.
[86] October 25, 1907.
[87] October 20, 1907.
[88] October 25, 1907.

have no recision, but is continuous, sweeping everything before it." The cause of this wave was quite simply "the abuse of power, the abuse of privileges, the wanton disregard of law, and the influence for harm the whiskey interests exert in politics." The whiskey power had laid hold on public office; it was felt "even in the house of God." The people would tolerate such conditions no longer. They had tried for years to minimize the effects of the liquor traffic on their communities and to drive whiskey out of politics. They had seen the evils of the traffic increase and "the whiskey interests getting more entrenched and more difficult to drive from cover." They had decided that

there is but one way to end it all, to restore city government back to the people, and to make conditions once more normal and tolerable, and that is to drive whiskey out, and the only way to drive it out, is to vote it out.[89]

Election day was cold with a stiff breeze blowing, but the voters of Jefferson County were too excited to notice the weather. By eight o'clock that morning thousands of women and children had turned out to parade the streets of Birmingham, singing, to the tune of "Gathering in the Sheaves," "Jefferson is going dry," and bearing banners with such slogans as "Down with Booze," "Boys or Beer," "Save the Boys," "Save the Girls," "Vote for the Home," "Down with the Saloon," "We Pray for You." Divided into four battalions, the parade visited the four voting places in the city, and left in each place a squad of eager women and children who served coffee and good advice to the voters, pinned white bows on coat lapels of converts, and kept up their theme song, interrupted only by frequent addresses by prohibition leaders. Some claimed that the women were intimidating voters and threatened to carry the matter to the courts, but the ladies, with the children beside them, kept up their vigorous work until the polls were closed.[90]

Thousands of voters thronged the polling places all day. Businessmen left their shops and offices to watch the excitement. Almost every minister in the city was on duty. Dr. J. H. McCoy, president of the Methodist College at Owenton, led a parade of his student body which was punctuated with college yells and the vigorous singing of "Jefferson is going dry." P. G. Bowman, a local attorney, stumped the polling places all day, and was at much pains to deny that he had said on the preceding Saturday night that ninety per cent of the working people of the county got drunk every pay day. That statement was a fake and a fraud.[91]

The circular which caused Bowman's embarrassment was one of the efforts of the liquor forces to stem the tide of prohibition sentiment. Another pamphlet, widely distributed on election day, warned the voters that the banks, fearing prohibition, had unanimously agreed not to pay more

[89] *Montgomery Journal*, October 23, 1907.
[90] *Montgomery Advertiser*, October 29, 1907. See also *ibid.*, October 23, 1907.
[91] *Montgomery Advertiser*, October 23, 1907.

than $50 a day to any depositor. The Reverend Frank Willis Barnett, speaking from his buggy, branded the statement as a lie and quoted President John Frye of the Traders' Bank to prove it. The crowd roared its approval.[92]

When the smoke of battle had cleared away, official returns showed that the prohibitionists had carried Jefferson County by a majority of 1,750. Thanksgiving services at the churches celebrated the victory.[93] Even the opponents of the measure were inclined to think that "all differences and animosities" should be forgotten and "every effort . . . be made to enforce the law."[94]

The *Alabama Baptist,* hailing the victory in Jefferson as "the greatest victory for civic righteousness which has ever been won in the history of Alabama," sounded also the keynote for the next effort of the prohibition forces. The governor of Alabama, said the *Baptist,* always a friend of prohibition, had had ample opportunity, as he cast his vote in Birmingham, to see "what the people want." The next step was very clear:

Now let the Legislature rise to its opportunity and give us statutory prohibition and provide a way to let the people vote on constitutional prohibition.[95]

Successful local option elections gave new courage and boldness to the prohibition forces. When in late summer of 1907 Governor Comer made known his intention of calling an extra session of the legislature to consider railroad legislation, the prohibitionists, flushed with victory, saw their opportunity. They brought pressure upon the governor to include state-wide prohibition in his call, but Governor Comer was cautious. He issued a statement recalling to the voters his position in favor of local option and his support of the law as passed by the regular session of the legislature. He was of the opinion that the law should stand "until the people have an opportunity to vote on the question as a state policy." Therefore, he said,

In the call for an extra session I would not embody a prohibition call and would not advise a state prohibition law.[96]

Undaunted, the temperance workers continued to press for immediate action. If prohibition was a good thing for a community, city, or county, declared the *Birmingham News,* it must follow that it would be a good thing for a state. A general prohibition law enacted now would "undoubtedly voice the will of a large majority of the people of Alabama."[97] The *Birmingham Ledger* also took up the cause. To all members

[92] *Birmingham Age-Herald,* October 29, 1907.
[93] *Montgomery Advertiser,* October 30, 1907. Reverend J. O. Haynes occupied the pulpit at the service held at the Wesley Chapel Methodist Church. The woman's central campaign committee had a special prayer meeting.
[94] *Birmingham Age-Herald,* October 29, 1907.
[95] *Alabama Baptist,* November 6, 1907.
[96] *Birmingham Ledger,* September 26, 1907.
[97] September 24, 1907. The editorial was entitled "State Prohibition."

of the legislature it sent a questionnaire, asking: "1. Will you cast your vote for a bill providing for state prohibition? 2. Will you, through the *Birmingham Ledger,* petition Governor Comer to include in the call for the proposed extraordinary session . . . the subject of statutory prohibition?" "While we have an opportunity to be rid of the liquor evil," urged the *Ledger* editor, "let us be up and doing."[98]

The Baptist Church, always active in the temperance cause, threw its considerable influence behind state prohibition. The editor of the *Alabama Baptist* urged his readers to "get to work at once, to send resolutions and petitions to the Governor and, to work upon their senators and representatives." Governor Comer, he believed, could scarcely veto a bill for state prohibition if the will of the people was made clear.[99] The Baptist State Convention had endorsed state-wide prohibition and local associations followed suit, among them the Harris Baptist Association, the Eufaula Baptist Association, the East Liberty Association, and the Chilton County Missionary Baptist Association. State-wide prohibition, in the minds of the members of the last-named association, was "the will of God and also our fellow men."[100]

The proclamation[101] convening the legislature "in extra session," which Governor Comer issued on October 9, did not mention a general prohibition law. The Governor admitted a few weeks later, however, that, if prohibition laws were inadequate, he favored strengthening them and declared:

I, the Governor of the State, will call the Legislature together as often as it is necessary to see to it that the laws of the State are upheld.[102]

Before the extra session assembled, new local option victories[103] and the surge of public opinion had made it a foregone conclusion that the bill the temperance forces were demanding would be brought before the lawmakers. It would be, predicted the *Montgomery Advertiser,* the first bill introduced, and by July 1, 1908, state prohibition would be in effect. Eugene Ballard

[98] September 25-30, 1907, *passim.*
[99] October 16, 1907.
[100] *Minutes* of the Harris, Eufaula, East Liberty, and Chilton Baptist Associations, (1907).
[101] *House Journal, Extra Session,* (1907), p. 3.
[102] *Alabama Christian Advocate,* October 24, 1907.
[103] Counties holding local option elections, October 9 to November 7, were:

County	Date	For Prohibition	Against Prohibition	Majority For
Lowndes	October 11	411	266	145
Lee	October 14	1,041	299	812
Calhoun	October 15	1,843	227	1,616
Wilcox	October 26	677	86	591
Jefferson	October 28	5,640	3,843	1,797
Etowah	October 29	1,632	474	1,158
Tallapoosa	November 2	1,520	240	1,280
Shelby	November 4	1,263	160	1,103
Fayette	November 4	1,113	132	981

would introduce the bill, the *Advertiser* thought. Its success might be somewhat threatened because "Speaker A. H. Carmichael has temperance strength which will not be behind the prohibition act. . . . On the other hand, it is possible that several band-wagon riders have climbed aboard the water wagon, on seeing that prohibition is stronger than it was in July."[104] Dr. W. B. Crumpton, president of the Alabama Anti-Saloon League, said unofficially that he believed that he spoke for every member of the League in endorsing the proposed bill as the *Advertiser* outlined it. The League had been accused by its enemies of opposing such a bill in July, Crumpton admitted; but the time was not then ripe for it. Now that the temperance forces had measured arms with the liquor power at its strongest point, the whole state was ready for a general law.[105]

The governor bowed to necessity. Two days before the extra session convened, Senator H. F. Reese of Dallas County, meeting Governor Comer in the lobby of the Exchange Hotel said, "By the way, Governor, I have heard a number of people say you would veto a State Prohibition Bill." The governor replied:

> I don't see how they could say that. My position on the question is well known. I stood for local option. It was put in the platform, and I favor carrying out the platform. But if the Legislature passes a prohibition bill and the time comes when I must line up with either the temperance people or the other side, why, nobody could doubt where I would stand.[106]

His words dashed the hopes of the liquor dealers and gave to their opponents a clear signal to go ahead. On the first day of the extra session the prohibitionists acted. A. H. Carmichael, speaker of the House, introduced a bill

> To prohibit the manufacture, sale, barter, exchange, giving away to induce trade, the furnishing at public places, or otherwise disposing of any alcoholic, spirituous, vinous, or malt liquors, intoxicating bitters or beverages, or other liquors or beverages by whatsoever name called which if drunk to excess will produce intoxication, except the sale of alcohol in certain cases upon certain conditions, and except the sale of wines, for sacramental purposes.[107]

Stubborn opposition from Mobile developed as the committee on temperance considered the Carmichael bill. A night session brought a delegation of that city's businessmen to plead that such a law would ruin the port of Mobile, since foreign ships would not come to a port where liquor might not be sold, and would also ruin the schools of the county, since their revenue which kept them running was largely derived from liquor licenses.[108] "It would certainly be an act of tyranny, very un-Democratic

---

[104] *Montgomery Advertiser*, October 30, 1907; see also *ibid.*, October 27, 1907.
[105] *Ibid.*, October 30, 1907.   [106] *Ibid.*, November 6, 1907.
[107] *House Journal, Extra Session* (1907), p. 31.
[108] *Montgomery Advertiser*, November 12, 1907. Among the delegation from Mobile were Albert Bush, D. R. Burgess, E. D. Ladyare, Mayor Pat Lyons, LeBarron Lyons, and J. Howard Wilson.

indeed," protested the *Mobile Register*, "to force prohibition upon Mobile without giving the Mobile people an opportunity to say whether they want it or not. . . . The Legislators have no commission from the people to force prohibition upon any county."[109] "Unless anti-prohibitionists win today," President M. J. McDermott of the Bank of Mobile wired Senator Max Hamburger as the fight neared its end,

> please give notice that Mobile is prepared to secede from the State of Alabama and organize home government and cease to be dominated by our country cousins, whose efforts to paralyze Mobile will not be tolerated.[110]

The *Register*, quoting McDermott's outburst, was inclined to think this was going just a little too far![111]

The House committee on temperance brought in a favorable report on the Carmichael bill on November 12,[112] and on the following day it was passed by a vote of 66 to 25. A. S. Lyons of Mobile had made a desperate effort to block it on the grounds that it had not been included in the governor's call and had been irregularly handled since its introduction. R. T. Goodwyn had attempted to amend the bill to make it effective on passage instead of on January 1, 1908. Lyons's effort had been ignored and Goodwyn's amendment tabled.[113]

The *Birmingham Age-Herald* made one last attempt to have the bill killed in the Senate. It reminded its readers that the passage of the Carmichael law would "stop the sale of liquor in the state for at least four years, regardless of any revulsion of sentiment that might take place." Local option was more flexible; the question of license or no license might be settled every two years under that system; but if the legislature acted, and its action were proved unwise, the people would have to wait for four years to have it reversed. "State prohibition," said the editor, "would be legislation with a vengeance. The Senate should reject the statutory prohibition bill and the *Age-Herald* believes it will."[114].

The *Age-Herald* was wrong. With much less trouble than had developed in the House, the Senate passed the Carmichael bill by a vote of 32 to 2 on November 19. It had amended the bill so that it would take effect upon the 31st of December, 1908.[115]

The signing of this bill on November 23 was carefully staged by the friends of prohibition, conscious that they were making history and

---

[109] November 9, 1907.
[110] McDermott was one of the largest real estate dealers in Mobile, a leader in civic affairs, and a conservative citizen. *Montgomery Advertiser*, November 20, 1907.
[111] *Mobile Register*, November 21, 1907.
[112] *House Journal, Extra Session* (1907), p. 85.
[113] *Ibid.*, pp. 125-132. Lyons had claimed that the bill had been introduced without receiving a two-thirds vote of the House, that it was introduced and referred to a standing committee without any vote whatever, and that it did not receive a favorable two-thirds vote of a quorum of the committee considering it.
[114] *Birmingham Age-Herald*, November 14, 1907. See also *Montgomery Advertiser*, July 9, 1907.
[115] *Senate Journal, Extra Session* (1907), p. 195.

feeling the eye of posterity already upon them. Reverend Brooks Lawrence, Speaker A. H. Carmichael, legislative leaders, and W.C.T.U. workers were present in the solemn semi-circle gathered to watch Governor Comer as, with a stroke of his pen, he made the measure the law of the state. For the ceremony Mrs. J. B. Mell handed to the Governor a handsome gold pen, given to her on her wedding day twenty years earlier and never before used. The Governor carefully traced "B. B. Comer" on the dotted line reserved for the signature of the state's chief executive and wiped the pen on a fresh linen handkerchief that Mrs. Chatfield, president of the W.C.T.U., had provided for the occasion. A virgin piece of blotting paper, furnished by Mrs. Mell, was used to dry the important signature. Pen, wiper, and blotter were carefully preserved as mementoes of the day. General hand-shaking and mutual congratulations upon the victory over the demon rum ended the great occasion.[116] Alabama had written prohibition into her laws.

The special session which passed the Carmichael Statutory Prohibition law, acted also to stiffen law enforcement. It passed an act whereby prosecutions for violations of laws regarding the sale of liquor might be instituted by affidavit or indictment.[117] It forbade "drinking intoxicating liquors in the presence of passengers on the railway passenger cars or street cars in the state of Alabama," fixing a fine of $10 to $50 and imprisonment not to exceed thirty days for disobedience to this law.[118] Concerned with the problem created by law-breaking by federal license holders, it memorialized Alabama congressmen, begging them to "use all honorable means to secure the early passage of a law prohibiting the issuance . . . [of internal revenue liquor license] where the sale of such liquors is prohibited by law."[119]

Then, since the Carmichael law was not immediately effective and temperance forces in counties not yet "dry" were impatient, the lawmakers heard and acted upon a number of petitions for special prohibition acts. Bullock County was one of the petitioners. The probate judge of this county had ordered a local option election for October 26; but this election had been stopped by an injunction issued by Supernumerary Judge A. H. Alston on the ground that the Merritt Amendment to the Lovelady Law, making it possible to vote on "dispensaries or no dispensaries," was illegal. The citizens of Bullock now asked, and received, of the legislature special action to make their county dry.[120] Pike County got a special enactment

[116] *Montgomery Advertiser*, November 24, 1907.
[117] *Acts, Special Session* (1907), pp. 189-190. When prosecution was begun by affidavit, the person charged did not have the right to demand that a grand jury prefer an indictment.
[118] *Ibid.*, p. 87. The provisions of this law did not apply to smoking compartments, closets, dining, or buffet cars. The police powers given and exercised by the conductors of railway passenger cars under Section 3457 of the Code of Alabama applied to this act.   [119] *Ibid.*, p. 68.
[120] *Montgomery Journal*, October 21, 1907. For Bullock's special bill, see *Local Acts, Special Session* (1907), p. 17.

authorizing an election for December 16, "for the purpose of determining whether or not intoxicating beverages of any kind should be sold in Pike County."[121] A similar act for Crenshaw County was passed calling for an election on December 30.[122] Lee County and Pickens County got legislation to prohibit both the manufacture and sale of liquor within their limits.[123]

New local option elections during the last month of 1907 added new dry territory.[124] They were generally landslides for the temperance forces, but the anti-prohibitionists put up a stiff fight to the end—not always a good-tempered fight. When Cullman County voted, on December 9, a free-for-all fight developed over the question whether the ladies of the W.C.T.U. should remove from the courthouse grounds the tent set up there as their headquarters. When the ladies refused to remove the tent, a crowd of men from the courthouse took it down by force. A few moments later a heavy shower came up and the ladies, left shelterless, tried to take refuge in the courthouse. The anti-prohibitionists tried to keep them out. The *Cullman Tribune* reported that "G. Badder was struck, and Asa Fuller's finger was bitten." Only when a prominent citizen "thrust a pistol in the face of the crowd and ordered it to stand back," was the traditional courtesy extended to the ladies.[125]

By January 1, 1908, only seventeen of Alabama's sixty-seven counties permitted the sale of liquor.[126] Twenty-nine counties had become dry by special legislative enactments; twenty-one by the exercise of the local option rights.[127] It was small wonder that the liquor interests renewed the energy of their campaign for life.

The constitutionality of the local option law was their point of attack. Lowndes County was the first battleground. The election, said the anti-prohibitionists in December, 1907, had not been properly advertised, and they claimed also that the law was a local, not a general, measure. They offered to Probate Judge J. C. Wood the license fees for the dispensaries at Hayneville and Fort Deposit, asserting that the provisions of the local option law did not apply there. When the judge refused the fees, they

---

[121] *Ibid.*, p. 41.
[122] *Ibid.*, pp. 35-36.   [123] *Ibid.*, pp. 39, 61.
[124] Walker and Cullman voted on December 9, 1907; Pike on December 16, and Crenshaw on December 30. All elections were landslides for temperance. The vote in Cullman County was 1,493 for and 726 against prohibition. Cullman and Vinemont alone of the twenty-four beats in the county failed to give a majority for prohibition. At Garden City, the vote was a tie, 30 to 30.
[125] *Cullman Tribune*, December 8, 16; *Montgomery Journal*, December 16, 1907.
[126] *Annual Report of State Auditor*, pp. 732-739. The counties operating dispensaries in 1908 were Macon, Winston, Elmore, Bibb, Limestone, Madison, Perry, Colbert, and Coffee. The counties with saloons were Montgomery, Dallas, Cleburne, Covington, Mobile, and Baldwin. Counties having both dispensaries and saloons were Barbour and Marengo.
[127] *Local Acts* (1880-1907), *passim. Alabama Citizen*, February 1, 1908. Two hundred and eight saloons and thirty-five dispensaries were closed in the twenty-nine counties which became dry on December 31, 1907.

applied to Circuit Judge J. C. Richardson for a mandamus to compel him to accept the license money. Almost simultaneously, the dispensers of Luverne, in Crenshaw County, applied for a second mandamus to force the probate judge of Crenshaw to accept dispensary fees on the grounds that the local option law was unconstitutional. Judge Richardson denied both petitions. He based his decision on his belief that the dispensary law, tending to create a monopoly, was contrary to the spirit and letter of the constitution.[128]

The saloon keepers of Birmingham took similar action, applying for a mandamus to compel Probate Judge S. E. Greene to issue to Ben Meyer of Meyer and Marx Liquor Company a license to sell liquor. The mandamus was denied and the case appealed to the Supreme Court. Judge D. W. Speake handed down a similar decision when the saloon keepers of Decatur in Morgan County asked for a mandamus to compel Probate Judge W. E. Skeggs to issue saloon licenses. He stated clearly his reasons for his decision and his pronouncement was hailed as a great victory for the drys. He said:

The first question is whether what is called the county local option law approved February 26, 1907, is constitutional. It is a rule of all county, and especially of lower or *nisi prius* courts, not to declare a statute unconstitutional in case of doubt. Furthermore, I am not of the opinion that the state prohibition bill approved November 23, 1907, takes notice and account of the election that was held in this county on November 9, 1907, and itself puts prohibition in force in this county under section 13, on January 1, 1908, whether the local option act was valid or not. It appears, therefore, that the probate judge had no authority to issue a license to sell liquor and where a license is issued it would be no protection to one who might thereunder sell intoxicating beverages.[129]

The Supreme Court, to which the case was appealed, sustained Judge Speake's decision.[130]

At Mobile the attack was slightly varied. The liquor interests sought to have the Lusk Early Closing Law declared unconstitutional, largely on technical grounds. A bartender, Z. Frank Fourment, employed in the Bienville bar, was arrested for violating the Lusk Law.[131] His case, *ex parte* Fourment, defended by the anti-prohibitionists, reached the Supreme Court, where the earlier vigorous decision of Judge Semms in the lower court was sustained and affirmed.[132]

The liquor dealers of Cullman County had a brief moment of success.

[128] *Montgomery Advertiser*, January 1, 1908.
[129] *Birmingham Ledger*, January 7, 9, 1908. *154 Alabama*, 249.
[130] *151 Alabama*, 249.
[131] *Montgomery Advertiser*, February 7, 1908. Saloons were required to close at six, eight, or nine o'clock according to the population of the places in which they were located. The claim in this case was that the act was void because there was a difference in the title of the bill as passed by the Senate and as amended by the House. One title called for the closing of "saloons" and the other "places" where liquor was sold. [132] *155 Alabama*, 109.

They succeeded in getting a mandamus against Probate Judge Burke; and the judge, upon reading it, issued the desired licenses. Saloons in Cullman thereupon opened on January 1, 1908. There was a storm of protest and nine liquor dealers were arrested. Governor Comer at once sent Circuit Judge Speake to hold a special session of court to settle the matter. The Governor made his own position clear. He said that "the fact that the Probate Judge issued a license to these men does not mean that they are operating under the protection of the State. The licenses mean no more than if they were issued by a private citizen." But the saloon men of Cullman continued to defy the law, confident that they could win the case in court.[183]

The special term of Judge Speake's Circuit Court convened on February 4, and the judge forthwith instructed his jury to proceed as if no licenses existed, inasmuch as Judge Burke had issued them without authority. Thirty-eight indictments were returned against the saloon keepers.[184] The nine liquor dealers convicted appealed to the Supreme Court which heard the case and affirmed the Circuit Court's decision on June 18. The decision handed down by Justice Simpson, in the case of Al Richter v. the State of Alabama, effectively dashed the hopes of the saloon men.[185] It effectively disposed of all the arguments which they, through Richter's counsel, had counted on to win the day for them.

The general prohibition act, Richter's counsel had contended, conflicted with the principles of local option. To which Justice Simpson replied:

This court has recently, after careful consideration, sustained the validity of said general prohibition law and has distinctly held that the provisions of Section 13 of said act, providing that said law should go into effect on the first day of January, 1908, in all counties in which an election shall have been held on or before December 12, 1907, does not require that said election shall be valid, the court saying: "It follows, we think, that the condition to the going into effect on January 1, 1908, of the State prohibition law in counties etc., does not import more than an election—an expression of the popular will—which was had in both counties named. Hence, where the local option law be valid or invalid, is not a vital inquiry."

To what was said in the case may be added that if the election, under a valid law, the provision in the general law would be meaningless, for in that case prohibition would necessarily be already established in the counties referred to by virtue of the local option law, without any aid from the general prohibition law. This is persuasive to show that the object of referring to such election in Section 13 was to cure any defects in the local option statute or in the steps attempted to be taken in pursuance thereto, and to base the going into effect of said law on January 1, 1908, merely upon the fact that the people of said locality had expressed their will by an election.[186]

To the contention that the validity of the law was destroyed because "thirty days" had not elapsed between the call and the election, Justice Simpson replied:

[183] *Montgomery Advertiser*, January 4, 1908.
[185] *Montgomery Advertiser*, June 19, 1908.
[184] *Ibid.*, February 5, 1908.
[186] *Ibid.*

If such had been the intention of the statute, it would have been very easy to have stated it, but that was not done. It is simply not to be less than thirty days, so that if, according to the law, the time at which the election was held could be said to be thirty days from the time of the order, it certainly could not be less than thirty days. From what has been heretofore said on the subject of the time of the notice to call and the special term of the court, it is evident that the ninth day of December was thirty days from the ninth of November, and as the law takes no notice of fractions of a day the first hour of the day was thirty days and the last hour was not more than thirty days.[137]

The defendant's counsel had argued that the probate judge and not the probate court, as required by law, had ordered the election; Justice Simpson declared that court and judge were one and the same. He ruled that the posting of a notice prior to an election was not essential but directory. He closed his opinion with the declaration that the holding of a license by the defendant was immaterial "as it could not confer an authority to sell liquor contrary to law."[138]

Justice Simpson's decision, coupled with a pronouncement from the Supreme Court, written by Justice T. C. McClellan and concurred in by all members of the tribunal, that the local option law, the general prohibition law, and the early closing law were all valid, and that the court upheld "all laws aimed at whiskey" completed the triumph of the prohibitionists. The liquor men had used the ablest attorneys they could hire to find some flaw in the law. They had failed and it was apparent to them that hope no longer lay in that direction.[139]

But the establishment by the highest court in the state of the validity of prohibitory laws did not secure their enforcement. Sheriff Higdon of Jefferson County was one of the officials bedeviled by law-breakers. Things got so bad that Higdon appealed to Governor Comer begging him to call a special session of the legislature to put the prohibition "dodgers" out of business. He declared that if "the present status of affairs continues there will soon be more whiskey and intoxicants sold in the county without revenue, than were ever sold under the old saloon regime." In support of his statement he sent along to the governor a list of clubs organized ostensibly "for the advancement of literature and culture" but which had, among their members, a suspicious number of ex-saloonists and liquor men and which were really only a cover for law breaking. He had tried without success to get an opinion on the legality of these clubs from judges and others. He was at a loss how to cope with the situation. He only knew that the governor ought to "give the people of Alabama the protection to which they were entitled."[140]

The *Alabama Courier* was quick to point out that the law was a complete failure. One could get all the "booze" he wanted in any prohibition

[137] *Montgomery Advertiser*, June 19, 1908; *156 Alabama*, 127.
[138] *Montgomery Advertiser*, June 19, 1908.
[139] *Birmingham Ledger*, April 9, 1908.
[140] *Birmingham Ledger*, March 14, 1908.

town. "Prohibition that is not backed by the people is mighty poor prohibition,"[141] said the editor, and he was very sure that public opinion was not behind this movement. "Prohibition has proven a rank failure in every town . . . where it has been tried," he said; and he urged again that "high license or a dispensary, with good police restrictions is the best manner of disposing of the liquor question."[142] The *Birmingham Ledger* uncovered a "bootleggers union" in that city. Many of the union's members were caught and fined, and such hazards of the "profession" raised the price of a pint of whiskey from eighty cents to one dollar.[143]

The prohibitionists were fully conscious of their obligation to make the laws they had fathered work. In Birmingham, on April 5, they held a mass meeting to plan a campaign against locker clubs and "blind tigers" in Jefferson County. Judge S. D. Weakley, their attorney, declared his willingness to prosecute all law-breakers and advised officers raiding illicit clubs to exercise their right to arrest operators and seize the liquors. Governor Comer, the last speaker of the evening, pledged the full support of the legislature. "It is the best legislature the state ever had," he said. He was quite willing to call it into extra session at any time if necessary for the enforcement of the law.[144]

Law and Order Leagues sprang up in various counties. They were organized to keep a watchful eye on the operation of all the laws, but the enforcement of the liquor regulations claimed their first attention.[145] The *Birmingham Ledger* thought they were on the right track—that they were sounding "the death knell of the 'blind tiger' in Jefferson County." "Attend the meeting of the Law and Order League tomorrow," urged the editor, "and give assistance by your presence to the efforts of those who

[141] *Alabama Courier*, August 12, 1908. "Where the public opinion is not behind the movement, it is impossible to enforce the measure, and prohibition that does not prohibit, is worse a thousand times than the open bar room." *Ibid.*, August 26, 1908.
[142] *Ibid.*, September 23, 1908.
[143] *Birmingham Ledger*, March 24, 1908.
[144] *Birmingham Ledger*, April 6, 1908.
[145] *Montgomery Advertiser*, January 20, 1908. In an address to the citizens of Montgomery County, the president of the League said:
    The Law and Order League of Montgomery County, as its name indicates, is organized for the purpose of aiding and enforcing our laws, protecting our homes, and preserving public security throughout the bounds of our county. Supplemental to its main object . . . , and absolutely essential to the complete accomplishment of that purpose, this League intends to emphasize and promote the growth of wholesome sentiment which shall uphold the majesty of the law, and not only give a hearty support to our officers, in its enforcement, but demand, if need be, that it be enforced thoroughly and impartially. We shall emphasize, if need be, the duties and obligations of citizenship and seek to stimulate an intelligent and alert interest, and cooperation on the part of each individual citizen in those things which are essential to clear and honest government and efficient enforcement of the law.
    The president of this League appointed a committee of 21, one for each beat in the county. Each committee member was supposed to organize his own territory. He would be ex-officio member of the Central Committee.

are determined that the laws shall be enforced."[146] The Law and Order League of Birmingham had its hands full during 1908.[147] The illegal liquor traffic steadily increased and, on August 11, a mass meeting at the Bijou Theatre considered new plans to "stop lawlessness." Governor Comer, who had just issued a proclamation urging the people of Alabama to aid in law enforcement, received the commendation of this meeting.[148]

Meanwhile the religious bodies of the state were inclined to think that prohibition was moving forward in a very satisfactory manner. The Alabama Baptist State Convention pledged itself "not only to be diligent in the enforcement of prohibition laws, but to work and vote for the enactment of constitutional prohibition in order that the matter may be removed from the constant agitation of the peanut politicians and ward heelers."[149] The North Alabama Conference of the Methodist Church was profoundly grateful "for the defeat and legal destruction of every saloon in our state after January 1, 1909, which we regard as the greatest victory in the history of our state."[150]

Was prohibition a "rank failure" as its enemies claimed, or a blessing as its friends insisted? Records of crime in certain Alabama localities during 1908 would seem to support the latter claim. The *Alabama Citizen* published comparative figures on arrests in eighteen towns in the two years, 1907 and 1908. Arrests for all causes in these towns were 23,044 in 1907; 12,907 in 1908. Arrests for drunkenness dropped seventy-five per cent in the same period, or from 6,830 to 1,536.[151]

Birmingham police records showed 11,417 cases on the docket in 1907; 7,255 in 1908. Arrests in that city climbed steadily during the last months of 1908, as the number of "blind tigers" increased, but, even so, the year's total was low enough to support the prohibitionists' claim that under prohibition, crime would be reduced thirty-five to fifty per cent. In 1907, 2,423 persons were locked up in the Jefferson County jail for drunkenness; only 725 met this fate in 1908, a decrease of sixty-seven per cent. Disorderly conduct cases and affrays, which the policy considered as usually caused by drink, decreased from 1,628 in 1907 to 955 in 1908.[152]

Records like these encouraged the temperance forces. Only one more step remained to complete their self-appointed task of driving liquor from Alabama. It seemed that facts justified their actions and that the people of the state were solidly behind them when they moved to take this final step —to write into the Alabama constitution a prohibition amendment. But they had reckoned without the liquor interests, now fighting desperately with every weapon they could command for their very life.

[146] *Birmingham Ledger*, March 7, 1908. See also, *ibid.*, April 6, 1908.
[147] *Birmingham Ledger*, December 30, 1908.
[148] *Ibid.*, August 12, 1908.
[149] *Alabama Baptist State Convention*, (July 22-24, 1908), p. 48.
[150] *Journal of the North Alabama Conference* (November 18-23, 1908), pp. 70-71.
[151] *Alabama Citizen*, February, 1908.
[152] *Ibid.*

CHAPTER VII

THE CONSTITUTIONAL PROHIBITION ELECTION OF 1909

Prohibition by constitutional amendment was no new idea to the people of Alabama. As early as 1890 the legislature had received a petition from the Alabama Temperance Alliance asking that the question be submitted to the people.[1] In the extra session of 1907 a bill calling for an election on a prohibition amendment on the first Monday in November, 1908, had been favorably reported by the temperance committee of the House and then, to the great disappointment of its promoters, indefinitely postponed.[2] And through all these years temperance speakers and temperance writers had kept before the people the idea that only through constitutional amendment could prohibition be made secure from the tampering of "peanut politicians and ward heelers"—as the Baptist Convention had phrased it.

The Alabama Anti-Saloon League began active battle for such an amendment when, on December 15, 1908, its trustees met in Birmingham and decided to invite to a state convention to be held in that city the following February four or five representatives of every church, Sunday school, young people's society, W.C.T.U., and every other temperance organization in the state.[3]

The League's president, W. B. Crumpton, presided over the convention when it met. And among the "large number of delegates from all over the state" were the familiar veterans of the movement. Dr. P. A. Baker, National Superintendent of the League, "inspired his audiences by his report from a nation-wide field." Reverend Brooks Lawrence, superintendent of the Alabama League, directed procedure. Eugene Ballard, chairman of the legislature's committee on temperance, was on hand, "full of fight." Birmingham sent Mrs. W. H. Jeffries of the W.C.T.U., F. M. Jackson, financier and manufacturer, and Judge S. D. Weakley, author of the statutory prohibition law. Dr. A. P. Montague, president of Howard College, contributed to the discussions and lent his influence to the cause.[4]

Resolutions which thanked "Almighty God for the achievements and victories of the past"; commended friends of temperance both in and out of the state; congratulated the city of Birmingham that it had not been "ruined after one year's experience of prohibition" as wet prophets had declared it would be; begged the support of the Sunday schools in the fight ahead; and memorialized Congress to prohibit the shipment of liquor into dry territory were adopted. The convention recorded its determination to

[1] *House Journal, Regular Session* (1890-1891), p. 887.
[2] *House Journal, Extra Session* (1907), pp. 29, 177.
[3] *Citizen,* January, 1909.   [4] *Ibid.,* April, 1909.

work toward "putting it into our organic law that no liquors be manufactured or sold."[5]

By April, 1909, a special session of the legislature was in prospect. Prohibition laws were not working well and remedial enforcement measures seemed necessary. "The Legislature had been insulted by this lawless element, and it is imperative that they take steps to pass such legislation as will curb the lawlessness of the liquor men and their friends," said Brooks Lawrence.[6]

Decisions of the Supreme Court in the spring and early summer[7] seemed to Lawrence and other temperance workers to play into the hands of their enemies. The court ruled unconstitutional ordinances in Bessemer and Birmingham prohibiting storage of liquors in soft drink stands. Presumably, said Judge Weakley, proprietors of such stands were not selling intoxicants and might keep on their premises liquor for their own use.[8] This was, to Lawrence, "an attempt on the part of the Court to invade the realm of legislation," and he said so, to the consternation of many of his friends.[9] "It has been the history of many worthy reform movements that they have had to carry the burden of ill-advised and more or less harmful utterances from enthusiasts," said the *Birmingham News*, adding: "We hope that the statement of Mr. Lawrence will not injure the cause of Temperance."[10] "Superintendent Brooks Lawrence has been in hot water for several days," said the *Montgomery Advertiser*. "His roast of the Alabama Supreme Court has been a boomerang. The conservative element of the League has been very much dissatisfied with their superintendent's indecent criticism."[11]

But there were many who stood with Lawrence when he declared: "If Court decisions against us are ever well founded on constitutional inhibitions, then the people of Alabama will change the constitution of the state to meet the situation. The day of the saloonkeeper, gambler, harlot, and pimp domination in government is drawing to a close in Alabama."[12] They waited eagerly for the governor to call the extra session.

Governor Comer acted on July 15. His proclamation convening the legislature in extra session on July 27 contained sixty-five sections, nine of which concerned prohibition. In the third section he recommended the

Proposal of the submission to the qualified electors of the State of an amendment to the State Constitution so as to prohibit the manufacture, sale, and

[5] *Ibid.*
[6] *Citizen*, May, 1909.
[7] *164 Alabama*, 699.
[8] *Birmingham News*, July 7, 1909. The judge thought the decisions had been "greatly misunderstood." They were not "nearly as far reaching as may have been supposed." The cases did not "involve the locker clubs." And moreover, "the opinion concedes that an ordinance prohibiting the keeping of liquors with intent to sell it, though no sale be made, could be properly enacted, and that a statute to that effect would be valid."
[9] *Ibid.*, July 3, 1909.
[10] *Birmingham News*, July 5, 1909.
[11] *Montgomery Advertiser*, July 7, 1909.
[12] *Birmingham Age-Herald*, July 1, 1909.

keeping for sale of alcoholic and malt liquors and other intoxicating liquors and beverages, with such exceptions as may be specified therein, and providing for the designation in the amendment or by the Legislature of places where such liquors and beverages may not be stored and kept.[13]

The state was in for "as much prohibition legislation as a man can shake a stick at," declared the *Montgomery Advertiser*. Prohibitionists seemed ready to put a patch on any piece of prohibition legislation that seemed to need it after the Supreme Court had finished with it. The superintendent of the Anti-Saloon League, said the editor, had now enlisted the aid of the governor in his threatened campaign to change the constitution where it did not suit him. The governor, sworn to support local option, had betrayed the people. "The Governor displays a willingness to allow the agitators to rewrite the constitution. Will he assist them farther in their declared program of changing the supreme court to get men who will do their bidding?"[14]

The *Birmingham Age-Herald* was apprehensive about the special session, for it believed that "all radical legislation that can be enforced only with difficulty should be left where modification would be easy and feasible." "To put it in the constitution while it is in an inchoate and tentative state would be the height of unwisdom," said the editor.[15]

The *Mobile Register* saw in the move an alliance between the governor and the extremists to punish the Supreme Court because it would not render decisions according to dictation. The governor stood ready, said the *Register*, to plunge the state into the throes of disorder; it was time for Alabamians to rise in protest.[16]

The governor's action brought commendations as well as condemnations. The *Birmingham Ledger* was somewhat lukewarm. "The expected has happened and happened as expected," was the editorial comment. The governor's call was partly good, partly bad, and partly mixed, "a very human document." But the *Ledger* promised its hearty support to the prohibition measures recommended "for the good of the common people and all people."[17]

"The people of Alabama have deliberately decided that they want prohibition, and the lawmakers, in strengthening the laws relating to the subject, will be carrying out the will of those whom they represent," said the *Birmingham News*.[18] The *Alabama Christian Advocate* thought the chief executive had proved the good faith of his "pledge to do his part in making effective the prohibition law of our State." It suggested that papers opposed to prohibition but professedly in favor of law enforcement, such as the *Age-Herald* and the *Advertiser*, now had a chance to prove their sincerity.[19]

[13] *House Journal* (1909), p. 4.
[15] July 17, 1909.
[17] July 21, 1909.
[19] *Alabama Christian Advocate*, July 22, 1909.
[14] July 16, 17, 1909.
[16] *Mobile Register*, July 17, 1909.
[18] July 27, 1909.

Before the legislature convened the organizations which were to lead the fight were already in battle position. Against the well-established Anti-Saloon League, the opponents of constitutional prohibition organized the "Safe and Sane Business Men's League," with Judge Leon C. McCord, clerk of the Supreme Court for six years, as its head. Judge McCord opened headquarters in Montgomery, and announced that "the safe and sane business men of Alabama, tired of discord, agitation, and fanaticism, are going to fight constitutional prohibition to the finish." Some five thousand Alabamians were behind the movement already, he claimed, and he called upon "every lover of liberty, every old-time democrat, every safe and sane business man, to unite . . . to defeat the men who make their living by agitation."[20]

Immediately, the Dexter Avenue Methodist Sunday School demanded that Judge McCord stop teaching his large class of young men.[21] It was evident that emotions were to reach a high pitch before the issue was fairly before the people.

The legislators, meeting for the special session on July 27, found on their desks Anti-Saloon League literature and newspaper articles warning them of the dangers threatening the amendment they were called to consider.[22] They also read the taunt of the *Montgomery Advertiser* that the control of the legislative power now admittedly rested, not in their hands, but in the hands of the governor and the superintendent of the Anti-Saloon League.[23] And in the lobby they met excited delegates from Mobile who had turned out in large numbers to make it clear that the "Gulf City" wanted to regulate its own liquor business, and the legislature had better keep hands off.[24]

Governor Comer's message frankly declared the statutory prohibition law "inadequate of enforcement." Open defiance of the law was manifest in many places, and the blind tiger was abroad in the land. "You should not shoot tigers with blank cartridges or bird shot," advised the governor. "It only tends to make them more vicious." He urged firm action, adding:

In the violation of your prohibition law it has almost come to the point when you must determine for the people whether whiskey shall dominate and control the State, or the State dominate and control whiskey. I assure you that the open, persistent disrespect of any law engenders serious conditions, and you had better never have touched the prohibition question unless you make the penalty for violations prompt and sure.[25]

Toward such enforcement the legislators directed their first attention. Speaker Carmichael introduced a drastic bill which was hailed as the

[20] *Montgomery Advertiser*, July 21, 1909.
[21] *Ibid.*, July 23, 1909.   [22] *Ibid.*, July 28, 1909.
[23] *Montgomery Advertiser*, July 27, 1909. "There are not a dozen members of the House and Senate who have thus far sought to impress their views upon the bodies of which they are members," declared the editor.
[24] *Ibid.*
[25] *Birmingham Age-Herald*, July 24, 1909. *House Journal, Extra Session* (1909), pp. 31, 32.

THE PROHIBITION MOVEMENT IN ALABAMA 133

"finest that had ever been drawn in all the attempts of the various states to ... enforce the statutes enacted against the storage and sale of alcoholic concoctions."[26] It passed both House and Senate almost without opposition.[27] J. T. Fuller of Bibb County, without waiting for the vote on the Carmichael bill to be taken, proposed yet more vigorous measures. His bill,[28] providing for searching, raiding, and confiscating of property of law-breakers, was described as "the most drastic prohibition bill ever brought to the attention of any legislature."[29] This measure the legislature passed without difficulty.[30] By August 2 it was ready to turn its attention to the more controversial problem of a constitutional amendment.

Governor Comer had told the legislature where he stood in his mes-

[26] *House Journal, Extra Session* (1909), p. 39. *Birmingham News*, July 28, 1909.
[27] *House Journal, Extra Session* (1909), pp. 189, 178. The vote in the House was: yeas, 75; nays, 19; in the Senate, yeas, 28; nays, 2. The bill became a law on August 9, 1909, when it was signed by Governor Comer. *Acts, Special Session* (1909), pp. 8-13. The Carmichael Bill of 1909 was designed "to promote temperance," suppress the evils of intemperance, and to prohibit the manufacture, sale, offering for sale, and keeping for sale, of intoxicating liquors. Any one selling distilled spirits or wines in less quantities than five gallons at one time was deemed a retail dealer. However, the Carmichael law did not prohibit the social serving of liquors or beverages in private residences in ordinary social intercourse. Wine could also be sold for sacramental purposes. Penalties for the violation of this act were severe. The violations were considered misdemeanors punishable by a fine of not less than $50 nor more than $500 to which might be added, at the discretion of the judge, imprisonment for six months for the first conviction. For the second conviction, an additional fine or confinement at hard labor for from three to six months was to be given. It was unlawful to carry on the business of a brewer, distiller of spirits, rectifier of spirits, or vender of intoxicants. Every day any of these businesses was conducted constituted a separate offense. Any club that violated the provisions of this act forfeited its charter.
[28] *House Journal, Extra Session* (1909), p. 242.
[29] *Montgomery Journal*, August 5, 1909.
[30] *Acts, Special Session* (1909), p. 119. This was a sweeping bill. Buildings should not be let for the sale or making of intoxicants or such violation permitted in them. Tenants violating this act forfeited their leases. Under Section III it was made unlawful to advertise liquor in any public place. The keeping of liquors in any place but a residence was *prima facie* evidence that they were kept for sale, or intended for sale. Delivery of liquor to any public place was an evidence of sale. It was a misdemeanor for any railroad or boat employees to be intoxicated while on duty. In case of injury to any person caused by one who was drunk, damages could be obtained from the man who sold the liquor. Heavy fines were imposed for selling liquor from behind screens or other obstructions. Judges were required to charge, and grand juries which had testimony had no discretion but to indict. Witnesses who refused to testify were in contempt of court, and even servants could not be excused from testifying against principals. Storage of liquor in any public place was a violation of the law. The law prohibited soliciting from without the state. Sheriffs were authorized to procure lists of United States liquor licenses every month and have them published in heavy black type, with the name and location of the business. Prohibited liquors were contraband when they were stored in violation of the law. Search could be made by warrant, and the presence of government license was *prima facie* evidence of guilt. Druggists were protected if they were engaged in *bona fide* business. A charter could not be issued to any firm or corporation except with the stipulation that it should in no wise violate the prohibition laws, and such charter was forfeited if there was any violation. Fines were graded from $50 to $200 and imprisonment might run to six months in each case. The bill received executive approval August 25.

sage. He had noted a "general demand throughout the State that the people be permitted to vote on the question." He thought this demand should be heeded. He said:

> When you enacted the State-wide prohibition law, I take it, you did not intend it to be ephemeral—a statute of a day. Undoubtedly, you intend a revolution in the relation of our State to liquor, and the law was intended to fix it so that Alabama would never again have saloons or liquor licenses. . . . I believe you could render no greater benefit to every business interest of the State than to enable the people to settle this question once for all times. If it could be written in the Constitution, agitation would stop.[31]

Eugene Ballard introduced the anticipated bill on August 2,[32] and three days later opened debate upon it, declaring: "The people have only one more obstacle to overcome before entering an era of peace and plenty." When he ended his speech with the assertion if the "Democratic party stands for whiskey, I am not a democrat," he was greeted by both applause and hisses.[33]

"Gentlemen," shouted William H. Long, Jr., of Morgan County, "this means the disruption of the Democratic party!" The proposed measure would not, in his opinion, strengthen the cause of temperance at all. He was against it. Excitement ran high. The House became unruly. Speaker Carmichael thumped with his gavel and declared that he would suppress any unreasonable demonstration on either side. The Senate adjourned its session to attend the House argument. Men and women vitally interested in the fate of the bill crowded the galleries. It was a dramatic moment when Speaker Carmichael brought the argument to a close and the question was called for vote.[34] The bill passed by a majority of 70 to 29. Six days later the Senate affirmed the House decision by a vote of 23 to 10.[35]

"The same emotional tactics that carried the day for state-wide prohibition put through the constitutional submission bill yesterday—members excited more greatly than spectators," said the *Mobile Register*.[36] And similar charges of emotionalism appeared in other opposition papers. The

---

[31] *House Journal, Extra Session* (1909), pp. 33-34.
[32] *House Journal, Extra Session* (1909), p. 146. The following are the provisions of the amendment:
Section 1. The manufacture, sale, and keeping for sale of alcoholic and malt liquors and other intoxicating beverages shall be forever prohibited in this State, but alcohol may be sold for medical, scientific, and mechanical purposes, and wine for sacramental purposes, under such regulations as the Legislature may have prescribed or may hereafter prescribe.
Section 2. Nothing in the Constitution of Alabama shall be construed to prevent the Legislature under the police power from designating places where such liquor may not be stored or kept.
[33] *Birmingham News*, August 5, 1909.
[34] *Ibid. Montgomery Journal*, August 5, 1909.
[35] *House Journal, Extra Session* (1909), p. 251; *Senate Journal, Extra Session* (1909), p. 275.
[36] *Mobile Register*, August 7, 1909. The *Montgomery Advertiser* commented on August 6: "The members were swayed by emotions—the prohibitionists seized upon the time as a good one to make the supreme test, and victory rewarded their efforts."

Birmingham News approved the move. It was a good thing to let the people decide for themselves; they had a right to decide every issue affecting their moral and material welfare. The editor noted the "overwhelming public sentiment" for prohibition and the desire of the people to "put an end to all strife and turmoil." He ventured to predict:

that the people will approve the amendment. It also believes that its adoption will put an end to the fight and do much to restore political peace to the State.[87]

The editor of the *Birmingham Ledger* also believed that a determined public had decided to put its prohibition laws beyond easy repeal. He did not put much faith in the talk of a great whiskey fund; he thought that anyone who hoped to be bribed was due for disappointment.[38]

Using the pen which had signed the statutory prohibition bill two years earlier, Governor Comer affixed his signature to the Constitutional Amendment Bill on August 18.[39] Then, turning to the ladies of the W.C.T.U., he said: "You ladies must get behind this amendment and adopt it. The fight is not yet over. It is only started, and we need your efforts." The ladies, in turn, gave evidence of their good will and cooperation; they presented to the chief executive a bouquet of roses, with a card of scriptural quotations.[40]

Neither the prohibitionists nor their adversaries really needed the Governor's reminder that the fight was "only started." Both sides moved at once to mobilize all their forces and to use to the fullest extent the technique they had developed in the local option campaign. Almost simultaneously in mid-September, the two factions laid out strategy for the struggle.

The anti-amendment forces[41] met in Montgomery on September 15, with 1,500 delegates representing every county in the state. Frank S. Moody, of dispensary fame, was elected chairman. Emmet O'Neal sounded the keynote of the campaign and gave his listeners their slogan when he said: "If this amendment is ratified, it means the legislature can invade the home." "The sanctity of the home must be kept inviolate," swore the delegates, and they prepared to ring the changes on this theme.[42]

The delegates declared that no partisanship for the saloon, nor anti-temperance feeling motivated this convention. They had no desire to see saloons reestablished. They deprecated the efforts of those who were trying to make political capital out of the amendment issue. But they felt that it was unwise to write into the fundamental law of the state legislation still in an experimental state. These new laws *"should be given a full and fair trial,"* they insisted. The amendment would not insure enforcement

[37] *Birmingham News*, August 12, 1909.
[38] *Birmingham Ledger*, August 21, 1909.
[39] *Acts, Special Session* (1909), pp. 20-21.
[40] *Birmingham News*, August 19, 1909.
[41] *Birmingham Age-Herald*, August 22, 1909. The call was issued in August by a group led by Emmet O'Neal of Florence.
[42] *Alabama Citizen*, November, 1909.

of the laws nor add anything to their strength. It was "unnecessary." The delegates considered the submission of the amendment to the voters an unjustified expense to taxpayers. The question could just as well have waited for the general election scheduled for the following year. With special "alarm" the delegates viewed the second section of the amendment: "Nothing in the constitution of Alabama shall be construed to prevent the legislature, under the police power, from designating places where such liquors may not be stored or kept." This clearly opened the way for the invasion of the rights of citizens in their homes. Certainly no free and democratic people would stand for that. Homes must not be subjected to "the humiliation of search and seizure."[43]

To command their ranks the anti-amendment forces chose J. Lee Long of Butler County. With him worked an executive committee of seventy-one prominent men, four from the state-at-large and one from each of the counties. F. S. Moody of Tuscaloosa, Charles Henderson of Pike, J. F. Stallings of Jefferson, and A. G. Smith of Jefferson were the four committeemen-at-large, and they, with Long, carried major responsibility for the direction of the movement. The plans called for the appointment of a chairman for each congressional district, who would have under him three workers for each beat. Anti-amendment rallies were scheduled for every county. No opportunity was to be overlooked to arouse the people to action in defense of "the sanctity of the home."[44]

"Today's conference will become historic," declared the *Birmingham Age-Herald*, "for it will mark the beginning of a campaign that will result in the triumph of right and justice over injustice and oppression. . . . We are face to face with the greatest peril that has confronted any southern commonwealth since reconstruction days."[45] The *Montgomery Advertiser* also proclaimed the beginning of a crusade. "The conference marks a new era in the politics of Alabama. Aroused patriotism and aroused ability are enthusiastically at work. The dead line for fanatical recklessness has been reached."[46]

Meanwhile the call had gone out for a meeting of the trustees of the Anti-Saloon League to be held in Birmingham, September 16.[47] That organization was naturally assuming leadership in the new campaign. Even before the session began Brooks Lawrence declared that every county and beat in the state had been organized; two thousand speakers were ready to take the stump.[48]

The call had stated that friends of the amendment would be welcome, and five hundred people turned out for the first meeting, held at the First Christian Church in the afternoon. Nearly a thousand gathered for the

[43] *Montgomery Advertiser*, September 16, 1909.
[44] *Montgomery Advertiser*, September 16, 1909.
[45] *Birmingham Age-Herald*, September 15, 1909.
[46] *Montgomery Advertiser*, September 15, 1909.
[47] *Ibid.*, September 17, 1909.
[48] *Montgomery Advertiser*, September 15, 1909.

evening session in the First Baptist Church. Dr. Crumpton opened the meeting, and J. F. Thompson of Bibb County was elected chairman.

"The issue is the same as in the past; liquor or no liquor," Thompson asserted; and ringing speeches by Speaker Carmichael, Representative Jerome T. Fuller, and State Treasurer W. D. Seed reiterated this theme and drove into the minds of their listeners the fact that they were fighting to decide the question of whiskey or no whiskey. Resolutions declared that public sentiment was unmistakably against the liquor traffic and that the "continued activity of the whiskey element in political affairs" could mean only determination to thwart public will. "This pernicious and persistent activity . . . hiding behind specious subterfuges and masquerading under false guises," would continue until the matter was finally put beyond the reach of the "lobbyist and political manipulator." This was a "fight in the last ditch of the whiskey forces," and they were trying to becloud the issue by introducing all kinds of irrelevant matters. Specific denial that there was any ground for apprehension about the invasion of the rights of citizens in their homes went into the resolutions, and a final appeal to "all people, regardless of political affiliation, to help us, . . . with supreme confidence in a glorious victory, and asking the aid of Almighty God. . . ."[49]

F. M. Jackson, chairman of the executive committee of the Alabama Anti-Saloon League, was elected campaign chairman. Assisted by Lawrence and Crumpton he began at once to organize with chairmen for every district, county, and beat, and to arrange prohibition rallies which, at the height of the campaign, would hear pro-amendment speeches at the estimated rate of one hundred a day.[50]

Both sides launched a barrage of publicity. The *Alabama Citizen* declared at the end of October that "the liquor dealers of the United States have been sending out over the signature of one Leon McCord, from Montgomery, ever since the representatives of the people submitted the prohibition question to the people, a large lot of indecent cartoons and printed falsehoods. The cost to mail to the voters is about $1,000 for postage and another $1,000 for help, printing, envelopes, etc."[51] On the other side, an address to the people issued by the Anti-Saloon League was widely circulated. It warned against "misrepresentation, personal abuse, prejudice and politics . . . all being freely used." It reiterated the statements of the convention resolutions regarding the "last ditch" campaign. It scoffed at the claim that the amendment would "mean nothing to prohibition."

[49] *Alabama Citizen*, October, 1909. Among those presented were Kyle B. Price of Coffee County; Mrs. J. B. Chatfield of the W.C.T.U.; Reverend S. E. Wasson, known as the Anti-Saloon League pioneer; Mike Solley of Dale County; N. L. Miller, State Senator from Jefferson County; and F. M. Jackson.
[50] *Birmingham News*, September 29, 1909.
[51] *Alabama Citizen*, October, 1909.

It means something so terrifying to the whiskey and beer trusts that before the special session of the legislature met it was heralded through friendly newspapers that these trusts had employed a bright young lawyer to lead a campaign to defeat it, and would put half a million dollars at his disposal.[52]

Another effective bit of pro-amendment publicity carried on one side of the leaflet the text of the amendment and on the other these stirring words:

> The Real Issue of Alabama is Liquor or no Liquor; saloons or no saloons; homes, our womanhood, and children, vs. the saloon and wretchedness, suffering, and want. Which shall rule, the saloon or the people?

One hundred thousand copies of this leaflet went out.[53] The *Alabama Citizen* estimated that "a million pages of literature" was in circulation.[54]

Both sides sought the support of the press by methods open and methods not so open. The *Alabama Citizen* published a report that on August 18 the editor of *Free Press,* a weekly of Barbour County, had had an offer from one Dr. W. H. Williams of Houston County who wanted to lease the paper for use against the amendment.[55] From the Wiregrass section J. E. McCants, editor of the *Hartford Herald,* reported a similar offer—but from the other side; an Anti-Saloon League member was willing to pay to have the editorial columns of the *Herald* go for the amendment.[56]

Past policy for the most part, however, seems to have determined the stand of the newspapers. Most of the influential dailies were opposed to the amendment. The *Montgomery Advertiser* thought it should be defeated as a matter of "principle," and "as a rebuke to the men who proposed it" who should most emphatically have known better than to "put the state to the expense of an election this year."[57] The *Birmingham Age-Herald* branded the amendment as the product of "political greed . . . and scheme . . . of fanatics and small-minded men who are easily caught up by the talk of paid agitators."[58] The *Mobile Register* also smelled politics in the proposition. Its editor, watching the Anti-Saloon League meeting, said: "Politics sticks out of that Birmingham meeting like quills from the back of a fretful porcupine. . . ." It was high time for "people of common sense and patriotism" to "rescue the state from the adviser of

---

[52] *Alabama Citizen,* October, 1909.
[53] *Limestone Democrat,* September 30, 1909.
[54] *Alabama Citizen,* October, 1909.   [55] *Ibid.,* September, 1909.
[56] *Montgomery Advertiser,* August 20, 1909.
[57] *Ibid.,* September 2, 1909. Other comments by opposition papers were: *Luverne Journal:* The Amendment will be defeated because it is wrong and is also unwise and has for its main purpose the endorsement of a misguided administration. November 4, 1909. *Florala Democrat:* You cannot make a man good by legislation. . . . We have state-wide prohibition as it is, so why not take it for what it is worth, and enforce the laws we have. As the matter now stands the law can be changed; the amendment would render this difficult though, should it be a failure. October 14, 1909. *Andalusia Star:* Prohibition is a dream of the sentimentalists. Local option is the slogan of Jeffersonian democracy. November 25, 1909.
[58] *Birmingham Age-Herald,* September 21, 1909.

THE PROHIBITION MOVEMENT IN ALABAMA 139

lawbreaking."⁵⁹ The course of these three leading journals was followed by many less prominent papers.⁶⁰

The *Birmingham News,* consistent friend of temperance, stood by the pro-amendment forces,⁶¹ and so did the *Birmingham Ledger,* whose editor believed "the ratification of the amendment and the banishment of the saloon forever from the borders of Alabama will make for good citizenship."⁶² Other pro-amendment dailies were the *Montgomery Journal,* the *Selma Journal, Opelika News, Gadsden Times, Tri-Cities Daily,* and the *Troy Messenger.*⁶³ Many weeklies⁶⁴ took the same position, and the church journals of the Methodist and Baptist denominations lent their support.

As was to be expected, the churches in general favored the amendment. Some acted directly through their official bodies. The Baptist State Convention pledged "hearty support to the effort to get this provision embodied in the organic law of the state,"⁶⁵ and this action was reenforced by resolutions from such local associations as the Birmingham Association and the North Liberty Association.⁶⁶ The Methodists post-

⁵⁹ *Mobile Register,* September 21, 1909.
⁶⁰ Other papers opposed to the Amendment were the *Abbeville News, Andalusia Star, Attala Herald, Cullman Democrat, Demopolis Times, Dothan Home Journal, Eufaula Daily Times, Fort Deposit Vindicator, Gainesville Times, Goodwater Enterprise, Green County Democrat, Greenville Living Truth, Hartford Times-News, Huntsville Democrat, Huntsville Mercury-Banner, Luverne Journal, Marion County News, Marion Standard, Mobile Item, Pine Belt News, Rockford Chronicle, Sand Mountain Record, Thomasville Echo, Troy Herald, Walker County News,* and *Wilcox Progressive Era.*
⁶¹ *Birmingham News,* September 3, 1909.
⁶² *Birmingham Ledger,* November 11, 1909.
⁶³ *Alabama Citizen,* October, 1909.
⁶⁴ *Alabama Citizen,* October, 1909, lists the following amendment weekly papers: *Abbeville Times, Alabama Dispatch, Alexander City Outlook, Anniston Star, Ashland Standard, Asheville Aegis, Athens Democrat, Atmore Spectrum, Baldwin Times, Brewton Standard, Brundidge News, Choctaw Advocate, Citronelle Call, Clanton Record, Clayton Record, Cleburne New Era, Clio Free Press, Columbia Breeze, Conecuh Record, Coosa Argus, Coosa River News, Cullman Tribune, Dadeville Courier, Decatur Telegram, Decatur Times, Dothan Siftings, Dothan Eagle, Elba Clipper, Enterprise Ledger, Eutaw Whig and Observer, Fayette Banner, Florala News, Ft. Payne Journal, Florence Times, Florence Herald, Greensboro Watchman, Greensboro Record, Greensboro Beacon, Greenville Advocate, Guntersville Democrat, Gurley Herald, Huntsville Tribune, Jackson South Alabamian, Jacksonville Record, Jasper Eagle, Lafayette Sun, Lineville Headlight, Livingston Southern Home, Marengo Democrat, Marshall Banner, Monroe County Journal, Moulton Advertiser, Northport Breeze, Opp Herald, Ozark Tribune, Prattville Progress, Randolph News, Red Bay Gazette, Roanoke Leader, Russell Register, Samson Ledger, Tallapoosa Mountain Home, Thomaston Post, Tuskegee News, Union Springs Herald, Union Springs Breeze, West Alabamian, Wetumpka Herald, Wilcox Banner,* and *Winston New Era.*
⁶⁵ *Minutes of the Alabama Baptist State Convention* (July 20, 1909), p. 51.
⁶⁶ The Birmingham Association resolved that "... we endorse the pending amendment to the constitution and pledge our support to its adoption." *Minutes of Birmingham Baptist Association* (September 21, 1909), pp. 25, 26. The North Liberty Association endorsed "the efforts being made to engraft into the state constitution an amendment prohibiting the manufacture and sale of intoxicating liquors." *Limestone Democrat,* September 23, 1909.

poned the Alabama Conference called for November, because, as Bishop P. C. Morrison announced, the ministers were all expected to be "in the field to work for the prohibition amendment next week, which is the final week of the campaign."[67] Bishop Morrison had earlier asked full support of his churchmen. "I am sure you will do your full duty and be ready to meet your God on this tremendous issue," he wrote in October. "Pray, work, speak publicly, talk privately, and vote the doom of Rum in Alabama for all time to come."[68] The Presbyterians of the North Alabama Presbytery also formally approved the action of the legislature "in . . . thus presenting to the people the bare issue of prohibition without entangling it with any party, faction or personal politics," and declared that the "adoption of the amendment will greatly strengthen the cause of temperance, promote the purest and best interests of our homes and redound to the welfare and prosperity of our people."[69]

Church efforts were encouraged, aided, and abetted by W.C.T.U. with mass meetings, prayer meetings, and other propaganda.

Less expected was the backing of the Confederate Veterans of Jefferson County who, meeting in Birmingham on October 27, resolved full support of the amendment, with a scornful blast at the sincerity of the advocates of the "sanctity of the home."

When in the history of Christian civilization did the liquor sellers ever defend the home? They never waited for law to authorize the invasion of the home, but have lawlessly invaded the home and dragged away to poverty and debauchery the husbands and fathers, and left the wives and children to rags and beggary. They have tempted the boys from homes of happiness and plenty to the gambling room, to the saloon, to vice, and to theft.[70]

The stand of the churches drew caustic criticism from those good "democrats" who, according to the *Mobile Register,* deplored the idea of the church's mixing in politics, a practice which history had proved pernicious and which could only cause confusion in the state and misfortune to the church itself.[71] At an anti-amendment meeting in Birmingham, Jesse Stallings put the matter in far stronger terms. He warned against turning over civic government "to the cheap class of preachers." He advised his hearers:

Do not fear them. When they strike, you strike, and in so doing do the country a service in whipping the political preacher back to his pulpit. Decent people can't follow that sort of gang any further. Tell them to tend to their flock in the old fashioned way or you will cut off their quarter. Remove the fire from the boiler and see what happens.

[67] *Montgomery Advertiser,* November 18, 1909.
[68] *Alabama Citizen,* October, 1909. The North Alabama Conference, meeting after the election, expressed regret that "Alabama has failed to write prohibition in her organic law," but believed that the time would "come yet when our fair state will endorse constitutional prohibition." *Journal of the North Alabama Conference of the Methodist Episcopal Church, South* (1909), p. 77.
[69] *Birmingham News,* October 29, 1909.
[70] *Alabama Citizen,* November, 1909.   [71] *Mobile Register,* August 30, 1909.

THE PROHIBITION MOVEMENT IN ALABAMA 141

Never hesitate to strike the "cloth" when the "cloth" strikes at the constitutional rights of Alabamians.[72]

"I love preachers," said ex-Congressman Howard, "but a number of them have descended from the pulpit to the dirty mire of politics."

To all of which the *Alabama Christian Advocate* replied that the men who wanted to "drive the preachers back to their pulpits" were, in general, the men whose lives and influence had been against the church for a long time. The editor said:

> We do not accept orders from those men, and put them now on notice that the preachers propose to stand always for the best interests of the people. If that calls them to take the stump in any moral issue, they will go out in that service to the people, conscious that they still represent their Lord and the church in service to their state and in the fight against liquor.[73]

It was a hot campaign, and it was a brilliant one. Both sides were able to draw to their support distinguished and prominent men, who toured the state, addressed meetings, lent their full prestige and influence to the cause on one side or the other. Dr. Crumpton, writing later of the Amendment Campaign of 1909, was inclined to believe that "the greatest good which came to the prohibitionists was the development of men to fight our battles."[74]

Among those men were Governor Comer, Judge S. D. Weakley, Speaker Carmichael, and Congressman Richmond P. Hobson. When Judge Weakley threw the full weight of his legal and judicial experience as former chief justice of the Alabama Supreme Court into debate with an anti-amendment speaker, crowds turned out to hear him. Fifteen hundred came to the "battle royal" at Huntsville when he matched his wits with Senator Spragins. "When the smoke cleared away," said the *Birmingham Ledger*, "there was much speculation as to who should wear the laurels of the victory."[75] It was at this meeting that Senator Spragins electrified the crowd by the direct charge that Governor Comer had at one time sold liquor in Barbour County.[76] Hobson brought to his campaigning the glamour which surrounded him as a Spanish-American War hero and the recognized master of oratory in the state of Alabama.[77] He had never taken sides on the question before, though he was a total abstainer; but study had convinced him that prohibition of the liquor traffic was the

---

[72] *Birmingham Age-Herald*, September 14, 1909; see also *Alabama Citizen*, October, 1909.
[73] *Alabama Christian Advocate*, October 21, 1909.
[74] Crumpton, *op. cit.*, p. 30.
[75] *Birmingham Ledger*, September 23, 1909.
[76] *Ibid.* The Governor had charged that Spragins was a representative of the liquor interests. See also *Birmingham News*, October 1, 1909, for account of debate between Judge Weakley and Emmet O'Neal, afterwards elected governor by the anti-prohibition forces.
[77] Hobson joined the campaign in September. *Birmingham News*, September 29, 1909.

"only way to preserve the nation from destruction,"[78] and he spoke with the zeal of a new personal convert.

Congressmen John L. Burnett and J. Thomas Heflin both voluntarily entered the fight in October. Burnett vowed that he would support the amendment even if it meant his own defeat. The important question, he said, was not his election to office but "whether the people will allow the liquor forces to continue battle in Alabama."[79] Heflin said he would speak for the pro-amendment side, but he did not question the motives of the antis and he would not deal in personalities.[80]

Against names like these and personalities with such power, the opponents of the amendment pitted their own galaxy of stars. They made much of the fact that Senator Moody, recognized for many years as a temperance leader, was on their side and that he believed the constitutional amendment radical.[81] Ex-Governor W. D. Jelks, who considered the measure extreme and unnecessary, carried weight also.[82] Two other ex-governors, Rufus W. Cobb and William C. Oates, were on the speakers' list of the antis, as were also S. H. Dent, John B. Knox and ex-Congressman M. W. Howard. And when, in September, Senator John Bankhead and United States Senator J. F. Johnson came out for the anti-amendment position the gathering strength of the anti-amendment forces was apparent.

Senator Bankhead's statement reads:

You may announce that I am opposed to the amendment. It is unnecessary and, under the conditions that exist in Alabama, it is extreme. The question of prohibition is not involved in this campaign. . . . A useless and unnecessary fight has been forced upon the people. . . .[83]

The Senator had, as he said, "supported prohibition whenever the issue was raised." The announcement of his position in the campaign was indeed a staggering blow.

Senator Johnson opposed the amendment simply because he saw no need for it, inasmuch as the existing laws disposed of the saloon. "If the amendment were defeated, the present laws would still be in force. I see no reason for the adoption . . . of the proposed amendment, and . . . shall cast my vote against it."[84]

Other influential men lent not only their names but also their voices to stop the amendment's passage. Ex-Congressman Sidney J. Bowie argued that prohibition laws had no place in the constitution—they came under the

[78] Crumpton, *op. cit.*, p. 30.
[79] *Birmingham Ledger*, October 9, 1909.
[80] *Ibid.* In commenting on the speech that Heflin delivered at Lanette before a large crowd, the editor said that he "presented one of the best legal arguments that has ever been made for ratification of the prohibition amendment. His address was free from personalities. . . ." *Ibid.*, October 27, 1909.
[81] *Birmingham News*, September 29, 1909.
[82] *Montgomery Advertiser*, October 31, 1909.
[83] *Ibid.*, November 5, 1909.
[84] *Ibid.*, November 7, 1909.

police powers of the state. The constitution had been too much amended already. He ridiculed the fear lest existing laws be repealed. "Suppose a legislature does repeal them, are not the legislators chosen by the people?" he asked. Congressman Henry D. Clayton took the ground that prohibition laws were adequate and a constitutional amendment unnecessary. He thought the people had some reason to fear that the second section of the measure did in reality threaten "the sanctity of the home." And he was against this irregular, off-season election anyway.[85]

Some of the speakers did not limit themselves to such theoretical and moderate statements. The pattern of much of the campaign argument was set when, in September, Judge Leon McCord met the Reverend Kyle B. Price in a debate at Autaugaville. McCord directed his attack chiefly at Governor Comer, with Brooks Lawrence as a secondary victim. The Governor and his allies, said McCord, had bankrupted the state. They were dead politically and they knew that constitutional prohibition was the only plank on which they could rally support. McCord reminded his hearers that Price had just been given an office by Comer, and he insinuated that no one believed in the amendment unless he, like Price, had been paid to believe in it. Comer's constitutional prohibition policy was breaking up the Democratic party in Alabama, and people like Brooks Lawrence were helping to do it. To which Price replied only indirectly. He called upon his hearers to protect their homes from "the whiskey demon," and charged that Judge McCord and his followers were "whiskey bought."[86]

Charges against Governor Comer figured largely in the campaign. He was coupled with Lawrence and Weakley, and all three were said to be out for their own interests—"the celebrated firm of Comer, Weakley & Lawrence," the *Age-Herald* scornfully called them.[87] Early in the campaign Judge McCord wrote:

> It is unwritten history that Comer would not have called the extra session if he did not have assurance of a victory for biennial sessions. Without biennial sessions his last opportunity to run for United States senator would have fled. . . . It was glorious for him to throw all his power into the movement for constitutional prohibition and plunge the state into the bitterest campaign the state has ever known. . . . But what of the Governor's reward. . . .[88]

And toward the close of the battle ex-Congressman Howard was still ringing the changes on the accusation. "Weakley wants to be governor; Comer wants to be United States senator. What does Lawrence want? . . . Comer is as ambitious as Julius Caesar and as determined as Hannibal."[89]

Insinuations and direct accusations that the Governor had been in-

[85] *Montgomery Advertiser*, September 12, November 18, 1909.
[86] *Montgomery Advertiser*, August 27, 1909.
[87] *Birmingham Age-Herald*, November 25, 1909.
[88] *Ibid.*, August 22, 1909.   [89] *Ibid.*, November 3, 1909.

volved in the liquor traffic himself also continued. P. G. Bowman had gone so far as to tell an audience of five thousand in Birmingham that the chief executive had not only sold liquor but had sold it illegally.[90]

To the charges of political ambition Governor Comer found it advisable to reply during the last weeks of the campaign. He said:

> Behind the amendment I hide no political aspirations. I am in no sense a candidate for the United States Senate or for any other office. I regard and respect that section of our constitution which provides that the governor shall not be eligible to election or appointment to any office under this state or to the Senate of the United States during his term and within one year after the expiration thereof.

The amendment was not an administration measure, Comer added.

> It was suggested and urged by the prohibitionists of the state for the purpose of safe-guarding our homes, our women and our children. It is not Comer or the Comer administration that is on trial.[91]

Great heat developed, as the anti-amendment forces had intended it should, around the issue of the "sanctity of the home." "Are the people who own their homes ready to have them under the eyes of the constabulary?" ominously inquired the *Age-Herald*. "The law means that a home may be seized and searched whenever any enemy of that home may desire."[92] "A vote for the amendment," declared the *Alabama Courier*, "is a surrender of the bill of rights making your home your castle in Alabama."[93]

The *Birmingham News* thought such statements merely attempts to becloud the issues and to mislead the voters. "Not only is the provision authorizing the search of the home in operation in the law of every state in the union, but in Alabama and everywhere else the provision has been in operation for decades," said the editor in a statement headed, "Sanctity of the Home." Only when this provision was directed, or about to be directed, toward the illegal handling of liquor had any objection been raised. Most of the men in the state who were "deeply stirred up about it" were simply anxious "that there shall be some way left open whereby they can violate or evade the prohibition laws."[94]

But there were, said the defenders of the home, other infringements on "personal liberty" implied in the amendment. No man in his senses would think of giving over to civic authorities the right to determine what he should eat and what he should wear, said the *Montgomery Advertiser;* the same kind of shackling of the individual was implied in this measure.[95] "Under the law as it is now you are not allowed to make blackberry

---

[90] *Birmingham Ledger,* October 4, 1909.
[91] *Alabama Christian Advocate,* November 11, 1909.
[92] *Birmingham Age-Herald,* October 10, 1909.
[93] *Alabama Courier,* November 10, 1909.
[94] *Birmingham News,* October 1, 1909.
[95] *Montgomery Advertiser,* October 6, 1909.

cordial so necessary in every home where there are children," complained the *Alabama Courier*. It indignantly added:

> Neither are you allowed to make from your grapes wine for your own use and pleasure. Perhaps it won't be long under the guide of Carpetbagger Lawrence, who comes from Ohio to teach the people of Alabama manners and morals, until you will not be allowed to have a little Peruna. Lawrence, it is said, is getting six thousand dollars a year to establish a code of manners and morals for the people of Alabama, and it may be he is trying to earn his money. When Alabama wants a hired man to teach her people manners and morals, she ought to get one from a state where the intermarriage of whites and negroes is not permitted and practiced. Yet the legislature elected on a distinct local option platform built by his excellency (?) B. B. Comer, let this carpet-bagger lead them around as if they had a ring in their nose. Shades of Houston, Morgan, and Pettus, whither are we drifting?[96]

This was nonsense, said the prohibitionists. The amendment would infringe on personal liberty no more than the law against stealing and murder. Any civilized society found it necessary to protect people from the weaknesses inherent in the "state of nature" by prohibitory laws. Said N. D. Godbold:

> The amendment certainly does not invade individual liberty. Its passage by the people does not mean that the legislature cannot then modify the statutory laws if they are found to be too far-reaching. It means that the general agitation will cease, the final step will be taken, and Alabama committed to prohibition by a vote of the people. Can any true prohibitionist object to this?[97]

Accusations of lavish expenditure for campaign purposes were made on both sides as the fight developed. The prohibition forces asserted that the liquor interests of Missouri, Indiana, and Kentucky were pouring money into the state to defeat the amendment.[98] Alvin Roberts, staff correspondent of the *Birmingham News*, knew just how it was done. He said he had toured the liquor strongholds and discovered that the money was coming in through the Safe and Sane League of Alabama. That League had $300,000 behind it, and not much of it had come from the dollar-a-man dues in Alabama. People had suspected this, but now Roberts was able to prove it. Not that the thing really needed proof, said the *News*.

> There cannot be the shadow of a doubt that the brewery and liquor interests are spending vast sums of money in Alabama to defeat the amendment. There is all the evidence an intelligent and observant man would ask. He does not have to go through the files of a newspaper which has long been defending the brewery and liquor interests to confirm his views on this subject, although he may get a little more accurate information from such a source as to the amount being appropriated. . . .[99]

[96] *Alabama Courier*, October 13, 1909.
[97] *Alabama Citizen*, October, 1909.
[98] *Birmingham News*, November 16, 1909.
[99] *Birmingham News*, November 17, 1909. See also, *ibid.*, November 4, 6, 1909. The plans of the Safe and Sane League were fully described. "He (McCord)

According to the antis, "the amenders were spending money like water in Jefferson County during the closing days of the campaign." For instance, they rented the Hippodrome Theatre for seven days at a cost of $100 a day. Ten thousand dollars in that one county in two weeks time—so the antis claimed—had gone into the fight. Said one prominent opponent of the amendment, "the amenders have spent dollars where we have spent dimes." The *Montgomery Advertiser* thought this ten-to-one ratio probably correct. And, like the amendment advocates, their adversaries were suspicious that the money was not all home grown. Said the *Advertiser*:

> It is foolish to say that the enormous amounts spent in Alabama have been raised by the collections at their churches and political meetings. There has been an endowment, a big gift from the outside. The Anti-Saloon League, if it dealt fairly with people, would make a statement of its financial resources and expenditures.[100]

Near the close of the campaign the brewers admitted that they were backing the fight in Alabama, and the pro-amendment forces made excellent capital of this admission. An editorial in the *American Brewer* was taken as conclusive evidence of this outside and interested support. It read:

> Providing constitutional prohibition is not secured by the "drys" of Alabama. strenuous efforts will be made at the forthcoming session of the Legislature of Alabama to secure modification of the new liquor law of that State. This measure represents about all of the iniquities that are harbored in the more or less narrow minds of the prohibition fanatics. Framed and fastened on the State in hysteria, these impossible regulations have evoked such a widespread revulsion of feeling that there is no doubt but that the entire law will be practically nullified by amendment.[101]

That, said the prohibitionists, is what you vote for when you vote against the amendment—emasculation of the law in the interests of the brewers.

November 29 came on and the bitter, hot, expensive campaign drew to its close. The day preceding the vote was observed as Temperance Day in most of the churches. Prayer meetings were held in the early afternoon and were followed by parades of the wearers of the white ribbon. In Birmingham the parade was more than a mile long.[102]

---

further went into full details as to their plans of operation. He stated that they were going to commence work then, paving the way towards election of a legislature that would be favorable to their interests. In fact he went so far as to say that they would organize every county in the state and put out candidates for every office, even down to constable—in each case men who would favor their interests. I said that all this would cost a tremendous sum of money and he replied that his people knew it and that they were prepared to spend at least $300,000 if necessary to win." *Ibid.*, November 27, 1909.

[100] *Montgomery Advertiser*, November 27, 1909.
[101] *American Brewer*, November, 1909.
[102] *Birmingham News*, November 29, 1909.

Both sides went to the polls confident of victory. Intense excitement marked the day, but excellent order was maintained on the crowded streets and at the polls.[103] Probably the anti-amendment forces were only a little less surprised than the prohibitionists when the official count of that day's votes showed 72,272 against, and 49,093 for the amendment.[104] No one had foreseen so overwhelming a defeat for the measure.

The amendment lost in all but six counties, and in these six the total favorable majority was only 467. Mobile had returned the largest majority against the amendment—2,918; only 884 votes among the city's 4,789 favored the measure. Jefferson and Montgomery counties each gave better than 1,700 majorities against the amendment. Four other counties turned in majorities of 800 or more. All of the large urban centers voted against the amendment.[105] The will of the people seemed clear.

Fraud had won the day, the prohibitionists immediately charged. According to Brooks Lawrence, it had been a matter of falsehoods told, deceit, crooked methods, and the prostitution of hitherto respectable agencies to the foul purposes of the liquor traffic. Men had been bought with money, he declared, and with promises of office. Thousands of illegal votes had been cast and counted.[106] Frank Leslie thought the money spent by breweries had had its effect; illegal votes had added to the result; and, in addition, many people had misunderstood the whole thing.[107] The *Alabama Baptist* said that the defeat was due to "puerile personal politics."[108]

On the other side, Leon McCord, secretary of the Safe and Sane League, had his own explanation of the affair. He gave it in a public statement just after election returns were known. He said:

> It has been in many ways the most remarkable campaign that the state has ever known. Statesmen, tried and true, have been slandered by the hypocritical oligarchy, deliberate falsifications and misrepresentations having a field day of their degenerate sport. But the will of the sovereign people has gone out to rebuke the individual and the small mass of Alabama citizens who thus turned loose the flood gates of vilification and libel. Everyone is happy that the state has been redeemed, that prosperity has been quickened . . . and foreign capital stands invited to Alabama. . . .[109]

[103] *Ibid.*, November 30, 1909.
[104] "The Official Returns of the Election for Constitutional Prohibition," November 29, 1909. The largest majorities for the amendment were 144 in Lee, a southeastern county; and 139 in Sumter, a southwestern county. The counties polling more than 800 majorities against the amendment were Bibb, 900; Pike, 887; Cullman, 882; and Walker, 860. Four of the six counties voting for the amendment were located south of an east-west line drawn through the center of the state. No county in either the northern or the southern extremity of the state voted for the amendment.
[105] Birmingham, Mobile, Montgomery, Huntsville, etc.
[106] *Alabama Citizen*, December, 1909.
[107] *Alabama Christian Advocate*, December 2, 1909.
[108] *Alabama Baptist*, December 15, 1909.
[109] *Birmingham Age-Herald*, November 30, 1909.

To which J. Lee Long, campaign chairman, added:

I desire to congratulate the people of Alabama in that their victorious fight was conducted on a high plane, and that they stood arrayed in solid phalanx against the vituperation and personal abuse of those who opposed them in their efforts to maintain the sanctity of their homes and preserve that liberty for which their fore-fathers bled.[110]

With less eloquence but more analytical reasoning, the press offered various explanations for the outcome of the vote. The *Limestone Democrat* attributed it to "fear of changing the organic law of the state, together with a hundred or more deceptive fake issues . . . very adroitly raised by the opponents of the amendment."[111] Irrelevant matters had indeed played a large part in the struggle, agreed the *Birmingham News*. Many of the voters had hardly considered the main proposition, but had voted as their personal feelings dictated, or because they thought they could get the saloon back in Alabama by defeating the proposed amendment, or had otherwise made a side issue the determining factor in their vote.[112]

From the vantage point of a later day the forces which sent that amendment to overwhelming defeat are more clearly seen. Five facts stand out, and taken together they undoubtedly account for the outcome. First, the anti-prohibitionists had the better organization. Second, the most influential newspapers of the state were on their side. Third, the most powerful politicians of the state threw their influence in that direction. Fourth, the people of Alabama were reluctant to amend the constitution. Fifth, the people had come to believe that the prohibitionists were asking too much—were hurrying them to action for which they were not ready.

Although the drys had failed to write prohibition into the constitution, they still had the state-wide prohibition laws on the statute books. Their next fight was to maintain these laws.

[110] *Birmingham News*, November 30, 1909.
[111] December 2, 1909.   [112] November 30, 1909.

CHAPTER VIII

REACTION AND RETURN TO COUNTY LOCAL OPTION, 1910-1915

The interval between the election for constitutional prohibition and the opening of the gubernatorial campaign in 1910 was only a lull in the agitation of the prohibition question. The line of cleavage between the prohibitionists and local optionists was never changed. Each side continued to fight as vigorously as ever, and to choose as candidates for public office those who were in sympathy with its views. When the contest for the governorship opened, those in favor of prohibition professed themselves willing to grant that the amendment was dead. But the local optionists were not content to rest the matter thus. They were flushed with victory and wished to be rewarded for saving the state from the "diabolical amendment."

Many leaders on both sides considered running for governor that year. Judge S. D. Weakley of Birmingham announced and then withdrew. Senator Spragins of Huntsville, who had actively opposed the amendment, was mentioned but never formally announced. Speaker Carmichael of Tuscumbia, a zealous prohibitionist, aspired but did not announce. Walter D. Seed of Tuscaloosa, a rampant prohibitionist, and Perry Thomas, of Eufaula, a local optionist, both wanted to be governor but contented themselves with candidacy for the lieutenant governorship. Charles Henderson, of Troy, a local optionist, withdrew from the race because, he said, "those who financed the anti-amendment campaign are demanding compensation for the part they took and the contribution made, and are now making a fight for control of both the executive and legislative branches of the state government."[1] Only Emmet O'Neal of Florence, the most active opponent of the amendment, and Hugh S. D. Mallory, of Selma, perhaps its most active supporter, actually stayed in the race as final candidates. Thomas and Seed became their respective running mates for the office of lieutenant governor.

In formally announcing his candidacy, O'Neal pledged that if elected, he would adhere to the constitutional oath, enforce the laws in the statute books, so administer the duties of the office as to restore tranquility to the state, and secure to every interest equal and exact justice under the law. Any defender of the constitution, he declared, must uphold the prohibition laws then on the statute books. These laws were entitled to a full and fair trial. Until the people, through the legislative department, expressed their will to revise, modify, and repeal them they must be enforced.[2] The

---

[1] *Selma Times*, February 9, 1910.
[2] *Birmingham Age-Herald*, January 9, 1910.

Montgomery Advertiser thought O'Neal's statement showed him to be conservative. This paper regarded him as a man of high purpose and decided ability. It remarked that he was known throughout the state and that he had been one of the first to declare against the amendment, even when it was pending in the legislature.[3] The *Age-Herald*, the *Florence Times*, the *Mobile Register*, and the *Limestone Democrat* agreed substantially. O'Neal had, they said, directly, simply, and unequivocally placed before the voters a strong platform which gave a straightforward account of the issues and his stand on them. He seemed to these editors attractive and conservative, and an able politician.[4] The *Limestone Democrat*, however, was inclined to think that O'Neal's position was somewhat weakened by the opposition of influential leaders of his own faction. The *Democrat* noted also that, although he was running on a platform declaring for a fair trial of the prohibition laws, it was well known that he was *heartily* against prohibition.[5]

O'Neal's opponent, Colonel Mallory, who announced his intention of doing his own thinking, also said that he believed in giving state-wide prohibition a fair trial. He was quite willing to regard the amendment issue as dead. Although he was a staunch advocate of prohibition, he did not intend to press for more legislation on that subject.[6] The *Selma Times* considered Mallory's platform a strong one, a vote-winner, a broad and true foundation for the future speeches of the campaign. There was not a radical word in it.[7]

With so much similarity in the platforms before them, the voters quite naturally turned major attention to the past records of the candidates, rather than their campaign statements.[8] Mallory, although he continued to repeat that prohibition was a dead issue, was known as a life-long friend of prohibition, probably more responsible than anyone else for submitting the amendment referendum. O'Neal, on the other hand, had done more than any other individual in the state to defeat the amendment, and his campaign utterances emphasized his conviction that the prohibition laws were unconstitutional and a complete failure. The prohibition question would not down. It became the most important issue in a spirited campaign.

Mallory was an able and convincing speaker. His favorite method of oratory was to make a definite statement and then fortify it with facts logically arranged. An address delivered at Birmingham is typical of his

[3] *Montgomery Advertiser*, January 10, 1910.
[4] *Birmingham Age-Herald*, January 9, 1910; *Florence Times*, January 19, 1910; *Mobile Register*, January 11, 1910; *Limestone Democrat*, January 13, 1910.
[5] January 13, 1910.
[6] *Selma Times*, February 25, 1910. [7] February 25, 1919.
[8] So true was this that the Anti-Saloon League of Alabama declared in January, 1910, that it had no active interest in the gubernatorial campaign since the platforms of the candidates were satisfactory to the League. Therefore, it did not intend to endorse or support any candidate. *Montgomery Journal*, January 28, 1910.

campaign speeches, and the arguments they set forth. In it he stated his policy of state-wide prohibition. Under just and equitable legislation, properly enforced by a friendly hand, he declared state-wide prohibition would be a great benefit. He told his audience that he knew they desired success for that law, and he promised again that under his administration it would be given a fair and impartial trial. This would take time, for the policy must be tested long enough to adjust itself to the varied conditions of society and to be shaped by legislation as appeared wise and best. Here was a matter too important to be swung back and forth by politicians. It was the people's business to see that the liquor question was settled in a safe, conservative, and intelligent way.

O'Neal, Mallory reminded his listeners, had frequently and publicly opposed state-wide prohibition. Granted that O'Neal had a right to his own opinion, was it wise to entrust administration of the prohibition laws to a man frankly hostile to them? Wasn't it more reasonable to suppose that these laws would have a fairer chance to show their true merits if tested at the hands of friends? Surely the people of Alabama, whatever had been their attitude towards the proposed amendment, did not desire the return of the open saloon. Mallory charged his opponents with harping on the dead amendment. They gave, as their sole reason for opposing him, his championship of that amendment. The amendment question was dead, not to be revived, Mallory repeated; none knew that better than the men who were trying to keep the differences of the late campaign alive for partisan political purposes.[9]

O'Neal used more subtle and effective strategy, with frequent and skilful appeal, not only to reason but also to public emotion. The amendment had been, he declared, the worst encroachment upon "personal liberty" ever perpetrated in the annals of history. Human "rights" figured largely in his oratory and he condemned the Fuller and Carmichael prohibition laws as abridgments of the right of trial by jury. In a speech at Montgomery he defended the home and individual liberty, saying,

> I believe in temperance and sobriety. I do not believe in force as a moral agent. I do not believe in liquor in every home. I do believe that the consensus of opinion in Alabama is that the use of liquor results in mental and physical deterioration. But I believe that if you want liquor in your home, that is your affair and not mine. Let very man be his own prohibitionist.[10]

These were arguments that spoke to the hearts of the people.

Mallory and his supporters had tried several times to cast popular suspicion on O'Neal's party regularity. They claimed that he had bolted the party in 1896 by voting for Palmer and Buckner instead of Bryan and Sewell, the party nominees. An affidavit signed by nineteen citizens of Florence made this accusation.

[9] *Montgomery Advertiser*, March 15, 1910.
[10] *Montgomery Advertiser*, March 15, 1910.

We, the citizens of Florence, who participated in the presidential election in 1896, make the statement that Col. Emmett O'Neal openly and publicly espoused the cause of Palmer and Buckner. It has been publicly and repeatedly charged ever since that time that he voted for Palmer and Buckner, and we have never heard the charge denied or challenged.[11]

Mayor A. E. Walker of Florence inserted a card in the *Florence Times* to deny the truth of this affidavit. On the election day referred to, said Walker, he and O'Neal had ridden to Memphis together to get the election returns. While they were on the train O'Neal had told him that he had voted an open ticket for Bryan.[12] W. A. Mooers, of the *Florence Herald*, who wrote an editorial, "Antidote, not Anecdote," against the truth of Walker's card, got a horsewhipping for his pains. But O'Neal apparently thought it necessary to devote a goodly part of an address at Camden to a defense of his vote in 1896. He claimed he had voted for Bryan.[13] C. G. Simmons had a story to add about O'Neal's getting lost in Monroeville. He would not swear that O'Neal had been drunk at the time; but he could say that O'Neal was "about the best lost fellow" he ever saw in a place of that size. While walking about the business part of town, Simmons related, O'Neal had wandered into the kitchen of Mrs. P. R. Finklea, and, being asked what he wanted, had said that he was looking for his room at the Wiggins Hotel. He had left Mrs. Finklea's kitchen with the required directions, only to turn up a minute later knocking at her front door. Mrs. Finklea met him and invited him in, but he gave no answer and made no motion to enter the door. Instead he walked out in front of the house and looked up and down the street "as though he was completely lost."[14] Simmons thought his story cast some doubt upon O'Neal's rationality. The *Huntsville Daily Times* published an article declaring that leading brewery companies had put up $10,000 to elect O'Neal and a legislature friendly to him.[15] When O'Neal's chairman denied the accusation, affidavits were presented which implicated the Cook Brewing Company through its representatives. Affidavits were also secured that declared that a representative of Cook's company said his company had contributed $25,000 to defeat the amendment.[16]

The largest and most influential daily newspapers and some of the weeklies endorsed Emmet O'Neal, basing their endorsement squarely on the candidate's strong fight against the amendment. If he could be elected governor, these newspapers believed, no further legislation would be enacted on the question for at least four years. As secondary reasons for their support, these editors offered various arguments. The *Mobile Register* regarded O'Neal as the most available candidate, and as a man who had much to recommend him both in his family and in his personal attainments. He was, moreover, well informed on public affairs, a good cam-

[11] *Florence Herald*, April 14, 1910.
[13] *Selma Times*, April 23, 1910.
[15] April 27, 1910.
[12] *Montgomery Journal*, April 14, 1910.
[14] *Selma Times*, April 28, 1910.
[16] *Montgomery Journal*, April 27, 1910.

paigner with a strong following in all parts of the state. Enthusiastically this paper urged all the O'Nealites—"old, middle-aged, prime-of-lifers, young and youngsters"—to participate in a torchlight parade, and to make it such a celebration as would show the state that Mobile had "woke up" politically.[17] The *Montgomery Advertiser* claimed that while exercising its right to its own opinion in supporting O'Neal, it would nevertheless treat Mallory fairly and justly in its news columns.[18] The *Birmingham Age-Herald* represented O'Neal as a champion of personal liberty, a broadminded statesman, and an earnest patriot who stood for conservatism as against radicalism. His doctrine of local option, thought this editor, was the only sane democratic doctrine.[19]

The daily newspapers which endorsed Mallory, although not as large or as influential as those which supported O'Neal, were more numerous and just as earnest. The *Selma Times* called Mallory the most evenly balanced man in public life in Alabama, and asserted that its editors would trust his judgment over that of any other man in the state. He was a man of great wisdom, conservative in all things; he loved men, and was loved by them; his honesty of purpose was admitted by all; his public and private record was without spot; he respected the opinion of others; and he was a Democrat who believed that when the majority had spoken, the minority should submit.[20] Even the *Advertiser*, the *Times* noted, impliedly confessed that Mallory was the more eminently fitted for and deserving of the office and frankly admitted that it had intended to support him.[21]

The *Birmingham Ledger* also favored Mallory's election. No one, the editor commented, after hearing his Oneonta speech, could think of him as radical. With him as governor, Alabama would have a strong, fair, and conservative business administration.[22] The *Florence Herald* stated that Colonel Mallory, though he regarded the issue of constitutional prohibition settled, still believed that prohibition should remain the fixed policy of the state.[23] The *Montgomery Journal* pointed out that both O'Neal and Mallory were good men, honest, fearless, upright, and well fitted for the office. But in the matter of temperament Mallory had a decided advantage over O'Neal. Many thought Mallory was the one man who could unite the party after the bitter amendment campaign. Many thought that his high character, honesty, and conservatism assured a clean and calm administration.[24] Some newspapers were less temperate. To praise of their chosen candidate they added denunciation of his opponent. The *Andalusia Star*, for example, after it had endorsed Mallory, had much to say about O'Neal's quick temper. "He got scared and when he got scared

[17] February 3, 1910; April 10, 1910.
[18] February 22, 1910.
[19] April 8, 1910.
[20] February 6, 1910.
[21] *Selma Times*, February 9, 1910
[22] February 23, 1910.
[23] February 24, 1910.
[24] *Montgomery Journal*, February 28, 1910.

he went to 'cussin,' " said the *Star*. In a day when a well-poised, calm man was needed as governor, this lack of self-control disqualified O'Neal.[25]

Strong men from the anti-amendment ranks gave help to Mallory. Such anti-amendment leaders as ex-Governor Jelks, Senator Frank S. Moody, ex-Congressman Sidney J. Bowie, Charles Henderson, president of the Railroad Commission, and Ray Rushton were outspoken in their support. Ex-Governor Jelks had written the resolution, in the shape of a platform adopted at the anti-amendment convention at Montgomery in September, 1909, and Senator Moody had been chairman of the same convention. They had both stumped the state in opposition to the measure. They and others like them now took as enthusiastic a stand in support of Mallory as they had in their opposition to the amendment. None of them considered the defeat of the amendment an endorsement of O'Neal for governor.[26]

Both sides fought an active battle. The O'Neal supporters were sure that his broad, progressive policies, and his part in the crushing defeat of the amendment would bring him victory. They conceded Mallory's personal, moral, and intellectual fitness, but they distrusted him as a radical who had wanted to write state-wide prohibition into the constitution. In his last speech before the election, O'Neal spoke for his conservative supporters when he said that the election of Mallory would mean the endorsement of "that thing which has cursed and disgraced the state, Comerism, Brooks Lawrenceism, and all the other isms."[27]

Mallory's friends waged their campaign on the ground that existing prohibition laws should be given a trial by their friends rather than by their open enemies. They believed that Mallory could harmonize all interests whereas the election of O'Neal would lead to the return of legalized sale of liquor in the state of Alabama.[28]

On the eve of the election both sides predicted victory. Manager J. Lee Long claimed O'Neal would be elected by an overwhelming vote. He ventured to prophesy that his candidate would carry sixty-six counties, and that only Dallas would go for Mallory. Manager James B. Ellis claimed that Mallory would get majorities in forty counties, and be elected.

Both claims were overoptimistic, but Long came nearer the truth. The election, held on May 2, was orderly. When the final vote was counted, the results showed that O'Neal had defeated Mallory by a vote of 70,734 to 57,734. He had carried forty counties to Mallory's twenty-seven. He had received his largest majorities in Mobile, Montgomery, and Jefferson counties, the urban centers of the state.[29]

The *Montgomery Advertiser* declared that the mass of voters had lost sight of the personalities of the candidates in their concern for the great

[25] *Andalusia Star*, March 10, 1910.
[26] *Montgomery Journal*, March 12, 1910.
[27] *Birmingham Age-Herald*, May 1, 1910.
[28] *Ibid.*
[29] *Alabama Official and Statistical Register* (1911), p. 32.

issue. Neither O'Neal nor his followers had sincerely believed that the spirit of the amendment was dead. The Democrats in Alabama, by their votes, had showed that they shared this opinion. The voters had cast their ballots against Mallory because they believed that his election would again bring to positions of influence the leaders of the previous amendment campaign, and they knew that in a very short time the old question would again rise to harass and disturb them.[30] The *Birmingham Age-Herald* declared that the extremes of state-wide prohibition had been clearly discredited by the election.[31] The *Birmingham News* interpreted the vote as an expression by the people of Alabama of their disapproval of the prohibition laws passed by the last legislature. Important changes should now be made in these laws.[32] The Alabama Anti-Saloon League naturally did not so interpret O'Neal's success. The League was willing to trust his statements that he favored a fair trial for existing laws and to issue a formal statement of confidence in him, but it did not believe his nomination showed that the people were tired of prohibition.[33]

The *Selma Times* declared editorially that, regardless of who had been elected governor, the question of the sale or non-sale of whiskey in Alabama was certain to be reopened. The editor regretted that this was true. The everlasting discussion, he declared, converted no one but disconcerted everyone. By the time the newly elected legislature convened in January, 1911, state-wide prohibition would be two years old, certainly not old enough to have given final proof of its worth. Undeniably, that law had reduced drunkenness, freed the public roads of disgraceful scenes, and reduced the attendance on police court. On the other hand, it must also be admitted that laws were violated, perjury increased, vile concoctions dispensed, men and boys led to excessive drinking, and commercial interests injured. The democratic state convention at its next meeting, this editor predicted, would readopt local option into its platform. Then, no matter who was governor, the legislature could provide machinery whereby any county desiring to suspend the Carmichael and Fuller laws could do so.[34] The *Southern Democrat* feared that O'Neal's election meant more radical legislation. There would, no doubt, be an effort to repeal the state-wide prohibition law; but such a movement would meet with rigid opposition in the Senate if not in the House.[35] The *Florence Times* believed that Seed's handsome majority indicated that the people of Alabama had not deserted prohibition.[36] The *Alabama Christian Advocate* deplored O'Neal's victory: "We consider his nomination a real calamity to the state."[37]

In response to many requests, the *Alabama Courier* carried a list of the names of the candidates for state offices indicating the stand of each

[30] May 3, 1910.
[31] May 3, 1910.
[32] May 5, 1910.
[33] *Walker County News* copied by *Montgomery Advertiser*, June 10, 1910.
[34] *Selma Times*, May 5, 1910.
[35] May 12, 1910.
[36] May 13, 1910.
[37] May 5, 1910.

on the prohibition amendment. Many voters, this paper noted, would not vote for any man who aligned himself with the opposition to the amendment.[38] The opposition, however, elected their candidates to all the other state offices except two.[39] The election clearly showed definite reaction against prohibition.

Prohibition was also the main issue in the legislative campaign. Many candidates openly announced that they either favored the continuation of the prohibition laws or that they favored repealing them. Some straddled the issue. Norman D. Godbold was elected to the Senate from Wilcox County on the prohibition ticket.[40] J. E. Horton was elected to the House from Limestone County on the local option ticket.[41] Senator Robert Spragins, local optionist and an advocate of the dispensary system, was reelected from Madison without opposition.[42] E. B. Almon was elected to the House on the local option ticket.[43] Frank S. Moody, father of the dispensary system in Alabama, was reelected to the Senate from Tuscaloosa County.[44] The general election held in November returned to office only ten members of the Comer legislators.[45]

Although O'Neal had made his campaign on the Montgomery platform of September, 1909, and had on many occasions expressed a willingness to see the prohibition laws given a fair trial, the State Democratic Convention which met in Montgomery on May 17, 1910, repudiated the state-wide prohibition plan and O'Neal's campaign pledges and adopted by an overwhelming vote the following local option platform:

> We favor temperance and sobriety as promotive of good government; but we deplore legislative attempts or other disposition of intoxicants of liquor against the expressed wishes of the communities affected, and we re-affirm our adherence to the principle of local option approved in the platform of the party adopted in 1906, believing that a departure in practice from the principle then announced was a departure from the time-honored democratic doctrine of local self-government, and was not in furtherance of the cause of temperance.[46]

The *Birmingham Ledger* charged that the Democratic majority in this convention was advised in the preparation of this local option plank by one Charles Lewis, an agent of the breweries. This, the editor thought,

---

[38] April 27, 1910.
[39] *House Journal*, (1911), pp. 84-85. The candidates elected by the anti-amenders were Cyrus B. Brown, Secretary of State; R. C. Brickell, Attorney-General; Brooks Smith, State Auditor; Henry J. Willingham, State Superintendent of Education; Leon McCord, Railroad Commissioner; Frank N. Julian, Railroad Commissioner; Ormond Sommerville, Member of Supreme Court; and John C. Anderson, Member of Supreme Court. The two candidates elected by the prohibitionists were Walter D. Seed, Lieutenant-Governor and John Purifoy, State Treasurer.
[40] *The Citizen*, February 25, 1911.
[41] *Alabama Courier*, March 30, 1910.
[42] *Huntsville Weekly Mercury*, January 10, 1910.
[43] *Montgomery Advertiser*, February 10, 1911.
[44] *Senate Journal* (1911), I, 3-5.
[45] *Senate Journal* (1907), I, 3-5; *House Journal* (1907), I, 3-5; *Senate Journal* (1911), I, pp. 3-5; *House Journal* (1911), I, 3-5.
[46] *State Democratic Platform*, May 17, 1910.

made honors even, for on the other side Brooks Lawrence had been charged with bringing on all the prohibition trouble.[47] The *Florala Democrat* declared that the Democratic convention had disgraced the citizenship of Alabama. Pledges had been violated, and whiskey boodle money accepted.[48]

Under an unsympathetic governor the prohibitionists already recognized that they would have difficulty in maintaining the *status quo*. The action of the Democratic convention added to their worries. They knew that the incoming legislature would be composed largely of new men and old opposition members who had been renominated. While local optionists began confidently to lay their plans for modification the prohibitionists admittedly faced an uncertain future.

During the summer Brooks Lawrence held out a ray of hope to them by declaring that the Anti-Saloon League had tested the nominees to the legislature and found that prohibition had a good working majority in both houses.[49] Later in the year the Anti-Saloon League, meeting in Birmingham on December 29, 1910, launched a campaign against the repeal of the prohibition laws. Brooks Lawrence, in his annual report at this convention, called on the members not to be discouraged. No church, he asserted, was more interested in the salvation of souls than was the Anti-Saloon League. "Our situation today," he said, "finds us facing a crisis and the trouble is simply lack of confidence on the part of temperance forces themselves."[50]

In its report on temperance in 1910, the members of the Alabama Baptist State Convention were also optimistic. They rejoiced in what had already been accomplished. They believed that the demand for intoxicants was decreasing and were gratified over the enactment of legislation outlawing the saloon in the state. They deplored the fact that the prohibition laws were being violated, but they noted with satisfaction that, in spite of imperfect enforcement, there was less crime under these laws than when the liquor traffic was legalized. They understood that the incoming administration was pledged to a "fair trial" of the prohibition laws before repealing them, and they pledged their cooperation to make such a trial work.[51] President Crumpton, reporting to the Anti-Saloon League in December, was able to say that out of seventy-one Baptist Associations in Alabama, seventy had adopted resolutions against the return of saloons.[52]

Similar support of prohibition came from the Methodists. The Alabama Conference of the Methodist Episcopal Church, South, memorialized the legislature not to alter the state-wide prohibition laws.[53] The North

---

[47] *Birmingham Ledger* copied by *Alabama Courier*, June 1, 1910.
[48] *Florala Democrat*, copied by the *Montgomery Advertiser*, June 2, 1910.
[49] *Florence Times*, August 26, 1910.
[50] *Montgomery Advertiser*, December 30, 1910.
[51] *Annual Report of Alabama Baptist State Convention* (1910), pp. 56-57.
[52] *Montgomery Advertiser*, December 30, 1910.
[53] *Minutes of the Alabama Conference of the Methodist Episcopal Church, South* (1910), pp. 40-41.

Alabama Conference expressed its unalterable opposition to any legislation looking to the reestablishment of the legalized sale of liquor in Alabama.[54] The Alabama Conference of the Methodist Protestant Church appealed to the legislature to let the state-wide prohibition laws remain on the statute books.[55]

On the eve of the meeting of the legislature, Hugh W. Roberts wrote that, following the O'Neal inauguration, a caucus would be held to determine administration policy. At this caucus, he said, a plan would be adopted to move against state-wide prohibition. The first step would be toward putting into effect the local option plank of the Democratic platform. Each county, through its representatives, would be given just the kind of legislation it wanted.[56]

Governor Comer defended his administration in a message to the legislature on January 11, 1911. Some people claimed, said the governor, that it was impossible to enforce the prohibition laws. He did not believe that this was true. If honest and capable law officers were serving the state, prohibition laws could be enforced in any place in Alabama. He justified the submission of the amendment. It had been submitted to a referendum of the voters so that the people might have an opportunity to say whether or not the sale of liquor should ever again be licensed in the state. Had they accepted the amendment, they would have lost none of their rights as citizens. Because the state had prohibited by statute, the governor continued, a higher ideal for home life and citizenship had been set up. To permit liquor and beer manufacturers north of the Ohio River to dictate Alabama's prohibition laws would be, he declared, a humiliation not to be borne by Alabama men.[57] The *Age-Herald* picked up this last statement, commenting that Comer attributed the loss of constitutional prohibition to the efforts of the liquor and beer manufacturers north of the Ohio River, but failed to point out that the votes had been cast in Alabama by Alabamians, and corruptly cast.[58]

Governor O'Neal came out strongly for local option as soon as he took office. In his inaugural address he declared his belief that prohibition should be the established policy of the state, under a general local option law to take effect at the next general election. Local option, he insisted, recognized the right of the unit affected to control the liquor traffic, either by absolute prohibition or regulation as the people in that area desired. The people could voice their will by electing representatives whose position on the issue were well defined and publicly avowed, or by the various methods which they could use to judge and estimate public sentiment. Liquor interests and politics should be eternally divorced, O'Neal declared,

[54] *Journal of the North Alabama Conference* (1910), p. 61.
[55] *Minutes of Alabama Conference Methodist Protestant Church* (1910), p. 24.
[56] *Birmingham Age-Herald*, January 7, 1911.
[57] *House Journal* (1911), I, 25-26.
[58] *Birmingham Age-Herald*, January 12, 1911.

and this happy event could be accomplished were the governor empowered to appoint an excise commission, subject to removal, which, under the restrictions of certain general laws, should be vested with plenary power in the management and control of the liquor traffic in the communities where the sale was authorized. Such a commission, he believed, should prohibit the sale of all spirits compounded wholly or in part of alcohol, which were produced in any other way than by the legitimate methods of distillation and aging as required by the most advanced pure food laws.[59]

The *Advertiser* considered Governor O'Neal's forceful plea for the keeping of the party faith the highest and best note of his inaugural, and approved his apt reference to the repudiation by the people of Alabama of the men who had violated their party pledges in 1906. The new governor, said the *Advertiser*, had declared that "Alabama must aim either at the abolition or the regulation of the liquor traffic," that since prohibition had utterly failed in some of the larger cities of the state, there was no other policy left but regulation. Such regulation should be worked out by the locality involved, and in the interest of temperance, law, and order, in compliance with the will of the people.[60]

The *Birmingham Ledger*, on the other hand, accused the governor of broken faith. Thousands of citizens had given O'Neal their support trusting in his promise that he would not lend his influence to the repeal of the prohibition laws. The Montgomery conference, which was the basis of O'Neal's candidacy, had distinctly stated that the prohibition laws would be given a fair trial. Every observant citizen who was not blinded by self-interest, or prejudice, and in whose views the taste and effects of rum had no voice, knew that this had not been done.[61]

On January 17, Governor O'Neal delivered a seventy-five page message to the legislature. He discussed almost every social, economic, and political problem confronting the people of Alabama. Prohibition loomed large in this report. The governor reviewed conditions in the large cities and analyzed to the people the meaning of the Fuller and Carmichael bills. "The remedy then is to carry out in good faith the declaration of the party platform and to restore local option and the right of self-government as the wisest and best solution of this problem." Local option, he explained, did not necessarily mean a referendum of the people; it meant ascertaining and carrying out their wishes in some proper and lawful manner. But if the representatives of the communities affected were in doubt as to the wishes of a majority of their citizens a referendum would be necessary in compliance with the party pledges.[62]

The *Mobile Register* approved of the governor's message. The views which O'Neal had held on the liquor question prior to the adoption of the Democratic platform on May 17, the editor noted, were personal, and they

[59] *Montgomery Advertiser*, January 17, 1911.
[60] *Montgomery Advertiser*, January 17, 1911.
[61] January 16, 1911.   [62] *House Journal* (1911), I, 188-263.

must now be subordinated to his duty as governor to carry out the will of the people.⁶³ The *Birmingham Ledger* believed Governor O'Neal wanted the liquor laws repealed, or materially modified. It added the comment that the legislature could repeal or modify those laws as it pleased. It was not bound by the ideas of the governor. Each and every member of it had made his distinct pledge to the people who had elected him, and each one had a responsibility to keep his pledge.⁶⁴

The *Citizen* charged that the governor in his message had shown himself neither logical nor consistent. He had declared that prohibition should be the established policy of the state and, in the next breath, had advocated a general local option law. In violation of the provisions of the Montgomery Anti-Amendment Conference platform, he had shown himself willing to deliver the state of Alabama into the hands of the brewing and distilling interests and to bring back the hated saloon.⁶⁵ The *Southern Democrat* called Governor O'Neal the first bolter of the platform on which he had been nominated. He had advocated the establishment of saloons by legislative enactment in cities of over 13,000 inhabitants. He had condemned the state-wide prohibition law because it had not been submitted to the people, yet he would force saloons on the cities without a vote.⁶⁶

Lobbyists were naturally and inevitably prominent among the group newly assembled at the state capitol. Charlie Lewis and other paid agents represented the liquor interests. Brooks Lawrence was the most noted representative of the Anti-Saloon League. On the third day after the legislature met in January, Representative A. C. Sanders of Pike County brought in a resolution that, since lobbying by partisan organizations could not be regarded as acting for the whole people and might tend to influence adversely the peoples' representatives, all parties and organizations should refrain from lobbying in or about the capitol during the session. This resolution requested the governor to use all legal means to prevent such lobbying so that the affairs of the state could be attended to with calm deliberation and sober judgment. Passed on January 20, this measure excluded lobbyists from the floor except when the privilege was extended by a unanimous vote of the House.⁶⁷

Brooks Lawrence, accused of dominating the committee on temperance, was generally thought to be the chief object of this anti-lobbying resolution. But on January 13, while the resolution was under consideration, the *Montgomery Journal* carried a letter from Lawrence denying the accusation. Lawrence said he supposed the rule was intended, not for him, but for the sheriff's organization which had been unusually active in the legislature.

Local optionists in both houses scored a victory as temperance com-

⁶³ January 18, 30, 1911.
⁶⁴ January 17, 1911.   ⁶⁵ *Citizen*, January 21, 1911.
⁶⁶ *Southern Democrat* (Oneonta), January 26, 1911.
⁶⁷ *House Journal* (1911), I, 78, 307.

mittee appointments were made. In the House Speaker Almon selected twelve of the nineteen committeemen from the anti-prohibition ranks. Six of these members were residents of Jefferson, Mobile, and Montgomery counties where public opinion for the return of liquor seemed strongest.[68] In the Senate Hugh Morrow, President pro tempore, appointed six local optionists and three prohibitionists. Of the six, Chairman Moody and Spragins, second in command, were strongly committed to the dispensary system; the other four urged quick and permanent "relief"—whatever form such relief might assume.[69]

As soon as the legislature was ready for work, the temperance committee began to consider the many bills which proposed changes in the prohibition laws. The most notable of these was one introduced by Senator Moody proposing a dispensary for every county in the state after the said county had held a local option election.[70] So many incompatible bills were introduced that the committee found it impossible to reconcile them. It decided to formulate for itself a bill certain to have the approval of Governor O'Neal. This general local option bill, known as the temperance committee bill, was introduced by Representative John V. Smith, the committee's chairman. It provided for regulation of manufacture and sale of liquor in cities of ten thousand inhabitants.[71] The new bill and one introduced by Senator Moody were placed before the legislature and the fight was on.

The people of Alabama took a lively part in the contest. In an editorial, "How to Browbeat a Legislature," the *Montgomery Advertiser* declared that the members of the legislature were being deluged with letters, most of them sent in through the influence of pressure groups, especially the Anti-Saloon League.[72] The liquor interests kept their lobbyists in action to influence the solons to enact legislation which would enhance their business.[73]

Meanwhile the existing prohibition laws were being openly and brazenly defied in many parts of the state, especially in Montgomery. Representative O. W. Mulkey of Geneva County, said that the Exchange Hotel had had a bar on the first floor but had moved it to the cellar.[74] Walker Percy of Jefferson County, declared that a waiter in a cafe in Montgomery had told him he had been instructed to throw everything wide open for the legislators.[75] Representatives declared this was an attempt to discredit the prohibition laws and bring pressure upon the lawmakers to repeal them. They disapproved such tactics. On January 24, Representative A. P. Fuquay of Tallapoosa County, introduced a resolution requesting the governor to take immediate cognizance of such notorious law-breaking,

[68] *Birmingham Age-Herald*, January 14, 1911.
[69] *Ibid.*, January 20, 1911.
[70] *Senate Journal* (1911), I, 235.   [71] *House Journal* (1911), I, 437-438.
[72] *Montgomery Advertiser*, January 24, 1911.
[73] Crumpton, *How Alabama Became Dry*, p. 22.
[74] *Birmingham Ledger*, January 28, 1911.   [75] *Ibid.*

and to begin immediate impeachment proceedings against every officer of the law who had known and permitted such violations.[76] During the heated discussion an amendment was offered and passed to make this a joint resolution.[77]

The smaller counties opposed the Smith bill because it included only cities of ten thousand population. Representatives from the large cities tried to nullify this opposition by assuring the smaller counties that they would later support their efforts to obtain dispensaries or any other local option laws.[78] The Smith bill, however, was defeated by the combined vote of the smaller liquor counties and the prohibitionists.

The legislature had been in session for seventeen working days and still the leading problem, liquor traffic, was unsolved. No bill had been devised satisfactory to a majority in a legislature divided into three factions—the administrative forces, the insurgents, and the prohibitionists.[79] Representative W. L. Parks of Covington County, attempted to meet the situation by introducing, on February 2, a straightout local option measure. He proposed to submit to the qualified electors of each county the question of whether or not the manufacture and sale of spirituous, vinous, or malt liquors should be legalized in the county; and whether or not such liquors should be sold by dispensaries or by private dealers under a license.[80] To test the reactions of the representatives and the senators, a caucus was held in the city council chamber the day the bill was introduced. Twenty members of the Senate and forty-four members and twenty proxies from the lower body attended, and harmoniously voted to endorse the Parks bill.[81]

The *Montgomery Advertiser* strongly approved this bill.[82] The *Birmingham Age-Herald* thought that it was thoroughly in accord with the local option plank upon which the legislators were elected.[83] The *Birmingham Ledger* continued to insist that Governor O'Neal and the members of the legislature who were favoring the Parks bill were violating their campaign pledges. O'Neal could not have been elected, the *Ledger* insisted, if he had publicly announced that he favored repealing the prohibition laws. Neither O'Neal nor any member of the legislature had the moral right to repudiate the pledges he had made to the voters.[84]

Realizing that the committees were organized against them, the prohibitionists decided to make their stand against the Parks bill on the floor of the house. Brooks Lawrence sent out notices and on February 9, the day of the final hearing, a large crowd assembled in the capitol. Prohibitionists with banners crowded the House gallery. W.C.T.U. workers

[76] *House Journal* (1911), I, 452.　　[77] *Ibid.*
[78] *Montgomery Advertiser*, January 26, 1911.
[79] *Birmingham Ledger*, February 3, 1911.
[80] *House Journal* (1911), I, 617.
[81] *Birmingham Age-Herald*, February 3, 1911.
[82] February 4, 1911.
[83] February 8, 1911.　　[84] February 3, 1911.

pinned badges on friendly representatives. "Vote against whiskey and the demon rum," urged a great banner suspended from the gallery and the white-riboned custodian of this flag alternately cheered and cried while the bitter debate was in progress. Women wearing white ribbons inscribed "For Prohibition," ranged themselves in a solid line at the front of the balcony. Messenger boys scurried about with telegrams for legislators before the session convened. Brooks Lawrence, wearing a white ribbon, superintended the marshalling of his forces both in the gallery and in the lobbies. Local optionists identified by red carnations or red neckties, were also much in evidence. The railroads brought large crowds from Birmingham, Mobile, and other places, indiscriminately accepting excursion fares from prohibitionists and local optionists alike.[85]

The local optionists were loud in defense of the party platform. They cheered Representative Pitts when he asserted that he would stand by it as long as he lived. The platform, Pitts insisted, had called for local option; it was the duty of loyal members to support the measure. Analyzing the Parks bill, Smith said it gave the qualified electors the privilege of expressing their opinions, and the qualified electors could be trusted to act wisely. On the other side, H. M. Merit, speaking for the prohibitionists, said that they were facing the liquor question only because it was forced upon them. He believed that every man in the House was under a solemn contract with his constituency not to violate his campaign pledges by voting for the repeal of the present state-wide laws. W. O. Mulkey of Geneva said that he had come to the legislature to fight the restoration of liquor to the state. The Parks bill, he declared, would make it possible for saloons to open at every crossroads in every county. He could not betray the trust of the people of his county by voting for it.[86] When the debate was concluded, Speaker Almon called for the vote. The Parks bill passed by a vote of 58 to 45.[87]

The House opponents of the Parks local option bill branded it a dangerous measure, said the *Birmingham Ledger*, because its passage, prior to the enactment of statutes for restriction and regulation, would pave the way for the open saloon. Moreover, if saloons were established in some counties, the people in the adjoining counties would have no protection. One of the greatest objections to the Parks bill, the *Ledger* editor thought, was that it had been backed by "Cousin Chawles" and the liquor trust. If the Parks bill should become a law, he predicted the people could expect a large increase of drunkenness and crime.[88] The *Twin City Telegram* thought that the Parks bill would only complicate matters by further and unnecessary elections, and that the liquor question would continue to disturb the peace of Alabama.[89]

[85] *Montgomery Journal*, February 9, 1911; *Montgomery Advertiser*, February 10, 1911. [86] *Birmingham Age-Herald*, February 10, 1911.
[87] *House Journal* (1911), I, 756. [88] February 10, 1911.
[89] *Twin City Telegram* (Decatur), February 10, 1911.

Favoring the Parks bill, the *Age-Herald* stated the belief that a return to local option meant a gain for the cause of real temperance, which was unquestionably gaining strength in Alabama and in the nation.[90] The *Mobile Register* saw in the passage of this bill a return to the Democratic policy previously recognized as the best for handling questions relating to the domestic affairs of the people.[91]

The Senate, receiving the bill from the House, referred it to the temperance committee. It was early apparent that the fate of the liquor question in the upper house would probably be in the hands of Moody and other dispensary advocates. If this group and the prohibitionists could have formed a coalition, they might have passed the Moody dispensary bill.[92] On the 17th of February the Parks bill came up in the Senate for final vote, after a hard but orderly fight lasting several hours. Moody, speaking for his dispensary bill, opposed the Parks measure.[93] But when the vote was taken the dispensary bill was tabled by a vote of 20 to 14. The Parks bill was then adopted by a vote of 21 to 12.[94]

Since the Parks bill was only a general measure, discussion inevitably centered on prospective legislation which would provide the local option machinery to regulate the sale of liquor. Many representative businessmen were outspoken in favor of saloons for Birmingham, but the *Age-Herald* thought they did not speak for the majority of that city. Most Birmingham citizens, the editor believed, preferred the dispensary plan because it would be a great revenue producer for the county.[95] He regarded the local option bill as sound Democratic doctrine and considered its adoption merely a reaffirmation of the Democratic platform. He hoped that a special bill would be passed to establish a dispensary in Birmingham without another election.[96]

The Parks law made no provision for the regulation of the liquor traffic. It was, therefore, imperative that such legislation be promptly enacted. Representative Smith of Montgomery County, drew up a regulation bill, which he introduced on February 22.[97] He proposed that the cities of Alabama be classified according to size. Birmingham, a city of over seventy-five thousand population, would be permitted one saloon to each three thousand population and each of these saloons would be required to pay a license of $3,000 annually. All towns and cities with populations ranging from one thousand to seventy-five thousand might

---

[90] February 10, 1911.   [91] February 10, 1911.
[92] *Birmingham Ledger*, February 11, 1911. About this time Brooks Lawrence wrote a letter in which he declared that if the Parks bill should pass the Senate it would be by the most corrupt methods. His letter created considerable discussion and gave the liquorites a strong weapon with which to fight for the Parks bill. While Lawrence's statement was made without the consent or knowledge of the prohibition forces, it nevertheless caused them some embarrassment.
[93] *Montgomery Advertiser*, February 18, 1911; *Birmingham Age-Herald*, February 23, 1911.   [94] *Senate Journal* (1911), I, 643-644.
[95] February 11, 1911.   [96] *Ibid.*
[97] *House Journal* (1911), I, 1034-1035.

have one saloon for each thousand population and the license fee for these saloons would be fixed at $1,500. Towns of less than one thousand population could have one saloon paying a license fee of $900. An excise commission would be created to supervise the wholesale and retail liquor establishments in the several counties. Salaries for members of the commission were fixed by terms of the act. Applications for licenses, to be issued by the probate judge upon order of the excise commission, would have to be endorsed by twenty householders and freeholders. Only domestic corporations with authorized charters would be eligible for licenses. Any qualified elector would have the right to file written objection against the granting of a license and to have such objection heard by the commission. Only one license could be issued to any one individual, firm, or corporation during any year, and such license would apply only to business conducted at the location specified in the application. License holders would furnish bond for the faithful performance of his duty. The excise commission, authorized to revoke or suspend licenses for certain misdemeanors, would be required to furnish to the sheriff a list of licenses, and the sheriff must visit all such places at least once a month, either in person or by deputy, and report all violations to the excise commission. No appeal would be permitted from any judge or decision of the excise commission to suspend or cancel a license and the notice of such revocation would have to be published. The liquors sold would be carefully described in the license, and must fully meet the requirements of the pure food laws. Twice each year the excise commission would be required to have an analysis made of the liquors sold, and defective liquors were to be destroyed by the sheriff. All agreements to buy or sell exclusively the output of beer, malt, or other spirituous liquors of any particular firm or corporation would be null and void. The act fixed the hour of opening at 6 a.m. and that of closing at 11 p.m.; and prohibited the sale of liquor to minors or persons of intemperate habits, the employment of any minor or woman to sell liquor, and the sale of liquor to white people and Negroes in the same room. Penalties for violation of these provisions ranged from $50 to $500 and hard labor for the county, or imprisonment in the county jail for not less than thirty days nor more than six months. The penalties were to increase upon the second conviction. The act further stipulated that all rooms in which liquor was sold at retail be on the ground floor, fronting the highway, and they should not be screened to obstruct the view from the outside. For violation of this provision, fines were set at from $50 to $500 for the first offense; for the second offense hard labor might also be added. This section, the act noted, was not to apply to bona fide hotels and restaurants. Retail dealers would not be allowed to sell liquors in quantities less than a quart on credit, nor to sell, give away, or otherwise dispose of liquors on election day or after six o'clock on election eve. The governor or the mayor of any city might under this act close all saloons, if necessary, in case of riots. The remaining sections of the bill from forty-two to ninety-four inclusive dealt with provisions for dispensaries and followed the provisions of the Moody dispensary bill.[98]

The Smith bill was read the third time and passed by the house on March 3, by a vote of 58 to 27.[99] The Senate debated it and amended it through its Committee of Conference and then passed it on April 5, by a vote of 20 to 9.[100] On that same day the House concurred in the Senate amendments by a vote of 57 to 42.[101] Governor O'Neal at once signed the bill, and it became a law on April 6.[102]

Even before final passage of the Smith bill the *Citizen* complained that Governor O'Neal was using all his political influence to force it through the legislature. "He has used threats and abusive language to influence and intimidate the votes of the legislature, but wherein is he to be censured for this; was he not bound by the party convention to deliver the state to the domination of the liquor traffic?"[103] The *Birmingham Ledger* declared that the new law made it possible for any hotel having thirty rooms to go into the liquor business, and become a menace to hundreds of young women in the community.[104] The *Alabama Baptist* then urged, "Let those who are against the legalized sale of whiskey get together and make a last ditch fight."[105] But the *Montgomery Advertiser*, a few weeks after the bill had become law, complimented and felicitated the state upon the political peace that had fallen upon the grand old commonwealth, and congratulated the legislature on the harmonious spirit marking its deliberations since local option had been adopted.[106]

Dr. W. B. Crumpton tartly summed up his opinion of the legislature thus:

Two-thirds of the time of the solons was given to the consideration of the question of liquor. Charles Lewis (connected with brewers), with his money bags, the Administration with unlimited patronage, the most experienced lobbyists of the nation, shrewdest lawyers of the state, some members of the Legislature, the party whip in the hands of the Chairman of the Democratic Executive Committee, who was always on hand, and the influence of the liquor press of the state were all combined to bring liquor back.[107]

Dr. Crumpton instituted *quo warranto* proceedings to test the validity of the Parks and Smith laws. The case was first tried in the Circuit Court of Montgomery County, with W. W. Pearson the presiding judge. The verdict was that the laws were valid with the exception of section 10½ of the Parks bill. Crumpton then appealed the case to the Supreme Court.

[98] *Montgomery Journal*, March 4, 1911; *Alabama Baptist*, April 12, 1911.
[99] *House Journal* (1911), I, 1311.
[100] *Senate Journal* (1911), II, 1810.   [101] *House Journal* (1911), II, 2255.
[102] *General Acts of Alabama* (1911), p. 315.
[103] *The Citizen*, March 18, 1911.
[104] April 8, 1911.   [105] April 12, 1911.
[106] *Montgomery Advertiser* copied by the *Limestone Democrat*, May 1, 1911.
[107] Crumpton, *How Alabama Became Dry*, p. 22; *Birmingham Ledger*, March 24, 1911.

In his petition he claimed that the respondents, Montgomery, Hails, and Banks, should be required "To show by what warrant or authority they claimed the right to hold said officers [excise commissioners], and respectively, to exercise the powers and privileges thereof and the rights and powers of the excise commission, and that on final hearing judgment be entered ousting said defendants from the said respective offices."

The Supreme Court rendered its decision on May 9, 1911. It said:

> Our conclusion is that the Parks and Smith Bills are not subject to the objections urged for appellant, and which we have considered and decided on this appeal. This conclusion coincides with that reached and pronounced by the trial court, with the exception that he ruled section 10½ of the Parks Bill to be invalid and so struck it from the act. Our view is that section 10½ is not invalid, but that it is a valid part of that act.[108]

The decision was a further victory for the local optionists, and they now began to circulate petitions in several counties for the local option elections.

The Parks law prescribed the conditions under which county local option elections could be called. The probate judge of any county, upon the written petition of forty-five per cent of the qualified voters at the last general election, was required to order an election within thirty days after the petition was filed. The election must be called within forty days from the time this order was issued, and announcement of such election must be published in a local newspaper or by posters at least twenty days before it took place.[109]

In elections which followed, the local optionists took the lead in getting petitions signed. Generally speaking, the local option campaigns were conducted by men who were well organized and who had economic interests at stake. On the other side were ministers and church members organized under the Anti-Saloon League and the W.C.T.U. Newspapers were, as usual, effectively used by both sides. The most prominent daily papers, such as the *Mobile Register, Montgomery Advertiser, Birmingham Age-Herald*, and the *Birmingham News*, all strongly endorsed the return to the legal sale of liquor; most of the weekly papers opposed it.

Colbert County was the first to act under the new law. During April, 1911, petitions were circulated to obtain signatures for the purpose of calling an election to determine whether the sale of liquor should be legalized and if so, whether it should be sold by dispensary or saloon. Signed by 525 voters the petition was presented to the probate judge on April 27.[110] The judge declared that, upon careful examination, he found it to contain more than the necessary forty-five per cent of voters and that he

---

[108] *Southern Reporter*, LIX, 295-303.
Section 10½ read as follows: "The sale of spirituous, vinous, malt and other intoxicating drinks and beverages enumerated in this bill, shall not be permitted outside the corporate limits of cities or towns, nor shall the sale of such drinks and beverages be permitted in any town which has not at least one policeman or marshall continuously employed."
[109] *Acts, General Session* (1911), pp. 26-27. [110] *Leighton News*, May 5, 1911.

therefore ordered the election to be held on July 1.[111] Of the three weekly papers published in Colbert County, the *Alabamian-Dispatch* (Tuscumbia) and the *Leighton News* both opposed the legal sale of liquor; the *Sheffield Standard* strongly favored it. All three papers were active in the fight. The local ministers, although they took a firm stand against liquor, failed to arouse much enthusiasm. "Our people seem to be taking very little interest in the matter," the *Alabamian-Dispatch* said ruefully, "and it is a matter of regret to the temperance people; however, it seems as if nothing is being done by the temperance forces to stem the tide of this great evil." The advocates of the open saloon, this editor observed, were letting no grass grow beneath their feet; they were working vigorously for the re-establishment of liquor.[112]

On the eve of the election, the *Sheffield Standard* condemned the state prohibition laws. No one, this editor declared, could have the temerity to say such laws had stopped the liquor traffic or in any way improved the morals of the people. On the contrary, they had bred lawlessness and disorder. Prohibition had failed in Colbert County just as it had failed everywhere else. County and towns had, during the experiment, been deprived of much income from liquor licenses and taxes. The county, alone, was out nearly $20,000 also in the costs of attempted enforcement and thousands of dollars more had been spent in court costs for trying violators of the prohibition law.[113] The *Alabamian-Dispatch*, on the other side, urged voters to consider prayerfully before they took the backward step toward the return of the saloon. Let them remember, the editor begged, that it would be a sad day for mothers, wives, and children when the saloon was opened again.[114]

The saloon triumphed in the election, but by no great margin. The local optionists defeated the prohibitionists by a majority of only seventy votes, and the saloon received a majority of only forty-six over the dispensary. Eight of the seventeen precincts in the county voted in favor of prohibition. The largest majorities in favor of the saloon came from Sheffield, Tuscumbia, Leighton, and Brick.[115] The temperance people conceding defeat before the election, realized too late that they could have won a victory if they had really worked for it.[116]

"Old Colbert has blazed the way to freedom from the regime of political intolerance and extremism," declared the *Sheffield Standard*, when the result was known. "Her example is an inspiration to the liberty-loving citizens of every section of the commonwealth."[117]

The campaigns in Mobile and Montgomery counties, where local optionists were recognized to be in an overwhelming majority, were never in question. In Mobile the prohibitionists hardly attempted to fight back

[111] *Alabamian-Dispatch*, June 8, 1911.
[112] *Sheffield Standard*, June 30, 1911.
[113] *Ibid.*
[114] July 7, 1911.
[115] June 22, 29, 1911.
[116] June 29, 1911.
[117] *Alabamian-Dispatch*, July 6, 1911.

The prohibition forces in Montgomery were organized by Reverend J. M. Dannelly, but they worked against tremendous odds. Local optionists won landslide victories in both the counties.

Jefferson County became, during the summer, the real center of the fight. This county contained both the largest population and the largest city in the state, and its election was naturally watched with keen interest. The local optionists began circulating their petitions in February. The probate judge declared the first petition inadequate because many of its signers were not qualified voters. The second petition, filed on July 6, met the legal requirements, and Judge J. P. Stiles then ordered the election to be held on August 24.[118] For more than two years the local optionists had been carrying on a systematic campaign to discredit the prohibition laws. They had been insisting that these statutes could not be enforced, and that failure to enforce them bred disrespect for all law. They had been claiming also that the city of Birmingham was losing a vast amount of revenue under these laws. The prohibitionists met such claims upon moral grounds. They contended that less liquor was consumed and less crime committed under the new statutes. They added that Birmingham had collected more license taxes under prohibition than it ever had under licensed saloons.

Unlike their fellow prohibitionists in Mobile and Montgomery, the Birmingham drys put strenuous effort into their fight. They launched their campaign with a meeting in the Chamber of Commerce auditorium on June 29.[119] Ex-Governor Comer, in a brief address at this meeting, said he was in the fight to help keep the saloon out of Jefferson County. Strong men were selected to lead the campaign. C. P. Beddow was elected permanent campaign chairman, Borden Burr and Dr. A. J. Dickinson, vice-chairmen.[120] The *Birmingham Ledger* considered Beddow an able and fearless lawyer, a citizen of high character, and a long-time vigorous enemy of the saloon. Vice-Chairman Burr, was, in the opinion of the same paper, also a lawyer of high attainment.[121] At a second meeting on July 8, the prohibitionists launched the Saloon Opposition League of Jefferson County, whose slogan was: "Favoring Local Self Government and Defending Our Homes Against Saloons." They also appointed at this time a committee of twenty prominent men to work in the city and every beat in the county to stimulate public opinion against liquor. The Saloon Opposition League opened headquarters in the First National Bank building[122] and sent speakers to all parts of the county. To provide funds for this work, two hundred men met at a "Dry Dollar Dinner," and free-will offerings came in steadily during the campaign. The *Birmingham Ledger*, a long-time champion of the cause, carried an editorial in almost every issue praising the achievements of prohibition in Birmingham. Birmingham was, this paper declared,

[118] *Birmingham Ledger,* July 21, 1911.   [119] *Birmingham Ledger,* June 29, 1911.
[120] *Ibid.*   [121] *Ibid.*
[122] *Ibid.,* July 8, 1911.

more sober, more orderly, more decent, and more free from crime since the saloons had gone. Defects in the Smith law furnished a favorite target for the prohibition forces. If any thirty-room house could operate a saloon, they claimed, saloons could easily be opened up in the residential sections. The old three-mile law at East Lake would be suspended if the Smith law passed, and saloons could then be established in the vicinity of Howard College.[123]

The local optionists were also well organized and active. Jones G. Moore, chairman of the local option committee, issued a proclamation, calling upon the voters to support the movement to establish saloons as the only hope for law and order.[124] Judge A. O. Lane, commissioner of public justice in Birmingham, announcing that he would support the licensed saloon, declared that every effort to suppress blind tigers in Birmingham had failed. He added that blind tigers were converting many young men into sneaks, undermining the social organism, and entailing heavy expense upon the city, county, and state. He cited some statistics on crime in Birmingham to fortify his statement. Between April 10 and August 10, 1,066 arrests had been made for violations of the prohibition laws. Convictions had been obtained in 668 of these cases, but 559 of these had been appealed, and only 109 had actually paid fines in money and labor. The prohibition laws simply could not be enforced, Lane declared. He used his own experience to prove his point. During one whole week in 1911, in the criminal court in Jefferson County, from the entire docket consisting of prohibition cases alone, not a single conviction had been obtained. Two weeks before these cases came to trial, Judge Lane had, he declared, detailed two officers to work up the evidence, but the offenders went scot free nevertheless. Lane also said he had employed ten patrolmen whose sole duty it was to run down blind tigers. They had done faithful and efficient work, but it had cost the city $900 per month to pay them. From April 10 to August 10 the number of arrests had steadily increased; the number of convictions as steadily decreased. Saloons controlled by expensive licenses seemed to the judge the only remedy against the blind tiger, for under such a system dealers would have an economic interest in running down illegal competitors and bringing them to justice.[125]

George H. Bodeker, chief of police, said that it was impossible to enforce the prohibition laws because blind tigers circumvented the law, leading even girls and women into crime.[126] The *Age-Herald* championed the optionist cause and favored the dispensary as the best method of controlling the liquor traffic. State-wide prohibition had been a miserable failure, but, said this editor, under the new local option law the liquor

[123] *Birmingham Ledger*, July 26, 1911.   [124] *Ibid.*, July 5, 1911.
[125] *Birmingham Age-Herald*, August 17, 1911.
[126] *Ibid.*, August 2, 1911. Bodeker's written statement follows: "Blind tigers and other forms of vice go hand in hand. For example, there is nothing more detrimental to our moral life than the sale of liquors by women and children and in places frequented by women and children. It is a matter of frequent occurrence to see respect-

THE PROHIBITION MOVEMENT IN ALABAMA 171

traffic would be rigidly regulated.[127] The *Birmingham News* said: "High license and strict regulation are the only remedies for the reign of chaos here."[128]

The local optionists carried the Jefferson election by a substantial majority. The official count gave the "wets" 6,490 votes and the "drys" 5,441, which meant a majority of 1,079 against prohibition; the saloon got 6,275 and the dispensary, 4,764, or a majority of 1,511 votes for the open saloon.[129]

The local optionists celebrated their victory with a monster torchlight procession, in which at least three thousand cheering and yelling people participated. This vast assemblage gathered at the Brown-Marx building and marched first to the residence of Judge A. O. Lane who addressed them. Before the *Age-Herald* building they were again addressed by Jones G. Moore, chairman of the local option campaign committee.[130] The throng then paraded the streets till the early morning hours. "It is safe to say that prohibition will never win another victory in Jefferson County,"[131] said the *Age-Herald* when the election was over.

Between July 1, 1911 and June 22, 1912, seventeen counties held local option elections.[132] The local optionists won only eight of these. Their victories were usually in the urban centers. Their most notable success was in Mobile County, where the vote stood about fifteen to one in favor

---

able looking white women brought into court for operating blind tigers. In many instances, girls of 12 years of age have been found serving drinks and 'sitting for company' in apparently respectable houses."
[127] July 18, 1911.
[128] July 18, 1911.
[129] *Birmingham News*, August 29, 1911.
[130] *Birmingham Age-Herald*, August 25, 1911.
[131] *Ibid.*, August 27, 1911.
[132] List of counties voting on local option:

Counties voting for saloons:

County	Date	Dry	Wet	Disp.	Saloon
Colbert	July 1, 1911	591	521	502	584
Mobile	July 6, 1911	188	2,872	179	2,826
Montgomery	July 17, 1911	467	2,230	335	2,084
Russell	July 17, 1911	184	416		
Jefferson	August 24, 1911	5,441	6,490	4,764	6,275
Pike	December 21, 1911	727	1,953	251	1,149
Cullman	May 20, 1912	813	1,461	354	1,377

County voting for dispensary:

Madison	August 21, 1911	1,388	1,768	1,617	848

Counties voting against the sale of liquor:

Covington	August 21, 1911	1,189	737	716	740
Tallapoosa	August 21, 1911	1,495	864	646	882
Houston	September 2, 1911	1,386	846		
Morgan	September 11, 1911	1,637	1,202	1,025	1,189
Crenshaw	September 25, 1911	838	531	178	674
Lauderdale	October 5, 1911	1,172	658		
Barbour	October 9, 1911	914	552	303	663
Etowah	April 8, 1912	2,105	1,416		
Tuscaloosa	June 22, 1912	1,999	885	767	723

of private license. Their closest victory was in Colbert County where they carried the election by only seventy votes. The advocates of the dispensary won only in Madison County. Local option as a policy in government seemed suited to large cities where people were accustomed to vote frequently and impatient of restraints upon their personal liberties. Possibly also urban centers felt the loss of the revenue from liquor licenses in the operation of local government more keenly than rural centers. And probably also the residents of urban centers with police protection were less annoyed by disorderly conduct of drunken men than those of rural communities whose public meetings were often disturbed by inebriates. The prohibitionists were usually more successful in rural counties. Their greatest victory was won in Tuscaloosa County where the vote stood a little more than two to one in their favor.

Retail liquor dealers continued to purchase licenses from the United States Government during the years 1910 to 1915. In 1910, while the state-wide prohibition laws were in force, 846 retail dealers secured such licenses.[133] The next year the number had increased to 1,832.[134] As the sale of liquor in the large cities of the state became legalized in the next three years, the number dropped to 500.[135] It is a striking fact, however, that there were more registered retail liquor dealers in the state in both 1911 and 1912, after the prohibition laws had been repealed, than in 1910 during prohibition. Practically all of them were located in the three largest cities of the state.

The number of wholesale liquor dealers also increased between 1910 and 1915. In 1910 there were 18[136] paying revenue to the United States Government. The number increased to 92[137] in 1913, but declined the next two years, when only 60[138] dealers were registered. With the introduction of legalized liquor traffic in 1911, the number of retail dealers in malt liquors steadily declined from 1910 to 1915. In 1910 there were 264,[139] but only 52 in 1915.[140] Meanwhile the number of wholesale malt liquor dealers increased. In 1910 there were 37[141] registered; by 1915 there were 43.[142] Two breweries were operating annually from 1910 to 1915.[143]

On October 1, 1911, sixty-one counties of the state were under prohibition, three under license. Two more counties had voted for private license and one had voted for dispensary. Eighty-five saloons in the state

---

[133] *Annual Report of United States Commissioner of Internal Revenue* (1910), p. 174.
[134] *Ibid.* (1911), p. 174. [135] *Ibid.* (1915), p. 234.
[136] *Annual Report of United States Commissioner of Internal Revenue* (1910), p. 174.
[137] *Ibid.* (1913), p. 202. [138] *Ibid.* (1915), p. 234.
[139] *Ibid.* (1910), p. 174. [140] *Ibid.* (1915), p. 234.
[141] *Ibid.* (1910), p. 174. [142] *Ibid.* (1915), p. 243.
[143] *Annual Report of the Commissioner of Internal Revenue* (1910-1914), *passim*.

were located in three counties.¹⁴⁴ Mobile and Montgomery had each licensed forty-two saloons and Colbert County one.¹⁴⁵ Thus far, two counties out of the sixty-seven contained practically all of the saloons in the state. There were also eleven wholesale liquor dealers, Mobile having seven and Montgomery four. Montgomery also had four social clubs. By 1914 the number of retail and wholesale liquor dealers and social clubs had considerably increased. The state then had 230 registered retail and 64 wholesale liquor dealers, and 31 social clubs. Jefferson County licensed 83 saloons; Mobile, 63; Montgomery, 43; Colbert, 10; Cullman and Pike, 4 each; Russell, 3; and Madison, 1 dispensary.¹⁴⁶ Jefferson had the most wholesale establishments, a total of 27, and Russell came second with 14. Practically all of the social clubs were located in the three largest cities. Jefferson County registered 13; Mobile, 8; Montgomery, 7; Cullman, 2; and Russell, 1.¹⁴⁷

The seven counties having saloons and the one having a dispensary represented a substantial part of the wealth of the state. However, they did not contain anything like half of the population of the state. Out of a total population of 2,138,038, there were 546,424 persons living in these eight counties, or about twenty-six per cent of the people of the state. A minority had legalized liquor in a state where the majority was against it.¹⁴⁸

The *Report of United States Commissioner of Internal Revenue* shows that 683 persons or firms in Alabama purchased internal revenue licenses to retail liquor during the fiscal year ending June 30, 1914.¹⁴⁹ During this same period there were only 332 registered liquor establishments operating in the state. Therefore, 351 federal licenses were issued to persons or firms who had not secured state licenses. Evidently the Federal government had granted licenses to 351 violators of the law of Alabama. The *United States Commissioner of Internal Revenue* in 1911 and in 1912 listed Alabama among the states in which illicit distilling was most prevalent.¹⁵⁰

One of the strongest arguments local optionists had used to gain their victory was that the legalized liquor traffic would put the blind tigers out of business. Experience soon proved the falsity of this claim. Almost as soon as saloons were opened in Montgomery, their keepers began to complain about blind tigers. D. J. Banks said in October, 1911, "We are troubled by the continued operation of blind tigers, but plans are on foot to eradicate the parasites which must result in success." He said that the

¹⁴⁴ *Annual Report of the State Auditor of Alabama, for the Fiscal Year ending September 30, 1911*, pp. 480-483. ¹⁴⁵ *Ibid.*
¹⁴⁶ *Annual Report of the State Auditor of Alabama, for the Fiscal Year ending September 30, 1914*, pp. 448-451. ¹⁴⁷ *Ibid.*
¹⁴⁸ *Official and Statistical Register* (1927), pp. 270-271.
¹⁴⁹ P. 208.
¹⁵⁰ *Annual Report* (1911), p. 25; *ibid.* (1912), p. 25. During the two-year interval, 1912-1914, the Circuit Courts of Alabama disposed of 4,643 cases of prohibition law violations, and 2,043 of them resulted in convictions. *Biennial Report of the Attorney-General* (1912-1914), p. 454.

bootleggers argued that if they could sell at will when such sale was contrary to law, certainly they could sell without license when the traffic was legalized. Banks was hopeful, however, that judges would some day mete out sentences to the culprits.[151]

Prohibitionists claimed that legalized liquor had resulted in an increase of drunkenness. The newspapers quoted a widow from Huntsville who claimed that, in her town and along the road from Huntsville to Monrovia, drunken white men and Negroes, swearing and shouting, raced their horses and mules and shot off their pistols from three o'clock in the afternoon until late into the night. More drunken and drinking men were seen in Huntsville on one day in December, 1911, she claimed, than had been seen during the whole period of prohibition.[152] The police records gave color to such claims. According to such official reports Birmingham, during the Christmas holidays of 1911, celebrated disreputably. The city had nine homicides, the victims being five whites and four Negroes. The streets presented a pagan spectacle. Drunkenness and disorderly conduct were common along the thoroughfares, in the hotels, the cafes, places of amusement, and wherever the surging Christmas crowd was to be found. Hilarious revelers marched unchecked, completely forgetful of the Christmas spirit. The police made forty-six more arrests in that three-day celebration than they had made during the holidays of the previous year, and the greatest number of these arrests were for drunkenness and disorderly conduct.[153]

During the O'Neal administration, the prohibition movement received its strongest motive power from the churches and their members, with the Anti-Saloon League and the W.C.T.U. acting to coordinate and strengthen their efforts. As usual Christian ministers led the movement and kept alive the agitation against the saloon. The Baptists, Methodists, Presbyterians, and the Disciples of Christ took the most aggressive part in this movement to outlaw the liquor traffic.

In Dr. W. B. Crumpton, the Baptists had an able and tenacious leader, always ready to deal telling blows in any fight against liquor. And the official conventions of that denomination followed his lead. In 1911, the Baptist State Convention, representing 185,000 people, called upon all good people everywhere to work against the return of the legalized whiskey traffic to Alabama. The Convention reaffirmed its continued support of temperance, prohibition, and the enforcement of law.[154] In its annual report on temperance in 1912, the same body condemned the Parks and Smith laws. These laws, said the churchmen, had completely failed to destroy the blind tiger, and the only recourse was to return to state-wide prohibition.[155]

[151] *The Citizen*, October, 1911.   [152] *The Citizen*, December, 1911.
[153] *Birmingham Ledger*, copied by *The Citizen*, January, 1912.
[154] *Annual of Alabama Baptist State Convention*, (July 20-22, 1911), p. 51.
[155] *Ibid.*, (July 24-26, 1912), pp. 46-47.

The Methodist Church, acting with its usual vigor, took an active part in preventing the return of the legalized liquor traffic in fifty-nine out of Alabama's sixty-seven counties. Every annual conference between 1910 and 1915 adopted resolutions urging church members to employ all lawful means to extirpate the liquor traffic. In 1911, the Alabama Conference rejoiced to observe a decided reaction in favor of prohibition in the state and prophesied that the next legislature would reenact state-wide prohibition. The same Conference recorded approval of the many papers of Alabama and West Florida which had consistently and energetically fought liquor, and disapproved of the five great dailies of Alabama which had given themselves up to the support of this "enemy of humanity."[156] When the North Alabama Conference met in 1912, it adopted a report declaring that saloons were a miserable failure in suppressing blind tigers, drunkenness, and associated vices. Therefore, the Conference resolved to urge Alabama Congressmen to vote and work for the passage of the Kenyon-Sheppard Anti-Shipping bill then pending. Ministers and church members were asked to write to these Congressmen and express their wishes in the matter.[157]

In 1913 the A.R.P. Synod of the South heartily endorsed "the effort to make this a saloonless nation by 1920."[158] The next year the Presbyterian Church reaffirmed all former deliverances of the General Assembly on temperance. The Synod went on record as unalterably opposed to the liquor traffic in any form.[159]

Writing in the *Alabama Christian Advocate,* William Irwin said that prohibition was a fundamental necessity in the South because of the ever-present race question. In every low Negro dive in the South, he said, certain unmentionable brands of gin were sold, containing drugs that stimulated the low passions which had made the race problem such a dreadful thing in the South.[160] Such liquor must be removed from the reach of Negroes.

The *Alabama Baptist* fought consistently for prohibition. Through its editorial and news columns it emphasized the necessity for individual abstinence and the careful training of the youth in the principles of temperance.[161] It favored the enactment of the Kenyon-Sheppard Anti-Liquor Shipping bill, which would prevent the shipment of liquors into regions where local laws prohibited such traffic. This bill could be passed, declared the *Baptist,* if its friends made their congressional delegations realize that they were in earnest.[162] The *Alabama Baptist* and the *Alabama Christian Advocate* continued to agitate for state-wide and national prohibition.

[156] *Minutes of the Alabama Conference of the Methodist Episcopal Church, South,* (December 6-11, 1911), pp. 42-43.
[157] *Journal of the North Alabama Conference,* (November 20-25, 1912), p. 187.
[158] *Minutes,* (November 6-10, 1913).
[159] *Minutes of the Synod of Alabama* (1914), pp. 200-201.
[160] *Alabama Christian Advocate,* January 23, 1913.
[161] *Alabama Baptist,* November 6, 1912. [162] *Ibid.,* January 1, 1913

CHAPTER IX

RETURN TO STATE-WIDE PROHIBITION, 1915-1920

Throughout Governor O'Neal's administration the prohibitionists worked steadily on plans to regain control of the executive and legislative branches of the state government. Ex-Governor Comer and Lieutenant-Governor Walter D. Seed from the prohibition ranks, Charles Henderson representing the local optionists, and Reuben F. Kolb an extreme whiskey man, were the four gubernatorial candidates in 1914. The prohibitionists went into the contest in a fighting mood, determined to overthrow local option, which they considered a complete failure. The Anti-Saloon League fought vigorously to elect a governor, a state legislature, and a delegation to Congress who were in sympathy with their views. From the beginning of the campaign, it was evident that the prohibitionists were at a disadvantage, for Comer and Seed opposed each other as bitterly as they did either of the other candidates, and thereby succeeded in splitting the ranks of their followers. A majority of the local optionists gave their support to Henderson.

Although prohibition was the principal issue in the campaign, Comer's entry introduced into it another fundamental issue. Comer felt that his constructive program had not been given a fair trial by the O'Neal administration. He proposed, if elected, to mature that program, to impose more rigid regulations on railroads, to advance the cause of education, and to enforce the prohibition laws. His opponents called this program "Comerism" and were ready to fight fiercely to prevent its author's return to office. The campaign became in part at least, a struggle between liberal and conservative Democrats for control of the state.

All four candidates conducted active speaking campaigns. Ex-Governor Comer spent most of his time defending his administration. Henderson vigorously attacked the Comer policies and charged that the ex-governor had violated the local option plank of the Democratic platform of 1906 when he signed the state-wide prohibition law. Seed favored a return to state-wide prohibition and promised that, under him, the state would have a businesslike administration. Kolb, still chagrined over having been "cheated out of the governor's office" in 1892, made his final appeal for recognition. Seed and Kolb both attacked Comer and "Comerism."

The Anti-Saloon League endorsed both Comer and Seed as trustworthy friends of advanced temperance legislation.[1] The *Birmingham Ledger, Montgomery Journal,* and the *Mobile Register* all favored Comer. The *Advertiser* declared that approximately seventy-five per cent of the

---

[1] *Birmingham Ledger*, February 4, 1914.

weekly papers supported Comer. The *Birmingham Age-Herald, Birmingham News, Gadsden Times,* and *Montgomery Advertiser* all advocated the election of Charles Henderson.[2] The *Advertiser* was the most outspoken of these papers. It declared that the election of Comer meant endorsement of state-wide and constitutional prohibition and other evils attendant on Comerism; and it urged the election of Henderson as a repudiation of Comerism.[3] The election of Henderson would prove that the people of Alabama desired to return to peace, quietude, and prosperity.

When Henderson announced his candidacy he clearly defined his position on the liquor question. Since early manhood he had recognized the baneful influence of the whiskey traffic. He was convinced that the surest way to eradicate such evils was by local option with the county as a unit. If he were elected, he promised, he would impose rigid regulations upon the retail liquor dealer and would revoke his license if he did not live up to it. The whiskey dealer should not use his license to make himself a political leader; neither should outside influences be permitted to make him such a figure.[4]

"Mr. Henderson is for local option. In Alabama that means saloons," commented the *American Issue,* reminding its readers that, although Henderson in 1909 was a member of the convention whose declared purpose was not to bring back saloons or the legalized liquor traffic anywhere in Alabama, seven counties now had saloons and one of these was Henderson's home county, Pike.[5]

Ex-Governor Comer expressed himself as satisfied with the present prohibition conditions, but he said that, if the legislature were to pass a state-wide prohibition bill or any other prohibition bill, he would sign it.[6] "Mr. Comer was and still is, a believer in the policy of local option," said the *Mobile Register.* Comer's signing of the state-wide bill in 1907 had been, this paper considered, merely a "common sense" act inasmuch as the bill had been passed already by an almost unanimous vote.[7]

In a speech at Troy early in March, Comer inquired why Samuel Kennedy, Henderson's campaign manager, had gone to Nashville to confer with Charles Lewis on January 16, 1914. He implied that this conference was an attempt to swing the liquor vote for Henderson. Comer's enemies at once countered by accusing him of trying to get the liquor vote for himself.[8] Will T. Sheehan, editor of the *Montgomery Advertiser,* issued a statement on March 8, charging that Comer had negotiated a secret deal with Charles Lewis for the beer and whiskey vote of Alabama. Sheehan declared that he and Kennedy had gone to Nashville to protest

[2] *Montgomery Advertiser,* February 4, 1914.
[3] *Ibid.*
[4] *American Issue,* May 15, 1913.
[5] *Mobile Register,* March 4, 1914.
[6] *American Issue,* May 15, 1913.
[7] *Birmingham Ledger,* March 4, 1914.
[8] *Montgomery Journal,* March 11, 1914.

to Lewis against such a trade.⁹ The purpose of such accusations, it appeared, was to cast suspicion on Comer's sincerity as a friend of prohibition.

In the first primary held on April 6, none of the candidates received a majority. Comer led the ticket; Henderson ran second; Seed and Kolb were eliminated. A second primary, ordered by the State Democratic Executive Committee, was held five weeks later. During the interval between these primaries the battle became even more acrimonious. Comer charged that Henderson, as railroad commissioner, had lost millions of dollars for the state through his railroad rate surrender.¹⁰ The *Mobile Register* tried to convince both the local optionists and the other voters of Mobile County that Comer was the more dependable candidate, and that Henderson could not be trusted even by the local optionists. Henderson was at heart a prohibitionist, the *Register* claimed. It quoted him as saying that a liquor trust, the like of which the world had never seen, reached all over America, debauching government and citizens and taking a death toll appalling to any thoughtful man;¹¹ and it cited as proof a statement in the *Tuscaloosa News* that Henderson was "at all times opposed to the licensed saloons in his home town."¹² If Henderson was what he pretended to be, said the *Register* editor, he would contradict such misrepresentations as were made about him in Mobile; if he did not refute these statements, he was a party to a fraud and deception that bordered on falsehood.¹³

The militant and bitter gubernatorial campaign ended with a peaceable election on May 11. Henderson defeated Comer by a vote of 69,184 to 58,857.¹⁴ Kolb had asked his supporters to swing their votes to Henderson. Seed had remained quiet. He was known to favor Comer, but his home county, Tuscaloosa, voted for Henderson. Henderson's largest vote came from south Alabama counties. Comer's strength was in the northern part of the state.¹⁵

"If the Democrats of Alabama are on record against any one proposition, they are on record as being opposed to the fallacy of state-wide prohibition," said the *Montgomery Advertiser* when the election was over. The extreme prohibitionists claimed that the incoming legislature was wholeheartedly with them; but the *Advertiser* believed and hoped that the new legislators would drop the liquor issue and adopt a constructive program.¹⁶

Many complaints of fraud were made in different parts of the state, but most of them were indefinite. George M. Cruikshank, editor of the *Birmingham Ledger*, said that he witnessed ballots cast by men whose

---

⁹ *Birmingham Age-Herald,* March 9, 1914.
¹⁰ *Birmingham Ledger,* May 5, 1914.   ¹¹ *Mobile Register,* May 5, 1914.
¹² *Ibid.*   ¹³ *Mobile Register,* May 10, 1914.
¹⁴ *Alabama Official and Statistical Register* (1915), pp. 439–441.
¹⁵ *Ibid.*
¹⁶ *Montgomery Advertiser,* May 16, 1914.

names were not on the registration books and whose word was accepted by the election officials as proof of right to vote. Such a practice, he said, would make it quite easy for a man to vote in more than one place.[17] The *Luverne Journal* stated: "The man who buys votes makes himself ineligible to hold office. The editor of the *Journal* has positive proof that votes were bought with whiskey and money in Crenshaw County."[18]

The contest between Richmond P. Hobson and Oscar W. Underwood for the United States Senate was also a fight between prohibitionists and local optionists. Hobson, who had served in Congress since 1906, was a zealous prohibitionist and a brilliant speaker for the temperance cause. In 1913 he had offered a prohibition amendment to the Federal Constitution, but his action at that time had been denounced by a majority of the Representatives from Alabama. Representative Underwood had called it "an attempt to rob the states of their jurisdiction over police matters, in part to destroy the right of local self-government, and to establish a precedent that would concentrate the power of all government in the government established here in Washington." Passage of such a bill, Underwood declared, would not eliminate the evils of intemperance, but it would destroy local supervision for the liquor traffic and deprive the government of much revenue.[19] Only four of the ten Alabama Representatives voted in favor of Hobson's resolution.[20]

Throughout his campaign for the Senate Hobson charged that Underwood was dominated by the liquor interests and corporations.[21] Again and again he told his audiences that his opponent had voted against prohibition in Birmingham in 1907, and that he had never come to Alabama to fight the liquor traffic. He challenged Underwood to meet him in joint debate. Underwood declined. He knew he was no match for the fluent Hobson. Hobson made the most of this refusal. Underwood was afraid of him, he said.

Friends of Underwood offered in his defense his support in 1913 of the Webb-Kenyon Anti-Shipping Act which empowered states to regulate interstate commerce to the extent of prohibiting the importation of intoxicating liquors.[22]

The Anti-Saloon League of Alabama, through Dr. W. B. Crumpton and Brooks Lawrence, waged an aggressive campaign for Hobson. This organization regarded Hobson as a consistent and active friend of prohibition. That was why, they insisted, the bitter and malicious opposition of every agent and representative of the liquor traffic in Alabama and in America was directed against him. Underwood on the other hand, according to League leaders, was opposed to the principle of prohibition and

[17] *Birmingham Ledger*, May 13, 1914.
[18] *Montgomery Journal* copied by *Limestone Democrat*, May 28, 1914.
[19] *Congressional Record*, LII, 519-520.   [20] *Ibid.*, p. 616.
[21] *Tuscaloosa News*, October 7, 1913.   [22] *Ibid.*, January 11, 1914.

favored local option, and this made him acceptable to the liquor interests, whose agents were giving him their fullest support.[23]

The *National Bulletin*, published at Cincinnati, Ohio, by the Wholesale Liquor Dealers of America, naturally opposed Hobson. The Anti-Saloon League of Ohio was determined to force Hobson upon the people of Alabama as a Senator, this paper warned, and the National Prohibition party was also back of the move because they knew Hobson to be their pliant tool. Hobson was continually spending his time making speeches which paid him well. He was rarely in his seat except when he could further Anti-Saloon League demonstrations for his personal benefit.[24]

If Captain Hobson was the "pliant tool" of the Anti-Saloon League, commented the *Birmingham Ledger*, it would be quite appropriate to say the candidate supported by the *National Bulletin* was the pliant tool of the National Wholesale Liquor Dealers Association of America.[25]

Many of the Underwood papers charged Hobson with spending too much time away from his duties in Washington. "As a member of the House of Representatives Mr. Hobson had achieved distinction for one thing, and that is his persistent neglect of duty," said the *Birmingham News*.[26]

Hobson made a brilliant campaign, but Underwood defeated him by a majority of 34,732 votes.[27] Hobson blamed his defeat upon the liquor forces. Just after the election he made a public statement in which he said that Alabama had only begun to fight the liquor interests and that under God's Providence they would fight to the end and successfully.[28] Although the local optionists had elected both the governor and the United States Senator, the prohibitionists had not lost everything. Frank S. White, prohibitionist, had been given a majority over Ray Rushton and Watt T. Brown, local optionist, for United States Senator to fill out the unexpired term of Senator Johnson; and Thomas E. Kilby, prohibitionist, had been elected lieutenant governor by an overwhelming vote.[29] Hobson's brilliant campaign had stimulated new enthusiasm for prohibition in the state.

Shortly after the primary on April 6, the prohibitionists claimed that they had a majority in both houses of the incoming legislature. Many

[23] *Birmingham Ledger*, February 4, 1914.
[24] *Montgomery Journal*, January 2, 1914.
[25] *Birmingham Ledger*, January 2, 1914.
[26] March 18, 1914.
[27] *Alabama Official and Statistical Register* (1915), pp. 364f.
[28] *Mobile Register*, April 8, 1914. Hobson's statement was as follows: "Please say to the liquor interests of America that we have only begun to fight, that the work we have done can never be undone; that we will meet them again on the battlefield of Alabama and on a hundred other battlefields; that we expect under God's Providence to be in the battle when the thirty-sixth state ratifies the Hobson resolution placing national prohibition in the constitution of the United States. It will be a fight to the bitter end and I look for success. The fight has just begun."
[29] *Alabama Official and Statistical Register* (1915), pp. 406f.

THE PROHIBITION MOVEMENT IN ALABAMA   181

of the candidates for the legislature had been handpicked by Brooks Lawrence. Although most of them had not openly committed themselves in favor of a state-wide law, they had privately pledged themselves to support such legislation. The Democrats in 1914 had formulated neither state nor county platforms, and therefore the prohibitionists did not press their candidates to commit themselves openly. In many instances local optionists voted for prohibitionists.[30]

On June 3, 1914, Dr. W. B. Crumpton, President of the Anti-Saloon League, issued a statement calling upon prohibitionists to continue their fight upon liquor interests in Alabama and to support in the gubernatorial campaign the Democratic nominee, "who," he said, "is no friend of the liquor interests." "The work of agitation against our enemy, the liquor traffic, must go on," said Crumpton. No compromise could be made with that mightiest foe of humanity. The prohibitionists might expect to be misunderstood and sometimes misrepresented, but they must not swerve from their fixed purpose to destroy liquor.[31]

Confident that a majority of the new legislators favored a state-wide measure, the dry leaders laid their plans to swing Alabama back into the ranks of the prohibition states. And they determined to work through the churches. The keynote of the temperance reports adopted by the several churches in 1914 was state-wide and national prohibition. The Baptist State Convention declared that temperance advocates now had power to enact any laws they wished if they stood together. All candidates for offices in both houses of Congress, asserted this body, should be compelled to declare themselves for state and national prohibition.[32]

The Alabama Conference recorded its conviction that the recent election, where a majority of legislators chosen were prohibitionists, reflected the sober sentiment of the state. Surely the incoming legislature would not fail to pass a state-wide prohibition law, said the Conference; and it instructed its secretary to present to the lawmakers a memorial to that effect. One important legislative step, these churchmen urged, was the prohibition of liquor advertising in the newspapers of the state.[33] In 1913 the North Alabama Conference had said: "We are unalterably opposed to local option, as used by the liquorites, and do hereby execrate and repudiate their deceptive and diabolical purpose for which they now seek to foist the doctrine and practice of local option upon free sons of Alabama."[34] In 1914 this same conference again recorded its unequivocal stand for state-wide and national prohibition and its belief that the day was not far off when the state would be dry. The combined membership of these two

[30] *Birmingham News*, January 17, 1915.
[31] *Limestone Democrat*, June 4, 1914.
[32] *Minutes of the Alabama Baptist State Convention, (November 18-20, 1914)*, pp. 59-62.
[33] *Minutes of the Alabama Conference of the Methodist Episcopal Church, South, (December 2-7, 1914)*, pp. 45-46.
[34] *Alabama Christian Advocate*, November 5, 1914, December 17, 1914.

conferences was approximately 175,000.[35] The legislature could hardly afford to ignore the wishes of such a large number of citizens.

The Synod of Alabama heartily supported the movement toward the total prohibition of the traffic in intoxicating beverages. This body considered it deplorable that the saloon was intrenched within some of the towns and largest cities of the state, and expressed regret that some newspapers regularly introduced seductive advertisements of intoxicating beverages into the homes. The Synod looked to divine providence for guidance to banish liquor from the borders of the state.[36] The A.R.P. Synod of the South rejoiced that the legalized liquor traffic was rapidly receiving the death sentence, which it so justly deserved.[37]

The Presbyterian Church, U.S.A., reaffirmed former deliverances, forbidding the manufacture and sale of alcoholic stimulants as inconsistent with Christian duty; and it further urged that all officers and members of local churches be forbidden to aid or abet in any way the liquor traffic by signing liquor applications or by presenting them in court.[38]

The Disciples of Christ hailed with delight the growing sentiment in Alabama to overthrow the liquor traffic, which was a menace to the peace, prosperity, and safety of the people. This body pledged its influence in crystallizing the sentiment into mental activity by educational processes. The Disciples lent their encouragement to the movement which had been inaugurated to make the United States a saloonless nation by 1920.[39]

The Woman's Christian Temperance Union launched an extensive advertising campaign. Posters were displayed in conspicuous places and letters were sent to ministers asking them to influence their congregations in favor of state-wide and national prohibition. The women cooperated with public-school teachers in their temperance work. Some Unions offered prizes to school boys and girls for the best essays on temperance. Temperance calendars were made and distributed. Some Unions sent out post cards to voters just before elections, but their most effective work was among the children.[40]

Prior to the convening of the legislature in January, 1915, the prohibitionists held several conferences in different parts of the state. These conferences had a double purpose, said their promoters. The first was to settle the friendly rivalry between two avowed prohibitionists for speakership of the House and the three avowed prohibitionists for president *pro tem* of the Senate. In that aim, they were successful. The second was to determine the kind of prohibition legislation which their constituents wanted

[35] *Alabama Christian Advocate*, December 17, 1914.
[36] *Minutes of the Synod of Alabama* (1914), p. 200.
[37] *Minutes*, (November 4-8, 1914).
[38] *Official Pronouncements of the General Assembly of the Presbyterian Church in the U.S.A. Relative to Social and Industrial Relations and Social and Moral Welfare* (1910-1936), p. 65.
[39] *Minutes of Alabama Christian Missionary Co-Operation*, (November 13, 1914).
[40] *W.C.T.U. Minutes* (1914-1919), *passim*.

presented and supported. They agreed that such legislation would be introduced and passed upon, so far as they were able, at the earliest practicable moment. In none of these conferences was there a word of hostility toward Governor-elect Henderson or his administration. All the members recognized that prohibition should not be allowed to monopolize the time of the legislature, and declared that all departments should act in harmony in settling matters of constructive and remedial legislation.[41]

Governor-elect Henderson on January 10, said that an unprecedented situation had arisen which made it necessary for him to take a positive position in the organization of the legislature. Attempts were being made to thwart the expressed will of the people in this organization, he declared, and he called "on every friend and all in sympathy with my policies, to support Hon. Oscar S. Lewis for president *pro tem* of the senate with full power to appoint all committees, and Hon. E. D. Johnson for speaker of the house of representatives." "President Wilson has said the governor is a part of the legislature," he added in justification of his appeal.[42]

The legislators, meeting in caucus on January 11, declined to comply with Henderson's request. They elected an outstanding prohibitionist to preside over each house. A. H. Carmichael of Tuscumbia defeated Edward D. Johnson of Huntsville for speaker of the House by a vote of 71 to 30. By a unanimous vote, Thomas L. Bulger of Dadeville was elected president *pro tem* of the Senate over Oscar S. Lewis of Tuskegee, local option candidate. The prohibitionists were in the saddle. Their majority in each house was so great that they could easily pass any bill they favored over the governor's veto.[43] Henderson claimed that his opponents were unfair. They had come to him asking for cooperation but they expected him to do all the cooperating. The prohibitionists assured him, however, that when their favorite legislation was out of the way, they would concur fully with the administration.

The House of Representatives convened on January 12 and immediately took up the question of prohibition. Merritt of Macon County, introduced one bill for state-wide prohibition and another for rigid enforcement of such a law. Both were almost duplicates of the former Carmichael and Fuller bills.[44] Johnson of Madison, opened the debate in the House with a speech against the state-wide bill. Members of the legislature, he asserted, had not been sent there to change the prohibition laws. The results of the last four elections gave them no such mandate. The passage of the proposed bill would not settle the liquor question in Alabama because it was not in line with the expressed wishes of the people. Bart Chamberlane also opposed the measure. He said, "I have never come in contact with a steam roller of such modern type." Merritt, floor leader,

[41] *Birmingham Age-Herald*, January 1, 1915.
[42] *Birmingham Ledger*, January 11, 1915.
[43] *Montgomery Journal*, January 11, 1915.
[44] *House Journal* (1915), I, 223-224.

closed the debate in favor of the bill. He had no doubts about its enforceability. It was the easiest thing in the world, he asserted, to convict a man for selling liquor. "When we pass this bill, we will not need so many courts and will save expenses. We will not have so many law-breakers, either."[45] Hill asked that Montgomery County be exempted from the provisions of the bill. He also favored a popular referendum.

Both Merritt bills were passed on January 14. The state-wide measure was passed by 73 to 27, the enforcement bill 79 to 18.[46] The bills were ordered sent forthwith to the Senate without engrossment, and the Senate passed them on January 16, by a vote of 20 to 6 for the first, and 22 to 6 for the second.[47] The prohibitionists had intended to get their bills passed before Governor O'Neal left office. They hoped and believed he would veto them. Instead O'Neal left them for his successor, Charles Henderson, to handle. The retiring governor bitterly scored the legislature for having "wantonly ravished the cherished and inalienable rights of the people."[48]

Local optionists, watching the Merritt bills move through the House, described the legislature as the smoothest, best-oiled road roller that ever crushed its way to victory in the Alabama legislature. The victory of the prohibition forces, they declared, "was due largely to the failure of local optionists to organize weeks ago. They slept over their opportunities. They permitted the prohibition leaders to get the bulge on them." Senator Hartwell of Mobile, very much chagrined and keenly annoyed, acidly requested that local optionists should not be crushed but allowed to die slowly.[49]

In anticipation of Governor Henderson's veto, Brooks Lawrence wrote innumerable letters to prohibitionists throughout the state urging them to send letters and telegrams to keep their representatives in line. Lawrence said that Governor Henderson would almost certainly veto these dry laws on the grounds that the matter should be referred to the people for a vote. That was exactly what the liquor interests wanted. "On account of the corruption possible under our present election laws every prohibitionist in Alabama should unite in resisting such a movement," he warned.[50]

Governor Henderson acted as expected. He vetoed the state-wide prohibition bill, declaring that he believed local option was the best way to handle the difficult problem; but he offered an amendment providing that the measure be submitted to the popular vote.[51] The legislature disregarded the amendment and passed the bill over the governor's veto. The

[45] *Birmingham Ledger*, January 14, 1915.
[46] *House Journal* (1915), I, 259, 261.
[47] *Senate Journal* (1915), I, 328, 329.
[48] *Birmingham Ledger*, January 18, 1915.
[49] *Birmingham News*, January 12, 13, 1915.
[50] *Birmingham Age-Herald*, January 20, 1915.
[51] *Senate Journal* (1915), I, 465-570.

law was to become effective July 1, 1915; the liquor establishments in the state were to be legally closed on that day.[52]

The *Birmingham Ledger* thought that, by enacting the bill without the governor's amendment, the legislators were merely fulfilling their pledges to their constituents.[53] The local option press, on the other hand, was bitter in its denunciation of the measure. The *Montgomery Advertiser*, referring to the rejection of the amendment in 1909 and the defeat of the prohibition candidates for governor in 1914, taunted the prohibitionists with not daring to try a referendum.[54] The *Alabama Christian Advocate* commended the prohibition members of the legislature. It said: "Your patriotic manhood is a rich legacy . . . as you have shown to the world that liquor domination in Alabama is a thing of the past, thanks be to God."[55]

To place further restrictions on the consumption of liquor, the legislature passed an act in February, 1915, which prohibited liquor advertising in newspapers, magazines, on bill boards, or in any other form. Again Governor Henderson exercised his veto prerogative. He returned the bill with the comment that he did not think the law could be effective. Liquor advertising by mail would be protected by the interstate commerce laws of the United States. In this and other areas advertising could not be stopped by legislation. The law would be impotent. It could serve only as a means of further irritation. The House passed the bill over the governor's veto by a vote of 69 to 25.[56]

The *Decatur Daily* of January 28 gave qualified approval to the bill. It had, the editor pointed out, some undeniably objectionable features. Newspapers published outside of the state would be exempt from its provisions and Alabama papers would suffer in consequence. Moreover, newspapers publishing liquor advertisements would be forced by such a law into a role of virtue which they had no right or desire to assume. The Birmingham City Court declared the measure unconstitutional but the Alabama Supreme Court later reversed the decision.[57]

[52] *Montgomery Advertiser*, January 23, 1915.
[53] January 22, 1915.
[54] January 25, 1915.   [55] January 28, 1915.
[56] *House Journal* (1915), I, 1182-1183.
[57] *Southern Reporter*, Vol. 80, pp. 993-999. W. C. Delaye, operator of a newsstand in Birmingham, was selling newspapers and magazines published out of the state of Alabama. Hugo L. Black, Solicitor of Jefferson County, attempted to prevent, by injunction, the sale of papers containing liquor advertisements, which was denied by the City Court of Birmingham. Black appealed the case to the State Supreme Court which granted the injunction. The decision was as follows: "We, therefore conclude that the anti-advertising liquor law here under review does not contravene any of the provisions of the state and federal Constitutions, is a proper exercise of the police power of the state, and is valid and now effective throughout the entire state. The law provides for the mode of procedure here followed, and which authorizes injunctive relief as a means of obtaining the end in view. It follows, therefore, in our opinion, that the writ of injunction should have been granted by the learned judge [John H. Miller] below, and his order denying the same is

Within two years after Alabama had rejoined the ranks of dry states, the movement for national prohibition terminated in the submission of a constitutional amendment to the Alabama legislature for ratification.

This move toward national prohibition was no sudden development. Prohibition bills had been introduced into Congress as early as 1876.[58] Senator Blair of New Hampshire had offered such a bill in 1887,[59] and in 1914 Senator Sheppard of Texas and Representative Hobson of Alabama both had attempted to get congressional action against liquor. The W.C.T.U., the Anti-Saloon League, and the Prohibition party had been fighting for nation-wide prohibition for many years. Their goal came within reach at last when the United States entered the World War and the conservation of grain for food became a national necessity.

Protestant churches had played their full part in the struggle. In Alabama Baptists, Methodists, Presbyterians and Disciples of Christ were especially zealous. Their annual temperance reports between 1914 and 1919 almost invariably urged the incorporation of a prohibition amendment into the Federal Constitution. The *Alabama Baptist* and the *Alabama Christian Advocate* also championed the cause.

When the United States Senate adopted on August 1, 1917, a resolution which proposed a constitutional prohibition amendment, the Alabama senators were divided on the measure. Bankhead favored and Underwood opposed it.[60] When the House passed an amended resolution on December 17, 1917, Alabamians in that body were also divided. Huddleston and Heflin spoke against the proposed amendment, calling it a violation of state rights.[61] The Senate concurred in the amendment made by the House on December 18 and the resolution went to the state legislatures for ratification.

Thus in 1918 the prohibition issue was again before the people of Alabama. Would Alabama ratify the Eighteenth Amendment? Enemies of the measure were quick to set up what Dr. Crumpton called the "Scare-crow of . . . states rights."[62]

Prohibition forces of Alabama had been agitating for national prohibition ever since their victory of 1915. They were now ready for action. Dr. W. B. Crumpton and Reverend Brooks Lawrence, supported by many men and women, took the lead in perfecting an organization to execute their plans. They chose their candidates for governor and both branches of the legislature and threw the full weight of this organization behind them. They made full use of the argument ready to their hands that a nation at war must conserve its grain and employ its man power for other

---

hereby reversed, and one will here be entered granting the temporary injunction as prayed in the bill."

[58] E. P. Gordon, *Women Torch-Bearers*, p. 86.
[59] Cherrington, *op. cit.*, p. 232.
[60] *Congressional Record*, LV, 5,666.   [61] *Ibid.*, LVI, 457-470.
[62] Crumpton, *How Alabama Became Dry*, p. 24.

tasks than running distilleries. They also contended that the Eighteenth Amendment ought to be ratified because the consumption of liquor and crime had both decreased under prohibition. All over Alabama, said the *Montgomery Journal*, the jail doors were standing ajar for a lack of prisoners. The sheriff of Dallas County, this paper claimed, had seriously considered resigning because he had no prisoners to feed. The sheriff of Montgomery County suggested renting out his jail as a garage. Lawyers were complaining that there was less litigation in the state than ever before, and many of them were looking around for outside sources of income.[63]

Calling themselves real Democrats, the opponents of the measure held a meeting in Montgomery on April 4, and organized to defeat the proposed amendment, to save state rights, to keep faith with time-honored democracy, and to thwart "the vagaries and whimsies of the constitutional amendists."[64] They were not, they protested, trying to bring saloons back to Alabama. They knew the whiskey business in their state "was as dead as the men who lived before the flood." But the amendment must be defeated lest the Federal Government regain what the white man had taken back in 1874, and Federal rule in state affairs be fastened upon Alabama citizens forever and forever.[65]

Five gubernatorial candidates entered the contest of 1918. They were William W. Brandon, Thomas E. Kilby, Charles B. Teasley, John Purifoy, and John H. Wallace. Kilby, Brandon, and Teasley were the leading candidates. Kilby openly favored the prohibition amendment; Brandon straddled the issue; the other three candidates opposed it. The prohibition amendment became the campaign issue. The *Birmingham Ledger*, the *Montgomery Journal*, and the Anti-Saloon League supported Kilby, who in the end defeated Brandon by a 3,404 majority. The legislature also was strongly prohibition. That settled the matter, said the *Advertiser* in an editorial "Let us have peace." The amendment would unquestionably be ratified. The Reverend Brooks Lawrence was now undisputed political boss of Alabama. He had not only directed the nomination of Kilby, but, as some of his friends boasted, he had picked the entire ticket of state officers. "Will Brooks Lawrence dominate a majority in the next legislature?" asked the *Advertiser*. It answered its own question: "He will as certainly and as surely as President Wilson dominates a majority in Congress."[66]

The Eighteenth Amendment was an issue also in the congressional elections of that year. About half of the Congressmen from Alabama had voted against the submission of the Amendment, but none of them lost their seats in consequence of it. Senator John H. Bankhead, who had

[63] *Montgomery Journal*, June 8, 1918.
[64] *Montgomery Advertiser*, April 5, 1918.
[65] *Montgomery Advertiser*, April 5, 1918.
[66] *Ibid.*, August 18, 1918.

voted for submission, was a candidate for reelection. His friends wanted him retained without opposition. Ex-Senator Frank S. White, an elderly man, could see no reason for suppressing his personal ambition, however, and he entered the race against Bankhead and attempted to draw to his support advocates of local option and state rights. Senator Bankhead made no attempt to canvass the state, but he was reelected by a majority of 12,006 votes.[67]

On January 14, 1919, the Alabama legislature ratified the Federal prohibition amendment by a joint resolution of both houses. The vote of the House was 64 for and 34 against;[68] in the Senate, 23 for and 11 against.[69] The Amendment became a part of the Federal Constitution on January 16, 1920. The prohibitionists had finally reached their goal.

The *Birmingham News* prophesied much violation of the new law and great graft and corruption. These things could only mean a serious undermining of the authority and efficiency of law enforcement. Moreover, the *News* editor ventured to doubt that any of man's temptations could be entirely removed from his path by law.[70] The *Alabama Baptist* hailed ratification as a glorious victory which had taught the people that when united in the effort, they could accomplish anything they desired, and could destroy public evil and enthrone public good.[71]

Both the Alabama and the North Alabama Conferences thanked God that the Amendment had been ratified, and that they had had some part in achieving its ratification. The Alabama Conference expressed its sincere regret that President Wilson had vetoed the enforcement act, and they heartily commended the prompt action of Congress in emphatically and promptly overriding the president's veto.[72]

The legislature next took under consideration a drastic bone-dry enforcement bill. This measure was framed to prohibit the manufacture, sale, transportation, or storage of distilled, malt, or vinous liquors in Alabama. It stipulated that a judge who suspended a prohibition violation sentence would be guilty of a misdemeanor. The bill met with very little opposition in either house. While the men and women in the galleries cheered vociferously, the House of Representatives, by a vote of 53 to 19, adopted on January 18, 1919, the Weakley bone-dry prohibition bill, which earlier in the day had been acted upon favorably by the Senate by a vote of 20 to 6.[73] When the final vote was recorded, J. Lee Long of Butler County, leader of the opposition in the House, exclaimed, "My God, is there no stopping place?" Shaw at once remarked that the law was too dry for the gentleman from Butler, but that his own county needed such a law because of the operations of bootleggers. The legislature is revo-

[67] *Alabama Official and Statistical Register* (1919), p. 393.
[68] *House Journal* (1919), I, 66.
[69] *Senate Journal* (1919), I, 77.   [70] *Birmingham News*, January 17, 1919.
[71] *Alabama Baptist*, January 30, 1919.   [72] *Journals* (1919), pp. 26, 50.
[73] *Senate Journal* (1919), I, 135; *House Journal* (1919), I, 120.

lutionary, charged Truss of Jefferson; the people should have had a chance to express themselves on this most important matter, he declared. Ellis of Elmore "wept when Smith of Greene County described in a pathetic manner the cries of the dying persons who could not get a stimulant to keep them alive." He became so interested in the story he forgot parliamentary rules and stood on the floor till the speaker had rapped for order several times. Several of the women in the gallery burst into tears as Smith sought to show that physicians could not get whiskey for medical purposes.[74]

After July 1, 1915, no liquor was legally manufactured in Alabama. Exactly how much illicit distilling was done, cannot, of course, be determined, but there is every indication that there was a good deal. In 1915, 386 illicit stills were seized. In 1918 the number dropped to 340, but it increased to 1,380 in 1920.[75] This tremendous increase was probably due to the desire of bootleggers to reap the maximum profits while the country was in the midst of great post-war prosperity.

From 1915 to 1919 retail liquor dealers continued to purchase licenses from the United States Government. In 1915, 500 dealers were licensed; in 1917, 633; and 397 in 1919. The total number of licenses in that period was 2,234. The county sheriffs were required to get a list of the licenses from the United States Revenue Office in Birmingham, Montgomery, or Mobile and publish this list in the newspapers. All of these dealers, with the possible exception of a few druggists, must have been violators of the state laws, but only 214 arrests are recorded.

The *Biennial Reports* of the Attorney General of Alabama between 1914 and 1920 show a steady decline in criminal cases disposed of by Circuit Courts. Between 1914 and 1916 these courts handled 23,579 cases of which 4,178 were violations of the prohibition law and 833 cases of public drunkenness.[76] Between 1918 and 1920 only 10,607 cases were handled, 2,666 for violating the liquor law and only 273 for public drunkenness.[77] This marked decline of more than fifty per cent showed that prohibition was really working. One contributing factor in this decrease of crime was federal restriction of the manufacture and sale of liquor in 1917 and 1918, and the ban on the sale of intoxicants to soldiers. Another factor was undoubtedly the absence from the state during 1917-1919 of approximately 50,000 young men called to military service.

[74] *Birmingham Age-Herald*, January 19, 1919.
[75] *Annual Reports of U. S. Commissioner of Internal Revenue* (1915 to 1920), *passim*.
[76] *Biennial Report* (1914-1916), p. 575.
[77] *Biennial Report* (1918-1920), pp. 793-794.

CHAPTER X

ALABAMA UNDER THE EIGHTEENTH AMENDMENT, 1920-1933

National prohibition was a product of many forces. Legislation as well as temperance agitation and education had foreshadowed its coming. Twenty-six states were already dry when the United States declared war on April 6, 1917. Twenty-seven were dry before the proposed amendment was submitted for ratification in December, 1917. And by the time the amendment became effective, January 16, 1920, thirty-three states had adopted prohibition.

The war restrictions placed on intoxicants by the Federal government in May, 1917, also prepared the way for the measure. The regulations made from time to time under the Selective Draft Act of that month prohibited the selling of liquor to men in uniform. Later and more stringent provisions also forbade giving or serving liquor to these men. Areas around training camps and stations were made dry. By the time the Armistice was signed, on November 11, 1918, more than five million men in the combined forces of the army and navy were subject to these prohibitory regulations.[1]

As another war measure, Congress forbade the use of foods, food materials, fruits, and feeds for the production of distilled spirits for beverage purposes. This Food Control Act became effective August 10, 1917, and all distilleries were forced to close down on September 10, 1917. The President was empowered by this act either to regulate or prohibit the production of malt or vinous liquors,[2] and he used this power from time to time to conserve food and fuel.[3] Executive prohibitions were relaxed shortly after the Armistice.

The war prohibition restrictions of the agriculture appropriation bill passed Congress in August, 1917, but the entire bill did not become a law until November 21, 1918.[4] This bill prohibited the production of malt and vinous liquors after May 1, 1919, and the sale of all liquors after June 30, 1919, until the conclusion of the war and the demobilization of all military forces. Saloons were thus outlawed after June 30, 1919. The Volstead Act, designed to enforce war prohibition and also constitutional prohibition as soon as it should go into effect, was repassed over President Wilson's veto October 28, 1919.[5] Forty-six states had ratified the Eight-

[1] *United States Statutes at Large* (1917-1919), *passim.*
[2] *United States Statutes at Large* (1917-1919), *passim.*
[3] *Messages and Papers of President Wilson.*
[4] *United States Statutes at Large* (1917-1919), *passim.*
[5] *Congressional Record,* LVIII, 7632.

eenth Amendment when it went into effect. This would seem a clear indication that a majority of the citizens had accepted prohibition as the established policy of the nation. Many of those who had been opposed to it acquiesced in its observance. The *Cosmopolitan Magazine,* after conducting a survey in 1921, concluded that the number of drinkers had been reduced from 20,000,000 to 2,500,000.[6]

The liquor interests had claimed that the Eighteenth Amendment would cause rebellion and had prophesied that laboring men would refuse to work without beer. They used the best of legal talent to fight prohibition in the courts. They tried to discredit it in a campaign of propaganda, declaring that it had been put across contrary to the wishes of the soldiers and the majority of the people. Yet the first years of national constitutional prohibition produced such extraordinary benefits that they were described as almost miraculous. Unfortunately the benefits did not last.

The temperance reports of both the Alabama and North Alabama Conferences of the Methodist Episcopal Church, South were full of optimism as they reviewed the results of national prohibition in 1920. The latter conference declared that prohibition, even though imperfectly enforced under unfriendly officials, had proved itself one of the most humanitarian and uplifting events of the whole Christian era. From every section of the country came the same story. Drunkenness and crime had been greatly reduced. Jails and penitentiaries had fewer inmates. Poverty was decreasing; bank deposits increasing. Merchants everywhere were delighted as old accounts, considered uncollectible, were being paid. Homes were happier; families were better fed, clothed, and housed. The transformation was like a miracle of God.

The churchmen admitted that the liquor interests had not accepted defeat. The organized brewing interests of America were still financing and carrying on an aggressive fight for beer and light wines, which, if successful, would mean the nullification of the Eighteenth Amendment, and a return to the old conditions. The temperance committee warned prohibitionists to be careful to elect Congressmen in 1922 who would take no backward step. Let ministers and churches throughout the state, they urged, open their pulpits to the representatives of the Anti-Saloon League and give that organization the fullest cooperation possible in the closing years of the warfare against the greatest curse mankind had ever known. The members of the W.C.T.U. were commended for their part in the moral advancement of Alabama. As pioneers in the great reform, they should not be forgotten.[7]

By 1926 when the violations of the prohibition laws were increasing annually, the Alabama Conference became alarmed at the widespread disregard for law and order. If this evil were not checked, the Conference

[6] December, 1921.
[7] *Journal of the Alabama Conference* (1920), pp. 58-59; *Journal of the North Alabama Conference* (1920), pp. 56-57.

declared, it would ultimately destroy that safety and protection which the laws and courts of justice guaranteed to every citizen. The Conference thanked Colonel Bibb Graves, Governor-elect, for his emphasis upon the urgent need for rigorous enforcement of the Eighteenth Amendment, and pledged him their undivided support.[8]

In 1926 the North Alabama Conference took note of the effort being made to reestablish the liquor traffic in the United States. The people were warned not to be deceived. The church must continue to fight until the "bush-whackers" of the liquor traffic had been driven from hiding and forced to admit their deception. The same Conference the following year expressed alarm over the efforts of the liquor interests to nullify the prohibition law. It declared that every possible method was being used to deceive good people, to persuade them to vote against real prohibition, and thus unwittingly to help bring back the evils of the saloon.[9] The Conference declared that the church would support the Anti-Saloon League.

In 1923 the Baptist State Convention viewed with alarm the efforts to nullify the effect of the Eighteenth Amendment. The report stated that the enemy of prohibition "never sleeps," and that it had unlimited means at its disposal. Church members were urged to support every effort to put an end to the liquor traffic. The work of the W.C.T.U. and the Anti-Saloon League was highly commended. The convention acknowledged a debt of gratitude to Dr. Crumpton for his long years of usefulness in the liquor fight.[10]

The A.R.P. Synod of the South noted in 1926 that there was a persistent and well-organized effort of national extent to discredit and to eventually repeal the Eighteenth Amendment. The Committee on Reform suggested that all ministers and members of the Associated Reform Presbyterian Church stand firmly for the enforcement of the prohibition law and resist all efforts to have it modified or repealed.[11]

In 1922 the Disciples of Christ took cognizance of the attempts to nullify the prohibition laws. The following report on the subject was adopted: "Inasmuch as the enemies of prohibition are exceedingly active in their efforts to weaken and overthrow our temperance laws, we call upon our brethren everywhere to manifest their interest in prohibition and give it their zealous support."[12]

The W.C.T.U., called by one state president "an organized force against all that is untrue, unjust, and un-Christian," had achieved its principal legislative goal—national prohibition. But it did not cease to be active. In 1920 among its many departments were those dealing with

[8] *Journal of the Alabama Conference* (1926), p. 50.
[9] *Journal of the North Alabama Conference* (1927), pp. 76-77.
[10] *Annual of the Alabama Baptist State Convention, (November 13-15, 1923)*, pp. 67-70.
[11] *Minutes* (1926), pp. 158-159.
[12] *Alabama Christian*, XX, No. 4, p. 1.

child welfare, temperance and labor, health, Americanism, scientific temperance instruction, law enforcement, and the abolition of the drug traffic.

All branches of the Union distributed large amounts of temperance literature each year. The West End Union in Birmingham, for example, presented wall cards to public schools and Sunday schools. One temperance Sunday it distributed more than five thousand pages of literature and emphasized the spirit of the day by placing in the church a large jar of flowers bound with white crepe paper.[13] The pieces of literature distributed annually by the state secretary and the individual unions amounted to several thousand. Temperance newspapers, among them the *Union Signal* published out of the state, and the *White Ribbon,* published in Birmingham, were widely read and distributed by the members. Even anti-prohibition papers sometimes published temperance articles. The *Birmingham Ledger* championed the cause of prohibition until that paper was discontinued in 1922. The *Alabama Baptist* and the *Alabama Christian Advocate* both defended prohibition.

Throughout the period from 1920 to 1928 the W.C.T.U. urged men and women to vote for candidates who would uphold the dry law. They earnestly protested against the modification of the enforcement code that would legalize the manufacture or sale of wine and beer and would nullify the Eighteenth Amendment. They called upon every citizen and all organizations to join them in making a vigorous educational campaign to secure obedience to the prohibition laws.[14]

Having served as superintendent of the Anti-Saloon League of Alabama for sixteen years, Brooks Lawrence resigned from that office in 1922. He had served the organization well and faithfully, and his departure was a severe blow to the temperance forces of the state. After careful consideration the trustees of the Alabama Anti-Saloon League selected J. Bibb Mills to take up Lawrence's mantle. He filled the position with general satisfaction until 1938 when the organization was disbanded.

Both Democrats and Republicans avoided the prohibition issue in the 1920 campaign. Both chose to assume that prohibition was an accepted national policy. The Democrats boasted of the achievements of prohibition between 1913 and 1920, but did not mention prohibition in their platform. The Republicans were so much concerned with the return to "normalcy" that they also overlooked prohibition. The Prohibition party alone adopted its usual prohibition plank. In no uncertain terms it condemned efforts to nullify the Eighteenth Amendment; it accused the organized liquor traffic of attempting to nullify the Amendment by modification of the enforcement act; and it went on record as the only party which upheld national prohibition.[15]

As early as 1922 the *Montgomery Advertiser,* the *Birmingham News,*

[13] *W.C.T.U. Minutes* (1923), p. 23.   [14] *W.C.T.U. Minutes* (1924), pp. 27-28.
[15] K. H. Porter, *National Party Platforms,* pp. 442-447.

the *Birmingham Age-Herald,* and a number of the political leaders of the state began to boom Senator Oscar W. Underwood for the Democratic nomination for president. In 1923 the legislature adopted a joint resolution endorsing Underwood, "as our choice for president of the United States" and urging "that he be made the standard bearer of the next Democratic convention."[16] In further compliment to Senator Underwood the legislature passed an act providing that the person who carried the state for president in the primary might name the delegates to the national Democratic convention and thus be sure to have on the delegation men who would stand by him in the national convention as long as there was hope of his nomination.[17]

Unwilling to see Underwood nominated without opposition, L. M. Dinsmore of Birmingham, and L. B. Musgrove of Jasper, entered the race. Musgrove, an ardent dry, injected the prohibition issue into the campaign. He charged that Underwood had consistently voted against prohibition both in the state and in Congress.

The *Alabama Courier* considered Musgrove's move ill-advised. "In entering the race he brought to the fore the wornout and threadbare slogan 'Prohibition,' a thing that has wafted many incompetent demagogues into office which they are not large enough to fill, and which showed them up in their littleness to the world."[18]

Underwood claimed that he had come to accept prohibition as a national policy. The decision made by the people of this country when they adopted the Eighteenth Amendment had foreclosed the issue so far as he was concerned, he said at Montgomery on July 31. Now that prohibition was a supreme law of the land he was in favor of its complete enforcement. He went further and voiced his disappointment of the cry for light wines and beer. This cry misled a good many people, he said, and it was not attainable under his interpretation of the Constitution.[19]

Ex-Governor B. B. Comer protested the right of Senator Underwood, or the successful candidate for the presidency, to name all the delegates to the national convention. As a leader in state politics for many years, as a man who had served as governor and filled out an unexpired term in the United States Senate, he felt that he should have the right to name some of those delegates. To preserve harmony and to avoid legal technicalities, the Underwood forces agreed to let Comer name half the delegates, and to name also the Alabama member of the platform committee. Comer pledged himself publicly to name dry delegates. The manager of the Underwood campaign announced simultaneously that the Underwood committee would make an earnest effort to appoint, as their half of the delegation, men who would oppose any change in the Volstead Act or any light wine and beer measures, and who would favor the enforcement of the present laws.[20]

[16] *General Acts* (1923), p. 10. [17] *Ibid.*, pp. 269-270.
[18] January 17, 1924. [19] *Alabama Courier*, February 14, 1924
[20] *Montgomery Advertiser*, February 7, 1924.

The election, held on March 11, resulted in the expected victory for Underwood. He polled 64,915 votes; Musgrove, 37,217; Dinsmore, 1,994.[21] The *Alabama Christian Advocate* believed he owed his success to the concession made to ex-Governor Comer.[22]

The national Democratic Convention, which met in New York in 1924, adopted a plank condemning the Republican party for its attitude toward prohibition. The Republican administration had failed to enforce the prohibition laws, it charged, and had become the protector of the violators of the law. The Democratic party pledged itself to enforce all laws.[23]

As early as June, 1927, presidential candidates began to enter the ring for the next battle, and contests for the delegates to the national conventions soon began. Herbert Hoover, relief administrator to Belgium during the World War, had been regarded as presidential timber as early as 1920, when the democratic *New York World* spoke favorably of him. Governor Alfred E. Smith of New York had also been mentioned as a possible candidate in that year.

Hoover had publicly expressed his faith in prohibition in 1925. He said that there was no doubt in his mind that prohibition was making America more productive. Increased temperance over the land was to his mind largely responsible for the enormously increased efficiency in production which statistics, gathered by the Department of Commerce, showed to have followed the passage of the dry law.[24] He held this position consistently in the years that followed. When Senator Borah on February 23, 1928, asked whether he favored repeal of the Eighteenth Amendment, Hoover replied flatly that he did not. He stood for the efficient, vigorous, and sincere enforcement of the laws enacted thereunder. He solemnly believed that whoever was chosen president had, under his oath, the solemn duty to pursue this course of law enforcement.[25]

The national Republican convention adopted a bone-dry plank in its platform. It reads as follows:

The people through the method provided by the Constitution have written the Eighteenth Amendment into the Constitution.
The Republican party pledges itself and its nominees to the observance and vigorous enforcement of this provision of the Constitution.[26]

Hoover was then nominated on the first ballot.

Governor Smith took the opposite stand from Hoover. He had expressed his disapproval of prohibition as an infringement of personal liberty when he signed the New York state enforcement act in 1922. In

---

[21] *Montgomery Advertiser*, March 13, 1924. Though the count was incomplete in Lowndes, Russell and Shelby, Underwood showed a majority in all but eleven counties.
[22] *Alabama Christian Advocate*, March 20, 1924.
[23] Porter, *National Party Platforms*, p. 488.
[24] *Christian Science Monitor*, March 11, 1925.
[25] *Literary Digest*, July 14, 1928.   [26] *Republican Platform*, 1928.

1924 on the eve of the Democratic national convention, he had scored the hypocritical attitude toward the whole question of temperance. He thought Congress should fix a maximum alcoholic content and leave prohibition and its enforcement to each state.[27]

Early in January, 1928, the *Montgomery Advertiser* came out with an endorsement of Smith's candidacy, and urged the election of delegates to the national convention who were in sympathy with his views. The *Montgomery Journal* came out on the other side and led the fight for a dry delegation to the Houston convention. This paper recommended that all Democrats opposing Smith cast their ballots for Harry M. Ayres, Sidney J. Bowie, A. H. Carmichael, and T. S. Faulk as delegates from the state at large. Dr. L. C. Branscomb, president of the Anti-Saloon League of Alabama, urged dry Democrats to make a second-choice vote also, as the Smith forces had only four candidates in the field while the drys had ten candidates from the state at large. The *Journal* listed the names of the dry candidates from all ten congressional districts.[28] Meanwhile the faction of the Democratic party which had always opposed prohibition in Alabama made a desperate effort to elect Mayor W. A. Gunter of Montgomery, J. C. Henderson, F. B. Nihart, and Travis Williams.

In January, 1928, the *Alabama Baptist* predicted that, if Smith were nominated, the "solid South" would become fluid and votes would flow away from the Democratic candidate. "As to Mr. Smith, everybody knows that he is as wet as the ocean," said the same paper later in the campaign, for he has systematically voted against all forms of prohibition every time he has had the chance. Neither Smith nor any of his admirers need be surprised, said the *Baptist*, if the honest-to-goodness prohibitionists were unfavorable to his candidacy.[29]

On May 8, 1928, the voters of Alabama elected a delegation unanimous in its opposition to Governor Smith. Alabama voters were unmistakably dry in sentiment, no matter how many of them were personally wet. They were opposed to modification of the prohibition laws and they thought even poorly enforced prohibition better than no prohibition at all.[30]

Governor Smith stated on June 9, 1928, that, if elected, he would execute his oath to the limit of his ability without reservation or evasion. He admitted quite frankly that he believed fundamental changes should be made in the prohibition laws; everyone knew he believed that. Such changes could, of course, be made only by the people themselves through their elected legislative representatives, but a chosen leader of the people had an inescapable duty to point the way to a sane, sensible solution of a problem whose present handling he believed to be entirely unsatisfactory to the great mass of voters. Common honesty must surely compel people

[27] *Decatur Daily*, July 28, 1928.
[28] *Montgomery Advertiser*, January 13, 14, 1928; *Montgomery Journal*, March 9, 1928.
[29] January 10, February 2, 1928.   [30] *Limestone Democrat*, July 14, 1928.

to admit that corruption of law enforcement officials, bootlegging, and lawlessness were now prevalent throughout the country. Smith was convinced that the application of the democratic principles of local self-government and state rights could secure real temperance, respect for law, and the eradication of existing evils.[81]

The Democrats, like the Republicans, wrote enforcement of the prohibition laws into their platform.

> Speaking for the national Democracy this convention pledges the party and its nominees for an honest effort to enforce the Eighteenth Amendment and all other provisions of the Federal Constitution and all laws enacted pursuant thereto.[82]

Governor Smith was then nominated. The twenty-four Alabama delegates to the National Democratic Convention at Houston, Texas, had been instructed to vote against Smith, but they could not prevent his nomination by an overwhelming vote.[83]

With similar bone-dry planks in both party platforms, the campaign tended to center around candidates rather than platform promises. And those candidates, through pre-campaign pronouncements, had made prohibition the principal issue.

After the convention had adjourned, Governor Smith sent Chairman Joe Robinson a telegram which was generally interpreted by many prohibitionists as a repudiation of the dry plank in the platform.[84] He further antagonized many prohibitionists when he made John J. Raskob of Delaware national chairman of the Democratic party. Raskob was a Republican, a Catholic, and a pronounced wet who, as director of the Association Against the Prohibition Amendment, was considered a leading advocate of repeal. And when, in a Milwaukee speech, Smith declared that prohibition was a farce, that it was a source of corruption in public service, that it bred disrespect for all law and was the principal cause of the new form of crime called "racketeering," the rage of the drys reached new heights. Smith cited in this speech statements of General Lincoln Andrews and Chester P. Mills, Republican prohibition administrators. He declared that the Volstead Act set a dishonest and unworkable limit in its definition of *intoxicating beverages*. He suggested that Congress, by expert advice, provide for higher maximum alcoholic contents and let the states legislate as they saw fit. He came out openly in favor of another amendment restoring liquor control to the states, but prohibiting the return of the saloon. Nor did he retract any of his statements when he made his speech of acceptance on August 22.[85]

[81] *Literary Digest*, July 14, 1928.
[82] *Democratic Platform, 1928.*
[83] *Mobile Register*, July 1, 1928.
[84] Smith's telegram read: ". . . It is well known that I believe that there should be fundamental changes in the present provisions for national prohibition, based as I stated in my Jackson Day letter, on the fearless application to the problem of the principles of Jeffersonian Democracy. . . ." *Mobile Register*, July 8, 1928.
[85] *Decatur Daily*, August 23, 1928.

A few Alabama editors vigorously urged their Democratic readers to vote against Smith. Some were lukewarm in their attitude. But most of the newspapers of the state pleaded for loyalty to the Democratic ticket from top to bottom. The *Foley Onlooker* said: "We are going to do all in our power to defeat the Democratic presidential candidate because the ideals of the South and future welfare of the nation are far more important than the solidity of the Democratic party, the control of which has been temporarily gained by the most corrupt, vicious and lawless political machine of the nation."[36] "As we see it," said the *Abbeville Herald*, "the hour has struck when dry Democrats stand at the parting of the ways. To surrender now, to dance to the crack of the party lash, to bow our necks to the wet yoke of Tammany controlled democracy is asking Southern Democrats to surrender a principle too sacred to be cast aside."[37] The *South Alabamian* (Jackson) asked who was less a Democrat—the man who would not accept the party platform or the man who would not accept the party nominee? Did the nominee have a right to reserve exceptions to the party platform? If so, did the voter have a right to reserve exceptions to the party's nominee?[38]

"There is little doubt but Alabama is nearer this year to dropping out of Democratic ranks than the state has ever been before," said the *Decatur Daily*.[39] The *Roanoke Leader* which had opposed the nomination of Smith was temperate. "The first concern that should be given consideration by all of us is that we determine to consider carefully the issue involved, keeping a good humor, and resolve to allow the other fellow the right to act as he sees best in the circumstances."[40] The *Greensboro Watchman* regarded the insertion of dry planks in both the Democratic and Republican platforms as an acknowledgment that the people of the United States were for prohibition and strict enforcement of the liquor laws.[41] The *Limestone Democrat*, which had been a vigorous opponent of the Smith nomination, swung into line, saying "Governor Smith won in a fair fight, and this paper expects to support him for the election. It does not expect any considerable majority of Alabama Dry Democrats to leave the party, believing that they would rather stay inside the ranks and pin their faith on dry legislators."[42] And the *Mobile Register* declared: "The platform rings true to party profession, the party record and party principles. No platform could do more."[43]

"We are wondering how prohibitionists, men and women who favor the continuation of the prohibition laws, can bring themselves to support Mr. Smith's program of modification," commented the *Alabama Christian Advocate*. "Thousands of people have already solved this problem. They positively cannot support Governor Smith. They are loyal Democrats,

[36] *Mobile Register*, July 11, 1928.
[38] *Ibid.*
[40] *Ibid.*
[42] *Limestone Democrat*, July 5, 1928.
[37] *Mobile Register*, July 11, 1928.
[39] *Ibid.*
[41] *Ibid.*
[43] July 1, 1928.

have always stood by the party, believe in its principles, glorified its traditions and its past achievements, and hate far more than they can express to see it go again into defeat, but they cannot support Governor Smith."⁴⁴

The *Alabama Baptist*, while condemning the shrewd politics of the Republican party, conceded that that party had nominated an excellent man. It would not take conscientious prohibitionists long to decide between Hoover and Smith. Certainly such men could not vote for Smith. Party alignments would be thrown to the wind. Said the *Baptist:* "Mr. Smith is as sure to be defeated as two and two make four."⁴⁵

Many of the Protestant ministers of Birmingham and other parts of the state announced immediately after the Houston Convention that they would actively oppose Smith. The *Birmingham Post* took a poll which showed that two thirds of these clergymen would speak against Smith either directly or indirectly. Not one minister approached by the *Post* poll takers said he would support or vote for Smith.⁴⁶ "I do not see how any 100 per cent American can vote for Smith: I am against him to the end," Trevonor Mordecai, pastor of the First Presbyterian Church, declared.⁴⁷ The Reverend C. H. Mansfield, Methodist, said he would show in his sermon the following day that Christ stood for the best interest of the people as a whole and not for party. He believed that the people should vote for the best man and not necessarily for the party's choice. Dr. Arthur J. Moore, pastor of the Birmingham First Methodist Church, indicated that he would not vote for the Democratic nominee and that he might later have something to say about the campaign from his pulpit.

The *Montgomery Advertiser* disapproved of such statements. An editorial, "Protestant Bigotry in Birmingham," asserted that "all the political preachers," who considered prohibition laws the most important in the land, were stupidly flying in the face of the Bible and of God's plan of saving man. They were sinfully taking one of man's great temptations out of the way. This was one reason why prohibition had failed.⁴⁸

In Montgomery, Dr. John W. Frazer, pastor of the Court Street Methodist Church, predicted that, "the vast majority of protestant clergymen in the United States will vote for Hoover irrespective of party." Religion and politics were not separated interests, Dr. Frazer declared. Man's religious and political thinking was organically related, and the history of religion was very largely the history of political science. The *Montgomery Advertiser* thought Dr. Frazer's sermon was a moral repudiation of Jefferson's Virginia Statute of Religious Freedom; it was nothing less than a political address.⁴⁹

. The Woman's Christian Temperance Union of Alabama opened their fight against Alfred E. Smith on July 10, 1928, when Mrs. Mary T. Jeffries, President, called on the women of all reform groups to oppose the

⁴⁴ July 5, 1928.
⁴⁵ *Alabama Baptist*, July 19, 1928.
⁴⁶ June 30, 1928.
⁴⁷ *Montgomery Advertiser*, July 1, 1928.
⁴⁸ *Montgomery Advertiser*, July 3, 1928.
⁴⁹ *Ibid.*, July 4, 1928.

Democratic nominee. Women of the W.C.T.U., she said, had been taught to love and honor the Democratic party. They were deeply grieved that this party had nominated Governor Smith, of New York, an avowed enemy of prohibition. But inasmuch as Governor Smith had repudiated the party platform, Democrats were absolved from supporting him; he did not reflect the spirit of his party. The South would not vote for Smith, and the W.C.T.U., a million strong, would stand together against him.[50]

Anti-Smith forces from twelve states, mostly Southern, held a conference in Asheville, North Carolina, on July 18 and 19, 1928, to plan their campaign to win the South for Herbert Hoover. The 267 delegates were supposed to be dry anti-Smith Democrats bent on electing dry Democratic congressmen, and state and county officials. The conference planned to set up for each state an executive committee consisting of a man and a woman. The Alabama Division was under the leadership of L. C. Branscomb of Gadsden, and Mrs. Mary T. Jeffries of Birmingham. Headquarters were established at Richmond, Virginia, the home of Bishop James Cannon, Jr., of the Methodist Episcopal Church, South, who with Dr. A. J. Barton of Atlanta, a Baptist leader, had called the meeting. The delegates termed Smith's telegram to the National Convention "an action of brazen political effrontery," and charged that he had emphasized his opposition to prohibition to secure wet Republican votes especially in the North and East. They regarded Governor Smith as "aggressively, irreconcilably wet." "It is unthinkable," read their report, "that the moral, religious leadership of the South can be a party to the election of such a man as Governor Smith, thus being guilty of an open betrayal of the great social, economic, and moral reform which was won for our children and our homes after years of unselfish labor."[51]

This Asheville conference moved the *Mobile Register* to remark that prohibition, whether right or wrong, wise or unwise, had been written into the Constitution of the United States, and that no man was fit to hold any political office, who did not believe wholeheartedly in upholding that provision so long as it was a part of the Constitution, and who was not willing to take an oath to uphold it in its completeness.[52]

The anti-Smith Democrats of Alabama, under the leadership of J. Bibb Mills, superintendent of the Anti-Saloon League of Alabama, inspired by the Asheville convention announced on July 28, that they would hold a meeting in Birmingham on August 13, to start a campaign against Governor Smith. Mills announced that Bishop James Cannon, Jr., would attend the meeting.[53] When the convention met, it adopted ringing resolutions, denouncing Smith as an opponent of the platform and policies of the Democratic party and charging that his election would mean an abandonment of the party's pledge for the maintenance of white supremacy.

[50] *Mobile Register*, July 15, 1928.
[52] *Mobile Register*, July 22, 1928.
[51] *Ibid.*, July 20, 1928.
[53] *Ibid.*, July 28, 1928.

The delegates then addressed an open letter to the Democrats of the state urging them to join in a campaign for an electoral ticket which would support Herbert Hoover.[54]

Before these anti-Smith Democrats met in Birmingham, Hugh Locke had given out a statement to the press that he had been invited and would attend the meeting. He had been, he said, requested to explain his action publicly and he had no hesitancy in doing so. The Democratic Convention, he declared, had endorsed the Eighteenth Amendment and the acts passed in keeping with it, and had committed the party to their enforcement, with the adoption of the strongest prohibition plank ever set forth by any party. Smith's forces at Houston had studiously avoided the prohibition issue, until after his nomination. Then Smith, with his belated telegram of acceptance, had nullified the dry plank of the party platform and had attempted to commit the party to modification. He had no right to do this, said Locke. The nominee's duty was to lead party members toward the objects expressed in their platform. In repudiating the platform, Smith had rebelled against the lawfully expressed purposes of the party. As a Democrat Locke could not follow his example. He stood firmly, he declared, on that platform and he would fight for the integrity of the party. He would, nevertheless, support every local Democrat; they should not suffer defeat because of the "Tool of Tammany and of his appointee, Raskob."

Locke also defended the W.C.T.U. and the Christian ministry. They had, he said, aroused the laymen from their lethargy and had made the nation dry. In 1907 their critics had professed to fear that their activities would disrupt their congregations and ruin their churches, but those critics were wrong. They were now being bullied with dire warnings, when failure to fight would be evidence that they no longer cared for a great cause and that the liquor spokesmen had bullied them into silence. "This is no time for political cowardice," Locke concluded. "Let us not be

[54] *Mobile Register*, August 15, 1928. The resolution in the open letter was as follows: "Therefore, be it resolved by this the Alabama Conference of the anti-Smith Democrats that we do hereby officially proclaim to the white Democrats of Alabama:

(1) That we pledge our support to the congressional state and county nominees of the Democratic party in Alabama.

(2) That Alfred E. Smith has betrayed the Democratic party, that he has deserted the party by abandoning its platform, that our duty to restore the national Democratic party to its original purpose, and to reclaim its honesty and decency, and to insure the continuance of white supremacy demands the defeat of Alfred E. Smith.

(3) That the executive committee of this body arrange for the names of twelve leaders to conform to the views of this body on the ballot of the election to be held in November, 1928, and that the white Democrats in Alabama be and are hereby called upon to vote for and support said candidates.

(4) That in the absence of a Democratic candidate for the exalted office of the president of the United States, this convention endorses and pledges electors supported by this body to cast the electoral vote of the sovereign state of Alabama for the Hon. Herbert Hoover, for president of the United States of America."

bullied into silence. Let us dare to do right."⁵⁵ "The friends of temperance throughout the state were greatly heartened when they read the address of the jurist, long prominent in legal circles in this state," said the *Alabama Christian Advocate* after Locke's statement had been made public.⁵⁶

To win as many Democratic votes as possible, the Republican leaders of Alabama chose, on August 30, twelve persons who had been active in the Democratic party as their candidates for presidential electors. The Alabama conference of anti-Smith Democrats which had been formed in Birmingham about two weeks earlier, drew up this list and the Republican executive committee approved it. It named one elector from each of the ten congressional districts and two from the state-at-large. One Alabama legislator, J. O. Webb of Waverly, was included in the group; his name appeared as a Hoover and Curtis elector from the Fifth District. J. S. Benson of Scottsboro, who had been a delegate to the Houston convention and opposed the nomination of Smith, was nominated from the Eighth District. Mrs. Mary T. Jeffries of Birmingham, president of the Alabama W.C.T.U., and George H. Malone, of Dothan, who had taken a leading part in the organization of the anti-Smith Democrats, were the two electors from the state-at-large.⁵⁷

The *Montgomery Advertiser,* in an editorial, "The Klan Names Them," at once charged that Judge Oliver D. Street and the other leaders of the Republican party in Alabama had succumbed to the Klan and let it control the selection of candidates for electors. The slate included not a single old-line Republican, although some of the men on it had voted the Republican national ticket and others had been uncertain in their party allegiance. "Today Judge Street is walking arm-in-arm with Grand Dragon Jim Esdale and Dr. L. C. Branscomb, president of the Anti-

⁵⁵ *Alabama Christian Advocate,* August 9, 1928. Locke further said: "Furthermore, since his [Smith's] nomination the entire plan of campaign had been wet. He had appointed John J. Raskob national chairman who accepted, he said, in order to rid the nation of the 'damnable affliction of prohibition.' There was nothing in the platform justifying such a battle cry. Senator Reed, speaking in Missouri against Mr. Hayes, a dry candidate for the Democratic nomination for the senate, had argued in effect that to nominate a prohibitionist would be 'arguing with ourselves.' His meaning was clear that the Democratic party under Smith was the wet party. Senator Reed was well informed as to the Smith plan of campaign. Senator Copeland of New York, while speaking in Chicago, had said the Democratic party was the party of modification and the Republican party must face the issue. Senator Copeland was also well informed of the Smith plan of campaign. He was either entirely ignorant of or entirely ignored the wishes of the states which had consistently voted for democratic principles."

⁵⁶ August 16, 1928.

⁵⁷ *Mobile Register,* August 31, 1928. The electors from the other eight districts were as follows: First—Mrs. Martha Yeager, Mobile; Second—Dr. A. P. Webb, Atmore; Third—E. C. Glover, Abbeville; Fourth—Dr. M. J. Williams, Oxford; Sixth—O. C. Oakley, Centerville; Seventh—Mrs. J. B. Wadsworth, Gadsden; Ninth—Dr. J. M. Hankins, Birmingham; Tenth—Mrs. Zue Musgrove Long, Jasper.

Saloon League—another Catholic-hating organization. These two are out to nail Al Smith to a Crucifix while Judge Street holds the torchlight!"[58]

Interviewed by the *Mobile Register,* Senator J. Thomas Heflin stated that he was against Governor Smith, but he refused to say whether he would stay away from the polls in November, or go and vote for Hoover. He believed in cleaning house within the Democratic party, he said. Smith's stand on prohibition and immigration and his appointment of Raskob, in Heflin's opinion, furnished ground for any loyal Democrat to scratch the party nominee from the ticket. "They have asked me if I could not take my crow and eat it. I can. But I cannot eat buzzard served with Tammany sauce," Heflin remarked.

Ex-Governor W. W. Brandon had invited the Senator to speak under his and Congressman Oliver's direction. Heflin said he could not accept this invitation. He wired Brandon: "As one star differs from another star in glory, so the Democratic party of the South in purpose, practice, and principles differs from the Tammany-cratic party in the East." He closed his telegram with the announcement that his next speech would be delivered in Montgomery. Attacks on city and state Democratic leaders and the opposition press figured largely in this Montgomery speech. Heflin charged them with obtaining "sugar from the Pope." The Democratic party, he affirmed, would not be turned over to Tammany "so long as I can help it." When he finished speaking, there was no doubt that Senator Heflin had unequivocally aligned himself with the Alabama organization opposing the election of the Democratic nominee.[59]

Major Emmett P. Smith of Montgomery, attached to the Rainbow Division during the World War, attacked the prohibition stand of the Democratic standard bearer before a Republican rally in Mobile in Bienville Square on September 26. He declared that Governor Smith's record, as a member of the New York legislature and as Governor of New York, showed very clearly his enmity toward prohibition. Under his influence and with his consent, New York had repealed her enforcement laws and that state had thus become the wettest spot on the continent. When Governor Smith selected a dripping wet Republican, Raskob, to lead and direct the Democratic forces in the campaign, the Major asserted, he had sealed his own defeat in November.

Major Smith charged that certain supporters of Smith in Alabama had injected the religious issue in the campaign; among others he named ex-Governor W. W. Brandon, Forney Johnson of Birmingham and ex-Senator Underwood. The question had been first raised, he said, in 1924 when Forney Johnson, an Underwood delegate to the convention, hurled the firebrand of religious hatred upon the floor of the Democratic national convention in his speech nominating Senator Underwood. Applause greeted Major Smith's denunciation of the "liquor trinity," the *Birmingham*

[58] August 31, 1928.   [59] *Mobile Register,* September 21, 1928.

News, the *Birmingham Age-Herald,* and the *Montgomery Advertiser* There was laughter when he said that the *Advertiser* had bolted the Democratic party in 1896 and was "now trying to read me a lecture because I cannot and will not vote for Al Smith." "I always wash my hands with bichloride of mercury to eliminate any danger of contamination while handling that paper," he remarked. Then he summed up his position in the statement that Tammany Hall had wrecked the Democratic party and that the only way to get rid of Tammany control was to vote against Smith.[60]

The *Alabama Christian Advocate* declared that Christian people could not be expected to support a candidate who was openly against prohibition. "To do so would be to renounce, and trample under foot, all their former prohibition convictions." The important point at issue, this paper asserted, was not the election of any particular man, but the preservation of the prohibition laws and the strict enforcement of them. Thousands of Democrats would vote against Smith, but their action could not be called disloyalty to the party. The South's opposition to Smith on the prohibition issue amounted to a revolution, said the *Advocate;* it was doubtful that Governor Smith would carry a single state in the South except South Carolina.[61]

Some of the Baptist Associations opposed the election of Governor Smith. The Mobile Baptist Association, noting with concern that great influences were at work to elect a president "well known as a faithful friend of liquor and an inveterate enemy of prohibition," resolved that "no such man shall ever become president with our help," and pledged support to "all agencies and efforts that looked to the maintenance of the Eighteenth Amendment and the Volstead Act and complete enforcement thereof."[62] The Birmingham Baptist Association, on October 17, resolved that anyone who advocated the return of alcohol should be returned to private life, no matter what party he belonged to.[63]

The Democratic party had been in power in Alabama continuously since 1874. People had long since acquired the habit of voting the Democratic ticket. It seemed unlikely that the state would go over to the Republican party. Yet the leaders, seeing old loyalties falter, became apprehensive and acted to discourage and discipline bolters.

As early as July 4, E. W. Pettus, chairman of the state Democratic committee, announced in a public statement that Democrats were expected

[60] *Mobile Register,* September 27, 1928. Major Smith also stated that the day before the religious question was raised in the convention of 1924, he wired Governor Brandon, chairman of the Underwood delegation, and begged him not to permit the question to be raised. Smith declared that Brandon had it in his power to prevent "this political catastrophe." His failure to hold Johnson in check was responsible for the religious question being a burning issue in the campaign of 1928.
[61] *Alabama Christian Advocate,* July 19, August 9, 23, 1928.
[62] *Minutes, 1928.*
[63] *Alabama Baptist,* November 1, 1928.

to be Democrats whether or not the party caucus, convention or primary chose candidates personally acceptable to individuals. Any person in Alabama who voted against Governor Smith in the general election, he warned, would run the risk of being barred from participating in the Alabama Democratic primary in 1930, when a governor and other state officials would be elected.[64]

Some ardent drys, Senator J. M. Bonner among them, announced that they would support the ticket. Bonner was convinced, he said, that a division within the ranks of the party would practically destroy its usefulness. He warned the preachers against supporting Hoover and thus working to disrupt the party. Hugh Mallory of Selma, a Baptist and a dry, gave his wholehearted support to Smith. He considered him, he said, far superior to Hoover, and predicted that Smith would win and that the Democratic party would carry the solid South. T. D. Samford also remained loyal to the party.[65]

In close cooperation with Chairman Raskob, the Democratic executive committee functioned under the leadership of E. W. Pettus. To assist him Congressman W. B. Oliver was selected chairman of the state Democratic campaign committee. In Oliver the executive committee had selected an able leader, an efficient lawyer, a scholar, an excellent speaker, a Presbyterian and a prohibitionist.[66] Oliver's appeal to the Democrats of Alabama emphasized the importance of party loyalty and solidarity. He commented at great length on the high character and great attainments of Smith and discussed, frankly and with crushing force, the objections to the nominee on the ground that he was a Tammanyite and a Roman Catholic. He attacked the sincerity of Hoover's prohibition pretensions. Finally he declared, "You cannot separate the candidate from the party. . . . You cannot vote for Hoover without endangering the solid South. If you succeed in breaking the solid South, you will awaken to the fact that you have destroyed your party and will have none to which to return." The *Montgomery Advertiser* considered Oliver's appeal "one of the proudest, sanest, and most convincing documents from the standpoint of a Southern Democrat" which it had seen.[67]

Judge B. M. Miller stumped the state for the Democratic nominee. At Centerville he voiced his confidence in the honesty and patriotism of Governor Smith. He had been a life-long prohibitionist and one of the first circuit judges in Alabama to impose hard labor sentences on violators of the dry laws. Now he asserted boldly that he was not afraid of any move to repeal or modify the prohibition laws.[68]

Senator John H. Bankhead campaigned vigorously for party regularity

[64] *Montgomery Advertiser*, July 5, 1928.
[65] *Montgomery Advertiser*, July 25, 26, 27, 1928.
[66] *Ibid.*, August 16, 1928.
[67] *Montgomery Advertiser*, September 3, 4, 1928.
[68] *Ibid.*, September 4, 1928.

both with his voice and with his pen. Two elements of discontent, he pointed out, entered into the contest in the state—religion and temperance. But, he added, even if a man had opposed the nomination of Governor Smith, he could not remain a Democrat without supporting the party's nominee and voting the Democratic ticket.[69]

The prohibition question Senator Bankhead dismissed as irrelevant. A president, he remarked, could not change the prohibition laws, nor could he force Congress to accept his views on the subject. President Taft had vetoed the Webb-Kenyon bill—a prohibition measure. A Republican Congress, by more than a two-thirds vote, passed it over his veto. Each senator and each representative had his own views and commitments on prohibition and each was responsible to his constituents. His continuance in public life depended on how accurately he reflected the views of the people who put him into office. He was responsible to them, not the president. Bankhead believed that the prohibition laws would be safeguarded by Congress, regardless of which candidate was elected.

Bankhead met the allegation that Governor Smith had "bolted" the party platform by citing Senator Glass, of Virginia, dry leader and author of the party's prohibition plank. Moving the adoption of this plank, Glass had clearly said: "It does not commit anybody to the theory of prohibition. It does not restrain or constrain anybody of the opposite opinion."[70] These words, Bankhead pointed out, were spoken by a man recognized as one of the strongest prohibitionists among the Democrats of the nation.[71]

Speaking at the courthouse in Tuscaloosa, Judge Bernard Harwood used a different argument to secure party regularity. He reviewed the history of the Republican party. He recalled the dark days of Reconstruction when many of the best white men in the state were deprived of the franchise and when many public offices were held by carpetbaggers, scalawags, and Negroes. "The Republican party still smells strongly of the Negro," he said. He quoted at length A. B. Moore's description of the state officials and members of the general assembly during Republican rule in Alabama. The passage he selected could hardly fail to arouse the pugnacious instincts of any loyal Democrat.[72]

Every daily newspaper in Alabama and practically all of the weeklies

---

[69] *Decatur Daily*, August 21, 1928. Bankhead said: "I did not favor the nomination of Governor Smith. My position was given publicity before the primary. But I am a Democrat by inheritance and acquired faith. I do not propose to be herded into the Republican party. I shall continue to carry the Democratic flag with pride and satisfaction. The only way to be a Democrat is to support its nominee. . . . There is but one effective and legal way to remain a Democrat. This one and effective legal way is to vote the Democratic ticket."

[70] *Decatur Daily*, August 21, 1928.

[71] *Birmingham News*, August 20, 1928; *Decatur Daily*, August 21, 1928.

[72] *History of Alabama* (1927), pp. 591-593.

In addition to these speakers many other prominent men took the stump for Smith. Among them were W. W. Brandon, Leon McCord, A. H. Carmichael, Borden Burr, J. Manley Foster, John McDuffie, Henry B. Steagall, Harwell G. Davis, and Lister Hill.

endorsed Governor Smith. The *Mobile Register* and the *Alabama Journal* were fair to both sides but were committed to Smith. The *Montgomery Advertiser* strongly championed the cause of the Democratic nominee. Governor Smith's desire to modify the law had this paper's wholehearted approval: "He knows, as do all open-eyed, fair-minded observers that the present laws must be changed, if real enforcement is to be practicable." Smith's religious handicap worried the *Advertiser* more than his prohibition views. "He will lose some votes because of his views on the Volstead Act; he will lose more votes because he is a Roman Catholic."[73]

Ministers who opposed Smith came in for plenty of rough handling from the *Advertiser*, which accused them of "quitting" the pulpit and going into politics. Their sermons were a butt for ridicule. The Reverend Arthur Moore, one of Birmingham's pulpit bosses and pastor of the First Methodist Church of that city, the paper commented one day, made a speech for the Republican ticket in his church. The *Advertiser* added that the anti-Smith Democratic headquarters "thought so well of the political oration that they have sent out copies of it over the state."[74]

The Reverend Bob Jones also drew the *Advertiser's* fire. The paper called him "the plutocratic evangelist," and sarcastically commented that he had evidently tendered his services to the Republican cause on the plausible theory that a "fool was needed to pep things up in Alabama." The *Advertiser* in an editorial on "Big Hearted Bob" claimed that Jones had been allowed to assume a position of leadership with the "boss bolters" and that he had agreed to make a hundred speeches for the Republican party in Alabama. At Newville in Henry County, according to the *Advertiser*, he had made a characteristic speech full of shady misrepresentation of the Democratic candidate and vile attacks on the candidate's church. He had referred to the *Dothan Eagle* as the Dothan "Buzzard." He had called the *Advertiser* a "polecat." But such tactics were to be expected from Jones, as was hat-passing. It always cost a "wad of money to hear Bob speak no matter whether he was saving one's soul or country," was the *Advertiser's* caustic comment.

Everyone knew, the editorial went on, that the Ku Klux Klan had hired J. Thomas Heflin, United States Senator, to go up and down the country reviling Smith and his co-religionists. The Anti-Saloon League had long been known to make a practice of hiring such members of Congress as were open to propositions to work in the interest of that organization. Neither the Klan nor the League would hesitate to hire a thrifty bond-holding evangelist like Jones. In sarcasm, the editor remarked that the Republican managers must have lifted their brows and said, "That is strange," when they heard that Bob Jones was working for them without charge and even paying his own expenses.[75]

[73] *Montgomery Advertiser*, July 8, August 3, 8, September 5, 1928.
[74] *Montgomery Advertiser*, July 8, August 3, 8, September 5, 1928.
[75] *Montgomery Advertiser*, August 21, 1928.

The *Advertiser* was indignant that the anti-Smith forces had injected the religious issue into the campaign. It complained that at a Republican rally at Thorsby the speakers had definitely accentuated the religious issue. It noted that O. D. Street, Republican national committeeman, was accusing the Smith newspapers of denouncing the preachers who opposed their candidate. It charged that C. B. Kennemer, United States District Attorney for the Northern District of Alabama, had attacked Governor Smith on religious grounds, when he spoke at Gadsden.

Smith's religion was also attacked, the *Advertiser* reported, by anonymous literature coming into Alabama from blind addresses in New York and Detroit. From Detroit came the spurious "Knights of Columbus Oath," known by all informed persons to be a downright forgery, and this spurious document had been widely distributed. The New York literature upheld "two unwritten laws in America"; the first that no president should serve more than two terms, the second that no Roman Catholic should ever be president. Anti-Catholic agents were roaming through Alabama distributing these vicious tracts and making scurrilous verbal attacks upon Governor Smith's church. Some of them pretended to be former Catholics. Later in the campaign the Smith forces charged that the Republican campaign committee was persistently sending anti-Catholic literature to the voters in Alabama. The *Advertiser* reported that Oliver D. Street was sending out 200,000 circulars attacking Smith and his church.[76]

The National Committee for the Repeal of the Eighteenth Amendment distributed literature sometimes offensive to prohibitionists and embarrassing to loyal Democrats. Raskob, vice-president of the Association Against the Prohibition Amendment, declared that he had no connection with this committee. But the public found it difficult to keep the difference in names clearly in mind, and in spite of Raskob's repudiation of it, the National Committee for Repeal freely used the name of the Democratic nominee. Floods of postcards, bearing on the front in large letters "Smith elected will speed up the repeal of the Volstead act, but we must have the support of a majority of Congress," were distributed. On the other side of the card was the voter's pledge: "I favor repeal of the Volstead act, so that beer and wine may be legally sold and the government get the profits that now go to the bootleggers; I solemnly pledge that I will vote against congressmen who vote dry and drink wet, and all those congressmen who have received money or political support from the Anti-Saloon League, the W.C.T.U., or bootleggers, so there will be a liberal majority in the next Congress to help Al Smith give the people beer, by repealing the Volstead act."

Cartoons were freely used and circulated by the Democratic national committee in New York. One of them, insulting to every advocate of

[76] *Montgomery Advertiser*, August 12, October 4, 8, 1928.

prohibition in the United States, portrayed a woman labeled "Temperance" standing in the middle of a map of the United States. She was covering her ears with her hands and was evidently in great distress as she exclaimed: "Must we endure eight more years of this?" Around her were disreputable figures labeled "Demoralized Youth," "High Law Violators," "Racketeers," "High-Jackers," "Crooked Dry Agents," and "Bootlegger." This and other cartoons appear to prove conclusively that Eastern forces in charge of the party were doing all in their power to represent the Democratic party as the champion of the liquor advocates, and to represent prohibition as an unbearable nuisance.[77]

In the heat of the campaign crowds sometimes violently expressed disapproval of speeches by throwing eggs, bottles, and other missiles. The most notable case of throwing eggs at the speaker occurred in the Anniston high school on November 5. While Senator Heflin was delivering a bitter tirade against the Democratic nominee, the Catholic Church, and the *Anniston Star*, he was "showered with eggs." Several eggs fell around him and spattered his clothes. The *Montgomery Advertiser* had remarked that egg-throwing was about as good a way as it knew to start a riot. It urged the people to be good sportsmen and to give every speaker a fair hearing, whether or not they liked the things he said.[78]

The national election of November 6, 1928, resulted in overwhelming defeat for the Democratic ticket. The only surprise in the outcome was the size of the Hoover majority. Prohibition and Protestantism had proved too strong for the New York Governor. His untimely telegram to the National Convention, his selection of John J. Raskob as chairman of the national Democratic executive committee, and his adverse comments on prohibition before and during the campaign were fatal errors. They had all helped to crystallize the opposition against him. His selection of a Republican as his generalissimo had seemed to set his stamp of approval upon bolting one's party, and many of his fellow Democrats took the course suggested. Many Democrats had apparently voted the Republican ticket, but they had not thereby become Republicans any more than Raskob had become a Democrat when he aligned himself with Smith.

The Democratic nominee carried Alabama by a very small margin. The Democratic electors defeated the Republican electors by a vote of 127,696 to 120,725.[79] In an editorial, "Alabama in Smith Column," the *Decatur Daily* attempted to explain this vote. Both the religious and prohibition issues, the editor thought, had tended to weaken Governor Smith and to shift normally Democratic votes to the Republican candidate. Church leaders had demonstrated that their influence was of greater importance than political party lines. The editorial ended on an optimistic note:

[77] *Mobile Register*, August 8, October 16, 1928.
[78] *Montgomery Advertiser*, September 8, 1928; *Anniston Star*, November 6, 1928.
[79] *Alabama Official and Statistical Register* (1931), pp. 511-512.

"Turning from the South, for a moment, the election gives the prohibitionists of America much to be encouraged over."[80]

The *Mobile Register* remarked that one lesson had surely been learned for all time; it was that no candidate repugnant to an important section of the party membership could be crammed down the throats of the rank and file of voters.[81]

The *Montgomery Advertiser* considered the victory won by the militant and unfaltering Democrats of Alabama a tribute to the sanity and liberalism of the people of the state. Their verdict for Alfred E. Smith was evidence that the most stupendous and unscrupulous effort to deceive the people ever made in the history of the state had failed. The *Advertiser* believed that thousands of Alabamians who voted against Smith would live to see the error of their ways and to regret their hasty and ill-advised decision to follow the unworthy leadership which had tricked them into an attitude of irreconcilable hostility to that "great Democrat and genuinely good man."[82]

Although some prohibitionists, out of loyalty to party traditions, voted for the Democratic candidate, the *Alabama Baptist* commented, yet prohibition had been thoroughly vindicated by what was in effect a popular referendum.[83]

The committee on temperance at the North Alabama Conference, which met in Birmingham on November 7 to 12, congratulated the people of the country on the stupendous and glorious victory so recently and overwhelmingly registered by ballot for the preservation of the Eighteenth Amendment and for the cause of prohibition.[84]

The committee on social conditions and service at the Alabama Baptist State Convention reported that they had hailed with delight the dawn of the day of prohibition and they still rejoiced in it. Amid many difficulties and the embarrassments of enforcement, it had received its just acclaim from the American people, who had put brakes on the demoralizing habit of drinking. The chairman of the committee suggested that, now that the American people had given a new impetus to prohibition, it would be well for them to begin an educational program on the question of alcohol.[85]

The problem of the enforcement of the prohibition laws was an important one. During the administration of Governor Kilby, the legislature established a law enforcement department to supplement the efforts of county officers. The principal duty of this department was to bring to justice violators of the prohibition law. In his message to the legislature on September 14, 1920, Governor Kilby said that the law enforcement

---

[80] November 8, 1928.
[81] *Mobile Register*, November 10, 1928.
[82] *Montgomery Advertiser*, November 7, 1928.
[83] *Alabama Baptist*, November 15, 1928.
[84] *Journal of the North Alabama Conference, (November 7-12, 1928)*, p. 69.
[85] *Annual of the Alabama Baptist State Convention* (1928), p. 135.

department had been helpful but that the appropriation of $20,000 was inadequate and the force of ten men was too small to cope with the situation. He declared that daily calls were being made for men from this department but, since they were so few in number, they could respond only to the most urgent pleas. He recommended that the appropriation for the maintenance of this force be increased to $50,000 per year and that he be given authority to employ as many men as were needed to enforce the law.[86] The legislature passed the appropriation requested and authorized the governor to employ thirty men instead of ten.[87]

When W. W. Brandon became Governor in January, 1923, he was greatly concerned with the increase in prohibition law violations. He asked that the appropriation for law enforcement should be substantially increased. The legislature made an additional annual appropriation of $50,000 for the faithful execution of the laws.[88] Nevertheless, when Brandon left office in 1927, his message to the legislature showed that the prohibition laws were still unenforced. During the last three years of Kilby's administration 1,903 arrests were made for violating one aspect of prohibition laws; the number increased to 6,192 during the Brandon administration. Governor Brandon recommended that ten additional men be added to the law enforcement department.[89]

By the time Bibb Graves became Governor in 1927, the transportation of liquor by automobile had become a serious problem. The illicit distiller often transported his product several hundred miles to deliver it to dealers in urban centers. He could thus easily conceal his illegal and profitable business. To prevent this malpractice, the legislature in 1927 made it unlawful to transport, in quantities of five gallons or more, any of the liquors, or beverages, the sale, possession, or transportation of which was prohibited by law in Alabama. Any person convicted of violating the act was guilty of a felony and subject to imprisonment in the state penitentiary for a period of not less than one nor more than five years.[90]

The constitutionality of this act was upheld by the Alabama Supreme Court in 1930 in the case, Ray v. State. The law was declared air-tight, in full force and effect.[91]

The legislature of 1927 authorized the sheriff to confiscate all vehicles and animals used to transport liquor illegally. The state was not required to prove any actual movement of said vehicle or animal but only that it was loaded with prohibited liquors or beverages.[92]

In 1929 the dry laws were further strengthened by judicial interpretation. The Alabama Supreme Court declared in Jinright v. the State that the purchaser of liquor was as guilty of violating the law as the seller.

[86] *House Journal, Special Session* (1920), p. 21.
[87] *Acts, Special Session* (1920), pp. 8-9.
[88] *General Laws* (1923), p. 560.
[89] *Senate Journal*, I (1927), 63-65.
[90] *General Acts* (1927), pp. 704-705.
[91] *Southern Reporter*, Vol. 127, pp. 799-800.
[92] *General Acts* (1927), p. 715.

The *Alabama Courier* remarked at that time: "Alabama heads the list in the defense of the Volstead Act."[93]

During the thirteen years in which the Eighteenth Amendment was in force prohibition laws were often violated. The number of arrests annually by Federal agents varied from 594 to 1,615. The number of stills seized yearly was irregular. In 1920 the number of seizures was 1,380. This number declined to 716 in 1926, but reached the maximum of 1,716 in 1932. The quantity of distilled spirits seized also showed considerable variation, but the seizures reached a peak in 1932-1933. Federal agents reported the seizure of 1,507 gallons in 1920; 10,150 gallons in 1923; 5,999 in 1924; and 10,956 in 1933. No automobiles and trucks were reported seized prior to 1923; 40 were taken over in that year, 135 in 1927 and 276 in 1933.[94]

[93] *Southern Reporter*, Vol. 125, pp. 606-608.
[94] *A Statement of the Number of Arrests and Seizures by Federal Prohibition Agents in Alabama, 1920-1933.*

Year	No. Persons Arrested	Stills Seized	No. Gal. Distilled Spirits Seized	No. Autos and Trucks Seized
1920		1,380	1,570	
1921	594	1,180	3,449	
1922	663	777	4,119	
1923	857	934	10,050	40
1924	831	770	5,999	45
1925	642	793	8,755	29
1926	747	716	6,427	44
1927	989	1,009	10,969	135
1928	1,064	722	8,207	127
1929	620	439	7,091	90
1930	1,130	441	7,103	71
1931	1,167	1,167	6,664	105
1932	1,615	1,716	10,438	201
1933	1,579	541	10,956	276

CHAPTER XI

MOVEMENT TO REPEAL THE EIGHTEENTH AMENDMENT
1922-1933

During the 1920's prohibition was not generally an issue in the elections for state officers, although some candidates continued to declare their approval of prohibition and to make platform promises of rigid enforcement of the dry laws. In the two senatorial elections held in 1920, however, this issue played a major part. After the death of Senator Bankhead on March 1, 1920, Governor Kilby appointed ex-Governor Comer to fill his place temporarily and an election was held to select a man to fill out the remainder of the Bankhead term. Congressman J. Thomas Heflin, who had sometimes sided with the prohibitionists, defeated overwhelmingly ex-Governor O'Neal, ex-Senator Frank S. White, and Ray Rushton, all local optionists. Candidates for the long term were Senator Underwood, local optionist, L. B. Musgrove, and Judge S. D. Weakley, both prohibitionists. Musgrove ran on his record as a friend of prohibition and emphasized especially the importance of electing a dry Congress to prevent the breakdown of the prohibition laws.[1] But Senator Underwood won over his two opponents. The vote cast was Underwood 69,045, Musgrove 61,429, Weakley 30,975.[2]

Musgrove was candidate for the United States Senate again in 1926, and again made his prohibition record the most important plank in his platform. Some of his opponents also stressed their anti-liquor views. Hugo Black was endorsed as a sincere prohibitionist, and ex-Governor Kilby usually gave a brief history of his affiliations with the state prohibition forces in his paid political advertisements. But John H. Bankhead, Jr., although himself a prohibitionist, declared that the question had no place in the campaign. Judge James A. Mayfield, the fifth candidate, was an avowed local optionist. The vote was Bankhead, 63,865; Black, 84,877; Kilby, 39,710; Mayfield, 50,994; and Musgrove, 33,052.[3]

Reaction against prohibition was very evident by 1932. The A.A.P.R., newspaper propaganda, and the depression helped produce this reaction, as did also the mistakes and indiscretions of enforcement officers. Some of these officers were undoubtedly overzealous. Three state deputies were charged, for example, with raiding, without sufficient information, the homes of Messrs. Albert P. Bush and Henry Hall, both prominent citizens of Mobile. Bush was head of the T. G. Bush Grocery Company, and Hall was a former bank president. The matter was brought to the attention

[1] *Limestone Democrat*, February 12, 1920.
[2] *Alabama Official and Statistical Register* (1919-1920), pp. 406-407.
[3] *Ibid.* (1927), pp. 358-359.

of Governor Kilby, who ordered Conrad W. Austin, chief of law enforcement officers of the state, to dismiss these deputies. Austin refused to carry out the Governor's orders. He declared that these officers had reliable information that beer was being manufactured in both these homes, and that the search had proved their information authentic inasmuch as they had found prohibited liquors in each house. Austin further said, "I am unable to find in the law where anyone is exempt, whether he be high or low and that the man who makes home brew is equally as guilty as the man who makes 'wild-cat' liquor." Governor Kilby therefore dismissed Austin for insubordination.[4]

Some officers were charged with shooting illicit distillers in the back while they were attempting to escape arrest. Two deputies, W. H. Knox and A. W. Crow, shot and killed Lee Taunton in Elmore County under such circumstances. They were immediately arrested, lodged in jail, and indicted for murder. The killing of Taunton shocked the best people of the state and gave opponents of prohibition effective ammunition.[5] A similar incident occurred the same year in Lee County. Three state law enforcement officers shot Homer Phelps, a Negro, and wounded a young white man, as they were running away from the still. The deputies were arrested but allowed to make bond.[6] "There has been too much promiscuous shooting in Alabama and too many explanations which did not explain," said the *Birmingham Age-Herald*.[7]

State law enforcement officers, it was also charged, sometimes, without apparent cause, molested people who were driving along the highways. Two officers in Montgomery County pursued and fired upon a car occupied by two women rural school teachers. Both officers were at once discharged and indicted by the grand jury on the charge of assault with intent to murder.[8] Such incidents stirred a public disapproval and distrust which helped swell the tide of sentiment running strongly against the prohibition laws.

Certain political leaders were quick to sense this change in the current and to shift their positions accordingly. Five candidates filed in the senatorial campaign of 1932. They were Henry L. Anderton, anti-repealist, Hugo L. Black, John Morgan Burns, Thomas E. Kilby, and Charlie C. McCall. Anderton, Burns, and McCall were eliminated in the first primary on May 3.

Prior to the first primary, Kilby had completely reversed himself on the Eighteenth Amendment and came out in favor of a referendum on the question. Senator Black did not commit himself until after the primary, but in May he also declared before a large audience in Montgomery that, if reelected, he would vote in the United States Senate for a resubmission

[4] *Montgomery Advertiser*, July 27, 1921.
[5] *Ibid.*, September 21, 24, 1921. [6] *Ibid.*, November 22, 1921.
[7] *Birmingham Age-Herald*, quoted by the *Alabama Courier*, October 26, 1921.
[8] *Alabama Courier*, May 30, 1929.

of the Eighteenth Amendment to the states of the nation.[9] He said that he had always been a personal and political dry, and that he was confident that the states would retain the Eighteenth Amendment if they had a chance to vote on it. Senator Black's statement incensed the Anti-Saloon leaders. They had supported him in the first primary and believed that he should have indicated his change in view before the vote was taken. The headquarters committee of the Anti-Saloon League of Alabama called a meeting for the purpose of dropping Senator Black and throwing their support to Kilby; but after hours of debate, the meeting adjourned without action. Each voter was left to decide for himself which candidate to support.[10] Black had lacked only about 4,000 votes of a majority in the first primary. Kilby, therefore, withdrew from the race and a second primary was unnecessary.

In the gubernatorial campaigns during the 1920's, all candidates who expressed themselves came out for law enforcement. In 1922 Colonel Bibb Graves and Judge W. W. Brandon endorsed prohibition, and both declared themselves in favor of the keeping and strict enforcement of the prohibition laws. Judge Brandon won over Graves by a vote of 163,217 to 44,151.[11] Again in 1926 all four candidates, A. H. Carmichael, Bibb Graves, Charlie McDowell, and A. G. Patterson, favored the maintenance and enforcement of the dry laws. In a fairly close race, Graves was elected. Carmichael received 74,133 votes; Graves, 83,471; McDowell, 67,612; Patterson, 68,304.[12] In 1930 there were five candidates: Watt T. Brown, J. A. Carnley, W. C. Davis, Woolsey Finnell, Charlie McCall, and Judge B. M. Miller. Judge Miller, who had declared in his platform:

> Personally and politically, prohibition is favored by me. Whether in or out of office, my ideas of prohibition are the same. It is no "experiment." It is permanently fixed in our national Constitution and State statutes. Its enforcement is as easy as any other criminal statute in our Code.[13]

was elected. His victory was partly due to his stand on prohibition and partly to his promises of economy in government. The vote was as follows: Brown, 4,030; Carnley, 10,653; Davis, 81,639; Finnell, 29,187; McCall, 25,471; Miller, 87,060.[14]

In his inaugural address Governor Miller stated that the prohibition laws in Alabama were second to none in the Union; that prohibition was a noble principle written permanently into the national constitution and the statutes of the state. Prohibition laws, he declared, could be and must be enforced. If the sheriffs, solicitors, and judges were personally in accord with the prohibition statutes, if they acted without favor, and each

[9] *Montgomery Advertiser*, May 17, 1932.
[10] *Ibid.*, May 26, 28, 1932.
[11] *Alabama Official and Statistical Register* (1922), pp. 358-359.
[12] *Ibid.* (1927), pp. 362-363.
[13] *Alabama Christian Advocate*, August 7, 1930.
[14] *Alabama Official and Statistical Register* (1931), pp. 531-535.

obeyed the law himself, effective enforcement would follow as a matter of course. But no law could be enforced if officials directly or indirectly aided and abetted the violation of that law. Governor Miller believed that officers who failed to perform their duty should be replaced by those who would steadfastly and faithfully do so.[15]

The most important influence in the movement to repeal the Eighteenth Amendment was the Association Against the Prohibition Amendment. Its promoters declared that they simply believed in facing facts. But its enemies were not so sure of the purity of its motives. Louis C. Cramton, addressing the national House of Representatives on January 21, 1924, charged that this Association lived on crime and disorder because it favored making the Eighteenth Amendment inoperative, and advocated the violation of law.[16] The motives and methods of the men connected with the organization were repeatedly exposed. Insistently agents of the association spread propaganda to prove that the Eighteenth Amendment was a failure, that it was largely responsible for bootlegging, drunkenness and crime, and that it was one of the major causes of the depression. Solemnly they demanded its repeal for the sake of law and order, political purity, real temperance, and prosperity. The corrupt character of their methods was proved when in 1930 their files were seized by the Senate Lobby Investigation Committee.[17]

Certainly, they had warm support from the liquor interests. In October, 1922, the Wisconsin Malters' Club sent out an appeal for funds, declaring that the Wisconsin division of A.A.P.A. had done a wonderful work during the last primaries in electing eight wet congressional candi-

[15] *Alabama Baptist*, January 29, 1931.
[16] *Congressional Record*, Vol. 65, part 2, p. 1213, 68th Cong. His exact words were: "This day there meets in Washington the Association Against the Prohibition Amendment in a so-called face-the-facts conference. I would, therefore, call attention at this opportune time to some facts deserving consideration in connection with that association which has in its aims, its policies, and its methods more possibilities of evil for the future political, industrial and moral welfare of our land than any other organization now in existence. It is an organization opposed to law enforcement, promoting, thriving upon and rejoicing at triumph of crime and disorder over law and order.

From its beginning, the Association Against the Prohibition Amendment has proclaimed its nullification program. In its prospectus issued soon after the incorporation of the organization in April 1919, before the wartime prohibition measure had gone into effect, but some months after the Eighteenth Amendment had been ratified in the manner prescribed by the Constitution, it declared:

'This association has two immediate aims: (1) To prevent the county from going on a bone-dry basis on July 1, and (2) to make the Eighteenth Amendment forever inoperative.'

It daily prophesies failure, justifies violation of the law, opposes enforcement, throws its influence on the side of lawlessness when it ought to be on the side of law and order.

The leader in the whole movement to discredit the law and make it 'inoperative,' as originally promised by it, is the Association Against Prohibition Amendment."
[17] Hearing before a sub-committee of the Judiciary, United States Senate, 71st Cong., 2nd session.

dates out of ten named. The club asked its members to permit themselves to be assessed to help carry on the fight against the amendment.[18] In June, 1926, the Gottfried Krueger Brewing Company of Newark declared its deep interest in the Association Against the Prohibition Amendment and solicited donations for it from their many creditors, suggesting that those creditors would be greatly benefited if the prohibition laws were modified.[19]

After 1926, although Captain William H. Stayton remained as president of the A.A.P.A., the general control and management of the organization was taken over by a group of multimillionaires under the direction of Pierre, Irenee, and Lammot Du Pont, John J. Raskob, vice-president of the Du Pont Company, and Charles H. Sabin. These individuals and others contributed millions of dollars to fight the Eighteenth Amendment.

Fletcher Dobyns claimed that an outstanding achievement of the Association was its capture of the national machinery of the Democratic party. It had been able to do this through the influence of Al Smith, he said. As a representative of Tammany Hall, Smith was a militant wet and a strong supporter of the Association's program. When he ran for president in 1928 he selected as chairman of the Democratic national committee John J. Raskob, one of the most powerful and influential members of the A.A.P.A. After that election Jouett Shouse, who later became president of the A.A.P.A., succeeded Raskob as chairman of the national Democratic committee, and in the four years which followed Raskob and Shouse wrested control of the Democratic party from dry leaders and turned it over to the Tammany organizations in New York and other Northern cities which had resolved to repeal the Eighteenth Amendment.

Under the Du Ponts the Association perfected a propaganda machine which, for power and efficiency, surpassed any organization of this type yet encountered. The scope of its work is indicated in the Association's annual report for 1930. Three times as many people were reading news publications based on A.A.P.A. information in 1930, said this report, as were reading such material in 1928. Millions of copies of newspapers read every day in every community carried A.A.P.A. releases and stories based upon them. News men in Washington had found that A.A.P.A. influence could help them get valuable inside information, and they repaid such favors abundantly. Clippings, books, pamphlets, and cartoons gave publicity to the work. Prominent writers and artists lent the prestige of their names and the power of their tongues and pens.[20]

The Du Ponts had been prohibitionists before 1926. Why did they suddenly change their attitude? There seems but one answer. The record proves conslusively that they believed that if the liquor traffic were brought

[18] E. Gordon, *When the Brewers Had the Stranglehold*, pp. 216-217.
[19] Gordon, *op. cit.*, pp. 217-218.
[20] *Annual Report of the A.A.P.A.* (1930); Fletcher Dobyns, *The Amazing Story of Repeal*, p. 3.

back and taxed, the federal income tax, which they felt was falling heavily upon them, would no longer be necessary. Pierre Du Pont said as much in a circular which he mailed out to the large income taxpayers of the country. He said, "The British liquor policy applied in the United States would permit of the total abolition of the income tax both personal and corporate."[21]

Meanwhile, the church continued to defend prohibition. In 1929 the Alabama Conference of the Methodist Church denounced as wicked and pernicious all efforts to legalize the liquor traffic. Though a fight against the repeal might be called the "Church in politics," said these churchmen, the freeing of man from the liquor curse was the Church's mission; and her servants must continue to be indifferent to a wet press and liquor politicians.[22]

The North Alabama Conference in 1930 recognized that powerful forces were waging a costly and spectacular campaign against the Eighteenth Amendment. These forces, determined to bring back the liquor business, the Conference declared, had attempted and partly succeeded in subsidizing the public press and had aligned with them practically all the metropolitan daily newspapers, the leading magazines, and the weekly publications. They had furnished large sums of money to elect and influence candidates.[23] They were constantly trying to persuade people that the nation had tired of the Eighteenth Amendment and desired modification or repeal.[24] In 1931 the Baptist Convention observed that powerful interests were seeking to capture both political parties and, by the overwhelming vote of wet cities and states, to dominate the majority party of Alabama. Their scheme was to seize the party reins, write the party platform and name the party candidates, and then to defy Southern sentiment and depend on prejudice and the party lash to bring the voters into line in support of such men and policies even though their consciences were violated and their common sense offended.[25]

During the twenties persistent attempts were made to amend the state laws to allow the sale of non-intoxicating cereal beverages. Before the call for the extraordinary session of 1921 was issued, Governor Kilby was visited by a small group of citizens who requested him to include the subject of such beverages in his proclamation. The Governor at first declined on the ground that one house of the legislature had already passed unfavorably on the matter and that, therefore, submission of the question would be useless. Later, when pledges of eighteen senators and fifty-four representatives to vote for the measure had been placed before him, he acquiesced and the subject was included in the call for the special session.

[21] Dobyns, *op. cit.*, p. 22.
[22] *Journal of the Alabama Conference, (November 20-25, 1929)*, p. 58.
[23] *Journal of the North Alabama Conference, (November 5-9, 1930)*, pp. 78-79.
[24] *Annual of the Alabama Baptist State Convention* (1930), pp. 130-131.
[25] *Annual of the Alabama Baptist State Convention* (1931), p. 87.

THE PROHIBITION MOVEMENT IN ALABAMA 219

Instead of making a recommendation, however, the governor presented arguments both for and against the proposal. The arguments had been prepared by Victor H. Hanson of Birmingham, who favored the measure, and by Dr. W. B. Crumpton of Montgomery, who violently opposed it. The bill was defeated by a vote of 51 to 39. Apparently at least three of the members who had signed the pledge had changed their minds.[26]

Another attempt in 1931 to pass a near-beer bill was vigorously opposed by Governor Miller, and overwhelmingly defeated in the temperance committee by a vote of 12 for and 22 against.[27] A Birmingham paper criticized and even ridiculed the state legislature for not permitting the sale of near-beer in Alabama. Near-beer, declared this paper, had both nourishing and medicinal properties.[28]

After the National Democratic Convention of 1932 the near-beer advocates gained tremendous strength in the Alabama legislature. In September of that year they succeeded in enacting a law providing for the sale of cereal beverages containing not more than one half of one per cent alcohol. Governor Miller vetoed the bill, saying that, "This bill drives a wedge into our prohibition statutes with destructive force which, in my opinion, should not be permitted." The House then repassed the bill over the governor's veto by a vote of 64 to 30, and sent it to the Senate where it was again passed by a vote of 21 to 10.[29]

Artemus K. Callahan, a Tuscaloosa County representative who voted for the near-beer bill, was asked to resign from the board of deacons of the Holt Baptist Church when he got home. He did so immediately. He was a leading member, song director of the congregation, secretary of the board of deacons, and a faithful attendant of church services. It seemed a plain case of the church's attempt to punish a legislator for voting according to his convictions.[30]

Hoover's renomination by the Republicans in 1932 was considered inevitable. As a first-term president he had only to express his desire to run again, and logic and tradition entitled him to renomination by the party he represented.

In the Democratic party Alfred E. Smith and Franklin D. Roosevelt were candidates. Smith was an avowed wet. Roosevelt was also a wet, but he held more conservative views. The prohibition issue finally caused an estrangement between these two men. Raskob and Smith desired to commit the party in favor of repeal and make it the leading issue of 1932. Roosevelt had committed himself in favor of modification in 1930, but he opposed making the amendment the dominant issue of the campaign.[31] He preferred to emphasize economic questions. When John

[26] *House Journal* (1923), I, 13-16.
[27] *Alabama Christian Advocate,* April 16, 1931.
[28] *Ibid.,* April 23, 1931.
[29] *Senate Journal, Special Session* (1932), I, 581-582; *Acts, Special Session* (1932), p. 56. [30] *Decatur Daily,* October 17, 1932.
[31] E. K. Kindley, *Franklin D. Roosevelt,* pp. 275-276.

J. Raskob attempted in March, 1931, to get the national Democratic committee to make a declaration against prohibition, Roosevelt checkmated him. He requested James Farley, New York State Democratic chairman, to call a meeting of his committee and to adopt a resolution against a declaration in advance of the national convention. This act met with widespread approval, and Raskob failed to get the national committee to make the declaration he desired.[32] Because he had successfully thwarted the Smith-Raskob liquor program, Roosevelt came to be looked upon in the South and West as a real dry. Wishful thinking helped to spread and exaggerate the report that he was dry. Walter Lippmann, a wet, declared, "The notion, which seems to prevail in the West and the South, that Wall Street fears him is preposterous. Wall Street thinks that he is too dry, not that he is too radical."[33] Southern Democratic leaders, the *Christian Century* commented, had "turned comfortably to Governor Roosevelt for whom plausible claims will be made on the liquor issue that he is as dry as President Hoover."[34]

A primary election was held in Alabama on May 3, 1932, to elect delegates to the Democratic National Convention. Eight delegates were to be elected from the state-at-large, out of nine candidates. These candidates, as well as those from the congressional districts, were committed to Roosevelt, and Alabama's delegation went to the convention instructed for him.

The Republican National Convention met in Chicago on June 14 and adopted a stand-pat platform with one exception—the prohibition plank. The party declared opposition to nullification but proposed the submission of a repeal amendment which would give the Federal government power to prevent the return of the saloon. The platform stated:

... We do not favor a submission limited to the issue of retention or repeal, for the American nation never in its history has gone backward, and in this case the progress which has been thus far made must be preserved, while the evils must be eliminated.

We therefore believe that the people should have an opportunity to pass upon a proposed amendment the provision of which, while retaining in the Federal Government power to preserve the gains already made in dealing with the evils inherent in the liquor traffic, shall allow States to deal with the problem as their citizens may determine, but subject always to the power of the Federal Government to protect those States where prohibition may exist and safeguard our citizens everywhere from the return of the saloon and attendant abuses.

Such an amendment should be promptly submitted to the States by Congress, to be acted upon by State conventions called for that sole purpose in accordance with the provisions of Article V of the Constitution and adequately safeguarded so as to be truly representative. . . .[35]

---

[32] *New York Times*, March 3, 6, 1931.
[33] *New York Herald Tribune*, January 8, 1932.
[34] April 20, 1932.
[35] *Current History* (August, 1932), pp. 630-638.

Hoover would hardly fool anybody, thought the *Birmingham News*, with his attempt to minimize the party's departure from its dry position. The real drys must surely have seen that the Republican prohibition plank really meant a break with everything they and the Republican party had held dear in the past. The wets, on the other hand, at least the more militant among them, would as certainly be displeased with the failure of the convention to make a straightforward and downright statement. As a vote-catcher, the *News* considered the prohibition plank a sure failure; it would be acceptable to neither wets nor drys. With regard to the platform, Franklin D. Roosevelt remarked: "I suspect that those who wrote that plank thought that it would sound dry to the drys and wet to the wets. But to the consternation of the high priests, it sounded dry to the wets and wet to the drys. This was very serious."[86]

The platform out of the way, the Republican Convention then lived up to expectation and renominated Hoover.[87]

Eleven days after the Republican Convention had adjourned, the Democrats met, on June 27, also in Chicago. Roosevelt and his forces won a complete victory when the convention moved, on its second day, to elect a permanent chairman. Their candidate, Senator Thomas J. Walsh of Montana, who had presided over the Madison Square Garden convention of 1924, defeated Jouett Shouse, Smith's candidate, although John W. Davis and other leaders spoke in behalf of Shouse. Roosevelt's choice of Walsh, a staunch dry, for the permanent chairmanship further endeared him to the prohibitionists of the South.

A fiery debate on prohibition broke out when the platform committee made its report. The out-and-out repealists, led by ex-Governor Smith of New York, Governor Ritchie of Maryland, and Senator David L. Walsh of Massachusetts, engaged in verbal combat for hours with a minority group led by Senator Hull of Tennessee, and W. C. Fitts of Alabama, who favored submission.[88] The repealists won and the following plank was adopted:

We favor the repeal of the Eighteenth Amendment.
To effect such repeal, we demand that the Congress immediately propose a Constitutional amendment to truly representative conventions in the States called to act solely on that proposal.
We urge the enactment of such measures by the several States as will actually promote temperance, effectively prevent the return of the saloon, and bring the liquor traffic into the open under complete supervision and control of the States.
We demand that the Federal Government effectively exercise its power to enable the states to protect themselves against importation of intoxicating liquors in violation of their laws.
Pending repeal, we favor immediate modification of the Volstead Law to legalize the manufacture and sale of beer and other beverages of such alcoholic

---

[86] *Chicago Tribune*, August 28, 1932.
[87] *Birmingham News*, June 17, 1932.   [88] *Birmingham News*, June 30, 1932.

contents as is permissible under the Constitution, and to provide therefrom a proper and needed revenue.[39]

Alabama was one of eight states whose delegations recorded a majority against repeal.

The *Birmingham News* hailed the adoption of this plank as representing "the boldest and most advanced stand that it would be possible to take on this issue. It is a complete victory for the militant advocates of prohibition repeal." The *News* heartily endorsed the action of the Democratic Convention and applauded its courage.[40] "A better written platform has never before been adopted by either party," the *Montgomery Advertiser* declared. "The *Advertiser* opposed the adoption of the amendment and predicted the failure that has characterized its history. For several years the *Advertiser* has advocated the repeal of the Eighteenth Amendment and pending its repeal modification of the Volstead act."[41]

As soon as the platform was adopted, the convention turned to the selection of a standard bearer. Franklin D. Roosevelt, who had waged a brilliant pre-convention campaign, appeared to be the favorite among the six leading candidates. On the fourth ballot 1,148½ votes were cast. Two thirds of that number, or 766 votes, were necessary for nomination. Roosevelt received 945 and was therefore overwhelmingly nominated.[42] He came to Chicago on July 2 to deliver his speech of acceptance. In that address he expressed his views on prohibition, saying:

> I want to congratulate this assembly for having written into the platform what a great majority really thinks about the 18th Amendment. The party wants repeal; your candidate wants repeal, and I am confident the United States of America wants repeal. Two years ago the platform on which I ran for Governor contained substantially the same provision. I say to you now that from this day on the 18th Amendment is doomed. When that happens we as Democrats must and will rightly and morally enable the states to protect themselves against the importation of intoxicating liquors where such importation may violate their state laws. We must rightly and morally prevent the return of the saloon.[43]

A few weeks later, in a speech at Sea Girt, New Jersey, Roosevelt accused President Hoover of "evading and confusing the issue by the use of pussy-cat words." He urged the enactment by the several states of such measures as would actually promote temperance, effectively prevent the return of the saloon, and bring the liquor traffic into the open, and under complete supervision and control by the states.[44]

President Hoover in his acceptance speech admitted that prohibition had proved not to be "the final solution of the evils of the liquor traffic." He demanded at that time, and also in subsequent speeches, that the rights

[39] *Literary Digest*, July 9, 1932.
[40] *Birmingham News*, July 30, 1932.
[41] *Montgomery Advertiser*, July 1, 1932.
[42] *Ibid.*, July 2, 1932.
[43] *Montgomery Advertiser*, July 3, 1932.
[44] *Christian Century*, September 7, 1932.

of dry states be protected. But neither candidate was eager to campaign on the prohibition issue; it receded into the background as election day neared.

In an editorial, "Mr. Hoover Slips a Cog," the *Alabama Baptist* said that real prohibitionists were grieved because Hoover had retreated from his staunch position as a defender of prohibition. He seemed to be carrying water on both shoulders, or in plainer words, simply playing cheap politics. Nevertheless this editor was forced to conclude that "with reference to the matter of prohibition, we do believe that between the two evils, Mr. Hoover is the lesser.[45]

Between 1928 and 1932 the American people had gone through a severe depression. They were looking for some one to get them out of "sackcloth and ashes." They came up to the campaign of 1932 in a serious state of mind. President Hoover's analysis of the depression as a psychological phenomenon, and his optimistic faith that "prosperity was just around the corner," did not seem to them very convincing. To a worried people the principal issue was action to remedy the bad economic condition of the country. Every daily newspaper in Alabama and most of the weeklies endorsed Roosevelt, and even went so far as to insinuate by innuendo that President Hoover was responsible for the depression. The Democratic politicians in the state also used their influence in behalf of Roosevelt.

A woman's society organized in Birmingham to work for the repeal of the Eighteenth Amendment and the election of Roosevelt took an active part in the fight. It was a branch of the Woman's Organization for National Prohibition Reform, commonly referred to as the W.O.N.P.R. It had been introduced into Alabama by Mrs. Lawrence O'Donovan of Talladega and New York. Mrs. O'Donovan became state chairman for Alabama and appointed Mrs. Solon Jacobs chairman of the Jefferson County group.[46] The principles of the national organization were concisely stated on enrollment cards to be signed by prospective members. Lawlessness and crime, said this statement, were the result of national prohibition. The states, it asserted, should retain their power over prohibition.[47] Mrs. O'Donovan said that her group planned to organize every town and city in Alabama, so that women might have a fair representation. They would act, she said, to bring about the repeal of the Eighteenth

[45] *Alabama Baptist*, September 1, 1932.
[46] Some of the charter members of the organization were Mrs. Prescott Kelley, Mrs. Burr Ferguson, Mrs. Solon Jacobs, Mrs. Lawrence O'Donovan, Mrs. S. J. Bowie, Mrs. A. P. Hull, Mrs. Charles S. Leeper, Mrs. Fay M. Benton, Mrs. R. C. Bush, Mrs. W. B. Leedy, Mrs. M. D. Taylor, Miss Virginia Jacobs, and Mrs. D. H. Maring.—*Birmingham News*, June 30, 1932.
[47] The cards bore the following pledge: "Because I believe that national prohibition has increased lawlessness, hypocrisy and corruption, and because I believe that the cause of real temperance has been retarded, I enroll as a member of this organization which is pledged to work for the repeal of the 18th amendment and to return to each state its power to regulate the manufacture, sale and transportation of intoxicating beverages."—*Birmingham Post*, June 25, 1932.

Amendment, because they believed it had retarded the cause of temperance rather than helped it.[48]

Senator J. M. Bonner of Camden, urged prohibitionists to remain in the party. He pointed out that, if they bolted, they might bar themselves from participating in a convention when the issue would be "Repeal of the 18th Amendment." Only by remaining loyal to the Democratic party could men truly aid the cause of prohibition and fight effectively to retain the Eighteenth Amendment, he insisted. He concluded his letter by saying:

And I may say that this appeal comes to you from a prohibitionist who has fought liquor for a quarter of a century, in season and out of season, when it was popular and when it was unpopular, one who has known no "shadow of turning." And it comes to you from a prohibitionist who will cheerfully accept political annihilation before he will ever bend a knee before the liquor cohorts.[49]

The *Alabama Christian Advocate* did not oppose Roosevelt, but it did oppose the repeal plank. "Put on the Armor of God," this periodical headed one of its editorials. "We are for the Eighteenth Amendment," it declared. "We are against its repeal. So-called political leaders who have once been dry may be stampeded into the wet ranks if they will, but, under God, this paper will fight the liquor traffic as long as God lets it live."[50] Just before the campaign ended the *Advocate* said that it did not see how anyone who wanted to keep the Eighteenth Amendment could afford to vote for a candidate who favored its repeal.[51]

The Democrats carried the state by an overwhelming majority. The vote was 207,000 for Roosevelt and 34,000 for Hoover.[52]

The *Advocate* was quite willing to admit then that the desire for liquor had had some part in Roosevelt's election, but the editor did not think that had been the controlling factor. Inasmuch as Roosevelt had come out strong against the Eighteenth Amendment, it was natural to suppose that most of the wets had voted for him. But the *Advocate* believed that the best people in the South had also supported Roosevelt because a change of administration gave promise of a remedy for the great depression.[53]

The *Montgomery Advertiser* said the election proved that the people had definitely repudiated the prohibition experiment. Tired of prohibition, they wanted something else without quite knowing what. They wanted liquor sold legally and definitely put under social control, and they wanted to get rid of the present system. The settlement of the liquor question would require statesmanship, this paper declared.[54]

Alabama women working for "prohibition reform" asked Governor Miller to appoint a commission to study plans for state control of liquor.

[48] *Birmingham News*, July 3, 1932.   [49] *Decatur Daily*, July 20, 1932.
[50] *Alabama Christian Advocate*, July 7, 1932.
[51] *Ibid.*, November 3, 1932.
[52] *Alabama Official and Statistical Register* (1935), pp. 503-508.
[53] *Alabama Christian Advocate*, November 17, 1932.
[54] *Montgomery Advertiser*, November 12, 1932.

"Since repeal within the next few years is almost assured, states must be getting ready now to cope with the new conditions," said Mrs. Jacobs.[55] Mrs. James H. Wideman, member of a committee appointed to call on Governor Miller to urge the appointment of a commission to study the prohibition situation in Alabama, reported that the Governor did not react favorably to such a project. Governor Miller believed if he were to name such a commission he would soon be deluged with petitions for other similar appointments.[56]

As repeal seemed to come more closely within reach, the W.O.N.P.R. intensified its efforts. The executive board was increased and the scope of the organization was extended to twenty-seven counties. The membership of the Alabama division had exceeded 3,000 by February 23, 1933, and plans were in progress to enroll still more members.[57]

Congress passed the proposed Twenty-first Amendment on February 16, 1933, by the following vote: Senate, 63 for and 23 against; House, 289 for and 121 against.[58] The Alabama delegation voted as follows: Representatives, 8 for and 1 against; Senators, both for.[59]

Immediately opponents of the Eighteenth Amendment in the Alabama legislature acted to secure a referendum. Senator J. Sanford Mullins of Tallapoosa County, recognized leader of the wet forces in the Alabama Senate, introduced a bill calling for a state convention, to be held in Montgomery in August, 1933, to vote on the proposed Twenty-first Amendment.[60] His bill was amended to provide that ninety days after the adjournment of the legislature an election should be held to choose delegates to such a convention. Delegates (except those from the state-at-large) were to be elected by the counties. A popular referendum, which should be binding on the delegates, was also provided for. The plan gave the large urban centers, such as Birmingham, Mobile, and Montgomery, a tremendous advantage over sparsely populated counties like Choctaw, Lowndes, and Wilcox. The prohibitionists at once objected, since the populous counties were known to be wet and the sparsely settled counties dry. The *Alabama Christian Advocate* declared, "the plan is atrociously unfair."[61] But the legislature passed the bill. The Senate voted 23 for and 6 against,[62] and the House 71 for, and 25 against.[63]

On March 28 Governor Miller vetoed the bill on the grounds that he considered the measure illegal, the provisions regarding the convention undemocratic, and the time not yet ripe for such a convention.[64]

[55] *Birmingham Post*, January 5, 1933.   [56] *Ibid.*, February 23, 1933.
[57] *Birmingham Post*, January 13, February 23, 1933.
[58] *Congressional Record*, Vol. 76, part 4, p. 4231, 72nd Cong., 2nd ses.
[59] *Ibid.*, p. 4516.
[60] *Birmingham News*, February 21, 1933.
[61] *Alabama Christian Advocate*, March 23, 1933.
[62] *Senate Journal, Special Session* (1933), p. 795.
[63] *House Journal, Special Session* (1933), pp. 786-787.
[64] *Ibid.*, pp. 920-922. Governor Miller said:
1. I do not think that the bill as passed by you provides for a convention as

The legislature promptly passed the bill over the governor's veto. Governor Miller then asked the State Supreme Court, on May 3, for an opinion as to the constitutionality of the Mullins Convention Act. The Court declared on May 10 that the measure did not violate Article 5 of the Federal Constitution. Moreover, since the act had a single subject clearly expressed in the title and the provisions of the act were germane to this subject, it could not be considered "violative of section 45 of the state Constitution."[65]

The state steering committee for repeal of the Eighteenth Amendment sent out a call, on May 6, for a state-wide mass meeting to be held in Montgomery, May 17. The call, signed by Frank P. Glass of Montgomery, Senator J. Sanford Mullins, and Mrs. Solon Jacobs, stated that the prohibition amendment, as a police regulation in the constitution, had been a mistake, that citizens were now able to return this power to the state, where it formerly resided, and where by consent of all political parties it belonged.[66]

Frank P. Glass, publisher of the *Montgomery Advertiser,* was unanimously elected permanent chairman of the Montgomery meeting, and A. M. Tunstall, veteran legislator, was named campaign manager. Judge Leon McCord of Montgomery County Circuit Court, keynote speaker, declared that citizens faced, not a question of strong drink but a question of state rights. A. H. Carmichael, long a zealous prohibitionist, was unable to attend the meeting. He wired his regrets, and he declared for repeal, saying that he had come to believe the adoption of the Eighteenth Amendment was an error.

Campaign manager Tunstall instructed his workers to conduct the campaign without bitterness and to take care that the main issue be kept before the people until the election of July 18. This main issue, he said, was whether or not the people of Alabama should govern their own affairs and let their neighbor states govern theirs; it was not a question of whiskey

---

intended by the Constitution of the United States with reference to amending the Federal Constitution and I do not believe that Alabama's action on the amendment either ratifying or declining to ratify would be legal under this bill. . . .

2. I think that the provision for a Convention in this bill is undemocratic, in that it binds the delegates elected from a county and representing a county, to vote according to the total state vote whether the county he represents voted that way or not. This destroys the democratic doctrine of local self-government. . . .

3. I do not think that the present is the time for a Convention to be held in Alabama to decide whether or not the 18th Amendment to the Constitution of the United States should be repealed. . . .

4. Under the Convention plan proposed by this Act only one man is necessary, if he can add and subtract. He could add up the votes of the State and subtract the pros and the cons or the cons from the pros and declare the result. . . .

For the reasons above stated, I cannot approve this bill.
                                              Respectfully,
                                              B. M. Miller,
                                                Governor.

[65] *Southern Reporter,* Vol. 148, pp. 107-111.
[66] *Birmingham News,* May 6, 1933.

THE PROHIBITION MOVEMENT IN ALABAMA 227

or no whiskey, barrooms or no barrooms. Tunstall said that he favored repeal simply because the National Democratic Convention endorsed it. Repeal would in no wise compel or authorize the opening of saloons or the sale of liquor in those states which had their own prohibition laws. The prohibition laws of Alabama would still stand and could be enforced. But with the repeal of the Eighteenth Amendment each state would regain the right to govern its own internal affairs. A vote for repeal of the Eighteenth Amendment, he insisted, was not to be interpreted as a vote against prohibition.[67]

Mrs. Solon Jacobs, introduced by Chairman Glass, said she spoke for an organization of six thousand Alabama women. These women realized that the Eighteenth Amendment was a failure, and they were fighting shoulder to shoulder with the men for its repeal. Prohibition, she asserted, had increased social drinking in the home; the movement for repeal was now the true temperance movement.[68]

Before the Montgomery meeting ended plans had been made to organize committees for repeal in every section of the state. Every county was to have a chairman, empowered to enroll as many helpers as he needed. A speaking campaign was planned, and many of the most able men in the state took the stump.

The *Montgomery Advertiser* thought that the cost of enforcing prohibition laws and the loss of revenue to the government were sufficient causes for repeal. Repeal was merely sound business. Any businessman realized that the lawlessness encouraged by prohibition overflowed into legitimate business channels, and caused a staggering extraneous loss. "In dollars and cents the economic cost of the prohibition experiment is COLOSSAL," thundered the *Advertiser*.[69]

The *Birmingham News* considered repeal practically a panacea, asserting that "law enforcement, temperance, state rights, party loyalty, patriotism, honesty, and general decency would be promoted—taxes would tend to be lowered as a result of new revenues accruing to the government—by repeal."[70]

A widespread national sentiment against the Eighteenth Amendment had been steadily growing. It was reflected in resolutions adopted by many representative national organizations, including the American Legion, the American Federation of Labor, and the American Bar Association.[71]

Even President Roosevelt took a hand in the Alabama movement. In response to a telegram he wrote to Judge Leon McCord asking Alabama Democrats to vote for repeal.[72] This was significant, not merely because

---

[67] *Birmingham News*, May 28, 1933.　[68] *Montgomery Advertiser*, May 24, 1933.
[69] *Ibid.*, July 2, 1932.　[70] *Birmingham News*, July 12, 1933.
[71] *Birmingham Age-Herald*, June 29, 1933.
[72] *Alabama Courier*, July 13, 1933. President Roosevelt's letter follows:
 "I have received your telegram of July 3 in reference to the repeal of the Eighteenth Amendment.
 "I think I have made it absolutely clear that the platform reads as follows, and

the President pleaded for good faith in the carrying out of the party pledge, but because this was the first time he had chosen to take a direct hand in molding public opinion in support of the new amendment.[73] James A. Farley also wired Judge McCord that he favored repeal. "The party is pledged to repeal," he declared. "President Roosevelt is earnestly advocating repeal, and I, as chairman of the Democratic National Committee, am wholeheartedly urging repeal."[74] Both communications had tremendous influence on the rockribbed Democrats of Alabama.

Meanwhile the churches stood firm. The Alabama Baptist State Convention, meeting November 15-18, 1932, appointed a committee to devise a plan to oppose repeal of the Eighteenth Amendment and modification of the Volstead Act. The committee recommended that the convention act to unite in one cooperative body all organizations, citizens, and forces that were ready uncompromisingly to fight every move of the liquor interests to manufacture, sell, or deliver to the American people intoxicating liquors. The plan was read before and approved by the Methodist Alabama Conference,[75] and the committee issued a call, inviting foes of repeal to a meeting in Birmingham on December 6.

The *Alabama Baptist* considered this gathering the "most enthusiastic prohibition meeting ever held in this state." It had been advertised to meet in the assembly room of the Tutwiler Hotel, but the hotel refused to permit the meeting to be held there. The delegates betook themselves to the auditorium of the First Methodist Church. State-wide organization to oppose repeal of the Eighteenth Amendment and modification of the Volstead Act became an accomplished fact. A constitution was adopted and trustees were elected for the purpose of legal incorporation. An executive committee composed of two members from each of the cooperating bodies and a steering committee appointed to form similar organizations in the various congressional districts were also chosen before the meeting ended. The organization of counties was postponed for later

---

should be carried out insofar as it lies in our power. The special session of the Congress has already translated into law a great majority of the pledges made.

"One of the pledges of the platform reads as follows: 'The Eighteenth Amendment. To effect such repeal we demand that the Congress immediately propose a constitutional amendment to truly representative conventions in the states called to meet solely on that proposal.'

"The Congress has acted on this and many states are now engaged in holding elections for the conventions proposed.

"Finally, I have made it clear ever since my nomination a year ago that I subscribed to the Democratic platform 100 per cent.

"In view of the fact that I have had so great a number of telegrams similar to yours not only from your state, but from Tennessee, Arkansas, Kentucky, and others, I am taking the liberty of giving this message to you to the press."

"Sincerely,
"FRANKLIN D. ROOSEVELT."

[73] *Birmingham Age-Herald*, July 10, 1933.
[74] *Ibid.*, July 15, 1933.
[75] *Journal of the Alabama Conference*, (November 17-20, 1932), p. 39.

consideration. Bishop W. N. Ainsworth and Dr. J. R. Hobbs greatly moved the vast audience with their eloquence. Telegrams were sent to the Alabama members of both houses of Congress urging them to remain dry and true to the people who elected them to office.[76]

The Anti-Saloon League of Alabama was not inactive. A special committee of the League sent a letter to the members of the Alabama legislature urging them not to concern themselves with regard to repeal, and to take no action pending further developments in Congress. Citizens of the state, said this communication, were not clamoring for ratification of the repeal amendment. There was no need for holding an expensive extra election for a convention when the state did not have sufficient funds to keep the schools open and pay the teachers.[77]

The opponents of repeal met again in Birmingham on June 7 and 8. Dr. F. Scott McBride of Washington, D. C., superintendent of the National Anti-Saloon League, reported encouraging news from nine Southern states. Among other notables attending this meeting were Dr. Ernest Cherrington, Westville, Ohio, chairman of the education bureau of the Anti-Saloon League and editor of its publications; Bishop Cannon; and the following state superintendents of the Anti-Saloon League: J. Bibb Mills, Alabama; Dr. Elam Dempsey, Georgia; Dr. Leon W. Sloan, Louisiana; B. F. Auld, Tennessee; N. S. Jackson, Mississippi; Atticus Webb, Texas; George J. Burnett, North Carolina; and John Glass, Arkansas.[78]

The Flying Squadron Foundation, a national dry organization, sent speakers to various communities in Alabama. Miss Norma C. Brown, secretary of this organization, speaking to a large crowd at the courthouse in Decatur, asserted that genuine party loyalty did not involve support of repeal. If liquor returned, warned Miss Brown, it would be a more deadly foe of civilization than it had been before. Automobiles had become more common and more speedy during prohibition days. Under the new conditions it would probably not be the drunkard who would do the most harm. He would rarely be able to enter the highway. But the moderate drinker, who had drunk just enough to make him uncertain, and not enough to make him drunk, would be a dangerous menace. Oliver W. Stewart, president of the Flying Squadron, also spoke at Decatur. Both addresses were a part of a state-wide campaign sponsored by the Alabama Temperance Alliance.[79]

Dr. George H. Denny, president of the University of Alabama, was asked to state in a few words why he favored retaining the Eighteenth Amendment. He replied that the return of the old regime would be a calamity. He was against the return of the saloon because he knew what

[76] *Alabama Baptist*, December 15, 1932.
[77] *Birmingham Post*, February 27, 1933.
[78] *Birmingham News*, June 8, 1933.
[79] *Decatur Daily*, June 27, 28, 1933.

the saloon was, and he knew that conditions were better since it had been outlawed.[80]

Senator J. M. Bonner, also a foe of repeal, told a gathering of several hundred like-minded persons in the First Methodist Church in Birmingham that if the anti-repealists would only "hold the line," Alabama would vote to retain the Eighteenth Amendment. "The responsibility rests on us and it is a glorious privilege," he said. "Can we hold the line? By the grace of God we can and will." Senator Bonner also rapped the claim of the repeal forces that prohibition repeal was an out-and-out party question. He had been a life-long Democrat, he declared, and he did not propose to be read out of the party because he was against repeal.[81]

The *Alabama Christian Advocate* charged that the repeal forces were backed by enormous contributions from wealthy businessmen, whereas the prohibitionists had to depend upon small gifts from many people to pay the actual expenses of the campaign. No great daily newspapers endorsed their stand. But one thing they did have for which they were grateful: a great host of God-fearing, home-loving, youth-protecting men and women, who, on election day, would go to the polls and vote against the return of the saloon. Upon such fine citizens the prohibitionists counted.[82]

The election, held on July 18, 1933, was not marred by disorders in any part of the state. Many people failed to cast their ballots, probably because of pressing business matters or insufficient interest. The repealists won the election by a vote of 100,269 to 70,631.[83]

"In the minds of the reasonable persons there has lately been no doubt of the inevitability of repeal," commented the *Birmingham News*, when the votes had been counted.[84] The *Limestone Democrat* refused to consider the vote proof that the people of Alabama wanted their state prohibition laws repealed. Many good men who had voted for repeal had stated emphatically in that editor's presence that they would not vote for a "wet" candidate the following year; they wanted to keep the present state-wide prohibition laws.[85]

[80] *Limestone Democrat*, August 11, 1932. Dr. Denny said: "There is every reason why the American people should resist every effort to bring back the saloon. No good purpose can be served by its return. On the contrary, the return of the old regime would be a calamity.

"I do not consider the prohibition question a political question. It is a great economic question. It is a great moral question. It is a great spiritual question.

"The public conscience needs to be aroused to the perilous question, that now confronts the entire country. The younger generation is apparently finding it difficult to realize just what those of us of maturer years witnessed during the days of the open saloon. My conviction is that the overwhelming masses of our people who have had experience with the wide open saloon will not find it difficult to decide that the present situation is infinitely to be preferred to the situation that obtained a quarter of a century ago."
[81] *Birmingham News*, June 20, 1933.
[82] *Alabama Christian Advocate*, May 4, 1933.
[83] *Alabama Official and Statistical Register* (1935), pp. 730-732.
[84] *Birmingham News*, July 19, 1933.
[85] *Limestone Democrat*, July 20, 1933.

THE PROHIBITION MOVEMENT IN ALABAMA

The Alabama Convention to Repeal the Eighteenth Amendment was held in Montgomery on August 8. The action to repeal was by unanimous vote, the dry delegates being bound by the rule which required that each delegate vote as did a majority of the people on July 18. The convention then adjourned, after a session of only a few hours, without considering any other matter.[86]

The dry forces did not propose to accept repeal without a fight. The Baptist State Convention deplored "the misleading methods used in bringing about the repeal of the Eighteenth Amendment," and earnestly requested the Baptist constituency to resist to the utmost every effort to repeal the state prohibition laws. The importance of educating the people as to the bad effects of alcohol on the human system and the incompatibility of its use with the teachings of the Scripture, should just now be reemphasized, resolved these churchmen.[87] The North Alabama Conference resolved that it would oppose and fight to the limit of its strength the return of any alcoholic beverages, and that it would also do all in its power to elect officials who would take the same stand.[88] Other dry forces also prepared to continue the struggle in Alabama.

[86] *Montgomery Advertiser*, August 9, 1933.
[87] *Annual of the Alabama Baptist State Convention*, (November 15-16, 1933), p. 68.
[88] *Journal of the North Alabama Conference*, (November 8-12, 1933), p. 61.

CHAPTER XII

REFERENDUM AND RETURN TO LOCAL OPTION, 1935-1937

Over the opposition of the Anti-Saloon League and the veto of Governor Miller, the Alabama legislature passed, in 1931, an act empowering circuit judges to suspend the sentences of persons convicted for violation of the prohibition laws and sentenced to serve not more than ten years and any person sentenced to hard labor for the county, and to place them on probation. The prohibitionists believed such a law detrimental to their cause and complained that it would render the prohibition laws ineffectual. In 1932 the legislature passed a near-beer bill over the governor's veto, and in 1933 the people voted to repeal the Eighteenth Amendment by a large majority. Step by step prohibition was losing ground. This had to be admitted on all sides by 1934.

Candidates for governor and the legislature in 1934, recognized the trend in public opinion as they framed their platforms. Practically all of them took their cue from the National Democratic Platform of 1932.

Three gubernatorial candidates, Judge Leon McCord of Montgomery, Major Frank M. Dixon of Birmingham, and ex-Governor Bibb Graves of Montgomery were in the race. Judge McCord stated his position on prohibition in his opening address at Athens on January 20. He believed the legislature should legalize the sale of light wines and beer as a temporary measure, but that the sale of hard liquor should not be permitted until the electorate had voted on the matter. Major Dixon concurred with Judge McCord regarding the sale of light wines and beer, and, like the Judge favored a referendum on the sale of hard liquor. He would, however, make the county instead of the state the unit for such a referendum.[1] Ex-Governor Graves stated his stand on this issue in his platform, and reiterated his convictions in his many campaign addresses. He declared that there was no question before the people upon which the opinion of every voter was so clear-cut and well defined as that of prohibition. He promised that, if he were elected governor, no change in the long-established prohibition policy of the state would have his support and approval unless, and until, the people should have first registered their decision. The people would be asked to vote on three questions: First, Shall our present prohibition laws be retained? Second, Shall light wines and beer be sold? Third, Shall hard liquors be sold? And, whatever the general outcome of the referendum should be, every county which voted

[1] *Limestone Democrat*, January 25, 1934.

to retain the prohibition laws, he promised, should be protected with all the power of state government.[2]

The future of the prohibition laws of Alabama seemed to hang in the balance. The election of a wet governor and wet legislature would mean that they would almost certainly be repealed. A wet governor would conclude that he had a mandate from the people and would act accordingly. In the election of a dry governor lay the only hope of safeguarding prohibition.

Two of the gubernatorial candidates, McCord and Dixon, openly favored repeal. The third candidate, ex-Governor Graves, would leave the decision to the people. Prior to his candidacy, Graves had always been a prohibitionist. Dixon had never held public office and, therefore, had no political record. McCord had opposed prohibition in earlier campaigns. In 1909 he had helped defeat the Alabama constitutional amendment, and in 1933 he had used his influence in Alabama against national prohibition. At the very beginning of his campaign he referred to this record, declaring, in an address at Athens, that he had never voted a prohibition ticket.

Graves was supported in the campaign by the prohibition forces, most of the schoolteachers, and the host of friends he had made during his first term in office. All the candidates had seen military service, and the ex-soldiers' vote was, therefore, divided among them, but Graves probably received the lion's share.

The most powerful daily newspapers in the state supported either McCord or Dixon. Many of the weeklies favored Graves. The *Alabama Christian Advocate* urged its readers to vote for Graves.[3] During the interval between the first and second primaries, the *Alabama Baptist* remarked, referring to Dixon and Graves, that it appeared "that the one, a wet, talks dryer than he is, to get dry votes; and the other, a dry, assumes an aspect of moistness."[4]

In the first primary, May 1, 1934, Graves led the ticket. Dixon polled 97,508 votes; Graves, 132,462; McCord, 75,208.[5] Graves' vote was less than a majority, and a second primary had to be held on June 12. Graves was then elected over Dixon by a vote of 157,140 to 135,309.[6]

That, said the *Alabama Christian Advocate*, settled the question of who would be the next governor but there was still doubt as to who would constitute the next legislature. That legislature would almost certainly be called upon either directly to legalize the sale of wine and beer, and perhaps, hard liquor, or to refer the matter to the people for a vote.[7] The *Advocate*, taking a poll of the electees to the incoming legislature, discovered that a majority of them expressed themselves, reluctantly in some cases, as favoring the sale of light wines and beer by legislative enactment.

[3] *Alabama Christian Advocate*, April 19, 1934.
[4] April 12, 1934; September 5, 1935.   [4] May 31, 1934.
[5] *Alabama Official and Statistical Register* (1935), pp. 574-575.
[6] *Ibid.*, pp. 630-631.   [7] June 21, 1934.

The *Demopolis Times* thought that the action of this group was "too previous" and was entirely against the spirit of the campaign in which they were nominated.[8]

Since the Eighteenth Amendment had been repealed, the wets were free to urge Governor-elect Bibb Graves to recommend a bill which, if enacted into law, would repeal the Alabama dry laws without a referendum. He steadfastly refused to grant their request, saying, "If they want war to the finish they can get it. . . . The voters have made it clear that they want a referendum on the whole business and I'll use the full power of the governor's office to see that they have it. In the meantime no beer, wine or liquor bill will be enacted into law if I can prevent it—and I believe I can." A merry scramble for leadership of the referendum campaign, declared the *Birmingham Post,* was under way in that city and reports were going the rounds that the beer interests would probably spend a sizable sum of money in the state, but that the liquor manufacturers were evincing scant interest. Money for a repeal fight, the *Birmingham News* stated, would be available as soon as those with the money could determine who was going to make the fight. The *Alabama Baptist* declared that, in anticipation of repeal, an Alabama company had already been organized for the purpose of making beer.[9]

The *Alabama Christian Advocate* used its editorial and news columns to oppose a referendum. Figures from the Birmingham Police Department were cited to prove that social conditions had been worse since the repeal of the Eighteenth Amendment. In the first half of 1933 arrests for all causes had totaled 4,852; whereas in the same period of 1934 since repeal, the number had mounted to 12,665. This was, said the *Advocate,* an alarming increase. For the first six months of 1933 the total arrests for drunkenness numbered 1,622; for the same period during 1934, 4,330. The arrests for liquor law violations during the first six months of 1933 totaled 904; in the same period during 1934, the number had jumped to 1,923. The traffic law violations showed even more marked increase, the total for the first six months of 1933 being 799, and the total for the same period during 1934, 3,926. Comparative figures for each month in the periods considered told the same story. The totals for each month in 1934 were higher than those for the same month in 1933. That Birmingham was suffering from the effect of National Repeal seemed an indisputable fact to the *Advocate*. If the state were to repeal her laws, or weaken them, that paper contended, the results would be inconceivably bad.[10] As further proof of the damage already done, the *Advocate* quoted part of Judge Henry B. Foster's charge to the grand jury in Tuscaloosa County. The Judge had told the jury that within a few days he would have been on the bench in Tuscaloosa County thirty-one years and that he knew

[8] *Alabama Christian Advocate,* October 11, 1934, quoted from the *Demopolis Times*. [9] December 13, 1934.
[10] *Alabama Christian Advocate,* July 19, 1934.

whereof he spoke when he said that crime conditions had been better under prohibition than under repeal.[11] The prohibition fight would have to be repeated, the *Advocate* warned. Prohibitionists must begin at once active efforts toward education and organization. Unlike the wets, they had little money to put into the fight, but what they lacked in money they could make up in prayer. Temperance, sobriety, and respect for law were at stake. It was inconceivable that Christian people should surrender to forces which openly despised these things.[12]

The North Alabama Conference adopted a report opposing the legalization of the sale of intoxicants. "No threats from any source, high or low, shall deter us from our God-impelled determination to prevent the legalization of this damnable traffic in our fair state," said the document.[13]

The W.C.T.U. expressed similar convictions:

> In view of the impending sessions of the Legislature of our beloved state and of the avowed purpose of bringing up for consideration the repeal of laws prohibiting the sale of beverage alcohol we take this opportunity to declare our opposition to repeal. And we urge upon our legislators their serious responsibility in dealing with this question.[14]

The Alabama Temperance Alliance, meeting December 5, 1934, at the First Methodist Church in Birmingham, took action to organize opposition to the repeal of the state prohibition laws. About a thousand people attended this meeting; they represented various religious denominations, the W.C.T.U., and the Anti-Saloon League. Harry Denman, business manager of the First Methodist Church, was elected president of the Alliance and Judge H. L. Anderton became state campaign manager for the fight to prevent repeal of the Alabama dry laws.[15]

The advocates of repeal organized their forces early in January, 1935. The League for Prohibition Repeal came into being as the spearhead of their movement. J. Sanford Mullins, of Alexander City, elected chairman of the League, was the ideal choice for the position. He had consistently worked against prohibition, both state and national, and had given conspicuous service in the campaign to secure Alabama's ratification of the federal repeal amendment.[16]

When the legislature convened on January 8, 1935, it was a foregone conclusion that a referendum bill would be passed. Both wets and drys were ready for the fight they knew would surely come.

Just before leaving office, Governor Miller sent a message to the legislature, reiterating his views on prohibition and urging that existing laws be retained. He moralized on the evils of the liquor traffic and was some-

---

[11] *Tuscaloosa News*, September 17, 1934, quoted by the *Alabama Christian Advocate*, September 27, 1934.
[12] *Alabama Christian Advocate*, October 25, 1934.
[13] *Journal of the North Alabama Conference, (November 7-11, 1934)*.
[14] *Report of the Alabama W.C.T.U., (October 9-11, 1934)*, pp. 50-52.
[15] *Alabama Baptist*, December 13, 1934.
[16] *Birmingham News*, January 13, 1935.

what inclined to blame enforcement officers for the failure of prohibition laws. The idea that legalizing and taxing the liquor traffic in the state for revenue would prove a good policy seemed fallacious to him. The governor's message probably had more influence on the voters of the state than on the members of the legislature.[17]

Governor Graves dealt with general principles in his inaugural address, but when he sent his first message to the legislature he made specific recommendations with regard to a prohibition referendum.

I think it advisable and necessary to the proper conduct of future legislation to enact as quickly as possible an act referring to the people prompt determination of the prohibition question. A bill indicating my views will be presented to your body at once with the hope that it will meet your approval and that we may submit this vexed question to be settled at an election and at a time to be set by you soon after the recess, and separate and apart from all other questions. I am sure that you know, as I do, that until this matter is definitely settled it will constantly recur and seriously affect much of the legislation that may be proposed.[18]

E. B. Parker, representative from Cleburne County, was quick to follow the governor's lead. At the very beginning of the session he brought in a referendum bill. It was referred to the Committee on Rules and favorably reported by that committee.[19] Parker's bill provided that the voters be asked first of all to decide whether they wanted the present laws retained. The advocates of modification declared that this provision put too much restriction on voters who might desire some changes in the present method of dealing with the liquor question, but who would strenuously oppose return of the open saloon. The first test votes in both branches of the legislature revealed considerable strength for the modificationists.[20] The bill was amended to meet their objections, and the House then passed it by a vote of 99 to 2.[21] Under its provisions, Alabama voters were to be asked to vote on three questions:

Question No. 1. Shall Alabama's present laws against the manufacture, sale and distribution of prohibited liquors be modified?
Question No. 2. Shall the manufacture, sale and distribution of beer (malt liquor) and wine (vinous liquors) be legalized in Alabama?
Question No. 3. Shall the manufacture, sale and distribution of hard liquors (spirituous liquors) be legalized in Alabama under strict State regulation, but under no condition any saloons?[22]

Senator J. M. Bonner, chairman of the temperance committee in the Senate, opposed the bill. It did not, he declared, give the drys anything to vote upon. He offered a substitute which would restore the original provisions of the bill, but his amendment was tabled.[23] His next move was

[17] *House Journal*, I (1935), 29-30.
[19] *Ibid.*, p. 89.
[21] *House Journal*, I (1935), 123.
[22] *Acts, Regular Session* (1935), pp. 5-6.
[23] *House Journal*, I (1935), 106-108.
[18] *House Journal*, I (1935), 76.
[20] *Decatur Daily*, January 18, 1935.

to introduce a petition signed by 30,000 men and women of Alabama who recorded their opposition to any changes in the bone-dry statutes. The W.C.T.U. workers were divided on the referendum bill. Mrs. F. W. Gist, of Montgomery, state legislative director for this organization, said she would urge Senator Bonner to desist from opposing a referendum. Mrs. Lamar Smith, state president, on the other hand, joined H. L. Anderton in supporting the Senator's position.[24] The bill, after debate and third reading, was passed by the Senate 29 to 3.[25]

The most influential daily papers favored the referendum and the repeal of the prohibition laws. The *Birmingham Age-Herald* summed up the arguments for repeal as follows:

> We need the revenue to be gotten from taxing the sale of liquor and beer. We need the self respect that will come from dealing boldly with an evil that overshadows our life. Drys keep on hammering away with the claim that repeal has not been an unmixed blessing. What has that to do with the situation in Alabama, a bootlegger's paradise under the nose of the driest governor the State has had? What has that to do when saloons are being specifically ruled out, when all that is being sought is to give a flourishing and irrepressible traffic the sanction and supervision of a law that can be enforced with the cordial co-operation of public opinion?[26]

J. Sanford Mullins declared that the wet forces would ask no quarter nor would they give any. He proceeded to perfect his organization and extend it into every precinct in the state. District chairmen were appointed for Birmingham, Montgomery, Mobile, and the Tennessee Valley. These district chairmen were assisted by county chairmen and they in turn were aided by precinct assistants. An effective liaison was maintained among all workers from the assistants to state headquarters in Montgomery.[27] Mullins said that he was particularly careful to select men familiar with the "deplorable conditions."

Meanwhile, the name of the state organization had been changed from the Alabama League for Prohibition Repeal to the Alabama League for Prohibition Modification. This, said Mullins, was a more accurate designation. Certainly it was calculated to attract voters who were opposed to outright repeal, but were willing to support modification.

W. O. Hare, secretary of the Alabama State Federation of Labor, called upon all friends of temperance to support the modification cause. Such action, he said, was in accord with the policy of the American Federation of Labor.[28]

Repealists made much of the contention that a great quantity of liquor was being sold in Alabama illegally under Federal license. Atticus Mullin said that Pensacola, Florida, was doing a land office whiskey business in

---

[24] *Montgomery Advertiser*, January 22, 1935.
[25] *Senate Journal*, I (1935), 108.   [26] January 19, 1935.
[27] *Birmingham Age-Herald*, January 26, 1935.
[28] *Montgomery Advertiser*, February 23, 1935.

Alabama. George Roak, City Manager of Pensacola, had jocularly remarked to Mullin: "It would not help us any for you to modify your prohibition laws in Alabama." The border counties of South Alabama were being flooded with Florida legalized beer and whiskey. They had been flooded with Florida moonshine while Florida was dry. Only repeal of the dry laws and the legal sale of liquor could remedy this condition.[29]

Since Alabama already had liquor, ran the argument of the wets, the state ought to get the revenue on it. Dry laws should be repealed to secure this end. Figures from the Internal Revenue Office in Birmingham showed 1,640 federal liquor licenses in effect in Alabama, valid till July 1, 1935. Six of these had been issued to hard liquor wholesalers, 71 to wholesale malt dealers, 669 to retailers of hard liquor, and 889 to retailers of malt liquors. This flourishing business had developed under the most rigid code of dry laws ever enacted, the *Birmingham News* noted, and under the most uncompromising dry governor the state ever had.[30]

The *Mobile Register* was convinced that repeal would relieve the heavy tax burden. Such benefits would moreover be cumulative. Breweries would be rehabilitated. Possibly new breweries would be built. Other industrial establishments would feel the effect of improved conditions. Taxable values of the state would mount.[31] J. Sanford Mullins estimated that the state would derive from $1,500,000 to $2,000,000 a year from the legal sale of liquor.[32] The *Mobile Register* believed that the prohibition law put too heavy a burden upon the taxpayers in consequence of sheriffs' liquor fees. This paper stated that William A. Holcombe, Jr., sheriff of Mobile County, had amassed, in search and seizure fees in liquor cases alone, about $80,000 during the four years he had been in office. That amazing sum was over and above the other emoluments of his office which were more than sufficient to pay him for the services he rendered.[33] The *Register* summed up its arguments in favor of repeal as follows:

(1) Public sentiment in this state, as expressed at the polls, is opposed to prohibition; (2) no law can be enforced in this state, or in any state, unless it has public sentiment behind it; (3) for twenty years prohibition laws in Alabama have been violated, openly and notoriously, in practically all parts of the state; (4) these laws have made lawbreakers out of citizens normally inclined to respect and obey the law; (5) liquor law violations have led to the violation of other laws, for lawlessness breeds lawlessness; (6) in the course of twenty years millions of dollars have been spent by the state, the counties and municipalities in a futile effort to enforce prohibition laws; (7) the existence of these laws, and the mockish effort to enforce them, have resulted in a criminal alliance between officers of the law and breakers of the law in some communities, thus sometimes corrupting the source of justice in the state;

[29] *Birmingham News*, February 3, 1935.
[30] *Birmingham News*, February 24, 1935.
[31] *Mobile Register*, February 15, 1935.
[32] *Birmingham News*, January 18, 1935.
[33] *Mobile Register*, January 12, 1935.

(8) in this same period millions of dollars worth of illicit and untaxed wines, beers and hard liquor have been smuggled into this state from other states and from foreign countries, to be sold and consumed in Alabama, and (9) in the meantime there has been a sharp increase in crime of all kinds, crimes against persons and crimes against property, with an alarming decrease in popular and general respect for the law, and we sometimes fear, a lowering of moral standards, usually, if indeed not always, the result of a loosening of legal restraints.[84]

The Reverend R. W. Hahn, pastor of the University Lutheran Church in Tuscaloosa took his stand with the repealists. He said: "There is nothing immoral in any alcoholic beverage; the morality depends upon the use or abuse to which the beverage is put; he who declares the sale and use of alcoholic beverages constitutes a sin against the moral law of God, perverts the law; he makes a sin of that which is no sin, and he usurps the authority of God in making laws for man." Here, declared the *Montgomery Advertiser*, was a telling lesson for those Christian ministers who held prohibition to be a part of salvation.[85]

Some women took the stump in behalf of modification. Miss Myrtle Miles, North Alabama Chairman of Women Modificationists, noting reports of sixty-one field workers,[86] predicted that the women in her district would give a large majority for modification. Strategic points in Jefferson County were visited the day before the election by the flying squadrons of Mrs. Lucy Wildman, Jefferson County Chairman of Women Modificationists. Mrs. B. M. Claypool went into St. Clair and Mrs. D. R. Smith into Marion County for final drives just before the election.

Eugene Connor, Jefferson County Chairman of the Alabama League for Prohibition Modification, directed an appeal to Alabama farmers. By voting for modification, he insisted, they would act to protect their children. Illicit liquor manufacturers exerted a debauching influence upon the youth of the rural districts. Children as young as eight years were being hired to scour the woods for pine knots for the fire at the still and to carry water for it from some spring. At first these children were paid ten to fifty cents a day; before long they were being paid in liquor. "I have seen more minors in the country villages under the influence of liquor than grown people in cities," Connor declared. "I ask the farmers of the state of Alabama were there any such conditions as these before prohibition?"[87]

The prohibitionists had also marshaled their forces. Anderton said that every county in the state had been organized for the battle with the wets.[38] County-wide meetings were held throughout the state. A campaign director was chosen for each county and was assisted by loyal workers in each precinct. The forces of the W.C.T.U. ably supported

[84] *Mobile Register*, January 26, 1935. [85] February 19, 1935.
[86] *Birmingham News*, February 25, 1936.
[87] *Birmingham Age-Herald*, February 15, 1935.
[88] *Birmingham News*, January 13, 1935.

Anderton, and young people's leaders also used their influence to oppose any changes in the dry laws.

Bishop Sam R. Hay urged the Methodists of Alabama to present a united front against any changes in the prohibition laws. He called a meeting of state denominational leaders on January 24 at the Dexter Avenue Methodist Church in Montgomery to organize their forces to fight repeal. All presiding elders, district lay leaders, district secretaries of all women's missionary societies, college presidents, and editors who were members of the Methodist Church were included in the call, and ministers and laymen of other churches were also invited. Paul T. Haley, president of the Anti-Saloon League, Mrs. Lamar Smith, president of the state W.C.T.U., Harry Denman, president of the Alabama Temperance Alliance, and campaign director Anderton were all speakers.[39]

The *Alabama Christian Advocate* noted that every speaker at this meeting was convinced that there were enough people in the state who hated liquor and who did not wish to see it legalized to win the fight if they would go to the polls. This constituted a challenge said the editor.

> This is a moral crusade free from politics. Nobody is running for office; nobody wants an office. It is a simple wet and dry fight. The wets want the prohibition laws of the state repealed so that beer, wine and liquor can be sold. The drys want to keep our prohibition laws so as to shield, as far as possible, our boys and girls from the temptations of alcoholic beverages. Everybody who believes in a temperate people, a Christian home and a saloonless nation ought to vote against the repeal of our prohibition laws.[40]

The *Alabama Baptist* proposed a plan of definite action to defeat repeal and urged "every lover of the dry cause to pass this word on." The plan contained seven points: (1) Register and pay poll tax. (2) Legalized liquor would not prevent bootlegging. (3) The return of beer and wine means the return of hard liquor. (4) It would not be desirable to operate schools on liquor tax. (5) Towns and cities would sell liquor and retain the revenue, but the youth of rural districts would be debauched. (6) Alabama should not become a bar-tender. (7) Prohibition in Alabama has been a success and not a failure.[41]

The Pastors' Union of Decatur appealed to the voters for the retention of the prohibition laws. Claims of the repealists that modification would end bootlegging ought to be disregarded, said these ministers. The only issue at stake was the protection of Alabama's boys and girls. A vote against modification was a vote for such protection.[42]

It was rumored that Governor Graves had sent word, by his lieutenants, that he wanted the people to vote for repeal. A delegation of forty drys, headed by Anderton, immediately called on him, asking him to confirm or deny this rumor. The Governor declared, "I am adhering in

[39] *Birmingham News*, January 13, 1935.
[40] *Alabama Christian Advocate*, January 31, 1935.
[41] *Alabama Baptist*, January 3, 1935.   [42] *Decatur Daily*, January 26, 1935.

every letter to the spirit of my campaign promise. I'm not taking any bets on the outcome. I have not directly or indirectly sent out word of any wish of mine and no one has authority to speak for me. I promised the people an untrammelled election and they will get one."[43]

Some out-of-state speakers assisted the drys in their fight. Dr. Mary Harris Armour of Atlanta, Georgia, lecturer for the W.C.T.U., and Sergeant Alvin York stumped the state. The *Montgomery Advertiser* ridiculed them in an editorial entitled, "The Drys and Local Talent." "If Alabama must have dry speakers to harangue innocent but mistaken widows and mothers, they should at least be from this state or home grown, so to speak." Sergeant York would have done better if he had stuck to his squirrel-shooting, said this editor.[44]

Dr. F. Scott McBride, general superintendent of the Anti-Saloon League of America, was another guest speaker. Seven counts in his indictment against the liquor program appeared in most of his addresses. Not one of the various methods of regulation or control adopted after repeal had proved successful or effective, he asserted. Drinking, drunkenness, and all evil effects of intoxication had invariably increased. Promises that the saloon would not come back had been promptly and shamelessly broken. Perfectly smokescreened by the legalized business, the illicit liquor traffic had continued its operations unabated. Promises to protect dry territory had been absolutely ignored. The cocktail hour had vastly increased drinking, particularly among young people and women. A colossal campaign of liquor advertising had revealed increasing indulgence and an expanded market.[45]

Ex-Governor B. M. Miller took his stand with the drys. "Wine is a mocker, strong drink is raging, and they that are deceived thereby are not wise," was the text of most of his addresses. For three years the liquor interests had been quietly bombarding the prohibition statutes of the state, he declared in a speech at Mobile. His concern for the happiness of Alabama's homes made him speak out and warn the people not to be deceived by the reports circulated by the liquor interests, that prohibition could not be enforced. He had been a circuit judge sixteen years and a judge on the state supreme court six years, he said, and he had never had any trouble enforcing liquor statutes. "But officials can't drink liquor and expect to enforce the prohibition laws," he added.[46]

The W.C.T.U. and other friends of temperance held a parade in Montgomery on February 22. Children carried placards begging the voters to "Save prohibition for Alabama." Other parade banners asked "What would Christ do?" The *Montgomery Advertiser* sarcastically remarked:

[43] *Decatur Daily,* February 9, 1935.
[44] *Montgomery Advertiser,* February 16, 1935.
[45] *Birmingham News,* February 22, 1935.
[46] *Mobile Register,* January 29, 1935.

Naturally the children who marched knew not what they were doing, and probably cared less. They were having a good time, making a white ribbon demonstration on the birthday of George Washington who owned a private distillery, and made his reputation fighting for freedom and the dignity of the individual.[47]

The campaign, however, seemed to stir only lukewarm popular enthusiasm. Several explanations were offered to account for this apathy. One was that the voters had already made up their minds. Another was that presentation of the issues had almost invariably been made by persons known to be either ardent prohibitionists or ardent liquor advocates; there had been nothing in the nature of a forum discussion. The advocates of retention, led by H. L. Anderton, had long been identified with the prohibition cause, and the exponents of modification, led by J. Sanford Mullins, had been perpetual opponents of both national and state prohibition.[48]

The election was held on February 26. Both Anderton and Mullins were confident of a decisive victory. Anderton was right. The official vote stood as follows: majority against repeal, 8,166; majority against wine and beer, 7,566; majority against hard liquors, 12,037.[49] Of the sixty-seven counties in the state, fifty-two voted to retain the prohibition laws. The largest majority against modification was 2,794 in De Kalb and the second largest was 1,671 in Walker.[50]

The repealists carried only fifteen counties which gave a total favorable majority of 27,919.[51] Jefferson County led with 10,767 votes for modification and Mobile County came second with a majority of 7,892. The highest percentage for modification was also found in Mobile. With the exception of Colbert, Madison, and Jefferson, all the counties which voted wet were located in the southern half of the state. The three largest urban centers voted overwhelmingly for modification; the rural counties in North Alabama in general rolled up large majorities against modification.

The *Birmingham News* congratulated the victors on their success, but could not congratulate the people on the outcome. A difficult situation had only been made worse. "It is no secret that some who had selfish interests in prohibition were in favor of retaining the dry laws," charged the *News*.[52] The *Alabama Journal* complained that the advocates of modification were making statements shocking to the sensibilities of many Alabama citizens. To characterize prohibition efforts as "revolting" and "obscene" was not calculated to win public approval, said the *Journal*. The cause of modification would have fared much better if other tactics had been used.[53] The *Birmingham Age-Herald* considered the dry vic-

[47] February 23, 1935; *Birmingham News*, February 23, 1935.
[48] *Alabama Journal*, February 25, 1935.
[49] *Alabama Official and Statistical Register* (1935), pp. 763-764.
[50] *Ibid.* [51] *Ibid.*
[52] *Birmingham News*, February 28, 1935.
[53] *Alabama Journal*, February 28, 1935.

tory a calamity. "Prohibition," it said, "as exemplified through the years in this state, has been repeatedly adjudged by the *Age-Herald* as a disastrous, compound failure."[54]

The *Alabama Baptist*, in an editorial written just before the election, declared that if the drys should win they would have wrought a great service to the state, to the youth, and probably to children yet unborn. But whether the drys won or lost, the editor added, all credit was due the little group of men in Birmingham who had dedicated their strength, time, and means to a noble cause. Chief among these men was Judge H. L. Anderton, who practically gave up his law practice to lead the fight.[55] The *Alabama Christian Advocate* hailed the election as "one of the most remarkable victories ever won over the brewers and distillers of the nation," adding, "the drys had a power that the wets had not reckoned with—the Lord God of Hosts was with us."[56]

H. L. Anderton remarked:

> The people have decreed through the ballot which is the only means at their command for speaking their will, that Alabama's laws shall not be modified. Every patriotic citizen should peacefully submit to this decree and turn his attention to the enforcement of the law. . . . Any citizen of Alabama who does not like the verdict of the people and who will not abide thereby should move out to wetter territory and build his breweries and distilleries. The liquor traffic will not be allowed to take the throne in Alabama.[57]

Before the official count had been made, the advocates of modification announced that they would go on fighting. Senator Isham Dorsey of Lee County, two days after the election, expressd his intention of introducing a local option bill when the legislature reconvened on April 30 which would legalize the sale of wine, beer, and whiskey in "all counties that went wet in the prohibition referendum." These counties deserved to have modification under strict state and county control, he said; and added: "I believe in de-moneytizing whiskey, that is, taking all the profit out of it and underselling the bootlegger and moonshiner."[58]

Since nearly half of the people in the state had shown themselves in favor of a change, said the *Birmingham News,* the difficulty of enforcing prohibition, particularly in the heavily wet centers, such as Birmingham, Mobile, and Montgomery, would be vastly increased. The statement of Senator Mullins that there should be "some relief" for these centers had merit. Doubtless Mullins had in mind some sort of local option provision. "It may be that this is the only practical solution to the liquor problem in Alabama."[59]

The *Alabama Journal* said that the preponderant majority for modifica-

[54] *Birmingham Age-Herald*, February 27, 1935.
[55] *Alabama Baptist*, February 28, 1935.
[56] *Alabama Christian Advocate*, March 7, 1935.
[57] *Decatur Daily*, February 28, 1935.
[58] *Ibid.* [59] February 28, 1935.

tion in the more populous counties deserved consideration from the legislature and no doubt the question would be warmly debated. Many citizens who had advocated the repeal of the federal amendment to the Constitution upon state rights grounds might well seek to apply the same principle of local self-government to county subdivisions within the state itself.[60]

The *Montgomery Advertiser* carried a front-page article saying that Alabama would get another chance to vote on beer. The headlines read, "Referendum slated in June under plan reputedly agreeable to the Governor." The voters had been confused in the February referendum, this paper believed, by the question relating to hard liquor. If the people were allowed to vote on beer only, they would favor it.[61]

M. E. Lazenby was disturbed because some newspapers reported that interested parties were already advertising local bills for counties that voted wet in the referendum. Nothing could be more absurd, he declared, than the idea that there could be local option in Jefferson, Montgomery, and Mobile counties without disadvantage to neighboring counties. He suggested that every reader of the *Alabama Christian Advocate* urge his representatives to vote against these local bills.[62]

When the legislature reconvened on April 30, the wets renewed the fight to legalize the sale of malt beverages. Senator C. M. A. Rogers of Mobile introduced a bill to authorize the sale of such beverages in counties that had a population of more than 75,000 people according to the last federal census. Proceeds from any such license tax were to be used for the benefit of the poor, needy, and unemployable people within those counties. The bill was referred to the temperance committee, which ordered it returned to the Senate with an adverse report. Senator Rogers' motion for further consideration of the bill was lost.[63] L. A. Sanderson of Montgomery County, introduced a similar bill in the House. It also received an adverse report from the temperance committee and was permitted to die without coming to a vote.[64]

Sanderson then introduced a bill to establish in every city, having a population of 60,000 or more, a dispensary for the sale of spirituous and vinous liquors. The temperance committee, to which the bill was referred, through its chairman Hamner, returned an adverse report on this measure also.[65]

W. C. Taylor of Mobile introduced a bill to authorize any municipality in the state to tax the possession, sale, and manufacture of spirituous, vinous, malt, or fermented liquors within its borders and police jurisdiction and to repeal all laws and parts of laws in conflict with such authority. This bill met the same fate as the others.[66]

[60] February 28, 1935. [61] March 28, 1935.
[62] *Alabama Christian Advocate*, April 18, 1935.
[63] *Senate Journal*, I (1935), 641, 673, 829.
[64] *House Journal*, I (1935), 506.
[65] *House Journal*, I (1935), 559, 672. [66] *House Journal*, I (1935), 1114.

The liquor forces were thwarted, at least temporarily. The referendum had gone against them, and the legislators were too sensitive to public opinion to enact either general or special legislation during the regular session in 1935. The drys were elated. But the wets continued to look to the future for what Mullins called "relief"—the right to sell liquor legally. The depletion of the state educational funds soon gave them their hoped-for opportunity.

The state superintendent of education had repeatedly stated that the funds were inadequate to operate the schools a normal term in 1935-1936. Governor Graves was determined to relieve the situation. He declared that an extraordinary occasion existed and issued a proclamation on February 8, 1936, calling the legislature in special session. Nothing was said in the call about any specific method of raising revenue, and a two-thirds vote would, therefore, be necessary to enact a law calling another referendum on the liquor question. Governor Graves later stated that unless the legislature voted either a sales tax or a tax on luxuries to provide the necessary funds for schools, he would veto any bill calling for a referendum.[67]

When the special session convened, Representative W. C. Harrison of Marengo County, at once introduced a bill to legalize and regulate the manufacture, sale, and possession of alcohol, and alcoholic and malt beverages. It proposed to create the office of Alcoholic Beverage Commissioner; to fix his salary and powers; and to provide for his appointment by the governor. A license upon the sale of alcoholic beverages would be levied and an excise tax would be imposed on such sale. Manufacture, sale, possession, and transportation of liquor would be regulated and general revenue provided for the state. All laws in conflict with the bill were to be repealed. Package sale of liquor would be allowed at an unlimited number of licensed stores; drinks might be sold at established clubs, and beer and wine dispensed freely. Whiskey would be taxed eighty cents a gallon, wine and beer ten cents, in addition to license taxes on manufacturers and wholesale and retail dealers. Total revenue to the state under such a law was estimated at $1,500,000.[68]

Representative Hamner opposed the passage of the bill. He declared: "The only things that can come from liquor are money and hell. It will bring only poverty, destruction, and misery." Hill Terry of Hale County, joined the fight saying, "Don't vote for this bill that will kill the two things we came here in special session to save—education and public health." A. L. Hanks of Talladega, declared that "The only success prohibition ever produced was Al Capone and his gang of racketeers."[69]

While the bill was before the House, more than five hundred prohibitionists, attending an Alabama Temperance Alliance mass meeting, marched on the capitol "to show the legislature we mean business against

[67] *Alabama Baptist,* March 19, 1936.
[68] *House Journal, Extra Session* (1936), pp. 547-584.
[69] *Huntsville Times,* March 20, 1936.

repeal." But when the marchers arrived both House and Senate were in their regular noon recess.[70]

The final vote on the bill was 64 for and 31 against, a bare two-thirds majority.[71] Speaker Harry Walker asked the Supreme Court for an advisory opinion as to its constitutionality. The opinion rendered upheld the referendum on repeal, because it involved primarily police power, and its revenue provisions were considered secondary.[72] The bill was then sent to the Senate where it received a vote of 19 to 14, less than the required two-thirds majority.[73]

During the debate on the bill wild confusion broke out in the Senate when J. Miller Bonner, prohibition chieftain, invited Tom Frazer of Bullock "outside," after an exchange of personalities. Both senators started for the door, but colleagues grabbed Frazer. Bonner walked to the rotunda, while Senator E. P. Russell, presiding, banged vainly for order. It took twenty minutes to get the two senators back to their seats.[74]

The *Alabama Christian Advocate* was thankful for the Senate's action. It remarked:

With the action of the state senate in defeating the proposed liquor legislation last week and the adjournment of the special session of the legislature, another crisis in the temperance affairs of Alabama was passed. . . . Let us be thankful that we are spared another strife-breeding contest on the liquor question at this time.[75]

The legislature adjourned on April 17. In its two-months session it had done nothing to enact the revenue legislation it had been called to devise. The merchants had vigorously opposed a sales tax, the prohibitionists were against a liquor tax, and the economy bloc probably did not want any tax the incidence of which might fall upon them.

What should be done about the depleted state treasury? The public health department was badly in need of funds and the public school situation was little short of tragic. In most counties the grade schools closed after terms of from five to seven months. In some communities the schools were continued by public subscription or by extra tuition fees. The *Alabama Christian Advocate* blamed "the determined opposition to any increase in taxation" for the plight of the schools.[76]

Although nothing could be done to relieve the situation after the legislature's fiasco, Governor Graves was determined to get some favorable financial legislation enacted in 1936-1937.

The drys were apprehensive that Governor Graves, noting the large majority favoring a liquor referendum in the legislature, might include a

[70] *Huntsville Times*, March 17, 1936.
[71] *House Journal, Extra Session* (1936), p. 587.
[72] *Ibid.*, pp. 627-630.
[73] *Senate Journal, Extra Session* (1936), p. 798.
[74] *Huntsville Times*, April 17, 1936.
[75] *Alabama Christian Advocate*, April 23, 1936.
[76] April 30, 1936.

liquor tax in his new call for a special session. Therefore, their leaders approached the governor in August with a promise to go "down the line" with him on any reasonable revenue program if he would omit from his proclamation the proposition of repeal of the state's dry laws. The governor made no reply to their proposal.

After this conference, Senator J. Miller Bonner, front-rank crusader for retention of the dry laws, warned the delegation that "if the Governor includes a liquor bill in his call, we cannot prevent its legislation." W. D. Graves, of Alexander City, told the same group, "We drys are not in a strong position to insist that prohibition repeal be omitted from the legislative call unless we agree to cooperate in finding such money as the state needs."[77]

The repealists had carried Jefferson County in the referendum of 1935, and most of that county's delegation had favored another referendum in 1936. Public opinion in the county and in the city of Birmingham was emphatically on the side of legal sale of liquor. The city fathers were quite responsive to the demands of the breweries and others for the legal sale of beer.

The city commission of Birmingham ordered an election to be held on August 18, 1936, to determine whether the laws on the statute books of the city against the sale of beer should be repealed. The election was carried by a vote of 11,099 to 758. W. O. Downs, police commissioner, thereupon instructed the police force not to interfere with the sale of beer in Birmingham. The state laws, however, had not been touched. They still prohibited the manufacture and sale of beer in Birmingham as elsewhere.

The Birmingham beer election was hailed by the wets as a great victory and they used every effort to make it an entering wedge to bring back legalized beer and hard liquors to Alabama. They declared that the election was a mandate to the legislature to repeal the state laws prohibiting the sale of beer. They urged the governor to include such legislation in his call for a special session so that it might be passed there by a simple majority without a referendum.[78]

The *Alabama Christian Advocate* had a different interpretation of the Birmingham vote. It declared, "The vote in this election indicates clearly that the temperance forces deliberately refrained from voting. They regarded it as a farce, a species of anarchy, and an affront to the law abiding citizens of the city and state."[79]

A rumor gained currency that Governor Graves had made a trade with the wets to include the legalization of the liquor traffic in his call, if they would vote for the administration's modified sales tax, or some other form

[77] *Montgomery Advertiser*, August 6, 1936; *Limestone Democrat*, August 6, 1936.
[78] *Alabama Christian Advocate*, August 27, 1936.
[79] *Alabama Christian Advocate*, August 27, 1936.

of taxation to provide money for education and public health. Dr. Seale Harris wrote:

> Personally, I will not believe that Governor Graves will intentionally offend the more than hundred thousand prohibitionists, who voted for him because they believe him to be a conscientious dry, until he has actually included the legalization of liquor in his next call for a special session of the Legislature.[80]

By the middle of November it was definitely known that the governor would call a special session. It was also currently reported that he expected to include in his official call a proposal for a referendum on the "State Store Plan" for legalizing the sale of alcoholic liquors. The *Alabama Christian Advocate* thought such a proposal jeopardized the youth of Alabama. "To enter upon such a terrible project for the sake of the revenue to be derived from the business is worse than Esau selling his birthright for a mess of pottage."[81]

Governor Graves' expected proclamation was issued. The sixth item reads as follows:

> To regulate the manufacture and sale of spirituous, vinous, or malt beverages through State owned and operated stores or other State supervision, and to provide for a referendum thereon to the electors of Alabama.[82]

When the legislature assembled on November 23, Governor Graves said in his message that he firmly believed that the long-established policy of Alabama on intoxicants should be changed only by the people. He did not favor having the people vote on a "cat in the bag." He preferred that some specific measure be presented to them.

The governor was insistent that any plan to legalize liquor should insure to the government all the profits from such traffic. A state store system might, he believed, yield the government two and one-half millions of dollars annually, if the state had the wholehearted cooperation of county and city governments. He urged the legislators to divide the proceeds, sixty per cent to the state, twenty per cent to the cities, and twenty per cent to the counties.

The revenue would be placed in the general fund and used for such purposes as health and welfare. The appropriation of the insane hospital might thus be increased. Educational and agricultural programs would be provided for in a special education trust fund.

In closing his message, the governor said that bills would be laid before the legislature which would carry out the general program. These bills would provide that established hotels, restaurants, and clubs might sell intoxicants in unbroken packages and would put no limitation on municipalities as to what license they might charge the venders.[83]

---
[80] *Alabama Baptist*, September 24, 1936.
[81] *Alabama Christian Advocate*, November 19, 1936.
[82] *Senate Journal, Special Session* (1936-1937), pp. 3-4.
[83] *Senate Journal, Special Session* (1936-1937), pp. 31-33.

The *Huntsville Times* favored legalizing and taxing the sale of alcoholic beverages in Alabama. Such action would bring revenue from a great business now operating scot-free of taxation. People who wanted to drink whiskey or beer, said the *Times*, were perfectly willing to pay a levy on these beverages. People who did not drink would not be affected by the new taxes. The editor estimated that the revenue derived from this source would range from $1,500,000 to $3,000,000 a year.[84]

On November 24, E. C. Boswell of Geneva County, introduced a bill in the House designed to meet the wishes of the governor. It was called "An Act to Promote Temperance and Suppress the Evils of Intemperance," and it provided for a county referendum to determine whether or not the liquor should be sold in each county. The bill proposed the creation of a department of Alcoholic Beverage Control and defined the functions, duties, and powers thereof. It provided for the appointment, suspension, removal, compensation, costs and expenses of such board and its members. It stipulated that beer and other beverages containing less than twenty-five per cent alcohol could be sold at retail by persons legally authorized in the counties voting for modification. The act was to be designated and cited as the "Alcoholic Beverage Control Act."

After its third reading, the House passed this bill by a vote of 54 to 32,[85] and sent it to the Senate. There it soon struck a snag. The temperance committee offered a substitute which was rejected. Certain senators complained that the bill would make possible "unbridled, political patronage." They opposed giving the governor unlimited power to appoint and remove members of the Beverage Control Board. The *Mobile Register* remarked: "The Graves administration's interest in repeal seems to be based largely on a desire for increased revenue and an opportunity to dole out more jobs to political favorites."[86] The *Register* thought that the principal reason for the defeat of the repeal bill in the Senate was the feeling of several senators that the Graves administration was bent on setting up a system which would result in widespread corruption. The governor was unwilling to permit the Senate to confirm his appointments, and therefore, several senators with wet sympathies joined with the drys to vote against the measure. The vote stood 13 for and 19 against the bill.[87]

The Senate, however, reconsidered its vote a few days later and set the measure down as a special order of business. The vote for reconsideration was 22 to 9. Anti-administration members who favored Senate confirmation of appointments to a Beverage Control Board urged a compromise. Senator Bonner charged that Governor Graves had exerted administration influence to force reconsideration and to swing votes from prohibition ranks.[88]

[84] November 15, 1936.
[85] *House Journal, Special Session* (1936-1937), p. 168.
[86] January 10, 1937.
[87] January 10, 12, 13, 1937.
[88] *Mobile Register*, January 13, 1937.

The Senate drew up a bill calling for a state referendum on a state liquor store system. Governor Graves called attention to this provision. The House, however, receiving the bill from the Senate, rejected it. Representative J. R. Wallace of Clarke County remarked that the dry vote in Alabama represented not only the opinion of sincere prohibitionists, but also of the bootleggers.[89]

A conference committee was then appointed to frame a bill satisfactory to both branches of the legislature. This committee agreed on a prohibition referendum by counties. Counties voting wet would be privileged to do away with prohibition regardless of the outcome of the total state vote in the referendum. Counties voting dry would be permitted to remain faithful to prohibition. This amounted to nothing more than a referendum on local option and was, therefore, pleasing to the largest urban centers of the state.[90]

Both the House and the Senate adopted the recommendation of the conference committee. Senator Bonner led a vigorous but losing fight against its adoption. The senators, he declared, were breaking faith with the people "who voted by an 8,000 majority in 1935 against any change in Alabama's prohibition laws."[91] But the bill, after its third Senate reading, passed by a vote of 20 to 13.[92] It was adopted in the House by a vote of 59 to 33.[93]

Governor Graves, however, vetoed the bill. He preferred, he said, the state-wide referendum as provided in the original Senate bill. He suggested that the bill be amended by incorporating a provision for such a referendum.[94] The Senate rejected the governor's suggestion by a vote of 20 to 13 and repassed the bill by the same vote.[95] The House took similar action, voting 30 to 66 against the revision and 65 to 32 to repass the vetoed bill.[96]

While the bill was under consideration, Edward F. Taylor, Clerk of the House of Representatives, stated that two agents of the Alabama and Florida liquor interests had told him they would give him $10,000 to have the legislature sustain the veto of Governor Graves. They also declared, Taylor asserted, that they had $100,000 to spend to keep Alabama dry. Taylor declared that he did not consider the offer a bribe but an effort to nire him to help defeat the bill.[97] Governor Graves thought a committee should be appointed to investigate Taylor's report, and the Senate acted to appoint such a committee, jointly with the House.[98] The resolution was referred to the standing committee on rules but no action was taken.

[89] *Mobile Register*, January 27, 1937.
[90] *Mobile Register*, January 29, 1937.   [91] *Ibid.*
[92] *Senate Journal, Special Session* (1936-1937), p. 647.
[93] *House Journal, Special Session* (1936-1937), p. 647.
[94] *Senate Journal, Special Session* (1936-1937), pp. 540-542.
[95] *Ibid.*, p. 543.   [96] *House Journal, Special Session* (1936-1937), pp. 702, 704.
[97] *Mobile Register*, February 2, 1937.
[98] *Senate Journal, Special Session* (1936-1937), pp. 534-535.

THE PROHIBITION MOVEMENT IN ALABAMA 251

The rejection of the governor's executive amendment to the repeal bill, said the *Mobile Register,* meant that on March 10, the sixty-seven counties of Alabama would have the opportunity to decide whether they wished to remain nominally dry or legalize the sale of alcoholic beverages within their boundaries.[99] "So we start toward common sense and genuine control and taxation in handling the traffic. And we may be sure that thus have the people of Alabama taken a great step forward,"[100] was the comment of the *Birmingham Age-Herald.* The *Montgomery Advertiser* remarked, "Any county that is tired of prohibition and its indecencies will now have an opportunity to vote itself under control of the proposed State Liquor Store's law."[101]

But the *Alabama Christian Advocate* deplored the turn of affairs. "We regret that it has come. There was no just cause for the referendum. After the referendum two years ago there should have been a cessation of the repeal agitation, at least during the remaining period of the present administration. . . . Let the church people and the moral forces of Alabama follow the leadership of Dr. Harry Denman, president of the Alabama Temperance Alliance. All other organizations will cooperate and we will win another victory for righteousness."[102] And the *Alabama Baptist* scored, as the "most iniquitous phase," the provisions of the bill that revenue from the sale of liquors would go to old-age pensions. This, said the editor, was a clever stroke by the wets to fasten the legalized liquor traffic permanently on the people.[103] And the editor of the *Limestone Democrat* said that, as a consistent dry, he would vote against the legalization of the sale of intoxicating beverages and would urge the electorate to do likewise.[104]

The "Alabama Beverage Control Act"[105] provided that the probate judge of any county, upon written petition of twenty-five per cent of the qualified voters of the county at the last general election, should be required to order an election not less than thirty nor more than forty-five days from the date of filing the said petition. He must give notice by publication in the county paper at least three weeks before the date of the election. If there should be no newspaper, publicity might be given by posting a notice at the courthouse. The ballot used in such elections had to follow this form: "Do you favor the legal sale and distribution of alcoholic beverages within this county? Yes...... No......." If a majority of the voters marked their ballots *yes* the county was to become wet and so remain until that county changed its status in a subsequent election. Elections could be held in any county six months after March

[99] *Mobile Register,* February 1, 1937.
[100] *Birmingham Age-Herald,* February 3, 1937.
[101] February 3, 1937.   [102] February 11, 1937.
[103] February 11, 1937.   [104] February 25, 1937.
[105] *General Acts, Special Session* (1936-1937), pp. 40-85. Cited hereafter as the ABC Act.

10, 1937. Thereafter, two years had to elapse between such elections in any county.

The Act created the Alabama Beverage Control Board, consisting of three persons appointed by the governor with the advice and consent of the Senate. The governor was authorized to designate one member of the Board as chairman. The members of the Board were to receive their actual expenses while engaged in the performance of their duties, and a per diem of $10 not to exceed $1,200 yearly. A member of the Board must have lived in Alabama for at least ten years before his appointment, and he must be a qualified voter in the state. The members were to be appointed for the following terms: one for two, one for four, and one for six years. Before entering upon his duties, each member was required to give bond with a surety or guaranty company to the state of Alabama, in a form approved by the attorney-general. Montgomery was designated as the headquarters of the Board. The Board was empowered to appoint an administrator to serve at the Board's pleasure and to receive a salary of $5,000 per annum. He must execute a $25,000 bond, payable to the state of Alabama. The administrator's powers were extensive under this law. He was to have authority to appoint clerks, stenographers, inspectors, chemists, and other employees of the Board. He was to act as manager, secretary, and custodian of all the records unless the Board otherwise ordered.

The Board was authorized by this bill to manufacture, buy, and sell alcoholic beverages; to control possession, sale, transportation, and delivery of beverages; and to determine the localities within which state liquor stores might be established and operated. It was authorized to provide for the maintenance of beverage warehouses; to lease, occupy, or purchase property; to grant, issue, suspend or revoke licenses; to appoint liquor store managers responsible for carrying out the provisions of the Act. With the approval of the Board, the manager might in turn employ additional helpers.

The Alabama Liquor Control Board would designate the hours for opening and closing its stores, but in no event might such stores remain open for business between 9 p.m. and 9 a.m. "Furthermore," said the Act, "there shall be no State Liquor Stores operated on Sunday, primary election day, general election day, or municipal election day under any circumstances."

Under this Act Alabama Liquor Stores would sell their goods at wholesale to the hotels, restaurants, clubs, railroads, Pullman and steamboat companies. All sales made by and through State Liquor Stores were to be for cash only. Every purchaser of liquor or of vinous beverages from a State Liquor Store would receive a numbered receipt bearing such information as the Board might deem necessary. "A duplicate record of all sales of liquor and vinous beverages from State Liquor Stores shall be retained by and shall form a part of the records of such store." No liquor could be sold, given, or served to any person under twenty-one, to any intoxicated person, or to an habitual drunkard.

Each State Liquor Store would be required to make daily deposits of receipts in a designated state depository. The manager of each State Liquor Store and the Board must make daily reports of all daily deposits to the State Comptroller. The net profits of these stores were to be distributed monthly, as follows: fifty per cent to the general fund exclusively for old-age pensions and other purposes of the State Department of Public Welfare; ten per cent to the general fund of the state which is distributed equally among the sixty-seven counties; ten per cent to the general fund of the state to be distributed equally among the counties for public health, old-age pensions, and for other purposes of the county departments of public welfare; twenty per cent to the municipality in which the State Liquor Store was located.

The Board was to be empowered to issue licenses to hotels, restaurants, and clubs. Such licensees might sell malt or brewed beverages as defined in this Act, not in excess of twenty-four per cent by volume. Applicants for such licenses were required to file with the Board a written application and pay a fee of $25 in towns of 4,500 to 25,000 population, and $100 in towns of more than 25,000 population. Every license issued under this Act had to be constantly and conspicuously exposed under transparent substance on the licensed premises. The Board was empowered to transfer licenses upon the collection of a $10 fee.[106]

Manufacturers of vinous, malt, or brewed beverages for sale were forbidden to do business in Alabama without a wholesale license. Every manufacturer had to keep a record showing the raw materials received and used in the manufacture of such beverages, sale of these goods, quantities of goods stored, and the names and addresses of purchasers. Licenses might be issued to corporations duly organized and registered under the laws of Alabama when it appeared that all officers and directors of the corporation were citizens of the United States, and at least fifty-one per cent of the capital stock was owned by citizens of the United States. Only malt or brewed beverages could be sold or distributed under the licenses granted to such wholesale dealers.

Every person or firm expecting to apply for a distributor's, wholesaler's, or retailer's license was required to file an application with the Board. Applications of distributors and wholesalers had to be filed at a time specified by the Board. At the time of filing the application, the applicant must pay the filing fee of $10. The application for licenses must contain the name and residence of the applicant, his place of birth, the place where the license was to be used, and the name of the owner of the property.

[106] *General Acts, Special Session* (1936-1937), pp. 40-85.

Certain prohibitions affected the granting of licenses. Retail dispensers could operate a number of places for the sale of malt or brewed beverages but they were required to have a separate license for each place. No person might possess or have issued to him more than one distributor's or wholesaler's license. Licenses might be granted only to reputable persons, associations, or organizations. The licensee whose retail license was revoked was ineligible to secure another license under the Act within three years.[107]

The repeal advocates and prohibition forces, traditional foes in Alabama politics, planned spirited campaigns in each of the sixty-seven counties which, on March 10, were to vote whether to remain under the state's twenty-two-year-old bone-dry statutes.

The repealists emphasized closely knit county organizations, and paid little attention organizing the state as a whole. They had carried only fifteen counties in 1935, but they confidently hoped to double this number in 1937.[108] Able men were carefully chosen for county campaign directors. Among these was Judge Norville R. Leigh, Jr., of Mobile County, who had the unqualified respect of the community. The directors appointed committeemen in each precinct.[109]

In Jefferson County repealists rallied their forces around a legalization league "to make them pay taxes" and to "rid the county of the insidious bootleg evils." Albert Boutwell, director of this league, announced that Jake R. Payne, widely known Birmingham attorney, had accepted the chairmanship of its young men's division and that he would start immediately to enlist young voters in every beat in the county.

The Women's Legalization League of Jefferson County also took vigorous action. Mrs. Lucy J. Wideman, chairman of the women's division, announced that headquarters had been opened at the Thomas Jefferson Hotel, that volunteers were pledging assistance, and that more speakers would soon be ready to take the stump.[110]

Taxation was everywhere the keynote of the repealist propaganda. Chairman Boutwell claimed that legalization would bring lower taxes on real estate. Illegal liquor traffic, he also claimed, was doing an annual business of approximately $25,000,000 and paying not one penny in taxes. Repeal of the dry laws would be followed by two beneficial results— decreased taxes on homes and additional revenue for the state's human welfare program.[111]

Moreover, said Boutwell, the trade of the Birmingham district would be improved if liquor could be legalized. Specifically he claimed that Jefferson County would enjoy even greater prosperity "if voters March 10, exchange the outmoded laws for an intelligent liquor control system." With paved highways converging in Jefferson County from all the North

[107] *General Acts, Special Session* (1936-1937), pp. 40-85.
[108] *Mobile Register*, February 7, 1937.   [109] *Ibid.*, February 9, 1937.
[110] *Birmingham Age-Herald*, February 19, 20, 1937.
[111] *Ibid.*, February 22, 1937.

Alabama counties, Boutwell remarked, nothing could prevent Birmingham and other cities of the county from attracting thousands of North Alabamians, once they were freed from the shackles of prohibition. Some North Alabama counties would probably vote dry, he explained, and a tide of business would then flow from such areas to Birmingham and adjacent towns. "The hotel operator may expect thousands of more guests annually from the dry areas for their respites here."[112]

The wets declared also that they favored repeal because they believed in law observance. Between 1917 and 1936 there had been 113,825 dry law convictions in Birmingham alone—a number equal to about one half of the city's population. Under the dry laws, drinking of bootleg liquors, as shown by annual police reports, had increased 500 per cent. A vote to retain the dry laws would be equivalent, said the repealists, to approving these flagrant violations of the law.[113]

Hugh Sparrow wrote that, during the last sixteen years of prohibition in Birmingham, dry law violations had apparently increased the number of white women arrested annually about 300 per cent. This was a much greater increase than that for white men arrested during the same period. Mrs. Claudia Williams, Birmingham policewoman, said the use of liquor by women during prohibition undoubtedly accounted for the increase of women arrested. Mrs. Williams said that her docket showed seventy white women arrested in February, 1937, and placed in the South Side jail; fifty-two of them had been arrested for drunkenness, and four more had been charged with driving while drunk. About half the number, she added, were middle-aged women and "the entire group was not confined to the lower class of women by any means." The annual reports of the Birmingham Police Department for the fiscal years of 1919-1920 and 1935-1936 show the tremendous increase in arrests of white women. In 1919-1920, shortly after the beginning of the prohibition era, such arrests aggregated 798. In 1935-1936 the number had mounted to 2,198.[114]

The *Montgomery Advertiser* considered repeal a panacea for all ills. Liquor could be removed from politics; bootlegging would be reduced to a minimum; temperance would be promoted; unemployment would be greatly reduced; taxes on real estate would be lessened; new revenue would swell the depleted state treasury; and the state would be saved millions in the cost of law enforcement and the maintenance of dry law violators in the penitentiary.[115]

The drys meanwhile moved to strengthen their state and county organizations. Harry Denman, president of the Alabama Temperance Alliance and state campaign director, called a temperance meeting at the Dexter

[112] *Birmingham Age-Herald*, February 23, 1937.
[113] *Ibid.*, March 2, 1937. [114] *Birmingham Age-Herald*, March 6, 1937.
[115] *Montgomery Advertiser*, February 1 to March 9, 1937, *passim;* *Birmingham News*, February 1 to March 9, 1937, *passim;* *Mobile Register*, February 1 to March 9, 1937, *passim.*

Avenue Methodist Church, Montgomery, on February 23, where Dr. L. L. Gwaltney, president of the Alabama State Baptist Convention and editor of the *Alabama Baptist,* delivered the keynote address. "If one county goes wet, Alabama will be a wet state," said Dr. Gwaltney. But that would not mean the issue was closed. "All we can do is bide the time until we can get men in office who will enforce the law. In the next election we will elect a governor and legislature who will do our bidding, and brother, don't you think I can't carry some votes in Alabama."[116]

The gathering discussed plans for prohibition campaigns in each county in the state, and for the thorough organization by the dry leaders of "every precinct." It passed a resolution calling upon Governor Graves to make public the results of the investigation into charges by Edward F. Taylor, Clerk of the House of Representatives, that the liquor interests had offered him money to work against the repeal bill.[117]

The tactics of the Morgan County dry organization were typical of the methods used by drys all over the state. Here prohibitionists launched their drive with a meeting at the Central Methodist Church in Decatur. A fair-sized crowd attended and heard various speakers predict confidently that Morgan would vote dry in the coming election. George T. Woodruff of Decatur and Elliott Peck of Hartselle were named co-chairmen to organize every beat in the county.[118]

Leaders of church young people's organizations attended a rally in Montgomery and took their stand with the foes of repeal. Their campaign added new methods to the drys' techniques. Radio programs were planned for Birmingham, Mobile, Montgomery, and Gadsden. Three-minute talks on the issues of the campaign were scheduled in various churches just before each Sunday morning sermon. Some of the young people solicited votes and distributed temperance literature.[119]

Senator Miller Bonner, addressing a Rotary Club in Montgomery which had invited him to speak on prohibition, made the bold prediction that, in 1938, "the prohibitionists would elect a governor who would enforce the prohibition law even if he had to call out the National Guard." The *Montgomery Advertiser* remarked: "We agree with the senator if he believes that the way to enforce prohibition is to establish martial law."[120]

The pastors of Montgomery issued a statement strongly condemning the liquor traffic and urging members of churches to vote against repeal. The statement was as follows:

We, the undersigned Christian ministers of the City of Montgomery recognize the liquor traffic as an age-old enemy of human welfare and the noblest

---

[116] *Birmingham Age-Herald,* February 24, 1937.
[117] *Birmingham Age-Herald,* February 24, 1937.
[118] *Decatur Daily,* February 9, 1937.
[119] *Birmingham Age-Herald,* February 27, 1937.   [120] February 26, 1937.

things of life; we deplore the fact that in our city our honored officials and some of our citizens have chosen to create the present lamentable situation in open opposition to the established laws of the Commonwealth; we recognize that liquor has no place in civilized society and as an evil is not necessary, and we pray God and call on all Godly citizens on March 10 with their conscientious votes to do their part to push the liquor traffic back into its Satanic lair from which it has crawled to our very doorways to plague our religious, domestic, political, social, and business life.[121]

The Pastors' Union of Birmingham adopted a similar resolution and issued an address to the citizens of Jefferson County.

Weaknesses in the bill itself were eagerly emphasized by the opponents of repeal. Dr. Gwaltney, co-director of their state campaign, urged the voters to read and study the bill with great care. "This act," he said, "puts into the hands of one man, the governor, whoever he may be, the most dangerous political control." The governor would have power to appoint and fire the control board at his pleasure and he could use this power to control the brands of liquor purchased and sold, the prices, the location of liquor stores, the purchase of all lands and buildings, all appointees and employees, the making of all rules and regulations for selling liquors, and the operation of breweries and distilleries. This was a dangerous power to give to any man.[122]

A vote for the bill, Dr. Gwaltney said, would be a vote for more tax money for the political bosses to spend and more political pie for them to distribute. Each wet vote would help to put the state into private business for the first time; and every citizen so voting would be a partner with the state in manufacturing and selling intoxicating liquors to debauch the people of Alabama. "Last, but by no means least," said Gwaltney, "let us always bear in mind that crime and liquor are inseparable. If we vote into Alabama more liquor, we vote for more crime with all its dangers and degradations."[123]

Ex-Governor Miller toured the state speaking against repeal. Judge Leon McCord introduced him when he spoke at the Dexter Avenue Methodist Church and emphasized his own record as a local optionist. "I have never voted a prohibitionist ticket and never broke a prohibition law, and I don't intend to," said McCord. "But this bill is not a local option bill. It sets me up in the liquor business. I am not aiming to sell it. I don't want the trade. But it gives me a bottle, and it gives me a store and says now sell it. I'm not 'gonner' do it."[124]

Establishment of a state liquor store would violate the democratic principle of majority rule, Miller asserted. The bill was deceptive and it would certainly make possible the creation of a political machine. It provided for a board that could open stores, put managers in them; and these

[121] *Montgomery Advertiser*, February 21, 1937.
[122] *Birmingham Age-Herald*, February 23, 1937.
[123] *Ibid.* [124] *Montgomery Advertiser*, March 3, 1937.

managers, in turn, could hire clerks. Only residents of the county and qualified voters were eligible for such appointments. That meant, the ex-governor said, that a political machine powerful enough to crush out all democracy in the state would almost inevitably come into being. Few counties, Miller predicted, would go wet and he nicknamed these counties "Alabama's babies." "Bibb Graves will be the pappy, the legislature will be the mammy. . . . And after they set up the Bibb Graves Alabama Liquor Stores then (they) will come along with a Bibb Graves Alabama Brewery. After that there will be a Bibb Graves Alabama Winery, and then there will be a Bibb Graves Alabama Distillery."[125]

Mrs. S. T. Slaton, chairman of the state woman's division against repeal, illustrated many of her campaign speeches with educational moving pictures showing the bad effects of intoxicants. Two days before the election she issued a call for prayer. "The Christian people of the state of Alabama," read this call, "are asked to meet in their churches Monday afternoon, March 8, at 2 o'clock, for united prayer that the state of Alabama may be kept from entering the liquor business."[126]

Mrs. George Adams of Andalusia, president of the Federation of Women's Clubs of Alabama, stated to the press her opposition to the liquor bill and sent out letters to the presidents of women's clubs urging their support in the fight. Mrs. M. E. Moreland, president of the Third District of Federated Women's Clubs, followed Mrs. Adams' lead in the district she represented. Mrs. Felix Jones, president of the Birmingham Parent-Teachers Association, also used her influence for the retention of the dry laws.[127]

The intensive, hard-fought campaign came to an end on March 9. On March 10 the voters went to the polls to vote on the following question: "Do you favor the legal sale and distribution of alcoholic beverages in this county?"[128] Twenty-four counties cast a majority vote for repeal; forty-three voted to remain dry.[129] The total vote in the state for repeal was 98,051; the total vote against repeal, 100,474. The drys had carried the state by a majority of 2,432. Since the twenty-four counties carried by the wets contained more than half of the state's population, it is evident that many people in these counties had voted against repeal.[130]

Six of the counties voting wet border on Florida. Thirteen others are contiguous to the six border counties. The claim was made that the influx of liquor from Florida influenced the vote of these counties. Only

[125] Ibid.
[126] Birmingham Age-Herald, and Birmingham News, March 6, 1937.
[127] Birmingham Age-Herald, March 5, 1937.
[128] General and Local Acts, Special Session (1936-1937), p. 81.
[129] Birmingham Age-Herald, March 13, 1937. Counties voting for repeal were Jefferson, Montgomery, Mobile, Baldwin, Barbour, Bullock, Colbert, Covington, Crenshaw, Dallas, Escambia, Etowah, Geneva, Greene, Henry, Houston, Lee, Lowndes, Madison, Monroe, Perry, Pike, Russell, and Washington.
[130] Birmingham Age-Herald, March 13, 1937; Limestone Democrat, March 18, 1937.

two counties in the Tennessee Valley, Colbert and Madison, voted for repeal. Apparently the race question did not figure in the election; for some of the counties having large Negro population voted for repeal. The *Birmingham Age-Herald* attributed the difference in the vote in the northern and southern sections to the difference in the cultural background of the people who settled these regions. In South Alabama, Gallic and Latin strains predominated and the people naturally took a different view toward drinking than did the much stricter Anglo-Saxons who had settled the northern section of the state.[131] The *Montgomery Advertiser* took some credit for the results. It said, "One of the deciding factors in repeal of Alabama's prohibition law, we think it fair to say, was the information that the *Advertiser* printed about the Virginia plan."[132]

"A smashing victory for reform, realism, and revenue," was the *Birmingham Age-Herald's* comment on the election returns.[133] The *Montgomery Advertiser* remarked: "Now we have established another type of control in Alabama. We who oppose prohibition have had our way.... The *Advertiser* freely grants that the 'wets' of Alabama, to whom it has been faithful for more than a century under more than a dozen ownerships, under more than a score of editorships, are now on the spot." If they did not accept their responsibility prohibition would be reestablished in Alabama.[134]

The *Alabama Christian Advocate* complained that prohibitionists had the bad habit of resting, even going to sleep, after a victory. They had become complacent after the referendum of 1935, whereas the booze advocates had been spurred to new effort, "and as a consequence, we have the present situation in our state."[135] The *Alabama Baptist*, regretting that twenty-four counties had voted to repeal the dry laws, nevertheless struck an optimistic note: "Temperance education and sane enforcement will swing the pendulum to prohibition."[136]

[131] *Birmingham Age-Herald*, March 13, 1937.
[132] March 13, 1937.
[133] March 11, 1937.
[134] March 12, 1937.
[135] March 19, 1937.
[136] March 18, 1937.

CHAPTER XIII

STATE LIQUOR STORE SYSTEM, 1937-1943

Although the advocates of the State Liquor Store had won elections in twenty-four counties on March 10, approximately two months elapsed before a store was opened. An appropriation had to be made for the initial purchases; buildings had to be rented and equipment installed; and suitable persons had to be employed before business could actually begin. Montgomery completed these preliminaries and opened the first State Liquor Store on May 5. Birmingham and Mobile were close seconds, opening their stores on May 7.[1] In Birmingham long lines of customers waited on the sidewalk for the door to open. Well-dressed men and women, as well as those whose general appearance indicated that they needed the necessaries of life instead of liquor, stood in these lines. Both white customers and Negroes waited their opportunity to purchase beverages.

Fifty-four stores were opened in twenty-five wet counties between May 5 and October 14, 1937. Those at Hartford and Samson in Geneva County were closed again on November 10, the day after the county changed its status from wet to dry in a special election. Cullman changed from the dry to the wet column on September 28, 1937, and Marengo made a similar shift on June 14, 1938. Of the fifty-two stores in operation on December 31, 1937, forty-one were retail only, one was wholesale only, and ten combined retail and wholesale business. Stores in large city areas were operated during the twelve-hour period allowed under the law, from 9 a.m. to 9 p.m. daily except Sundays, election days, and legal holidays. Local regulations governed store hours in the small cities and towns. The average daily number of store sales made during December, the peak month of 1937, ranged from 78 at Robertsdale to 2,386 at the Birmingham number eleven store. The average daily values of these sales were $88.10 and $6,270.61 respectively. The Robertsdale store was operated by one man; store number eleven in Birmingham employed nineteen persons.[2]

According to the provisions of the ABC Act, hotels and restaurants were permitted to procure licenses to sell wine, liquor, and beer. Since 1937 the ABC Board has issued annually more than two thousand licenses to retailers of beer. The liquor licenses come second but are not as numerous as those for beer. Wine licenses are very few. The following tables[3] show the number of private dealers, State Liquor Stores, volume of business, net profits, and allocation of the proceeds.

[1] *First Annual Report of Alabama Alcoholic Beverage Control Board*, p. 31.
[2] *First Annual Report of Alabama ABC Board*, p. 12.
[3] *Annual Reports of Alabama Alcoholic Beverage Control Board* (1937-1940), *passim*.

LICENSES

	1937	1938	1939	1940
Beer	3,272	2,794	2,481	2,229
Liquor	271	283	370	374
Wine	6	7	9	7

NUMBER OF STORES AND FINANCIAL DATA

Year	No. Stores at End of Year	Sales	Cost of Goods	Net Profit
1937	52	$ 5,963,941.30	$ 3,909,522.22	$1,420,420.93
1938	56	8,957,779.80	5,799,276.52	2,010,782.73
1939	55	9,674,086.54	6,255,680.51	2,432,643.73
1940	53	11,776,410.80	7,495,498.19	3,197,822.38
Total		$36,372,218.44	$23,459,977.44	$9,061,569.77

The total revenue going to the governmental agencies of Alabama during the four years of operation of the ABC Board may be summarized as follows:

Year	Stores' Profit	Beer Tax and License Income	County Licensing	Total ABC Revenue
1937	$1,420,420.93	$ 477,738.13	$ 60,561.02	$ 1,958,620.08
1938	2,010,782.73	267,436.56	60,887.51	2,339,106.80
1939	2,432,643.73	233,716.95	56,108.44	2,722,469.12
1940	3,197,822.38	214,544.69	58,386.34	3,470,753.41
Total	$9,061,669.77	$1,193,436.33	$235,843.31	$10,490,949.41

The total ABC revenue of $10,490,949.41 was allocated to beneficiaries under the Beverage Control Act as follows:

State General Fund, ABC Stores Profit	$ 3,931,923.71	
State General Fund, ABC Stores Profit, 1940 excess	997,822.38	
State General Fund, Beer Tax and License Income	1,193,436.33	$6,123,182.42
State Department of Public Welfare		786,384.73
Total to State		$6,909,567.15
Counties General Fund	786,384.73	
Counties Department of Public Welfare	786,384.73	
Counties Licensing	235,843.31	
Total to Counties		$1,808,612.77
Municipalities in which stores are located	1,572,769.49	
Incorporated Municipalities	200,000.00	
Total to Municipalities	1,772,769.49	
Total Revenue Allocated	$10,490,949.41	

The phraseology of the ABC Act was not clear on the possession of liquor which had been purchased from a State Store and then taken to a dry county. A case arose in the Circuit Court of Walker, a dry county. Welder Williams purchased some liquor from a State Liquor Store and returned to Walker with it. He was arrested and fined $50. He appealed the case. Judge Rice of the Court of Appeals, on January 11, 1938, wrote the decision which held that Williams should pay the fine. The Court also ruled that the possession of alcoholic beverages, including beer, in dry counties was illegal, although the beverages might have been legally purchased in a wet county. Thus the court held that the old state prohibition laws were still in force in counties which had failed to vote wet.[4]

The constitutionality of the Alabama Beverage Control Act was tested in the Circuit Court of Jefferson County in the case State *v.* Murphy, in 1939, and was declared valid by Judge John Denson. The case was then appealed to the State Supreme Court. The plaintiff, Horace C. Wilkinson, contended that the constitution of Alabama denies the state the right "to be interested in any private or corporate enterprise." Therefore, the state had no constitutional right to operate State Liquor Stores since they were forms of business. The Supreme Court ruled that in operating Liquor Stores the state was not in business, since the operation of these stores was unlike any regular business. "We conclude the trial court correctly ruled in sustaining the Act, and the judgment will accordingly be here affirmed," declared the Justices.[5]

The Alabama Temperance Alliance, precursor of the present A.T.A., was organized on a temporary basis to meet a specific election emergency, and its first constitution is dated December 5, 1933.[6] The first available minutes are dated March 13, 1935.[7] There is adequate evidence to show that it was functioning in the campaign to repeal the Eighteenth Amendment.

In 1936 the *Alabama Baptist* urged the prohibitionists of Alabama to form "an adequate temperance organization." The Anti-Saloon League of America and of the various states, said this periodical, should recognize that they could no longer lead the fight against liquor, and should voluntarily disband. The League had rendered valuable service to the cause of temperance in times past, but its day of usefulness was over. The editor suggested that the various religious denominations in the state appoint delegates to a meeting called to devise a plan for coordinating all the temperance forces in Alabama.[8] The imperative need of a vigorous Temperance Alliance, with a full-time secretary, was recognized by temperance leaders. Harry Denman, president of the A.T.A., called all friends of

[4] *Southern Reporter,* Vol. 179, pp. 915-920.
[5] *Southern Reporter,* Vol. 186, pp. 487-499.
[6] "Constitution of Alabama Temperance Alliance, Inc."
[7] "Minutes."   [8] August 13, 1936.

temperance to meet at the First Methodist Church in Birmingham on June 12, 1937. The present Temperance Alliance was organized at that meeting. The Alliance proposed to unite all the protestant churches and the several state-wide civic, cultural, educational, and character-building agencies into one solid front for a Christian solution of the liquor problem.[9] Instead of the Anti-Saloon League, long ineffective, unpopular even with many churchmen, weakened by its identification with politics, they would build a local, autonomous, non-political, energetic organization. Denman urged the maintenance of temperance organizations in all counties and their continued activity looking toward the elections of the next year. On June 22 he announced at a temperance meeting that a full-time director of the Alabama Temperance Alliance would be put into the field as soon as funds could be secured to pay his salary.[10]

Selection of a suitable person for this office took time and careful thought. Harry Denman and other A.T.A. leaders agreed upon the Reverend W. Earl Hotalen, evangelist of the North Alabama Conference, as an almost ideal candidate. Hotalen had a pleasing personality, aggressive and abundant energy, good common sense, tact, and an unassailable character. He was well educated, a good organizer, an excellent speaker, and an ardent dry. Late in June, 1937, the committee invited Hotalen to be its guest at a luncheon in Birmingham, and offered him the position of executive secretary of the A.T.A. Hotalen accepted and began work on July 1, 1937. The vigorous program desired by temperance advocates against the State Liquor Store and all other aspects of the liquor traffic was now launched in Alabama.[11]

Hotalen announced that an intensive organization campaign would be conducted in the sixty-seven counties of Alabama to mobilize the church people. A research department was to be established to gather data regarding violations of the law and to report this information to the people of the state. Hotalen kept in close touch with political movements and with the legislature when it was in session, and was thus able to keep his temperance forces informed of new trends.

In counties where the margin of dry votes was small in the March 10 election, the wets planned to hold referenda as soon as the law would permit, and hot campaigns would almost certainly be waged in those counties in the last four months of the year. In counties where the wet majority was small Hotalen planned to institute a fight to recapture those areas for the drys.[12]

The Alabama Beverage Control Act provided that counties might hold elections six months after March 10, 1937, to decide whether or not liquor, wine, and beer could be sold within their limits. Calhoun County's March

[9] "Minutes," June 22, 1937.
[10] *Alabama Christian Advocate,* July 1, 1937.
[11] *Alabama Christian Advocate,* July 22, 1937.
[12] *Alabama Christian Advocate,* July 22, 1937.

vote had been very close, showing a majority of only ninety-five against the legal sale of liquors. Therefore, Calhoun advocates of the ABC system began circulating petitions about the first of August. Walter Merrill, local attorney, was chairman of the group in charge of these petitions. Judge Thomas E. Coleman received the signed petitions, checked the number of signatures, and set September 28 as the date for the referendum.[13]

In an editorial, "The Next Election," the *Anniston Star* stated several reasons why such an election should be called. The close vote had left the losing side somewhat dissatisfied with the outcome; a second vote, whatever its outcome, would convince them of the people's will. Moreover, bootlegging was still flourishing. Law enforcement agencies unquestionably had been diligent in their efforts to dry up Calhoun, but it was manifestly impossible to rid the county of bootleggers until those who wanted the beverages could legally purchase them from licensed establishments. In summary the *Star* declared: "The question of escaped taxes, lost business that escapes to precincts that voted for repeal and the myriad other arguments in favor of abolishing an ineffectual statute have been repeated time and again. They are well known. It remains to be seen, on September 28, if Calhoun County citizens vote like they drink."[14]

Walter Merrill believed that repeal would win in the new election. He said, "Judging from the people who signed the petition, we can count in the repeal ranks some of the outstanding leaders in our business, civic, religious, and social life."[15] The repealists prepared for an aggressive campaign. One of the leaders confidently stated: "Businessmen who were not in the ranks before will be with us this time." The anti-repealists also marshaled their forces to resume their fight against the sale of liquor.

The advocates of repeal declared that the police force had been active since the March 11 election and had reduced the number of illicit dealers in the Anniston city limits. But, they asserted, bootlegging was decreasing partly because it had become less profitable since the opening of the State Liquor Store in Gadsden had reduced the local demand. More than a hundred Annistonians were reported to have visited the Gadsden store during a single week-end.[16]

Senator M. B. Wellborn assumed the chairmanship of the Calhoun County repeal campaign. He predicted that the citizens would vote for legal sale of all beverages. He said, "It is with reluctance that I enter any kind of campaign at this time, but I consider it a duty I owe to my town and county"; and he added, "Any visitor to Gadsden on week-ends will realize the amount of trade Anniston merchants are losing. We must awake and bestir ourselves!" Wellborn appointed a large committee of beat workers and speakers to aid in conducting an active campaign.[17]

[13] *Anniston Times*, August 27, 1937.
[14] August 26, 1937.
[15] *Anniston Star*, August 25, 1937.
[16] *Anniston Star*, August 25, 1937.
[17] *Ibid.*, August 31, 1937.

Early in September the anti-repealists announced, in the *Anniston Star*, that they would publish the names of persons who signed the election petition. Chairman Wellborn promptly accused them of trying to use intimidation. Signers of that petition, he declared, had only signified that they were in favor of another vote on the issue, they had not necessarily committed themselves for or against repeal. He added that the repeal forces would be very glad to have the public know the high caliber of those citizens who desired a new election, and he closed his statement with these words:

... we want to warn the "publishers" that the petition says that those signing it desire an election to determine the sentiment of the voters of the county on the question of legal control of alcoholic beverages. It does not state that those signing the petition favor repeal. There were many people signing the petition who stated at that time they were opposed to repeal, but they were willing for the voters of the county, in view of the closeness of the last election and small vote, to have another opportunity to express themselves. To those, we say we sincerely hope that the obvious attempt of the "publishers" to embarrass and intimidate them will lead to their voting and their friends voting, for legal distribution of alcoholic beverages in this county.[18]

The editor of the *Star* claimed that, under the prohibition regime, the Fourth Corps Area of the United States Army, comprising dry states in the South, had established a record for venereal disease which exceeded that of any other area in the country. Sadly the editor noted that Fort McClellan in Calhoun County had the worst record of any fort in this corps area. Official records of both the late Colonel George F. Baltzell and Colonel John W. Lang, the present commander, proved this to be true. Colonel Lang had said that illegal liquor joints, assignation houses, and taxi lines that transport lewd women had become a menace to the continuance of Fort McClellan in this nominally dry section. Prohibition had not and could not be enforced, said the *Star's* editor, and he ended his lament with the statement that the bootlegger "is one of the worst evils that ever infested civilized society. He is utterly without conscience and respects neither laws of God nor man.... He becomes a partner of every kind of evil in the category."[19]

With these facts in mind the *Star* could only endorse the repeal of prohibition laws. "Liquor Not the Issue" was the title of one of its editorials. The questions to be decided on September 28, said this paper, were clearly these: "Do we want to vote the bootleggers a new lease of life? Do we want to continue to send money to Gadsden to build up Etowah County? Or do we want to continue to keep the profits of a business, that already exists illegally, here at home to help support our own institutions, and at the same time to continue the work in the schools, church, the press, and the home to promote temperance?" Experience and mature

[18] September 10, 1937.   [19] *Anniston Star*, September 27, 1937.

deliberation prove that legalization is the best answer to a problem which has vexed good citizens throughout the ages, concluded the editor.[20]

Anti-repealists charged that advocates of the State Liquor Stores had stuffed the petitions "with the names of respectable citizens WHO DID NOT SIGN IT." Preachers, godly women, chairmen of boards of deacons and boards of stewards, officers of churches, and many others who were lifelong drys, they claimed, had been astounded and outraged to discover that their names had been forged to the petitions. The Calhoun County Temperance Alliance asserted that if the lists had been purged of forgeries and frauds the petition would not have contained sufficient names to meet the legal requirements for the referendum. Among the voters who actually did sign the petition, the Alliance said, was "every known bootlegger of Calhoun County."[21]

This same organization used its official *Bulletin* to present an impressive array of facts for the consideration of the voters. Among the arguments made were the following: In every wet county in Alabama traffic accidents and fatalities were increasing as the immediate result of increased alcoholic consumption. In Alabama cities where State Liquor Stores were located retail trade volume among legitimate businesses had suffered. Credit managers reported serious impairment of credit ratings for many people who were making their grocers, clothiers, landlords, dairymen, and other merchants wait for their money because liquor purchases required cash. Official reports of sheriffs, solicitors, state highway patrolmen, and other authorities, showed that "bootlegging had increased by leaps and bounds since the Alabama Beverage Control Act had become effective," and that crimes directly traceable to alcohol consumption were multiplying to such an extent as to give serious concern to law enforcement agencies. Dry counties, which the wets had promised to respect and protect, had been invaded by all sorts of wanton aggression by those who dealt in beer and hard liquors. Gambling casinos, bawdy houses, disreputable dance halls, and honky-tonks were flourishing as never before as a direct result of the sale of stamped liquor. Between March 10 and September 28, 1937, more than five thousand young women in Alabama had become engaged in the sale of beer and spirituous liquors—five thousand daughters of Alabama who ought to be in high schools and colleges were employed as bar maids.

The drys rallied to their banner. The *Bulletin* asserted that there were ministers, schoolteachers, physicians, merchants, industrialists, professional men and women, and Christian parents in the group. The wets had the support of some newspapers willing to put aside moral scruples for the sake of selling more advertising space; politicians eager to grab some of the graft always associated with liquor-controlled politics; hotel and cafe

[20] *Ibid.*
[21] *Temperance Bulletin Published by the Calhoun County Temperance Alliance,* September, 1937.

owners in avid search of more profits, whether the money they made be clean or dirty; gamblers, bootleggers, roadhouse operators and habitues; dance hall, night club, tourist camp managers and patrons; criminal elements, and all who saw in the legalization of alcoholic beverages some promise of pecuniary profit for themselves. Everyone would admit without argument, said the *Bulletin,* that the opposing camps were respectively composed of these elements. Which side, it asked rhetorically, could be trusted to tell the truth, publish the facts, and give the most trustworthy advice?[22]

With their phalanx of church and civic leaders, temperance advocates held prohibition rallies in virtually every community in Calhoun County. Two important rallies were held in Anniston during the closing days of the campaign. L. E. Barton, editor of the *Walker County Tribune,* and W. Earl Hotalen spoke at the courthouse on Saturday morning, September 25, and another meeting was scheduled for the following Monday night at which Dr. J. C. Cowell of Decatur would deliver the principal address. Dr. L. N. Claxton and J. A. Morgan addressed a rally at Shady Glen Friday night. Hotalen also spoke at a number of other places in the county.

Repeal forces, which had been less active than usual in the campaign, were understood to depend largely on the support of political machine groups. Their principal arguments were that repeal would result in increased farm trade and general business for Anniston, complete suppression of the bootlegger, and increased revenues for a depleted county treasury.

To the claim of increased business the temperance leaders replied that revenue from liquor sales was sent out of the state immediately, a very small part of it being retained in the form of taxes. Dr. G. F. Cooper declared that liquor sales in Gadsden in three months had totaled $102,000, but that only $4,280 had been paid in taxes to the city. Fully $90,000 had gone to eastern distilleries. Legal liquor sales were not only undesirable as a matter of principle, said the drys, they also constituted a serious drain on the pocketbook of local business.[23]

A number of influential men in Calhoun County threw their influence against legalizing the liquor traffic. Dr. Fred Cooper, Methodist presiding elder at Anniston, said that "a vote to repeal Calhoun's dry law on September 28, is a vote to flood our towns and county with more beer and hard liquor than we now have."[24] W. Bert Johnson, publisher of the *Anniston Times,* declared: "Regulation of the liquor traffic . . . has been an outstanding failure for hundreds of years in all parts of the world. It has not yet been demonstrated that any unit of government has helped itself through the recent changes; but it has been clearly demonstrated in many

[22] *Temperance Bulletin Published by the Calhoun County Temperance Alliance,* September, 1937.
[23] *Anniston Times,* September 24, 1937.
[24] *Temperance Bulletin Published by the Calhoun County Temperance Alliance,* September, 1937.

cases that legalization of liquor has brought both economic and moral loss to the community. The record, therefore, stands definitely in favor of retaining our prohibition laws."[25] J. A. Morgan, an industrialist of Anniston, insisted that it was better to remedy existing ills than to "fly to other ills we know are worse."[26]

In the referendum the anti-repealists polled 2,284 votes, the repealists 1,906, giving a dry margin of 378. This was an appreciable gain over the results of the March 10 election, when the dry majority had stood at 95. M. B. Wellborn, chairman of the repeal committee, said when the votes were counted: "I regret that the voters of Calhoun County prefer the illegal to the legal and it appears that Ephraim is still joined to his idols. The result of the election makes me sorry for Anniston." The loss of the election for repealists meant a loss of revenue for the city of Anniston which Wellborn estimated at $40,000 annually.[27] The *Anniston Star* thought that the vote could be interpreted in only one way—that a majority of the people of the county were opposed to the sale of liquor in this governmental subdivision. Enforcement authorities should heed this mandate and quicken their efforts to enforce the law to the letter. The *Star* considered it unfortunate that the division for and against legalized liquor was so close. This would make it, the editor thought, almost impossible to drive out bootleggers, as long as many people still demanded liquor and would continue to patronize such illegal dealers. "As a matter of fact there are probably enough bootleggers in the county at present to account for the result of the election, as the bootleggers certainly do not want their illegal profits withdrawn," remarked the *Star*.[28]

Another typical county local option election was held in Houston. On March 10, 1937, Houston had voted with the wets, by a vote of 1,731 to 1,269. The campaign had been marked by an intensive propaganda barrage by the wet politicians and liquor interests who solemnly promised that legalization of alcoholic beverages would stop bootlegging; reduce traffic accidents and fatalities; keep the schools plentifully supplied with money; provide immense revenues for city, county, and state treasuries; reduce crime; and promote temperance. Many ardent drys had given tentative credence to the reform promises of wet spokesmen in the state capitol, in the legislature, and in the daily press, and had been willing to vote to legalize liquor and to try the State Stores plan.

On June 15, 1937, State Liquor Store number 35 was opened at Dothan. A number of local establishments were licensed to sell liquor or beer. Others, not bothering to procure or unable to qualify for state licenses, hastened to get Federal licenses in order to be immune from Federal interference, and entered upon an unprecedented spree of overt bootlegging operations. The State Liquor Store supplied their wares. At

[25] *Ibid.*
[27] *Anniston Star*, September 29, 1937.
[26] *Ibid.*
[28] September 29, 1937.

night, on Sundays, and on holidays, these law-defying liquor dealers raised their prices and began to garner large profits. Roadhouses, tourist camps, dance halls, honky-tonks, and would-be night clubs sprang up all over the county. They catered especially to youth, enticing young people by every conceivable wile to become patrons of these unwholesome places of rendezvous. Hilarity reigned, drunkenness flourished, quarrels multiplied, brawling and fighting were common, vulgarity increased. Gambling, vice, prostitution, venereal disease, speeding and reckless driving on the highways, declared one temperance paper, "all . . . goose-stepped into our county with legalized liquor." In the unpoliced areas of the county citizens became increasingly alarmed. In Dothan arrests for drunkenness and disorderly conduct multiplied so rapidly that authorities, ashamed of the infamous records, began to book arrested drunks as "vagrants," and to deal with them in the justice of the peace court, so that the police records would not reveal the true condition.

As early as October, 1937, temperance people began to discuss a movement to rid the county of the obnoxious traffic. Churches denounced the bad effects of the liquor traffic and some ministers spoke out against the Liquor Store at Dothan. Two-fisted farmers met and talked things over, protesting ominously against the liquor-selling nuisances. Businessmen watched their cash registers and observed that many of their customers were spending their cash for liquor and making legitimate merchants wait for their money. These merchants were forced to recognize that the Liquor Store was a vicious and hard competitor.[29]

On January 10, 1938, about one hundred and fifty representative drys from every section of the county met at the courthouse in Dothan and organized the Houston County Temperance Alliance. Judge H. K. Martin was elected president; Oscar L. Tomkins, vice-president; Webb U. Miller, secretary; and John J. Fowler, treasurer. These officers were authorized to name committees on publicity, finance, speakers, and absentee ballots. The officers, together with the chairmen of the committees, formed the executive committee which conducted the campaign. Money to start the campaign was raised. Petitions were given to precinct committeemen for presentation to the voters. The referendum drive was launched. Fifteen days later the petitions were filed at the probate judge's office. The law required less than 900 names on the petitions but 1,606 voters had signed them.[30]

The *Dothan Eagle* remarked that, even if the drys of Houston County were to succeed in ending the legal sale of whiskey, only one thing of importance would be accomplished—six employees of the State Liquor Store would lose their jobs. The "victory" would be greeted with more enthusiasm by the bootleggers than by the drys, for the bootleggers would

[29] *Houston County Temperance Alliance Bulletin,* February, 1938.
[30] *Dothan Eagle,* January 6, 1938.

know that their greatest competitor—the Store with its low price—had been put out of business.[81]

Not only did the *Dothan Eagle* indorse the State Liquor Store, but it believed that such stores should be left open until 10:30 at night and should introduce a delivery system. Although many ardent and sincere prohibitionists would not believe it, this periodical asserted, liquor was offered guests in many homes as naturally as other forms of hospitality. On impromptu occasions a host might find himself without liquor. Moreover, said the *Eagle,* a great number of persons who drink did not openly patronize a Liquor Store. They preferred to telephone for what they wanted and the bootlegger was willing to serve them. A night delivery system in the Liquor Store would put the bootlegger out of business.[82]

During the campaign 10,000 copies of the *Houston County Temperance Alliance Bulletin* and thousands of other pieces of temperance literature were distributed by mail and at meetings. Pastors preached on the evils of alcohol. Temperance speakers went into every precinct. Sound trucks from which voices pleaded with the people to exterminate the evil toured the county. Drys bought considerable space in the daily newspaper and printed facts about the evils of alcoholic beverages. The radio broadcast information. Temperance workers made house-to-house canvasses, soliciting dry votes.[33]

The Houston County Temperance Alliance claimed that liquor was not paying its way in Dothan and the county. Much money was taken from the legitimate channels of trade and sent out of the state, leaving a comparatively small sum for local government revenues. This contention was lucidly set forth in the following paid political advertisement:

> From June 15th to January 1st the Dothan State Liquor Store made sales totaling $137,362. From the opening, sales steadily mounted as follows: June—one half month—$6,781; July, $16,094; August, $18,411; September, $20,133; October, $22,787; November, $22,574; December, $30,579; total for first six and half months, $137,362. The total profits from sales were $25,292. Of the profits $6,292 went to the City of Dothan, and $19,000 went to the State of Alabama. The State of Alabama paid back Houston County $4,240. Stated another way, Dothan received $6,292; Houston County received $4,240. Total profits received by Dothan and Houston County, $10,533. Amount paid to the State of Alabama over and above amount received by Dothan and Houston County, $14,759. In short, Houston County and Dothan, of the actual profits received, have paid back to the state $14,759 over and above the amount received by them.[84]

The *Dothan Eagle* denied such statements and claimed that a dollar spent for liquor in a State ABC Store went into the legitimate channels of trade. This periodical claimed:

[81] *Ibid.,* January 10, 1938.
[82] *Dothan Eagle,* January 11, 1938.
[83] *A.T.A. Bulletin, Number 8,* March, 1938.
[84] *Dothan Eagle,* February 7, 1938.

This dollar was not taken from business channels but directly from the bootlegger who cannot compete with the low price and the high quality of legal liquor that is available under the State Store system.[85]

When the probate judge called the referendum election in Houston County for February 28 there were only four days left in which to register and pay poll tax. Many hundreds of citizens, delinquent for several years in their poll tax payments, were unqualified for voting. The drys claimed that the wets promptly produced a huge slush fund, bargained with many of these people, and paid back poll tax for them in return for promised support of the wet cause, and that more than 1,200 voters were thus added to the registration lists. Prohibitionists declared that they had no funds for vote buying, nor would they have resorted to such corrupt practices if they had had the money. But, they promised, the drys could wage a vigorous campaign along honorable lines,[86] and they proceeded to make good that promise.

Executive Secretary Hotalen said the wets boasted that they had $25,000 with which to buy votes and control the election counting. The *Montgomery Advertiser* published a front-page article by Atticus Mullin asserting that the drys at Dothan had received $10,000 from the Anti-Saloon League for similar purposes.[87] Hotalen and the dry leaders were amazed at the effect of that article. Hundreds of nondescript citizens, Hotalen said, read it and at once approached these leaders, offering to sell them their votes if they offered a better price than the wets. He declared that this was the first and only time in all his life that people had asked him to purchase their votes.[88]

The A.T.A. charged that the wets were attempting to coerce some employees of the city of Dothan and of the State Highway Department to vote for and use their influence in behalf of the State Liquor Store. It claimed:

> Drunken men went to Dry Rallies and heckled speakers; among these hecklers were employees of the *Dothan Eagle*. Mr. William I. Truby, Director of Public Relations for the ABC Board at Montgomery, left his office duties, went to Dothan, spent several days assisting Julian Hall in preparing editorial appeals and arguments for the Wet Cause. Members of the Law Enforcement

---

[85] *Ibid.*, February 24, 1938. "Where $1 spent for liquor in a State ABC Store Goes":

Gross profit to state, county and city	$0.33.3
Federal government tax	.32.0
Bottling cost	.07.1
Freight	.01.6
Raw materials, merchandising	.24.5
Net profit to distiller	.01.5
	$1.00

[86] *A.T.A. Bulletin, Number 8*, March, 1938.
[87] February 27, 1938; *A.T.A. Bulletin, Number 8*, March, 1938.
[88] "Story of the Alabama Temperance Alliance, Inc." from July 1, 1937 to November 18, 1941.

Division of the ABC Board came to Dothan also, but NOT TO ENFORCE THE LAW. They ignored the numerous bootlegging establishments running wide open in the heart of Dothan; spent their time gathering votes for the Wet Cause. Employees of City, County and State who had signed the Dry Petitions, or had otherwise indicated their support of the Dry Cause, were threatened with loss of their jobs unless they switched to the Wets. An Election Manager, Dry, was told that his son would lose his job with the State Highway Department, unless he handled things for the Wets.[39]

The temperance forces declared further that numerous irregularities existed in the city of Dothan just prior to and during the day of the election. They asserted that

On Sunday, Feb. 27th, and on Election Day, Feb. 28th, bootleggers did a booming business. The Liquor Store was closed on those two days; but the bootleggers had bought huge supplies of hard liquor for sale at huge prices. This supply of liquor was openly used to influence and control voting at the polls. Liquor Store employees worked to carry voters to the polls. Men were discovered voting at each of several different boxes in Dothan, and buying votes, and tampering with Election Officers, and illegally marking ballots, and interfering with a fair count of votes cast. In some Beats these Ballot Crooks were driven from the polls by angry citizens. One Wet leader boasted that his crowd had the election in the bag; "a $20,000 bag." That frauds and illegalities and criminal methods were used in wholesale measure is common knowledge in Dothan.[40]

The drys lost their fight. Houston voted to retain legal liquor 2,910 to 1,949. Twenty-five of the county's thirty-four boxes returned a majority in favor of the State Liquor Stores. A gain of 439 votes in favor of legalized liquor had been made since the March 10 referendum. The majority in the February 28 election was 961. That in the March, 1937, election had been only 522.[41]

The *Dothan Eagle* made the following comment on the election:

Those who voted for prohibition and those who voted for continued legal sale are united on one important thing concerning alcoholic beverages; every Jouk in Houston County must be closed, and remain closed.
These bawdy, brawling places are not only Nuisances with a capital "n," but have no place in orderly, civilized society. . . .
As a newspaper that advocated continued legality, the *Eagle* pledges its whole-hearted support.[42]

One of the most important local option elections was held in Madison County on September 23, 1941. This was true because of the position this county had occupied in the history of the state. It is the second oldest county and has made many contributions to the cultural and political life of both the state and the nation. The early records show that strong drink was used in the twenties during political campaigns and at elections. Throughout its long history whiskey and other alcoholic beverages had

[39] *A.T.A. Bulletin, Number 8*, March, 1938.
[41] *Dothan Eagle*, March 1, 1938.
[40] *Ibid.*
[42] *Ibid.*

been sold legally in Madison except during state-wide and national prohibition. Madison County voted in favor of legal sale of liquor on March 10, 1937, by a large majority, showing that the people had not broken with the past. Since this election it has become the most highly industrialized center in North Alabama. It is the site of one of the Federal Chemical Warfare plants in which thousands of people are employed.

With such a background it seemed almost impossible to win an election against the State Liquor Store. However, certain things began to happen after its installation in 1937 which caused the people to doubt the value of the ABC Store. The most important result seemed to be the debauchery of young people, particularly girls. The *Voice of Temperance* carried an item on September 18, 1941, verifying this fact. The item stated, in part, that a businessman of Huntsville admitted he had voted wet in 1937. Upon his observation of growing liquor evils and his daily reading of the *Huntsville Times* he was convinced he had voted wrong. He stated that a few weeks previously the *Times* reported there were twenty girls in jail one Saturday night for drunkenness. Those girls were 15, 16, 17, and 18 years old. This man related similar instances of drunkenness. He stated that these things did not happen during prohibition times and he expected to vote dry on September 23.[43] Many people were growing tired of the things this businessman disliked.

The ABC Store was a liability and not an asset to the county. During the period 1937 to 1940 Madison County had spent approximately $2,402,750.51 for hard liquor and other beverages and received $91,152.63 as its share of the profits. Thus, more than $2,000,000 had left the county. The people were actually spending $26.35 for hard liquor and beer for each dollar received in return.[44] This was indeed an unfavorable balance of trade. These and other similar facts prepared the way for the temperance forces to agitate for an election.

For several months Executive Secretary Hotalen had been hearing complaints from Madison County against the State Liquor Store. After making a personal investigation, he was convinced that the people would vote dry if an election should be called. To help precipitate sentiment for an election, the Reverend Sam Morris, the "Wizard of Temperance," was asked to deliver several temperance lectures in the county. Following these speeches a petition was circulated and more than 2,200 signatures were affixed to it. Judge Thomas G. Jones examined the petition and found that it more than met the legal requirements. He set September 23, 1941, as the date for the election.[45]

The drys then organized to wage an intensive campaign. W. E. Butler, former probate judge, was elected chairman of the Madison County

[43] *Voice of Temperance* is published by the Madison County Temperance Alliance, Huntsville, Alabama.
[44] *Annual Reports of the ABC Board* (1937-1940), *passim*.
[45] *Voice of Temperance*, September 18, 1941.

Temperance Alliance. He was assisted by the Reverend T. J. Chitwood, vice-president; Professor Edward Anderson, secretary-treasurer; Dr. John J. Milford, chairman of the executive committee, and numerous other prominent citizens who formed beat chairmen and various active committees of the dry organization. In this way, and by the use of the local radio station, the drys contacted practically every voter.[46]

The advocates of the State Liquor Store conducted a quiet campaign, possibly believing that, upon the basis of past records, they could not lose. The *Huntsville Times* carried articles for both factions, but its editorial comments were favorable to legal sale. The wets also used the local radio station to reach the voters.

The election went off quietly and when the votes were counted the result showed that the drys had won the election by a vote of 2,150 to 1,787.[47]

In commenting on the election the *Huntsville Times* declared: "The qualified voters of Madison County made a grievous mistake yesterday, in our opinion, in casting out the State Liquor Store system, and again enthroning the bootlegger as the source of alcoholic drinks for those who want, and are going to have them."[48]

The exponents of the State Liquor Store charged the prohibitionists with frauds, forgeries, and misrepresentations in the petitions upon which the liquor election had been called, and filed proceedings in both the Probate Court and the Circuit Court at Huntsville. The first phase of the court battle was fought out in the Circuit Court at Huntsville on December 5, 1941. Hugh A. Locke, attorney for the drys, entered a demurrer to the wets' bill, which Judge Schuyler Richardson sustained. However, he granted a request by A. Berkowitz, attorney for the wets, that the matter be transferred to Chancery Court for an equity hearing. Thus the drys won the first round in the Madison County Court fight. At this writing the actions filed by the wets in the Probate Court were pending.[49]

The next two local option elections, held in Perry and Houston counties respectively, resulted in victories for the State Liquor Stores. Since the installation of the State Liquor Store in Perry County, the abuses of liquor had increased in large proportions. The docket of the Mayor of Marion and the sheriff's jail register showed the bad effects of the increased consumption of liquor. The drys made a careful survey of their voting strength and were convinced that they should win if they could break even in the city of Marion. One influential citizen of Marion declared that his business was disturbed by a near-by honky-tonk. The drys considered his influence invaluable to their cause. He inquired of the ABC Board as to what could be done to give him relief. The Board

[46] *Voice of Temperance*, September 18, 1941.
[47] *Huntsville Times*, September 24, 1941.
[48] *Ibid.*
[49] *Alabama Christian Advocate*, December 18, 1941.

closed the honky-tonk, thereby removing the nuisance. This individual changed his mind and suddenly began working for the retention of the ABC system. The drys lost the election, they believed, on account of the retraction of this influential citizen. The election held on January 20, 1942, resulted in the following vote: Dry, 617; wet, 726.[50]

After the drys of Houston County complied with the legal requirement for another election on the State Liquor Store, the probate judge set August 14, 1942, as the date for it to be held. The presence of near-by training camps, Napier Field and Camp Rucker, induced an alarming multitude of liquor evils, and many of the people of the county were greatly alarmed. The *Dothan Eagle* (usually wet) had, prior to the campaign, denounced in caustic language the frightful conditions of lawlessness, drunkenness, bootlegging and immorality in the city. The *Eagle* declared:

> Prostitution is rampant in Dothan. The gals of glamor timed their arrival with the opening of Napier Field and Camp Rucker—army posts to which thousands of United States soldiers have been assigned. They ply their trade under the auspices of pandering taxi drivers and brothel operators. They are a menace to public morals and health.
> Drunken soldiers walk the streets of Dothan. Ugly charges have been made that they have accosted respectable women in downtown Dothan. There have been fist fights. There have been brawls in public places which resulted in business houses closing their doors to prevent property damage. Many of these brawls, but not all, developed from imbibing too freely of liquor and beer. Drunk and rowdy soldiers are a menace to public morals and health.
> Bootlegging goes on in the streets of Dothan. The bootleg traffic is monopolized by prostitutes. Their period of greatest activity is after the State Liquor Store is closed for the night and before it opens in the morning. Most of the bootleg liquor is bought from the State Store in anticipation of the nightly demand. The bootlegger is a menace to public morals and health.
> Juke joints with a front of sandwiches and soft drinks screening the girls and beer and coin-in-the-slot machines are operating in and around Dothan. They are the scenes of many disorders which annoy law-abiding citizens. Many of them hold licenses from the State, City and County, to sell beer. They, too, are a menace to public morals and health.[51]

The editor believed that hundreds of people who voted wet in Houston County on February 28, 1938, would then vote dry. Leading churchmen, business and professional men and women, civic leaders and prominent members of society had united to form a central committee which was leading the movement for a dry county.

The drys were confident that they would win but they lost the election probably by their own fault. They distributed no literature and made not a single speech. Their organization was only perfunctory. Overconfident of winning, they decided not to agitate the issue but simply give the voters a chance to express themselves. The wets quietly capitalized on

[50] Hotalen, "Resume of the Alabama Temperance Movement in 1942"; *Marion Standard*, January 22, 1942.   [51] June 7, 1942.

this inactivity of the drys by thorough vote-getting efforts, and managed to win by a slender margin. The vote was: dry, 1,609; wet, 1,626—a wet majority of 17.[52]

The drys of Colbert County, galling under the effects of the State Liquor Store, petitioned for another local option election (the second since March 10, 1937), which was held on October 6, 1942. Throughout its history this county had never voted dry in a liquor election. Therefore, the drys knew that they had a hard fight on their hands. They constituted a closely knit organization, electing the Reverend J. Luther Gaines chairman. Under his and Executive Secretary Hotalen's leadership the temperance forces were welded into an aggressive fighting machine. Voters were contacted both directly and by speakers over radio. During the campaign thirty-four thousand pieces of temperance literature were distributed.[53] The wets also had an organization which reached practically every voter in the county. Tuscumbia's mayor and aldermen inserted a paid political advertisemen in the *Tri-Cities Daily* urging the retention of the State Liquor Store.[54] The *Sheffield Standard* used its editorial and news columns for retention of legal sale of liquor.[55] Exponents of the ABC system found a "Hardshell" Baptist preacher to champion their cause and put him on the "air" to prove by the Bible that it was all right to drink intoxicating liquors. The following excerpt was quoted from his radio address:

> You all recollect that the patriarch Noah planted a vineyard, and made wine, and drank thereof, and was drunk. But does the record say that God came down and made any sort of prohibition law to stop Noah from drinking. No! On the contrary, we find that God put a curse upon them that laughed at Noah.[56]

During the campaign an unfortunate incident occurred in Tuscumbia. On the night of September 28, 1942, several high-school boys made three assaults with beer, whiskey, and wine bottles upon the home of Reverend J. Luther Gaines, Pastor of the First Baptist Church of Tuscumbia and Chairman of Colbert County Temperance Alliance. Their car license number was taken and reported to the police, who refused to investigate the matter or to take any steps toward protecting the minister's home.[57] The incident helped to fan to white heat the anger of the citizens who were already indignant at the city officials and the police department personnel for their pro-liquor activities in the campaign. The official returns of the election showed that the drys had won by a vote of 1,750 to 1,665.[58]

In consequence of the increasing bad effects of the sales of the State Liquor Store, the citizens of Cullman County met the legal requirement

---

[52] August 16, 1942.
[53] *Alabama Christian Advocate*, October 15, 1942.
[54] September 23, 1942.   [55] October 2, 1942.
[56] *Alabama Christian Advocate*, October 15, 1942.
[57] *Ibid.*
[58] *Sheffield Standard*, October 9, 1942.

for their third local option election. This county had voted dry by a small margin on March 10, 1937, but reversed itself in another election held in September of that year. The probate judge set January 22, 1943, as the day for the election. In the previous elections the drys claimed that they had had the potential vote to drive liquor out of the county but due to inclement weather and faulty organization they had failed to capitalize on their real strength. In this contest the drys had an excellent organization. Secretary Hotalen coordinated all of the dry forces. During the campaign the pastors of all Protestant denominations, many members of women's missionary societies, some leading businessmen and farmers, and officers of the Cullman County Temperance Alliance worked energetically for a dry county. A prohibition newspaper, *The Voice of Temperance*, was mailed to every home in the county, and one hundred and four short radio addresses, at the rate of twenty-six a day for four days preceding the election, were "beamed" into Cullman County by the drys from broadcasting stations at Birmingham, Bessemer, Gadsden, and Decatur.[59] One of the strongest arguments used by the drys to influence businessmen was that of economics. The drys declared that, according to the records of the ABC Board, ninety-two cents out of every dollar spent for liquor by the people of Cullman County was taken away from circulation, resulting in a loss of $1,192,688.87 between 1937 and 1941.[60] The advocates of the State Liquor Stores also conducted an active campaign but worked quietly among the voters. Two of the local newspapers endorsed the ABC system. The *Cullman Democrat* declared that it stood where it had always stood "without equivocation or apology." It advocated the legal sale of tax-paid alcoholic beverages and drinks in regulated, licensed outlets as opposed to illegal sale of such beverages. Many people would have their liquor, so why not sell it legally and get the revenue.[61] The *Cullman Banner* favored retention of the State Liquor Store on account of the revenue that accrued to the county from the sale of liquor.[62] The editor stated that vast revenues were needed for contingent governmental expenses and if the tax on liquor should be lost, a tax would have to be placed on something else. The official count showed that the drys had won by a landslide. The vote stood: dry, 3,032; wet, 1,927.[63]

County option liquor election campaigns began September 28, 1937, and the last one prior to this writing was held January 22, 1943. The twenty-four elections which were held were real tests of prohibition sentiment. The drys won seventeen of the contests, having substantial majorities in most of the counties. The wets won only seven victories and four of them were marred by reduced majorities. The drys increased their total

[59] *Alabama Christian Advocate*, January 28, 1943.
[60] *Voice of Temperance*, January, 1943; *Annual Reports of the ABC Board* (1937-1941), *passim*.
[61] January 21, 1943.
[62] January 14, 1943.
[63] *Cullman Banner*, January 28, 1943.

vote in twenty-three of these twenty-four elections, while the wets increased their total in only nine. Two counties, Cullman and Marengo, have changed their status from dry to wet since the general referendum; however, seven counties, Geneva, Washington, Monroe, Madison, Colbert, Etowah, and Cullman have changed from wet to dry. Thus the drys hold the decided advantage in the county option elections.[64]

Public opinion has, quite evidently, been again turning against the legal sale of liquor. Editorials and news articles have appeared in many papers throughout Alabama demanding such reforms as the prohibition of the employment of "barmaids," hostesses, and "come-on" girls; the refusal of liquor or beer licenses to any place located outside of the police jurisdiction of incorporated municipalities; strict enforcement against the sale of liquor or beer to minors or to persons visibly intoxicated; bans upon the display of alcoholic beverages within public view in any restau-

[64] The counties and election results were:

Date		County	Official Vote Count		Majority	
			Wet	Dry	Wet	Dry
1937						
September	28	Calhoun	1906	2284		378
September	28	Cullman	2377	2062	315	
September	30	Dale	357	1526		1173
October	5	Autauga	438	724		286
October	19	Talladega	1279	2082		803
November	9	Geneva	1159	1500		341
1938						
February	28	Houston	2910	1949	961	
June	14	Marengo	1549	1258	291	
September	27	Shelby	752	1919		1167
November	8	Choctaw	729	813		84
November	8	Clarke	931	1206		275
November	8	Conecuh	593	1078		485
1939						
August	15	Elmore	973	2090		1117
October	10	Washington	315	1108		793
1940						
April	2	Cullman	3184	2930	254	
May	1	Tuscaloosa	3297	4189		892
July	9	Colbert	2050	1953	97	
September	3	Monroe	1171	1472		301
1941						
September	23	Madison	1787	2150		363
1942						
January	20	Perry	726	617	159	
August	14	Houston	1626	1609	17	
October	6	Colbert	1665	1750		85
December	1	Etowah	2517	4102		1585
1943						
January	22	Cullman	1927	3032		1105

rant, cafe, hotel, or other place of sale; and stricter limitations upon the advertising of intoxicants. Drys described this outburst of demand for reform in which wets joined as clamorously as drys, as caused partly by the people's growing indignation against intolerable liquor evils and partly by a disorderly retreat of wets who were desperately trying to save their vested interests.

Following the Madison County dry victory on September 23, 1941, churches in various parts of the state began to demand a ban on the Sunday sale of liquor, wine, and beer. This demand met with popular favor. The wets offered little resistance to it. The City Commission of Birmingham enacted an ordinance prohibiting Sunday liquor selling; similar action by authorities of Sheffield, Bessemer, and Selma soon followed. The movement had been under way only a few days when the Alabama Alcoholic Beverage Control Board made the reform state-wide with a new regulation that on and after January 1, 1942, no alcoholic beverages—whether distilled, vinous, or malt—might be legally sold on Sunday anywhere in Alabama. Another regulation, announced a little later to take effect on the same date, prohibited the public display of alcoholic beverages by licensed dealers.[65]

The State Liquor Stores played a part in the state elections of 1938. Five gubernatorial candidates filed in the Democratic primary of 1938. They were D. Hardly Riddle, James J. Arnold, R. J. Goode, Chauncey Sparks, and Frank M. Dixon. All of them made platform pledges about the liquor problem. Riddle declared:

I am opposed to State Liquor Stores and to any other plan of legalizing the traffic in alcoholic beverages. As a Senator, I voted against the Alabama Alcoholic Beverage Control Act. I favor submitting the question of its repeal and the reinstatement of the bone dry law to the people of the entire State.[66]

He favored rigid enforcement of the law, without fear or favor, and promised, if elected, to use the power of his office to protect dry counties. The *A.T.A. Bulletin* approved Riddle's platform pledge. It stated that his promises were in exact conformity with the objectives of the Alabama Temperance Alliance and thoroughly consonant with the earnest wishes of the prohibitionists throughout the state. "The sincere friends of temperance will heartily approve such statements," said the *Bulletin*.[67]

Arnold said he was opposed to the state's engaging in the liquor business and that he thought no person, firm, or corporation should be allowed to undertake the manufacture, sale, or use of liquor in the state, unless the people had approved such business at the polls. The *Bulletin* approved his stand against the sale and distribution of alcoholic beverages, but

[65] "The Story of the Alabama Temperance Alliance, Inc.," July 1, 1937 to November 18, 1941. See also, *Shelby County Reporter*, November 20, 1941.
[66] *Riddle's Platform*, 1938.
[67] *A.T.A. Bulletin, Number 8*, March, 1938.

noted that he did not commit himself to any program looking toward the legal extermination of the traffic.[68]

Goode declared his belief that the primary purpose of any legislation dealing with liquor should be the promotion of temperance, and that the people should decide on the best means of attaining this end. He promised to sign any bill passed by the legislature, whether it should involve state-wide prohibition, local option, or a referendum. He pledged himself to enforce such laws and to continue teacher training for the instruction of school children concerning the effects of alcohol. "Mr. Goode is a likeable gentleman, a personal dry; politically he favors local option and his platform pledge . . . is an evasion," was the *Bulletin's* comment. Legislation which legalized alcoholic beverages, this paper noted, though it pretended to promote temperance, had always fostered intemperance. "We want a governor who will actively exert his influence to rectify the legislative iniquity of February 2, 1937."[69]

Sparks said that he believed in giving the State Store system an honest trial, but that he was also convinced that the present law should be clarified and strengthened, and additional safeguards thrown around it in order to control the liquor evil. The principle of local self-government should be recognized, said he, but if the legislature should see fit to submit another referendum he would approve such a bill. The *Bulletin* remarked that Sparks' platform declaration was "ambiguous and equivocal. It certainly gives no hopes to the prohibitionists of Alabama."[70] His platform commitment regarding the State Liquor Store system obviously could not be approved by the A.T.A.

Dixon said that the present law, which had failed in many ways, was not the one he had advocated in his last campaign. He asserted that teeth should be put into the enforcement provisions so that dry counties might be protected. He was deeply concerned that the lack of law enforcement had brought into the state a vicious system of roadhouses and gambling houses, which were an affront to good people and a nuisance to youth. "These must be stamped out with adequate law enforcement," he declared. He asked the opportunity to try out an effectual control system with teeth in it. This would, he believed, promote real temperance in Alabama. He opposed issuing licenses in areas not having sufficient law enforcement. Only thus could highways be safeguarded and the public safety protected. The *Bulletin* declared that "Mr. Dixon was a wet gubernatorial candidate in 1934. His platform is wringing wet." On only one point did the paper agree with this candidate; it was quite willing to endorse his statement "that the Alabama Beverage Control Act is a failure." But the *Bulletin* pointed out that Dixon accepted the county

[68] *A.T.A. Bulletin, Number 8,* March, 1938.
[69] *Ibid.*
[70] *A.T.A. Bulletin, Number 8,* March, 1938.

local option principle in the ABC Act, a principle "adequately opposed by every sincere prohibitionist in Alabama."[71]

Political prognosticators, including some opposed to him, began to predict Dixon's election almost as soon as the campaign began. He spoke with the force of a crusader and appeared able to win votes in mass. Although some of the temperance leaders characterized him as the "wettest of the wets," drys as well as wets flocked to his standard, and his vote in the primary on May 3 was more than double that of his nearest rival. Arnold polled 1,201 votes; Riddle, 15,478; Goode, 70,287; Sparks, 74,554; Dixon, 152,860.[72] Riddle had been considered the most dependable dry in the race. He had a consistent record as a prohibition legislator. But he had been unable to make much headway as a campaigner. Harry Walker, editor of the *Limestone Democrat*, speaker of the House in Graves' second administration, and a consistent dry, said, "I do not believe the prohibition question was an important factor in the gubernatorial campaign of 1938."[73]

In his final message to the legislature, delivered on January 9, 1939, retiring Governor Graves said that, if the people were willing that intoxicating liquor should be legally sold in the state, he firmly believed the system provided for by the Alabama Alcoholic Beverage Control Act was the best available. Financially the administration of that act had been an eminent success, he declared; and then added, "And I believe that its administration has been as clean as a hound's tooth." Since its creation on February 2, 1937, he noted, the ABC Board had disbursed $4,176,378.75 in net profits to the state, the counties, and the municipalities of the state for the purposes provided by law.[74]

Governor Dixon, delivering his initial message to the legislature on January 17, 1939, devoted only two short paragraphs to the liquor question. He declared that Alabama had been exceedingly fortunate in the operation of the state monopoly system of liquor control. If adjustments were necessary in the system most of them could be made administratively. The administration license provisions probably needed tightening and action should be taken to secure a greater degree of law enforcement in dry counties. Any suggestions for minor amendments to the law, he said, would be considered later if it were deemed advisable.[75]

About three months later, on April 19, 1939, Governor Dixon was quoted in the Associated Press dispatches as saying: "It [the ABC Act] has solved our problems to the satisfaction of the people of Alabama."[76]

[71] *A.T.A. Bulletin, Number 8*, March, 1938.
[72] *Alabama Official and Statistical Register* (1939), p. 741.
[73] In a personal interview with the author.
[74] *Senate Journal, Regular Session* (1939), I, 44.
[75] *Ibid.*, p. 95.
[76] *Annual of the Alabama Baptist State Convention* (1939), pp. 99-100; *Montgomery Advertiser*, April 19, 1939; *Birmingham News*, April 19, 1939.

The governor had apparently changed his opinion since he framed his election platform.

The legislature evidently shared the governor's view with regard to altering the ABC law. This body had made only one change in the law since its passage in 1937. That amendment, effective January 1, 1940, changed the allocation of State Liquor Store profits so that incorporated municipalities in both wet and dry counties would receive a share of the profits. According to the provisions of the original act incorporated cities in wet counties without State Liquor Stores did not share in the profits. Under the new amendment the original distribution was to be followed in the payment of the first two million dollars of profit. The next two hundred thousand dollars of profit was to be distributed on a population basis, to all incorporated cities in the state. All profit above two million, two hundred thousand dollars, went into the state general fund.[77]

The State Liquor Stores were a factor in the state elections of 1942. In the Democratic primary election of May 5, 1942, there were five candidates for nomination to the governorship of Alabama, Chauncey Sparks, J. E. Folsom, Chris Sherlock, Hillry J. Carwile, and W. O. Broyles. Sparks, Folsom, and Broyles each publicly pledged that, if elected, he would see that the people are given a state-wide referendum on the liquor question. Those three candidates polled approximately 78 per cent of all votes cast in the election. Sherlock publicly stated that, if elected, he would allow no change in the present liquor laws of Alabama, but would retain the Alabama Beverage Control Act as it was. He polled barely more than 20 per cent of all votes cast. Carwile did not commit himself on a referendum. The people had a clear choice before them. Broyles received 2,157 votes; Carwile, 4,745; Sherlock, 53,448; Folsom, 73,306; and Sparks, 145,798. Thus Sparks polled 52 per cent of the total vote cast and was nominated to be the next governor of Alabama.[78] This seemed to be a mandate of the people to the 1943 legislature.

The drys also claimed a majority of both branches of the 1943 legislature. The Senate of Alabama has thirty-five members, nineteen of which represented wholly dry districts. Two of the senators represented districts composed each of three counties, two counties in each district being dry, and one wet. Three senators were from districts, each of which was composed of two counties, one county being wet and the other dry. In the distinctly wet territory, there were seven sentors representing districts composed of only one wet county. Two senators came from districts having three counties each, two of which in each district were wet. Finally, two senators represented districts each of which was composed of two wet counties. Consequently, the drys claimed that 60 per cent of the senators should vote dry.

[77] *General Act, Regular Session* (1939), pp. 526-527.
[78] *Birmingham Age-Herald*, May 12, 1942.

Alabama's House of Representatives has one hundred and five members. Sixty-four of these represented dry counties, and forty-two came from wet counties. As a result of these facts, the drys declared that they were entitled to a fraction more than 60 per cent of the votes in the House of Representatives.[79]

In his final message to the legislature, Governor Frank M. Dixon said the ABC law was not perfect in letter or application, but "It is far superior to the prohibition experiment which we tried and abandoned." He stated that the people of the state adopted the law "in an effort to alleviate the admittedly rotten conditions which prevailed under prohibition." This statement was heartening to the wets who claimed that people were more temperate since everybody could get all the liquor he wanted from ABC stores. They continued to assert that people were drinking less under the state store system than they drank during prohibition. According to the governor's own statement the revenue from the sale of liquor in Alabama increased annually by large increments. He announced to the legislature that the revenues from the ABC system in the state ranged from $2,666,360 in 1939 to $7,586,898 in 1942.[80] That did not look like an increase in temperance.

In his inaugural address January 18, 1942, Governor Sparks renewed his pledge for a referendum on the liquor question. He said that as for dealing with alcoholic beverages the purpose of the law was the "protection of public welfare, health, peace, and morals of the people of the state" and that this would be his guiding principle in dealing with the subject. He would regard it as a duty to ask the legislature to let the people say whether the laws had accomplished that purpose.[81] Thus the people could probably look forward to a referendum on the liquor question.

The campaigns of 1937 put upon the Alabama Temperance Alliance an expense burden which it was not strong enough to bear. In six elections the organization had spent more than $1,300 for campaign literature, travel, expenses, long distance telephone calls, and other incidentals. About this time the insurance company which had loaned the Alliance some office equipment asked that this furniture be returned. The A.T.A. was left with its records and meager supplies flat on the floor. Meanwhile, the Alliance's executive secretary was turning his salary back into operating expenses and borrowing against his life insurance reserve to continue his work. The A.T.A. came to the end of 1937 about $3,200 in debt. Early in 1938 it launched the first of its regular annual appeals that special offerings be taken in every Sunday school for the support of the state-wide temperance movement. Several hundred churches responded on the first quarterly temperance Sunday and the total of their offerings relieved the pressure of debts and enabled the Alliance to continue its work.

[79] *A.T.A. Bulletin*, January, 1943.
[80] *Birmingham Age-Herald*, January 13, 1943.
[81] *Montgomery Advertiser*, January 19, 1943.

The A.T.A. realized that it must become stronger and more efficient if it were to be any match for the wets. The rumors loosed by its enemies in some of the county campaigns stung the Alliance to action. The organization prepared to create an adequate research bureau, which it had for sometime been planning. Secretary Hotalen began an intensive organization in this field. The Alliance obtained membership in the National Safety Council, in the American Business Men's Research Foundation, in the Research Council on Problems of Alcohol—a unit of the American Association for the Advancement of Science—and in the Scientific Temperance Federation. It contracted for the *Encyclopedia Britannica Research Service,* and for the weekly, monthly, and annual publications of a multitude of governmental agencies such as the Bureau of Vital Statistics, the Bureau of Internal Revenue, and the Federal Bureau of Investigation. It subscribed to every trade publication issued by distilleries, vintners, and brewers in America, as well as to such dry publications as *The Union Signal,* the *National Voice,* and the Methodist Board of Temperance's *Voice.* It began building a library on alcohol, adding to it month by month every worthwhile book available on any phase of the liquor problem whether it voiced the views of the wets or the drys. The A.T.A. was getting ready to meet propaganda with facts, and to prove its statements anywhere and at any time.

During the winter of 1938-1939, A.T.A. Secretary Hotalen launched a state-wide movement toward education. Schools and churches were visited; talks, often illustrated with charts, were given; and the signing of total abstinence pledges was promoted. Response was far beyond even the most optimistic hope. Many young people's organizations unanimously accepted the total abstinence pledge and not a single youth group approached pledged less than 95 per cent of its membership. Approximately 30,000 young men and women had voluntarily subscribed to the total abstinence pledge by the end of the winter. That number has since been increased to more than 160,000.

Secretary Hotalen had in progress in February, 1943, an extensive educational program on the evil effects of alcohol. Equipped with visual aids, he went into schools and colleges, instructing thousands of young people about the evils of alcohol. Intensive training of Sunday school teachers in small groups began in 1940 and has since continued with notable improvement in the quality and effectiveness of temperance teaching. The A.T.A. collaborated with the Alabama W.C.T.U. in providing a scholarship fund for a selected public school teacher to pursue courses in narcotics at Northwestern University, Evanston, Illinois, preparatory to teaching those courses "to Teachers-in-Service in Alabama." Furthermore, arrangements were made with the authorities of Alabama College for Women for the inclusion of a special course in narcotics education at the 1943 summer school for teachers. Each teacher so trained was expected to serve as "Consultant in Narcotics Education" for the other teachers in the school system where she was employed. Through E. B. Norton, State Superintendent of Education, the A.T.A. offered twelve scholarships, each valued at twenty-five dollars, to teachers who qualified for them and agreed to conduct certain activities in anti-alcoholic education after completing the summer course at Alabama College for Women in 1943.[82]

Since 1937 the W.C.T.U. has placed considerable emphasis upon the educational aspects of temperance. Mabel Vitu Divelbliss, corresponding secretary, stated in her 1937 report that she had spent six weeks working in eight districts of the state, "majoring in membership and organization activities and assisting in institutes." Her itinerary had carried her approximately one thousand miles. With her had been Mrs. S. T. Slaton who presented the Educational Fund Program, and Mr. and Mrs. Ray Jewell, who gave motion picture demonstrations before institutes, high schools, colleges, CCC camps, mixed audiences, and educational leaders.

The summer months of that year, said the W.C.T.U. secretary, had been devoted to instructing and supplying the new unions with practical material; and to mailing literature, posters, and books to teachers and educational leaders. In September, in company with Mrs. McAdory and Mrs. Sisson, the corresponding secretary, spent a week attending six district conventions in the state. The programs at these meetings had been arranged and sent to each district president a month in advance.[83]

The legislative report for 1937 was also encouraging. Mrs. Gist, director of legislation for the Alabama W.C.T.U., reported that she had completed negotiations with Governor Graves and A. H. Collins, State Superintendent of Education, for the employment of Miss Estelle Bozeman as Alcoholic Educational Teacher for Alabama. Miss Bozeman, who had been trained for this work by the National W.C.T.U. in Evanston, Illinois, had already taken up her work with the state teachers and this work had become a definite function of the State Department of Education. Miss Bozeman's employment was sponsored by Governor Graves and Senator Graves and was to be financed by the governor. Alabama was the leading state in its effort to teach the effects of alcohol. Such teaching had been required in Alabama schools since 1891. Mrs. Gist said: "This phase of public education has not heretofore been undertaken in any State as an official action."[84]

The W.C.T.U. reports assert that training and education in the effects of alcohol on the human body have been steadily pushed. The columns of the *White Ribbon* have been used for this purpose. Personal letters have helped carry the message, and temperance materials in Sunday schools and junior missionary societies have further spread the information. In some

[82] Hotalen, "Resume of the Alabama Temperance Movement in 1943."
[83] *Minutes of the Alabama W.C.T.U.* (1937), pp. 19-20.
[84] *Minutes of W.C.T.U.* (1937), p. 32.

Sunday schools children have been encouraged to make temperance, as well as Christian and American, flags. Many pledges have been signed. Rallies, conferences, one-day camps, and children's meetings have all helped to stimulate and maintain interest in temperance.[85]

At the annual convention held in Tuscaloosa in 1941 the late Dr. R. C. Foster, president of the University of Alabama, praised the Union for what it had done to promote temperance in Alabama. He believed, he said, that the W.C.T.U.'s most effective work had been accomplished through education and he predicted that such education would continue to be the most satisfactory attack upon the liquor problem.[86]

The churches, as was to be expected, have opposed the State Liquor Stores. In 1937 the North Alabama Conference commended the fight being waged by the Alabama Temperance Alliance against legalized liquor traffic, and pledged financial support for this fight.[87] The same Conference a year later adopted a report which provided "for extensive educational and legislative programs" as the only adequate solution to the alcoholic problem. The presiding bishop was authorized at this time to appoint a temperance committee consisting of six laymen and six preachers to formulate plans to promote temperance.[88] In 1938 the Alabama Conference went on record as "condemning the officials of the state of Alabama who are responsible for imposing the present liquor law on the people," and appealed "to every voter at every opportunity to cast their vote for the repeal of the present law and the reestablishment of prohibition.[89] In 1939 the North Alabama Conference adopted a report setting aside February 4 as Temperance Sunday in Sunday schools, and asking that a special program and an offering for the Alabama Temperance Alliance be part of the observance of that day. This same conference sent a telegram to Governor Dixon protesting against the establishment of a State Liquor Store for women in Montgomery.[90] In 1940 both the North Alabama Conference and the Alabama Conference pledged the complete support of all their people in the effort to attain state-wide prohibition in 1943.[91] Both of these conferences anticipated a state-wide referendum in 1943 and urged the people to return an unprecedented majority in favor of state-wide prohibition.[92] In addition to the special collections taken on Temperance Sunday, the Temperance Board of the North Alabama Conference and

[85] *Report of W.C.T.U., October 10-13, 1939*, p. 44.
[86] *Birmingham Age-Herald*, October 11, 1941.
[87] *Journal of the North Alabama Conference* (1937), pp. 73-74.
[88] *Ibid.* (1938), pp. 70-71.
[89] *Journal of the Alabama Conference* (1938), pp. 40-41.
[90] *Journal of the North Alabama Conference* (1939), pp. 79-80; *Journal of the Alabama Conference* (1939), pp. 107-108.
[91] *Journal of the North Alabama Conference* (1940), pp. 76-78; *Journal of the Alabama Conference*, (1940), pp. 65-66.
[92] *Journal of the North Alabama Conference* (1942), p. 103; *Journal of the Alabama Conference* (1942), p. 64.

many Baptist churches made special donations to the Alabama Temperance Alliance.[93]

In 1937 the Alabama State Convention approved the work of the Alabama Temperance Alliance and urged its pastors and churches to support it with contributions. All Baptists were asked to support for public office only the candidates who definitely pledged themselves to vote to suppress the liquor traffic in all its forms.[94] In 1939 the same body adopted a report on social service which contained this declaration: "The ABC law has bred crime, corrupted politics, made bootleggers, increased insanity, doubled the number of drunken drivers, multiplied venereal disease, crippled normal moral business, ruined girls, produced inebriates, and debauched society." Churches must act to rid themselves of this baneful influence.[95] The Convention of 1940, in listing certain dangers to America, stated: "The liquor traffic is a moral and economic monster which threatens the foundation of government."[96] In 1941 the same body condemned legalized liquor traffic and approved the idea of a liquor referendum, state-wide in application. It also recommended the passage of U. S. Senate Bill 860, which sought to eliminate alcoholic beverages and immoraltiy from army camps.[97] In 1942 the Baptist State Convention adopted a report on temperance, which embodied the following statement: "Unless it is curbed, alcohol will destroy the United States. . . . Drunkenness cost us terribly at Pearl Harbor. Liquor is the patron saint at Washington." The report declared that liquor was protected by the President and the Secretaries of War and Navy, and feared by Congress; and the merry Devil's dance goes on debauching our soldiers and endangering our chances in the war. The governor was urged to give the people a referendum on the liquor question at an early date.[98]

In 1939 the A.R.P. Synod of the South declared that the whiskey traffic, responsible for promoting the grossest immorality, was being sponsored through governmental agencies. All professed followers of Christ should, the Synod urged, abstain from the use of intoxicating liquors and work to prohibit the sale of that which destroys the bodies and souls of men and women. "We should use every legal means to bring back sobriety by law and by such influences as the Church can use for the destruction of the drink evil and social evils,"[99] the report concluded.

The *Alabama Christian Advocate* worked energetically to drive liquor from the state. The temperance forces must be united in determination, said the *Advocate* in March, 1938, and that determination must express itself in action against the evils of liquor. Surely there were in the church

[93] *Journal of the North Alabama Conference* (1940), p. 87; *Annual of the Alabama State Baptist Convention* (1939), p. 51.
[94] *Annual* (1937), p. 51. [95] *Ibid.* (1939), p. 101.
[96] *Annual of the Alabama State Baptist Convention* (1940), p. 124.
[97] *Alabama Baptist*, November 20, 1941.
[98] *Annual of the Alabama State Baptist Convention* (1942), p. 107.
[99] *Minutes of the A.R.P. Synod of the South* (1938), pp. 305-306.

enough people who hated the liquor traffic and its train of evils to drive it out if they could be aroused to move in solid phalanx.[100] In 1940 the same periodical declared that "economically, socially, physically, and morally the liquor traffic is a millstone around the neck of many people."[101] Acton E. Middlebrooks, editor of the *Advocate,* declared in 1943, "We are fighting the liquor evil with all our soul, mind and strength."[102] Middlebrooks looked forward to the time when there would be no ABC stores in Alabama.

The *Alabama Baptist,* a champion of temperance since 1835, said in 1937 that the excesses to which the legalized liquor traffic would go would ultimately lead to its undoing. Many of those who had been deceived by insistent propaganda would return to the dry camp, and there renew the fight against the demon rum.[103] In 1940 L. L. Gwaltney, editor of the *Alabama Baptist,* remarked: "One of the healthiest signs of our times is the irrepressible sturdiness and strength of determination which characterizes the growing opposition of the people to the legalized liquor traffic."[104] Dr. Seale Harris said, "Worse than the old saloon is the Alabama honky-tonk; and as bad as the worst honky-tonk is the State Liquor Store for Women."[105]

The temperance forces were gaining ground at the end of seven years of the ABC system. The advocates of legal sale were aware of the rising opposition to their business and in a number of localities had placed restrictions on Sunday sales of liquor. The ABC Board had also recognized the trend of public opinion and had banned Sunday sales. In consequence of the foregoing, the Alabama Temperance Alliance, coordinating agent of all other temperance organizations, was making plans to swing Alabama into the dry column. Temperance reports of the churches and W.C.T.U. were in accord with the Alliance. Chauncey Sparks, candidate for governor in the election of 1942, favored a state-wide referendum on the liquor question. His stand harmonized with a temperance report recently adopted by the Alabama Baptist State Convention.

Between 1935 and 1941 there were 178 individuals who paid tax to the Federal Government for wholesale liquor dealers licenses to operate in the state of Alabama. During the same interval 8,465 retail liquor dealers paid taxes to the Federal Government. The largest number of retail licenses procured in any one year was 2,428 in 1938 and the smallest number was 491 in 1940.[106]

Federal law enforcement agents were active in Alabama between 1935 and 1941. During this interval they arrested 14,242 persons for violating

---

[100] March 17, 1940.
[101] *Alabama Christian Advocate,* May 23, 1940.
[102] *Ibid.,* January 28, 1943.
[103] *Alabama Baptist,* June 10, 1937.
[104] *Ibid.,* September 19, 1940.
[105] *Ibid.*
[106] *Annual Reports of the United States Commissioner of Internal Revenue* (1935-1941), *passim.*

THE PROHIBITION MOVEMENT IN ALABAMA 289

the alcoholic tax law. They seized 11,004 stills and 142,050 gallons of distilled spirits. During the same period 2,784 automobiles and trucks were confiscated.[107]

The Law Enforcement Department of the ABC Board had also been active in apprehending violators of the prohibition laws. The records for the years 1938 to 1940 showed substantial increases in dry law violations. During those years 7,314 court cases were handled; 3,064 stills and 61,951 gallons of "mooshine" whiskey were destroyed; 900 automobiles and other vehicles were confiscated. It was noted that the violations in each of these offenses in 1938 had more than doubled by 1940.[108]

The number of Alabama's convict population fluctuated between 1935 and 1942. In the seven-year period ending September 30, 1942, 14,934 persons had been sentenced to the state penitentiary on felony charges. Of these 2,943 were sentenced for violating the prohibition laws. The number of persons convicted for violating the dry laws increased during the first year that the State Liquor Store opened, but there was a notable recession in the number of convictions for this crime in 1941-1942. County prisoners sentenced to penal institutions during this seven-year period totaled 20,849, of which 3,844 were convicted of dry law violations and 3,824 for public drunkenness. County prisoners sentenced for violating the dry laws also increased in 1937-1938 but declined considerably in 1941-1942. The number of persons convicted annually of public drunkenness was irregular between 1935 and 1942. The total state and county prisoners for this period were 35,783. The total state and county dry law convictions were 6,767.[109]

[107] *Annual Reports of the Commissioner of Internal Revenue* (1935-1941), *passim.*
[108] *Annual Reports of the Alabama Alcoholic Beverage Control Board* (1938-1940), *passim.*
[109] *Annual Reports of the State Board of Administration* (1935-1938), *passim;* *Quadrennial Report of Department of Corrections and Institutions* (1938-1942), *passim.*
Number of state and county convicts received in the penitentiary October 1, 1935 to September 30, 1942

Year	State Convicts	For Violating Prohibition Law	County Convicts	For Violating Prohibition Law	Public Drunkenness
1935-36	2,288	385	3,249	736	305
1936-37	2,242	358	2,485	465	296
1937-38	2,547	479	2,728	495	386
1938-39	2,260	535	3,543	593	427
1939-40	2,006	470	3,449	654	432
1940-41	1,939	431	3,161	655	358
1941-42	1,652	285	2,234	226	224
	14,934	2,943	20,849	3,824	2,428

SUMMARY

Immediately on its entrance to statehood Alabama had been confronted with the problem of regulating the liquor traffic. In the early days men had expected the state to license and to regulate the traffic in liquor and to see that druken men did not disturb the peace; consequently, the number of acts restricting the conditions under which intoxicating liquors could be sold had increased from year to year. During the Civil War the state further extended its powers and the people consequently learned more about the possibilities of state control. In the distressing days following the war, men had realized the necessity of regulating the sale and consumption of liquor so that the Negro would not be a menace to white women or to the peace of the community. More and more was demanded of the state as a regulator of the sale and consumption of liquor as the struggle grew in intensity and as men become increasingly social-minded. By licensing, by local option, by special acts, by local dispensaries, and finally by state-wide prohibition, the power of the state over the liquor business was gradually extended. Politics, temperance, and business became inextricably mingled as the issue became more clear-cut.

In 1906 the temperance forces were successful in electing a governor and a legislature friendly to the local option movement; thus, they could look forward to the culmination of a movement which had begun in the decade of the fifties. Within sixty days after the convening of the 1907 legislature, a county local option law was passed. The first election, held in July, 1907, resulted in a land-slide vote for prohibition. Twenty other county elections were held in 1907, all of which voted out the saloon or dispensary. In the special session of the legislature of 1909 the prohibition forces had little trouble in passing more rigid enforcement laws, but a struggle of a more serious nature came when they tried to write prohibition into the constitution. In that struggle the prohibition forces were overwhelmingly defeated.

In addition to the state temperance societies, the press, the churches, and the schools played an important part in the prohibition struggle. The temperance forces aided in educating the people, and they were the primary agency in arousing the people on the temperance issue. In order to educate the public and thus to achieve their ends, these organizations presented in vivid colors, and with continuous propaganda, the evils of drink and the duty of the individual and the state to see that all men abstained. The aggressive W.C.T.U. and the powerful Anti-Saloon League fought with energy the battles which were necessary in order to bring the public and the lawmakers to desire complete and permanent prohibition. With them the force which began with the local temperance society reached its culmination.

Joining with the politicians, the temperance forces were victorious in the year 1907. It only remained to make the victory permanent by constitutional prohibition. But the prohibition forces had reckoned without the opposition. Those who were in favor of drink or who thought they saw their business ruined were willing to go to any lengths to strengthen their forces. This they did by building up a powerful organization of their own. In the contest, in which propaganda was used with great effectiveness by both sides, the anti-prohibitionists won, and the constitutional amendment was defeated in 1909.

An interesting phase of the temperance movement was the reorganized opposition. Many people opposed both the theory and practice of prohibition. The organized opposition, however, came from liquor dealers. As one would expect where a vested interest was involved, the contest was bitter and prolonged. And the saloons and distilleries were backed by immense wealth.

After the defeat of 1909, the prohibitionists doubted whether they could hold what they had gained; but the local optionists were greatly encouraged by the overwhelming defeat of the constitutional prohibition amendment. Each side prepared to elect a governor and a legislature, in 1910, pledged to do its bidding. The prohibitionists selected an outstanding dry for their standard bearer, while the local optionists chose the most prominent opponent of the amendment. The local optionists elected the governor and a majority of the state officers and legislators. Feeling that they had a mandate, the legislature, upon the recommendation of the governor, repealed the state-wide prohibition laws and passed a county local option act. During this quadrennium eight counties legalized the sale of liquor.

The drys laid their plans to regain control of the executive and legislative branches of the state government in 1914. In this contest the local optionists elected the governor, but the prohibitionists won an overwhelming majority in both branches of the legislature. When the legislature assembled, a state-wide prohibition law and rigid enforcement acts were immediately passed over the governor's veto. Thus the state re-entered the dry column on July 1, 1915, where it was to remain for the next twenty-two years. Ministers, church members, and the Woman's Chritsian Temperance Union were the principal actors in the movement to drive liquor from the state. The Anti-Saloon League of Alabama was the coordinating agency of all the temperance forces in these contests.

In 1918 the prohibitionists were again successful. They elected both a governor and a legislature in sympathy with their views. In this campaign the Eighteenth Amendment and state rights were the principal issues. When the legislature assembled in January, 1919, it forthwith ratified the

Eighteenth Amendment. The prohibitionists of Alabama had achieved all they had ever hoped for in legislation.

The temperance reports of the several denominations during the early 1920's indicate that the drys were well pleased with the progress of prohibition; but by the latter part of this decade these reports became less optimistic. Some indicate alarm at the flagrant violations of the dry laws and demanded more rigid enforcement of them.

In 1928 prohibition and religion were the most important issues in the presidential acmpaign, at least as it was conducted in Alabama. Emotionalism ran high and the people went through one of the most turbulent political campaigns in the history of the state. Many Democrats refused to vote for the party nominee, and the Democratic party carried the state by the narrowest margin since the days of Reconstruction.

Reaction against prohibition was evident in 1931. Courts became more lenient toward violators of the dry laws. The legislature gave circuit judges discretionary powers to suspend sentences for certain offenses involving the dry laws. Candidates began to embody repeal planks in their platforms. The National Democratic party climaxed the movement by declaring for outright repeal of the Eighteenth Amendment in 1932. The electorate of the state gave the Democratic nominee a landslide vote. In this campaign some churchmen and the church papers stood firm for the retention of national prohibition, but in 1933 the people of Alabama voted by a large majority to repeal the Eighteenth Amendment.

In 1934 the three candidates for governor favored a referendum on the liquor question but differed on details. Most candidates for the legislature also favored some form of referendum. Before the legislature convened in 1935 it was generally believed that the people would be given an opportunity to decide between retention of the dry laws and the legal sale of liquor. When it met, the legislature enacted a law calling for a referendum. The Alabama Temperance Alliance took the lead in opposing the legal sale of hard liquors, light wines, and beer, and the manufacture of liquor in the state. Most of the daily papers and many of the weeklies favored repeal of the bone-dry statutes. A number of the leading politicians also endorsed repeal. The results of the election showed that the drys had carried the election by substantial majorities.

The repealists, successful in fifteen counties containing the largest cities, were not satisfied with the results and introduced a bill in the legislature calling for county local option. The bill was defeated. The repealists then tried to get local acts through the legislature providing for legal sale in large cities. The drys contended that the legal sale of liquor in those centers would frustrate the bone-dry statutes, and defeated all repeal bills.

In 1936 the public health department and the public schools were in dire financial straits. In calling a special session of the legislature, the governor included the provision for another referendum. The legislature passed, over the governor's veto, a bill providing for the establishment of State Liquor Stores in counties voting in favor of legal sale. Twenty-four counties voted in favor of legal sale and State Stores were opened in May, 1937.

The contest between the opposing forces has been a long and bitter one, with first one and then the other in the ascendancy. While one side has been enjoying the victory, the other has been setting itself to undo the victory. Only time can tell whether a final solution to the issue can be found. In the meantime neither side has ever been the complete victor.

BIBLIOGRAPHY

I. Primary Sources
 1. Official
  A. Federal
   American State Papers. 38 vols. Washington: Gales and Seaton.
   Compendium of the Sixth Census of the United States, 1840. Washington: Printed by Thomas Allen, 1841.
   Digest of Accounts of Manufacturing Establishments in the United States and their Manufacturers. Taken from the 4th Census, 1820. Washington: Gales and Seaton, 1823.
   Manufacturers of the United States in 1860: Compiled from the Original Returns of the Eighth Census. Washington: Government Printing Office, 1865.
   Public Laws of the Confederate States of America. Passed at the First Session of the First Congress, 1862. 2 vols. Richmond: R. M. Smith, Printer to Congress, 1864.
   Twelfth Annual Report of the United States Department of Labor. Washington: Government Printing Office, 1898.
   United States Census Reports, 1820-1941.
   United States Commissioner of Labor, 12th Annual Report—Economic Aspects of the Liquor Problem. Washington: Government Printing Office.
   United States Congressional Documents, 1820-1941.
   United States Internal Revenue Reports, 1864-1941. Washington: Government Printing Office.
   United States Statutes at Large, 1789-1938. 50 vols.
  B. State
   Alabama Digest, 1820-1937. 19 vols. Covering Alabama Reports and Southern Reporters as well as Alabama Cases Decided in Federal District and Circuit Courts, Circuit Court of Appeals, with Current Cumulative Picket Service. St. Paul: West Publishing Co., 1837.
   Alabama House and Senate Journals, 1819-1939.
   Alabama Supreme Court Reports. 200 vols. 1819-1940.
   Alabama Official and Statistical Register, 1911-1939.
   Annual Reports of the State Auditor of Alabama, 1880-1940.
   Annual Reports of Alabama Alcoholic Beverage Control Board, 1937-1940.
   Annual Reports of State Board of Administration, 1922-1940.
   Biennial Report of the Department of Corrections and Institutions to the Governor of Alabama, 1938-1940.
   Comptroller's Reports of Alabama, 1848-1880.
   Educational Reports of Alabama, 1868-1942.
   Laws of Alabama, 1819-1939.
   Proceedings of the House and Senate. The Debate of the Upper Branch of the Legislature Upon the Statutory Prohibition Bill, 1907.
   Proceedings of the Annual Sessions of the Woman's Christian Temperance Union of the State of Alabama, 1884-1941.
   Rowland, D., *The Mississippi Territorial Archives, 1789-1803.* 2 vols. Nashville: Brandon Printing Company, 1905.

Rowland, D., and Sanders, A. G., *Mississippi Provincial Archives, 1704-1743*. 3 vols. Jackson: Press of the Mississippi Department of Archives and History, 1932.

Statutes of Mississippi Territory, 1798-1816. Natchez: Peter Isler, Printer to the Territory, 1816.

Toulman, H., *A Digest of the Laws of the State of Alabama*. Cahawba: Ginn & Curtis, 1823.

C. Special

Recopilación de Leyes de los Reinos de las Indias, Tomo Segundo, Leyes XXXVI and XXXVII.

D. Local

Codes of Ordinances of the City of Huntsville with Charter, 1861, 1870, 1891, 1899.

Code of Ordinances of the City of Decatur, 1891. n. p., n. pub.

Directory of Huntsville, 1859-1860. Huntsville: Coltart & Son, 1859.

2. Manuscripts

Bolling Hall Papers. State Department of Archives and History, Montgomery, Alabama.

Colonial Office (C.O.) 5: 574-635. Library of Congress, Washington, D. C.

Constitution of Alabama Temperance Alliance, 1935 and 1938.

Election Returns: Constitutional Prohibition Amendment, November 29, 1909. State Department of Archives and History, Montgomery, Alabama.

Executive Journal of Governor Holmes, Book 2. State Department of Archives and History, Montgomery, Alabama.

Minutes of the Alabama Temperance Alliance, 1933-1940. Headquarters of A.T.A., Comer Building, Birmingham, Alabama.

Minutes of the City Council of Huntsville, 1837-1848; 1858-1869; 1880-1909. City Hall, Huntsville, Alabama.

Minutes of the City Council of Decatur, 1871-1909. City Hall, Decatur, Alabama.

Minutes of the City Council of Montgomery, 1820-1854; 1858-1909. City Hall, Montgomery, Alabama.

Minutes of the Council of British West Florida, 1764-1779. State Department of Archives and History, Montgomery, Alabama.

Original Letters of Governor John G. Shorter. State Department of Archives and History, Montgomery, Alabama.

Original Vouchers of the LaFayette Entertainment Committees of Montgomery, Cahawba, and Mobile, 1825. State Department of Archives and History, Montgomery, Alabama.

Transcripts of British West Florida Assembly Records, 1763-1783. State Department of Archives and History, Montgomery, Alabama.

Records of Domestic Corporations of Alabama. 5 vols. Secretary of State's Office, Montgomery, Alabama.

Reports of Probate Judges of Alabama to the State Auditor on Liquor License, 1825-1908. State Department of Archives and History, Montgomery, Alabama.

Record of Licenses in Limestone County, 1875-1905. Court House, Athens, Alabama.

Record of Licenses of Decatur, 1897. City Hall, Decatur, Alabama.

Superior Court Minutes of Madison County, Mississippi Territory, 1811-1816. County Court House, Huntsville, Alabama.

Superior Court Minutes held for the District of Washington, Mississippi Territory at the Court House in the town of Wakefield, 1807-1811. State Department of Archives and History, Montgomery, Alabama.

Transcripts of Mississippi Territorial Records. State Department of Archives and History, Montgomery, Alabama.

Wills and Iventories of Madison County, 1820-1870. Court House, Huntsville, Alabama.

Wills and Iventories of Limestone County, 1826-1860. Court House, Athens, Alabama.

3. Temperance Literature

Centennial Temperance Volume, 1876. New York: National Temperance Society and Publishing House, 1881.

Cherrington, Ernest Hurst (ed.), *The Anti-Saloon League Year Books, 1909-1930: An Encyclopedia of Facts and Figures Dealing with the Liquor Traffic and the Temperance Reform.* Columbus: The Anti-Saloon League of America Publishing Co., 1910-1931.

"Constitution of the Huntsville Temperance Society," *Southern Advocate,* October 2, 1829.

"Constitution of the Matrons and Maidens of Temperance," *Crystal Fount,* April 2, 1852.

Cyclopedia of Temperance and Prohibition. A Reference Book of Facts, Statistics, and General Information on All Phases of the Drink Question, the Temperance Movement and the Prohibition Agitation. New York: Funk and Wagnalls, 1891.

Permanent American Temperance Documents. 3 vols. New York: Published at the Office of the American Temperance Union, 1861. [They contain the annual reports of the American Temperance Society 1831-1836, those of the American Temperance Union 1837-1859 and other valuable early material.]

"Proceedings of the Grand Division of the Sons of Temperance of Alabama," *Crystal Fount,* September 19, 1851.

"Proceedings of the Grand Division of the Sons of Temperance," *Southern Advocate,* October 2, 1847.

Proceedings of the Grand Lodge of the Independent Order of Good Templars, 1860, 1871, 1873, 1875. Public Library, New York City.

"Proceedings of Friends of Temperance," 1852-1853. In MSS. files, State Department of Archives and History, Montgomery, Alabama.

"Proceedings of the Alabama Templars of Temperance," *Huntsville Weekly Democrat,* June 13, 1877.

"Proceedings of the State Temperance Convention," *Alabama Courier,* August 18, 1881.

"Proceedings of the Prohibition Party," *Montgomery Advertiser,* July 8, 1886.

Wilson, Alonzo E., *American Prohibition Year Book.* Chicago: United Prohibition Press. Published annually after 1900.

4. Contemporary Essays, Addresses, Pamphlets, Sermons

Andrews, J. O., "Temperance and Politics," *Alabama Christian Advocate,* March 5, 1896.

Anderson, N. L., "Evils of the Liquor Trade," *Montgomery Advertiser*, October 22, 1907.
Bankhead, John H., "Reasons for Opposing the Amendment," *Mobile Register*, November 10, 1909.
Carmichael, A. H., "Address in the House of Representatives On the Bill for Constitutional Prohibition," *Montgomery Journal*, August 5, 1909.
Childers, J. W. L., "An Address Delivered Before the Citizens of Selma on the Organization of a Temperance Society," *South Western Christian Advocate*, February 1, 1840.
Clark, J. F., "The Saloon and Racial Equality," *Alabama Christian Advocate*, January 4, 1906.
Clayton, Henry D., "Governmental Prohibition," *Montgomery Advertiser*, December 22, 1907.
Clements, Jere, "An Address Delivered Before Huntsville and LaFayette Divisions Sons of Temperance," *Southern Advocate*, January 19, 1849.
Cruickshank, G. M., "Whiskey or no Whiskey," *Birmingham Ledger*, September 20, 1907.
Doughterty, Judge, "Temperance Laws," *Macon Republican*, April 7, 1853.
Finley, James, "Speech Delivered Before the New Hope Temperance Society," *South Western Christian Advocate*, July 3, 1841.
Furgerson, W. P. F., "Prohibition Party," *New Encyclopedia of Social Reform*. New York: Funk and Wagnalls Company, 1897.
Hare, F. W., "Why I Oppose the Proposed Constitutional Amendment," *Montgomery Advertiser*, October 1, 1909.
Heflin, J. Thomas, "Endorsed the Constitutional Amendment," *Birmingham Ledger*, October 9, 1909.
Howard, W. M., "Politics Figure," *Birmingham Age-Herald*, November 3, 1909.
Hubbard, Miss E., "An Address Delivered Before the Sons of Temperance at Fayetteville," *Crystal Fount*, June 20, 1851.
Jewett, Milo P., *Address Before the Sons of Temperance, Marion Division, No. 27*. Marion: Markham, 1848.
Knox, John B., "Argument against Proposed Amendment," *Montgomery Advertiser*, October 18, 1909.
McCord, Leon, "An Appeal Made to Safe and Sane Business Men to Fight Constitutional Prohibition," *Montgomery Advertiser*, July 21, 1909.
Jeffries, M. T., "Sketch of Alabama W.C.T.U."
Rhodes, Ruffus N., "Whiskey and the Negro," *Birmingham News*, September 5, 1907.
————, "Sanctity of the Home," *Birmingham News*, November 10, 1907.
————, "Showing Up the Brewers," *Birmingham News*, November 17, 1909.
————, "As to the Slush Fund," *Birmingham News*, November 17, 1909.
Screws, W. W., "A Sensation of Politics, Brooks Lawrence's Attack on the Supreme Court," *Montgomery Advertiser*, July 7, 1909.

Sheehan, Will T., "Southeast Alabama Chain of Dispensaries," *Montgomery Advertiser*, February 25, 1905.
Taylor, J. W., *An Address Before the Mt. Horeb Division of the Sons of Temperance, September 21, 1848.* Eutaw: Samuel M. Houston, 1848.
Warren, Jno. F., "The License System Again," *Crystal Fount*, September 12, 1851.
———, "Daughters of Temperance," *Crystal Fount*, April 21, 1852.
———, "Reasons for the Decline of the Sons of Temperance," *Crystal Fount*, October 3, 1851.
Wasson, S. E., "The Retail Liquor Traffic in Alabama," *Alabama Christian Advocate*, August 10, 1905.
———, "Alabama Anti-Saloon League," *Alabama Christian Advocate*, November 17, 1904.
———, "What the Alabama Anti-Saloon League Proposes," *Alabama Christian Advocate*, January 12, 1905.
Woods, N. M., "A Sermon, Reasons for Supporting the Amendment," *Montgomery Advertiser*, September 21, 1909.
Wright, Seaborn, "Fight Liquor Trust Not Local Saloon Men," *Montgomery Advertiser*, June 21, 1909.

5. Records of Religious Organizations. (Dates indicate years consulted.)
   A. Baptist
   Minutes of the Baptist State Convention, 1829-1941.
   Alabama Baptist Association Minutes, 1900-1907.
   Arbacoochee Baptist Association Minutes, 1907.
   Bessemer Baptist Association Minutes, 1901.
   Bethel Baptist Association Minutes, 1901-1907.
   Bethlehem Baptist Association Minutes, 1836; 1900-1905.
   Bibb County Baptist Association Minutes, 1904-1905.
   Bigbee Baptist Association Minutes, 1868; 1902.
   Birmingham Baptist Association Minutes, 1893-1896; 1903-1909.
   Blue Creek Baptist Association Minutes, 1904-1905.
   Butler County Baptist Association Minutes, 1906.
   Cahaba Baptist Association Minutes, 1906.
   Calhoun County Baptist Association Minutes, 1893-1907.
   Canaan Baptist Association Minutes, 1837-1883.
   Centennial Baptist Association Minutes, 1901-1906.
   Cherokee County Baptist Association Minutes, 1895.
   Chilton County Baptist Association Minutes, 1905-1907.
   Clay County Baptist Association Minutes, 1907.
   Clarke County Baptist Association Minutes, 1901.
   Coffee County Baptist Association Minutes, 1906-1907.
   Colbert Baptist Association Minutes, 1900-1907.
   Columbia Baptist Association Minutes, 1900-1907.
   Conecuh Baptist Association Minutes, 1898-1901.
   Coosa River Baptist Association Minutes, 1870-1904.
   Cullman Baptist Association Minutes, 1901.
   De Kalb County Baptist Association Minutes, 1905.
   East Liberty Baptist Association Minutes, 1907.
   Escambia County Baptist Association Minutes, 1907.
   Etowah Baptist Association Minutes, 1904-1906.
   Eufaula Baptist Association Minutes, 1886-1887; 1900-1907.
   Florence Baptist Association Minutes, 1901.
   Geneva Baptist Association Minutes, 1907.

Gilliam Springs Association Minutes, 1904.
Harris Baptist Association Minutes, 1895-1908.
Judson Baptist Association Minutes, 1901-1905.
Liberty Baptist Association Minutes, 1900-1906.
Marshall Baptist Association Minutes, 1905.
Mineral Springs Baptist Association Minutes, 1900-1905.
Mobile Baptist Association Minutes, 1904-1907.
Montgomery Baptist Association Minutes, 1905.
Mud Creek Baptist Association Minutes, 1904.
Mulberry Baptist Association Minutes, 1885-1886.
Muscle Shoals Baptist Association Minutes, 1902-1907.
New Providence Baptist Association Minutes, 1900.
New River Baptist Association Minutes, 1904-1906.
North River Baptist Association Minutes, 1900-1905.
Pea River Baptist Association Minutes, 1901-1905.
Pine Barren Baptist Association Minutes, 1858; 1891-1895; 1900-1907.
Randolph County Baptist Association Minutes, 1901.
"Round Island Baptist Church Minutes," Limestone County, 1820-1909. In possession of C. R. Jones, Athens, Alabama.
Shelby County Baptist Association Minutes, 1906.
Sipsey Baptist Association Minutes, 1904-1907.
South Bethel Baptist Association Minutes, 1886.
St. Clair County Baptist Association Minutes, 1904.
Sulphur Springs Baptist Association Minutes, 1901-1904.
Tallapoosa River Baptist Association Minutes, 1885.
Tallahatchee and Ten Island Baptist Association Minutes, 1886.
Ten Island Baptist Association Minutes, 1900-1907.
Troy Baptist Association Minutes, 1909.
Tuscaloosa Baptist Association Minutes, 1900-1907.
Tuskegee Baptist Association Minutes, 1904-1907.
Union Baptist Association Minutes, 1900-1906.
Unity Baptist Association Minutes, 1885; 1901-1907.
Weogufka Baptist Association Minutes, 1904-1907.
Yellow Creek Baptist Association Minutes, 1905.
Zion Baptist Association Minutes, 1907.

B. Congregational
Minutes of the General Conference, 1876-1930.

C. Disciples of Christ
Minutes, 1886-1940.

D. Methodist Episcopal, South
Doctrines and Discipline of the Methodist Episcopal Church, South. Nashville: Stevenson and Owen, 1854.
Doctrines and Discipline of the Methodist Episcopal Church. New York: J. Collord, 1832, 1840.
Journals of the General Conference, Methodist Episcopal Church, South, 1846-1858.
Minutes of the Alabama Conference, 1839-1940.
Minutes of the North Alabama Conference, 1877-1941.
"Minutes of the Blount County Circuit," 1832-1849. State Department of Archives and History, Montgomery, Alabama.
"Minutes of the Centerville Circuit," 1835-1849. State Department of Archives and History, Montgomery, Alabama.

"Minutes of the Montgomery Station," 1850. State Department of Archives and History, Montgomery, Alabama.
E. Methodist Protestant
Minutes of Annual Conference, 1880-1907.
F. Presbyterian
"Minutes of the Synod of Alabama," 1837-1940. All Minutes of the Presbyterian Church were found at the Historical Foundation of the Presbyterian and Reformed Churches, Montreat, North Carolina.
"Minutes of the North Alabama Presbytery," 1825-1844; 1876-1909.
"Minutes of the South Alabama Presbytery," 1827-1909.
"Minutes of the East Alabama Presbytery," 1842-1909.
"Minutes of the Tuscaloosa Presbytery," 1835-1909.
"Minutes of the Tuscumbia Presbytery," 1849-1868.
"Minutes of the Talladega Presbytery," 1852-1854.
Minutes of the Southern Synod of the Associate Reformed Presbyterian Church, 1862-1940.
G. Presbyterian Church U. S. A.
Minutes of the General Assembly, 1880-1924.
6. Newspapers. (Dates indicate files consulted.)
A. Secular
Alabamian-Dispatch, Tuscumbia, 1911.
Alabama Journal, Montgomery, 1827; 1849-1855.
Alabama Progress, Montgomery, 1882.
Alabama State Journal, Montgomery, 1869-1874.
Alabama Republican, Huntsville, 1882.
Alabama State Intelligencer, Tuscaloosa, 1829.
Alabama Beacon, Greensboro, 1843-1889.
Alabama Courier, Athens, 1880-1941.
Anniston Star, 1937.
Anniston Times, 1937.
Athens Weekly Post, 1869-1882.
Bibb Blade, Six Miles, 1880-1884.
Birmingham Age-Herald, 1887-1941.
Birmingham Ledger, 1892-1922.
Birmingham News, 1888-1941.
Carbon Hill Enterprise, 1903.
Chicago Tribune, August 28, 1932.
Christian Century, April 20 and September 7, 1932.
Christian Science Monitor, March 11, 1925.
Clarke County Democrat, Grove Hill, 1856-1897.
Cullman Tribune, 1907-1912.
Current History, August, 1932.
Daily Register, Mobile, 1897-1937.
Daily State Guard, Wetumpka, 1849.
Daily Times, Eufaula, 1882-1898.
Dallas Gazette, Cahaba and Selma, 1854-1909.
Decatur Daily, 1912-1938.
Democrat, Huntsville, 1832-1850.
Dothan Eagle, 1938.
Dothan Siftings, 1899.
Eufaula Times and News, 1880-1890.
Florence Herald, 1897-1911.

Greensboro Watchman, 1890-1909.
Greenville Advocate, 1880-1909.
Huntsville Tribune, 1900-1914.
Independent, Gainesville, 1854-1865.
Independent Monitor, Tuscaloosa, 1841-1871.
Jacksonville Republican, 1837-1893.
Laborer's Banner, Brewton, 1900-1902.
Limestone Democrat, Athens, 1890-1941.
Limestone News, Athens, 1873-1877.
Literary Digest, July 14, 1928; July 9, 1932.
Macon Republican, Tuskegee, 1837-1893.
Mobile Commercial Register, 1820-1837.
Mobile Daily Tribune, 1874-1876.
Montgomery Advertiser and State Gazette, 1854-1856.
Montgomery Advertiser and Mail, 1873.
Montgomery Advertiser, 1866-1941.
Montgomery Journal, 1897-1941.
Moulton Advertiser, 1880-1909.
Mountain Eagle, Jasper, 1903-1907.
National Bulletin, Cincinnati, Ohio, February 19, 1914.
New York Herald Tribune, January 8, 1932.
New York Times, March 3, 6, 1931.
North Alabamian, Tuscumbia, 1937.
Oakman News, 1903-1907.
Opelika News, 1900-1909.
Our Mountain Home, Talladega, 1886-1887.
People's Reflector, Centerville, 1892.
Pickensville Register, 1842.
Pine Belt News, Brewton, 1892-1902.
Selma Courier, 1829.
Sheffield Standard, 1910-1911.
Shelby County Reporter, 1937-1941.
Shelby Sentinel, Calera, 1875-1909.
Southern Advocate and Huntsville Advertiser, 1825-1851.
Southern Democrat, Oneonta, 1910-1915.
Southern Argus, Selma, 1869-1879.
Standard Gage, Brewton, 1888-1902.
Sumpter County Whig, Livingston, 1851-1856.
Troy Messenger, 1881-1909.
Tuscaloosa Blade, 1872-1875.
Tuscaloosa Gazette, 1899-1909.
Tuscaloosa News, 1899-1937.
Union Springs Herald, 1869-1909.
Weekly Tribune, Birmingham, 1900.
West Alabamian, Carrollton, 1869-1885.

B. Religious

Alabama Baptist, Montgomery, 1881-1899; Birmingham, 1899-1941.
Alabama Baptist Advocate, Marion, 1849-1850.
Alabama Christian Advocate, Birmingham, 1881-1941.
Earnest Worker, Richmond, Virginia, 1886.
Junior and Senior Sunday School Quarterlies of the Methodist Episcopal Church, South, 1885-1909. Nashville: Southern Methodist Publishing House.

South Western Baptist, Montgomery, 1852-1854; Tuskegee, 1854-1865.
South Western Christian Advocate, Nashville, 1833-1848.
C. Temperance
Alabama Citizen, Birmingham, 1906-1909.
Crystal Fount, Tuscaloosa, 1851-1852.
White Ribbon, Birmingham, 1903-1941.
D. Magazine Articles
(1) Favoring Prohibition
"Influence of Rum and Whiskey on the Commercial Life of the Colonies," by D. A. Wells, *Princeton Review*, March, 1884.
"Liquor and Labor," *Catholic World*, XLVII (1888), 539-544.
"The Dispensary System in the State of Alabama," *Outlook*, LXXI (1902), 454-455.
"Prohibition and the Negro," *Outlook*, LXXXVIII (1908), 587-589.
"Prohibition in Alabama," *Outlook*, LXXXVII (1907), 207.
"Prohibition in the Confederacy," by William M. Robinson, *The American Historical Review*, XXXVII (1931); XLVI (1932).
(2) Opposing Prohibition
Simpson, R. W., Jr., "Near Prohibition in the South," *Harper's Weekly*, LV (1911), 12-13.
Ball, S. Mays, "Alabama's Fierce Struggle Over Prohibition," *Leslie's Weekly*, CIX (1909), 652.
Gobel, Herman P., "The Personal Rights and Liberties of Man," *Congressional Record*, XLII (1908), 5380-5381.
The American Brewer, November, 1909.
7. Other Contemporary Accounts
Bartram, William, *Travels through North and South Carolina, Georgia, East and West Florida, etc., 1773-1778*. Philadelphia: James and Johnston, 1792.
"Collection of Letters Written by Mollie Johnston," Transcripts are in Athens College Library, Athens, Alabama.
Coxe, Tench, (Digest and Prepared); *A Statement of Arts and Manufacturers of the United States of America for the Year 1810*. Philadelphia: Printed by A. Corman, 1814.
Hall, Basil, *Forty Etchings, from Sketches made with Camera Lucids, in North America, in 1827 and 1828*. 3 vols. Edinburgh: For Cadell & Co., 1829.
McGuffey, W. H., *Third Electric Reader* (First Edition). Cincinnati: Van Antwerp, Bragg & Co., 1857.
Power, Tyron, *Impressions of America*. 2 vols. Philadelphia: Carey, Lea and Blanchard, 1836.
Romans, B., *A Concise Natural History of East and West Florida*. New York: Printed for the author, 1775.
Webster, N., *American Spelling Book Containing the Rudiments of the English Language*. Cincinnati: W. M. & O. Farnworth, 1826.
II. Secondary Sources
1. State and Local Histories
Betts, Edward C., *Early History of Huntsville, Alabama, 1804-1870*. Montgomery: The Brown Printing Co., 1916.

Blue, M. P., *History of Montgomery.* Montgomery: T. C. Bingham & Co., 1878.
Boyd, Minnie Clare, *Alabama in the Fifties.* New York: Columbia University Press, 1931.
Claiborne, J. F. H., *Mississippi as a Province, Territory, and State.* Jackson, Miss.: Power and Barkesdale, 1880.
Crumpton, W. B., *A Book of Memories.* Montgomery: Baptist Mission Board, 1921.
――――, *How Alabama Became Dry.* Montgomery: Paragon Press, 1925.
Dobyns, Fletcher, *The Amazing Story of Repeal.* New York: Willett, Clark & Company, 1940.
Dorman, Lewey, *Party Politics in Alabama from 1850 Through 1860.* Wetumpka: Wetumpka Printing Company, 1935.
Gordon, E. P., *When the Brewers Had the Stranglehold.* Alcohol Information Committee, 1930.
――――, *Women Torch-Bearers.* Evanston: National Woman's Christian Temperance Union Publishing House, 1924.
Hamilton, P. J., *Colonial Mobile, 1715-1821.* Boston: Houghton, Mifflin and Company, 1898.
Moore, A. B., *History of Alabama* (Second Edition). University: Alabama University Supply Store, 1933.
――――, *History of Alabama and Her People.* 3 vols. Chicago: The American Historical Society, 1927.
Owens, Thomas M., *History of Alabama and Dictionary of Alabama Biography.* 4 vols. Chicago: The S. J. Clarke Publishing Company, 1921.
Saunders, J. E., *Early Settlers of Alabama.* New Orleans: L. Graham & Son, 1899.

2. Histories of Religious Organizations

Bledsoe, Elder W. C., *History of the Liberty (East) Baptist Association of Alabama.* Atlanta: Constitution Job Office, 1886.
Foster, Henry B., *History of the Tuscaloosa County Baptist Association, 1834-1934.* Tuscaloosa: Weatherford Printing Co., 1934.
Holcombe, H., *A History of the Rise and Progress of the Baptists in Alabama.* Philadelphia: King and Baird, 1840.
Posey, Walter Brownlow, *The Development of Methodism in the Old Southwest, 1783-1824.* Tuscaloosa: Weatherford Printing Company, 1933.
Riley, B. G., *A History of the Baptists of Alabama, 1808-1894.* Birmingham: Roberts & Son, 1895.
Shackelford, Josephus, *History of the Muscle Shoals Baptist Association from 1820 to 1890.* Trinity, Alabama: Published by the Author, 1891.
Williams, Harriot Eunice, "History of Ruhama Baptist Church, Birmingham." In possession of the author, Birmingham, Alabama.

3. Temperance Literature

Black, James, *Brief History of the Prohibition Reform Party.* New York: The National Committee of the Prohibition Reform Party, 1880.
――――, *The National Prohibition Party,* reprinted from *One Hundred Years of Temperance,* 1885. New York: National Temperance Society Publishing House, 1886.

Colvin, D. Leigh, *Prohibition in the United States.* New York: Geo. H. Doran Company, 1916.

Dunn, James B., *One Hundred Years of Temperance.* New York: National Temperance Society Publishing House, 1886.

Hotalen, W. Earl, "The Story of the Alabama Temperance Alliance, Inc.," July 1, 1937 to November 18, 1941. In possession of the author at A.T.A. Headquarters, Birmingham, Alabama.

Krout, John Allen, *The Origins of Prohibition in the United States.* New York: Alfred A. Knopf, 1925.

4. Biographies

Birney, William, *James G. Birney and His Times.* New York: D. Appleton and Company, 1890.

Claiborne, J. F. H., *Life and Times of General Sam Dale.* New York: Harper & Brothers, 1860.

Kindley, E. K., *Franklin D. Roosevelt.* New York: Bobbs-Merrill Company, 1931.

Rowland, D., *Life, Letters, and Papers of William Dunbar.* Jackson, Miss.: Press of the Mississippi Historical Society, 1930.

"The Life of John T. Tanner," *Northern Alabama Historical and Biographical.* Birmingham: Smith & De Land, 1888.

INDEX

TO

HISTORY OF
THE PROHIBITION MOVEMENT IN ALABAMA,
1702-1943

By

JAMES BENSON SELLERS

INDEX

Abbeville, 93
Abbeville Herald, 198
Abstinence, for sake of others, subject of Sunday school lesson, 56
Accosted, respectable women, 275
Acrimonious, 178
Affrays, 9
African Baptist, use unfermented wine for communion, 64
Affront, for refusing social drinks, 26
Against intemperance. *See* Abstinence
Ainesworth, Bishop W. N., 229
Alabama Baptist, endorses temperance, 50, 64; favors keeping prohibition out of politics, 65, 101, 102, 118; attributes defeat to personal politics, 147, 176; hailed ratification of Eighteenth Amendment as glorious victory, 188, 193; predicts some Democratic opposition to Alfred E. Smith, 196; predicts Smith's defeat, 199; prohibition vindicated, 210; Hoover slips a cog, 223, 228, 234, 243, 256; advocates new temperance organization, 262; sees growing opposition to legalized liquor traffic, 288
Alabama Beacon, favors moral suasion, 50, 66
Alabama Beverage Control Act, establishes State Liquor Stores, 251, 263, 266
Alabama Beverage Control, 249; Governor appoints board, 252, 260; illegal to possess liquor in dry counties, 262
Alabama Christian Advocate, endorses temperance, 65; advocates local option, 72; whiskey power frustrates dry law, 77; opposes prohibition party, 84; for dispensary, 88, 91, 93; favors anti-saloon league, 102; commends governor, 131, 141; race question, 175; compliments legislature, 185; opposes Alfred E. Smith, 198; opposes repeal plank, 224; plan unfair, 225; liquor backed by wealth, 230; endorses Bibb Graves, 233; endorses prohibition, 234; election a farce, 247; prohibitionists complacent, 259; dispose of liquor, 287
Alabama Citizen, official prohibition publication, 104, 105, 113, 137, 166
Alabama Conference of the Methodist Episcopal Church, South, request denied, 17; oppose to repealing dry law in Macon County, 59; vote against liquor, 60; memorializes legislature, 157; majority of legislature for prohibition, 181; drunkenness decreasing, 191; condemns state officials for restoring liquor, 286
Alabama Conference Female College, 59
Alabama Convention, Eighteenth Amendment repealed, 231
Alabama Courier, 66; favors dispensary, 89; turn on the light, 92; prohibition a failure, 126; prohibition threadbare, 194, 212
Alabamian-Dispatch, 168
Alabama Division of Anti-Smith forces, 200
Alabama Good Templar, 65
Alabama Journal, opposes methods of wets, 242-244
Alabama League for Prohibition Modification, 237
Alabama Liquor Stores, policies, 252; a liability, 273
Alabama Presbyterian, 65
Alabama Prohibitionist, 65, 81, 102
Alabama Progress, 78
Alabama State Intelligencer, 25
Alabama State Temperance Association, meets in Tuscaloosa, opposes high license, 79; need for prohibition party, 79
Alabama Supreme Court, Jinright *v.* State, purchaser of liquor violates law, 211
Alabama Temperance Advocate, moral suasion stressed, 24
Alabama Temperance Alliance, opposes repeal of Eighteenth Amendment, 229; opposes repeal of state prohibition laws, 235; perfects organization, 262-263; employs W. Earl Hotalen as Executive Secretary, 263
Alabama State Temperance Society, formed and purpose, 21
Ale, 5
Alexander City, 235, 247
Allocation of profits, 280
Almighty God, 129
Almon, E. B., appoints temperance committee for House, 161
Almonds, liquor adulterated, 95
Aloes, liquor adulterated, 95
Alston, Judge A. H., issues injunction, 122
Amendment, prohibition, 128, 142, 147; Federal Constitution, 179
American Brewer, 146
American Issue, 177

American Spelling Book, lessons on temperance, 24
American Temperance Society, formed, purposes, 19-20
Americans, political party, 37
Ammunition, propaganda, 54; grounds for opposition to prohibition, 214
Andalusia, 73, 258
Anderson, John C., 156
Anderton, Judge Henry L., anti-repealist, 214; campaign manager, 235, 237; organizes forces, 239, 242
Andrew, Bishop James O., 16
Andrews, A. S., 79
Andrews, Lincoln, 197
Anecdote, 152
Anglo-Saxon, 75
Annihilation. *See* Senator J. M. Bonner
Anniston, voting for prohibition, 73
Anniston Star, favors legal sale of liquor, 264; bootlegger a menace, 265
Anniston Times, liquor regulation a failure, 267
Anonymous, whispering, 115; literature, 208
Anti-Catholic, opposition to Smith, 208
Antidote, 152
Anti-Liquor League, 102
Anti-Saloon League of America, 61
Anti-Saloon League of Alabama, organized, purpose, officials, 102-105, 129, 157, 160, 161, 167, 176, 179, 180, 191, 193, 196, 203, 207, 208, 215, 229, 232, 235, 262
Anti-prohibitionists, organized, 115
Anti-repealists, charge fraud, 226
Anti-Shipping, dry territory, 110
Anti-Smith, Democrats, 200-201
Appelant, Parks and Smith Bills constitutional, 167
Arkansas, 38
Arsenic, adulterated, 95
Asheville, North Carolina, 200
Armistice, 190
Armour, Dr. Mary Harris, W.C.T.U. lecturer, 241
Arnold, James J., candidate for governor, 279; defeated, 281
Ashes, get out of, 223
Assassin, like the blind tiger, 115
Assembly, British West Florida, 4
Associate Reformed Presbyterian Synod of the South, 50, 175, 192, 287
Association Against the Prohibition Amendment, 208, 216
Athens, 47, 64, 66; voted against prohibition, 73, 91
Athens Academy, 38
Athens Female Institute, act vetoed, 37, 38
Athens Division, Sons of Temperance, 44

Athens Post, 45, 50
Atlanta, Georgia, 200, 241
Atlantic Ocean, 79
Attalla, 64
Auburn, second dry area in state, 30
Auld, B. F., State Superintendent of Anti-Saloon League, 229
Austin, Conrad W., Law enforcement officer, dismissed, 214
Autauga, 107
Automobiles, confiscated, 212, 289
Avocation, 115
Avondale, 115
Ayres, Harry M., candidate for presidential elector, 196

Baggs, 166
Baker, Dr. R. A., Superintendent of Anti-Saloon League, 102, 129
Baldwin, 8
Ball & chain, punishment, 13
Ballard, Eugene, chairman of temperance committee, 107; offers substitute, 108, 119-120, 129; introduces bill, 134
Ballot box, puts out candidates, 34
Baltimore, 22
Baltzell, George F., on bootlegging near Camp McClellan, 265
Ban, unsound mind, 43
Bands of Hope, bad effects of liquor, 56; violate pledge, 62
Baneful, 177
Bankhead, Senator John H., Sr., opposes prohibition amendment to state constitution; for reelection, 187-188; reelected, 188
Bankhead, Senator John H., Jr., for party regularity, 205; prohibition irrelevant, 206; no place in the campaign, 213
Banks, D. J., bootlegging in progress, 173
Banks, T. C., delegate to Anti-Saloon League, 60
Banners, parade in amendment election, 117
Baptist, 16; sustain interest in, 48, 114
Baptist Associations, oppose return of saloons, 157; opposition to Alfred E. Smith, 204
Baptist State Convention, laments increasing intemperance, 28; adopts strong report on temperance, 57; lead movement for anti-saloon league, 102; optimistic, 157; alarmed at efforts to breakdown dry laws, 192; liquor interests active, 218; oppose repeal of the Eighteenth Amendment, 228; deplores method used to repeal Eighteenth Amendment, 231; approves financial support for the Alabama Temperance Alliance, 287; ABC has debauched

INDEX 309

society, 287; eliminate alcoholic beverages and immorality from army camps, 287
Barmaids, people demand reform, 278
Barnes, W. H., State Temperance Association, 79
Barrooms, opposition and egg-throwing, 71; not a question of, 227
Barry, R. J., secretary prohibition party convention, 82
Barton, A. J., 200
Barton, L. E., editor, 267
Battle, enters politics, 28
Bawdy, debauchery, 266; conditions in Houston County, 272
Beasley, Major Daniel, orders liquor for soldiers, 12
Beddow, C. P., Chairman for drys, 169
Beer, slaves not to buy, 5; opposed by Senator Underwood, 194
Belgium, 195
Bench, 34
Benson, J. S., opposes nomination of Alfred E. Smith, an Anti-Smith elector, 202
Berkowitz, A., attorney for wets, 274
Bessemer, 279
Bethlehem Baptist Association, abstain from trafficing in, 15-16
Beverage Control Board, 249
Bibb Blade, 66
Bibb County, 107, 133, 137
Bible, 15; temperance reading, 54
Bichloride, handled liquor trinity, 204
Bide, elects drys, 256
Biennial Session, 35; endorsed by Comer, 143
Biennial Reports, on crime, 189
Bienville, Jean Baptiste Le Moyne, on price of wine, 1; director, 2; bar, 124; Square, 203
Bills, Fuller and Carmichael, 159; Parks, 162
Birmingham, meeting of Catholic Total Abstinence Union, 53; W.C.T.U. meets, 54, 129; drys hold parade, 146; drys fight hard, 169; Anti-Smith Democrats meet, 201, 230, 232; opens state liquor store, 260
Birmingham Age-Herald, consistently wet, 109, 116, 121, 131, 136, 150, 158, 167, 194, 170, 171, 177, 204, 214, 242, 251, 259
Birmingham Baptist Association, opposes wets, 204
Birmingham City Court, anti-advertising bill, 185
Birmingham Ledger, 89, 104, 106, 116, 118, 127, 131, 153, 156, 159, 160, 169, 176, 178, 185, 187, 193

Birmingham News, 112, 118, 135, 139, 145, 148, 193, 199, 203, 221, 222, 234, 242, 243
Birney, James G., member of temperance society, 21
Birney, William, much drinking, 26
Black man, drunken, 51
Black, Hugo L., 185; prohibitionist, 213; favors resubmission, 214
Blackbelt, first temperance society formed, 20; local option impractical, 80-81; drunkenness along highways, 96; improved conditions, 101
Blackberry wine, not permitted, 144
Blackburn, Felix, 106
Blackwelder, W. M., 102
Blades. *See* Washingtonians
Blind tigers, flourish, 108, 115; local option ends, 173
Blue, M. P., editor, 25
Boats, 29
Bodeker, George H., chief of police, 170
Boiler, Jesse Stallings lampoons clergymen, 140
Bolted, 204
Bone-dry, enforcement, 188; planks, Democratic and Republican, 197
Bonner, Senator J. Miller, consistently dry, supports Alfred E. Smith, 205; urges party loyalty, 224; against repeal, 230; opposes referendum, 236; verbal clash, 246; discouraged, 247; charges against Governor Graves, 249; wages losing fight, 250; law to be enforced, 256
Book of Discipline, against sale of liquor, 49
Bootleggers, union, 127; prevalent, 197; postcards, 208; not to sign petitions, 266, 267, 272; flourishes, 275
Booze, slogan, 117
Borah, William E., inquiries of Hoover, 195
Boston, Massachusetts, 20
Boswell, E. C., author of ABC bill, 249
Bottles, throwing of, 209; at minister's house, 276
Bowie, Sidney J., opposes amendment, 142; dry presidential elector, 196
Bowie, Mrs. Sidney J., favors modification, 223
Bowling, Alexander, jug on his tomb, 26
Bowman, P. G., solicits votes, 117; charges against B. B. Comer, 144
Branch, Mrs. M. A., treasurer of W.C.T.U., 53
Branchville, 39
Brandon, W. W., non-committal, 187, 203; enforcement, 211; endorses prohibition, 215
Brandy 1, 5; prohibited, 9

INDEX

Branscomb, Dr. L. C., President of Anti-Saloon League, 200; delegate to anti-Smith convention, 200, 203
Brashears, T., Indian agent, 10
Brantley, 93
Brantley, W. T., 20
Brawling places, 272
Brawls, 26
Brazos, Texas, 19
Brewer, W. P., 102
Brewers, raised fund, 115, 145; make contribution, 152, 156, 166
Brewton, 66
Bribery, dispensary, 86
Brickell, R. C., 156
Bricklayer, no license, 5
Bridges, how built, 5
British, 3-5
British West Florida Assembly, restrictions, 3
Brooks, Major George, prohibition party, 82
Brothel operators, 275
Brother-in-law, 9
Brown, Cyrus B., 156
Brown, Miss Norma C., secretary of Flying Squadron, 229
Brown, Watt T., local optionist, 180, 215
Browne, Reverend J. J., Catholic Union, 53
Broyles, W. O., 282
Bryce, Dr. Peter, Superintendent of Insane Hospital, 79
Bulger, Thomas L., 183
Bulletin, 266
Bullock County, 72, 114, 122, 246
Bureau, A. T. A. research, 284
Burgess, D. R., 120
Burke, Probate Judge, 125
Burnett, George J., Superintendent of Anti-Saloon League, 229
Burnett, John L., Congressman, 142
Burns, John Morgan, 214
Burnt Corn Academy, dry territory, 38
Burr, Borden, 169
Bush, Albert, 120
Butler County, 113-114, 136
Butler, W. E., temperance committee, 273
Buzzard, *Dothan Eagle*, 207

Cabiness, E. H., trustee, 103
Cadillac, Governor Antoine de Lamothe, 2
Cadets of Temperance, 22
Cahaba, 26
Calera, 82
Calhoun County, 72, 73, 114, 263, 264, 266
Calhoun County Temperance Alliance, 266

Callahan, Artemus K., asked to resign, 219
Camden, 224
Camp Ground, temperance society, 20
Camp Rucker, 275
Camp McClellan, 265
Campaigns, 109, 156, 168, 178
Canaan Baptist Association, urges ministers, 48
Candidates, give liquor, 31
Cane, 40
Cannon, Bishop James, Jr., calls anti-Smith democrats together, 200, 229
Capone, A., racketeer, 245
Captains, of boats, 29
Carbon Hill, 73
Carmichael, A. H., trustee, 103, 107, 120; state prohibition, 121, 122, 132, 149; elected Speaker of House, 183; candidate for presidential elector, 196; candidate for governor, 215; Eighteenth Amendment an error, 226
Carnley, J. A., 215
Carpenter, 5
Carpetbaggers, 206
Carrollton, Baptist Church, 113
Carwile, Hillary J., 282
Cartoon, racketeers, 208
Casino, 266
Catholic, 15; Raskob, 197, 203, 209
Catholic Total Abstinence Union, 53
Centerville, 73, 205
Cess-pool, saloon, 101
Chadwick, J. S., on communion, 65
Chairman, John J. Raskob, 197
Challenge, 46
Chamberlane, Bart, 183
Chamber of Commerce, 169
Chambers County, 34
Chaos, remedies for, 171
Charlotte County, 3
Chase's Tavern, 22
Chatfield, Mrs. J. B., of W.C.T.U., 137
Chattahoochee, 8
Cheated, Reuben F. Kolb, 176
Cheered, custodian, 163
Cherrington, anti-saloon league editor, 229
Cheunnenuggee Female College, 38
Chicago, 220, 221
Chickasaws, Indian Congress, 6
Chief Mattaha, complains about liquor, 6
Children, temperance education, 50
Childs, Madam, 38
Chilton County, 72, 114
Chilton County Missionary Baptist Association, 119
Chitwood, Reverend T. J., 274
Choctaw Nation, 10
Christian Century, 222
Christian Church, 114

INDEX 311

Christian Missionary Convention, 62
Christian Observer, 50
Christmas dinner, wine served, 38
Christmas drinking, in Mobile, 70
Cincinnati, 115
Circuit Court, 77, 262
Circuit Judges, enforce law, 29
Claiborne, Governor William C. C., on selling liquor to Indians, 9-10
Clanton, 91
Clanton, J. H., Report on temperance, 35
Claret, 3
Clark County, 67, 250
Clark County Democrat, 66, 77, 80
Clark, J. F., on saloons, 101
Clarke, Thomas, 106
Claxton, L. N., 267
Claypool, Mrs. B. M., for modification, 239
Clayton, 88
Clayton, Judge Henry D., prohibition laws adequate, 143
Clayton Record, 88
Cleavage, 149
Cleburne County, 68, 72, 236
Clements, D. A., Grand Worthy Secretary, 52
Clergy, 34
Cleveland, Ohio, 60
Cliterall, A. B., 34
City Commission of Birmingham, prohibits Sunday liquor selling, 279
City Manager, 238
Civil War, temperance, 14, 40
Cobb, Rufus W., opposes amendment, 142
Coleman, J. A., 108
Coleman, Thomas E., probate judge, 264
Colbert County, 72, 73, 107, 167, 168, 172, 175, 242, 259, 276, 278
Collinsville, on communion, 63
Columbia, dispensary, 87, 91
Columbus, 208
Colvin, D. L., 86
Come-on girls, 278
Comer, Governor B. B., 74; elected governor on local option ticket, 104, 115; calls extra session, 118-119; signs bill, 122; proclamation, 130; laws inadequate, 132, 135, 141; aspires to United State Senate, 143, 145; stands for re-election, 158; candidate for governor, 176; defeated, 178; charges against Henderson, 177; favors dry delegation, 194; appointed to United States Senate, 213
Comerism, his policies, 176
Commandants, 2
Commissioners, dispensary, 87
Committee, on temperance, 121
Commonwealth, 168

Conecuh County, 75
Conecuh Star, 66
Confederate army hospitals, need whiskey, 41
Confederate Veterans, support amendment, 140
Conference, Methodist Episcopal Church, endorses temperance lessons for Sunday school, 55
Conference, North Alabama, endorses work of Anti-Saloon League, 103
Congress, 8, 13, 37, 79, 176, 181, 208
Connor, Eugene, for modification, 239
Cook Brewing Company, makes contribution, 152
Congregational Church, temperance through education, 61
Constitution, 128, 130
Constitutionality, referendum legal, 246
Constitutional amendment, 129
Consumption, 4
Convention, National Republican, 195
Convicts, violating dry laws, 289
Convington County, 72
Covington, Judge W. A., 115
Cooper, 5
Cooper, D. C., trustee, 103
Cooper, G. F., 267
Coosa County, 112, 113
Corn, distilled, 27, 40, 68
Cornfield, 96
Cosmopolitan Magazine, 191
Coulson, L. C., Republican, 83
Courts of Commissioners of Revenue and Roads, 35
Court Street Methodist Church, 199
Courturier, 2
Convington County, 162
Cowell, J. C., 267
Cox, W. J. E., 111
Crampton, Louis C., denounces A.A.P.A., 216
Crenshaw County, 123
Cried, 163
Crimes, 34, 51, 128
Cross plains, 53
Crow, take and eat it, 203
Crow, A. W., 214
Crozat, Antoine, 2
Cruikshank, George M., 178
Crumpton, W. B., candidate for governor, 85; calls meeting to organize Anti-Saloon League of Alabama, 102; lobbyist, 105-106; president of Anti-Saloon League, 120, 129, 137, 141, 166, 174, 179, 181, 186, 219
Crucifix, 203
Crusade, 111
Crystal Fount, 25, 30
Cullman, 125
Cullman County, 123, 124, 276, 277, 278

Cullman Tribune, 123
Cumberland Presbyterian Church, 102
Cunningham, G. J. L., 83
Curse, 53, 276
Curtis, vice-president, 202
Cyder, 5

Daily State Guard, 25
Daily Times, 66
Dale County, 72-73, 114
Dallas County, 15, 25, 31, 108, 120
Dannelly, Reverend J. M., 169
Danville, license required, 39
Dardanell, Arkansas, 38
Dauphin Island, 1-2
Davis, Harwell G., 206
Davis, W. C., 215
Dealers, retail, 27, 114, 172, 180
Death benefits, 23
Debauchery, Indians, 5; womanhood, 273
Decons, 219
Decanters, 26
Decatur, 98, 229, 267
Decatur Daily, 185, 198, 209
Decisions of the Supreme Court, 130
Declamation contests, prizes offered, 56
Decorum, agree to forfeit membership, 17
Defeat, not accepted, 191
Delaware, 197
Delegates, 46, 75, 135, 136
Demaree, T. B., comes to Alabama, 52
Demagogue, 31
Demobilization, no malt liquors to be sold, 190
Democrats, favor enforcement, 197
Democrats, dry, 198
Democratic Executive Committee, chairman uses pressure, 166
Democratic National Convention, delegates instructed for Roosevelt, 220
Dempsey, Elam, 229
Demopolis Times, 234
Denman, Harry, President of A.T.A., 235, 240, 255, 262, 263
Denny, George H., opposes return of saloon, 229
Denson, John, 262
Dent, S. H., opposes amendment, 142
Detroit, 208
Dexter Avenue, 43
Diary, 26
Dickinson, John V., 102
Dinsmore, L. M., 194, 195
Dinsmore, Silas, agent for Choctaw Nation, 10
Disciples of Christ, 182, 192
Discipline, whiskey rations taken away, 12, 17, 48, 63, 64
Dispatches, 281
Dispensary, 86, 87, 91, 93, 101, 104, 109, 114, 156, 161, 173

Distillers, 41, 115
Distillery, 68, 242
Divelbliss, Mable Vitu, 285
Dixon, Frank M., 232, 233, 280, 283
Dobbs, Reverend H. M., 115
Dobyns, Fletcher, 217
Dominated, 179
Donaldson, James, 19
Donoho, Jennie, 53
Dothan, 87, 88, 91, 269
Dothan Siftings, 88
Dothan Eagle, 207, 269, 270, 272, 275
Dowdell, J. F., 37
Downs, W. O., Police commissioner of Birmingham, 247
Druggists, 37
Drunkenness, 269
Dunbar, William, 3
Dunbar *vs.* Frazier, 69
Du Pont Company, 217
Du Pont, Lammot, 217
Du Pont, Pierre, 218

Earnest Worker, 56
East Birmingham, 115
East Lake, 115
East Liberty Baptist Association, 17, 18, 119
Eclectic, 67
Education, temperance through, 36
Eggs, throwing of, 71, 209
Eighteenth Amendment, 187, 208; doomed, 222, 231
Election results, 278
Election treating, with liquor, 32
Electioneering, barbecue and whiskey, 31
Ellis, James B., 154
Ellis, H. C., cried, 189
Elliott, Alonzo S., Editor, 45, 47
Elmore County, 83, 214
Encyclopedia Britiannica Research Service, 284
England, 1
Ensign, 1
Enterprise, 93
Episcopalians, 15, 103
Esdale, Jim, 202
Ethiopian, 75
Etowah County, 278
Eufaula, 66, 108
Eufaula Times and News, 85
Eufaula Weekly Times and News, 71
Eutaw Whig, 50
Evergreen, 66
Excursion, into politics, 28

Factories, dry territory, 43
Family, 5
Fanatic, ceased to be harmless, 28
Fancher, William, good when sober, 26
Farley, James A., urges repeal, 228

INDEX   313

Farce, prohibition party, 84
Faulk, T. S., 196
Fearn, Thomas, 21, 25
Federal Chemical Warfare Plant, 273
Federation, temperance society, 21; of labor, 237
Federal Government, internal revenue, 41
Federated Women's Clubs, 258
Furgurson, Mrs. Burr, 223
Finklea, Mrs. P. R., 152
Fennell, Woolsey, 215
Fine, 5
Fiske, Clinton B., candidate for president, 85
Fitts, W. C., presidential elector, 221
Florala, 98
Florence, voted dry, 73
Florence Democrat, 157
Florence Herald, 152
Florence Times, 155
Florida, 8, 79
Flushed, with victory, 149
Flying Squadron Foundation, 229
Folk, E. E., editor, 102
Foley Onlooker, 198
Fort Hampton, 45
Fort McClellan, 265
Fort Stoddard, 9
Folsom, J. E., 282
Foster, Henry B., 234
Foster, J. Manley, 206
Foster, S. J., 115
Foster, R. C., 286
Fourment, Z. Frank, *ex parte*, 124
Fowler, J. J., 269
France, 1
Franchise, drinking, 31, 206
Franklin County, 27
Fraud, 147
Frazer, John W., 199
Frazer, T. L., 69
Frazer, T. S., 246
Freeholders, 30, 36
Free Press, 138
Friend of Temperance, 47, 65
Fruit, distilleries, 68
Fry, John, 118
Fuller, Jerome T., author of prohibition law, 107, 133, 137, 159
Fuquay, A. B., 161

Gadsden, 53, 63, 91, 200, 208, 264
Gadsden Times, 139, 177
Gaines, Reverend J. Luther, 276
Gallery, 106-107, 163, 189
Gallon, 41, 289
Gals of glamor, in Dothan, 275
Galvez, Viceroy, 7
Gamblers, 267
Gathering in the sheaves, 117

General Assembly, 29, 32, 34, 35, 36, 37, 38, 42, 44, 57, 72, 79, 84
General Conference of the Methodist Church, 17, 63
Geneva, 91, 163
Geneva County, 249, 275
Georgia, 50, 115
Germain, Lord George, 6
Girls, juke joints, 275
Glass, Senator Carter, not committed to prohibition, 206
Glass, Frank P., 226
Glass, John, 229
God, 71, 83, 188, 191
Godbold, Norman D., not an infringement, 145; elected on prohibition ticket, 156
Good Templars, 45-47, 52, 75
Good Templar's Advocate, 45
Goode, R. J., temperance through education, 279-280
Goodwater, 93, 112
Goodwyn, R. T., 107, 121
Goose-stepped, vice, 269
Gorden, E. P., 186
Gothenburg, Sweden, origin of dispensary, 86
Gottfried Krueger Brewing Company, 117
Government, 4
Governor, 131
Governorship, 149
Grain, 40
Grand Division, 23, 45
Grand Dragon. *See* Jim Esdale
Grand Lodge of Alabama, 45, 46, 52
Grand Lodge of America, schism in ranks, 46
Grand Templar, 47
Grand Temple of Honor, incorporated, 23
Grand Worthy Chief Templar, 52
Grand Worthy Christian Templar, 45
Grape juice, for communion, 62-65
Graves, Bibb, enforcement, 192, 211, 215; favors referendum, 232-233; for repeal, 240, 245, 246, 249, 258
Graves, W. D., 247
Green, S. E., 115
Greene County, 189
Greensboro, 66
Greensboro Watchman, 198
Greenville, 71; votes wet, 73
Greenville Advocate, 66, 71
Gregory, O. F., organizer of Anti-Liquor League, 102
Grief, 19
Grip. *See* Sons of Temperance
Gubernatorial campaign, 36; prohibition the issue, 149, 176, 178, 181; Eighteenth Amendment the issue, 187

314 INDEX

Gubernatorial candidates, local option, 34
Gunn, Norman, 108
Gunter, W. A., candidate for presidential elector, 196
Gwaltney, L. L., on communion, 64; elect drys, 256; opposes repeal, 257; sees growing opposition to liquor, 288
Gwaltney, L. R., 75

Habits, drinking, 8, 43
Hahn, Reverend R. W., on the use or abuse, 239
Hails, Parks and Smith Bills valid, 167
Hale County, 245
Haley, Paul T., president of Alabama Anti-Saloon League, 240
Hall, Henry, home raided, 213
Hamburger, Senator Max, 121
Hamner, R. F., money and hell come from liquor, 245
Handley, L. S., prohibition party, 82
Handpicked, by Brooks Lawrence, 181
Handwriting, liquor dealers see, 111
Hanks, A. L., on racketeers, 245
Hannibal, Comer, ambitious as, 143
Haralson, K. L., 17
Hardaway, Colonel R. A., of the University, 79
Hardshell, favors sale of liquor, 276
Hare, W. O., urges modification, 237
Harrison, B. D. & Company, 24
Hartford Herald, 138
Hartselle, 82, 256
Hartwell, Senator, permit liquor forces to die slowly, 184
Harwood, Judge Bernard, 206
Hatton, Hugh, 53
Hay, Bishop Sam R., 240
Haynes, C. M., Grand Templar, 47
Haynes, J. O., prayer meeting held, 118
Hayneville, 25
Heflin, Senator J. Thomas, favors state prohibition amendment, 142; opposes Alfred E. Smith, 203, 207; eggs thrown at, 209; elected to United States Senate, 213
Hell, can not extinguish, 79
Henderson, Charles, opposes amendment to state constitution, 136; local optionist, 149; elected governor, 177-178; frustrated, 183; vote anticipated, 184
Henderson, J. C., 196
Henry County, votes wet, 73, 87, 114
Herndon, Thomas, urges voters to support prohibitionist for governor, 35
Hierarchical. *See* Sons of Temperance
Higdon, Sheriff, 126
High-Jackers, 209
Hilarity, reigned, 269
Hill, A. D., co-editor, 47, 184

Hill, Lister, 206
Hilliard, W. P., favors referendum, 25
Hillsboro, Ohio, 53
Hobbs, J. R., 229
Hobbs, Thomas Hubbard, Diary, 23
Hobson, Richmond P., supports state constitutional amendment, 141; candidate for United States Senate on dry ticket, defeated, 179; only begun to fight, 180
Hoffman, F. O., 107
Holcombe, Reverend Hosea, presents first memorial to General Assembly, 32
Holifield, R. C., Jr., editor, on drinking in Cahaba, 26
Holms, Governor David, 9, 12
Holt, B., 34
Honky-tonks, 266, 274, 275; worse than saloons, 288
Hopkins, Arthur F., 21
Hooper, J. J., on opposition to Sons of Temperance, 34
Hoover, Herbert, faith in prohibition, 195; Anti-Smith democrats support, 201, 202, 221, 223, 224
Horton, J. E., 156
Hosmer, S. M., trustee, 103
Hostesses, barmaids, 278
Hotalen, W. Earl, elected Executive Secretary of A.T.A. and announced plans, 263; financial condition, 263; conducts campaign in Calhoun County, 264-268; on campaign in Houston County, 271; in Colbert County, 276; in Cullman County, 277; education program, 284
Hotel, sell liquor, wine, beer, 260
House of Representatives, 283
Houston County, dry by special act, 114, 138, 145; election, 268, 275; Temperance Alliance, 269
Houston County Temperance Alliance *Bulletin*, 270
Houston, Texas, 196, 197, 201
Howard, M. W., Ex-congressman, 141; blast, 143
Howard College, 129
Hubert, Sieur, 1
Hughston, John L., 110
Hull, Cordell, 221
Humor, 3
Humphries, John R., 17
Huntsville, 25, 42, 45, 46, 47; license fee, 98, 141, 149, 183, 273
Huntsville Daily Times, 249, 273, 274
Huntsville Temperance Society, organization and purpose, 19, 20
Huntsville Times, 249, 273, 274
Hygiene, taught in public schools, 57, 59

INDEX

Illegal, buying makes, 179
Illicit distillers, shot while running away, 214
Inalienable rights, 184
Inaugural, Governor Graves favored referendum, 236
Increasing, deposits due to prohibition, 191
Income tax, Du Pont favors putting tax on liquor, 218
Independent, 25
Independent Order of Good Templars, formed and purposes, 24, 47, 52
Indians, debauched by liquor, 6; Spanish have legal system to protect, 7; Council of, 7; Chiefs complain about liquor, 9
Indulgences, 30
Inhabitants, 30
Iniquity, saloons, 101
Injected, religion into campaign, 208
Injunction stopped election in Bullock County, 122
Inmates, penitentiaries have fewer, 191
Inn, 26
Isinglass, liquor adulterated with, 95
Insubordination. *See* Conrad W. Austin
Internal revenue, 42
Interpreted, prohibition disapproved, 155
Intoxicants, 29
Iowa, 32
Irregularities, in Dothan, 272
Irwin, Williams, 175
Issue, Temperance a dead, 37, 156, 222, 265, 275

Jackson County, 27, 73, 83
Jackson Day letter, by Alfred E. Smith, 187
Jackson, F. M., 129; chairman of executive committee, 137
Jackson, N. S., 229
Jacksonville Republican, 21, 25
Jacobs, Mrs. Solon, charter member of W.O.N.P.R., 223, 225; Eighteenth Amendment a mistake, 226, 227
Jacobs, Virginia, 223
Jail, empty, 187, 191; register shows bad effects of liquor, 274
James, R. L., 25
Jasper, votes, 73
Jasper District, minister expelled for selling liquor, 17
Jefferson County, 83, 91; number of saloons, 100, 104, 107, 114; votes dry, 118, 126, 127, 136, 223, 242
Jeffries, Mrs. Mary T., opposes Alfred E. Smith, 199, 200; delegate from state-at-large, 202
Jeffries, Mrs. W. H., president of state W.C.T.U., 129

Jelks, W. D., ex-governor, opposes amendment to state constitution, 142; writes resolution, 154
Jinright *v.* the State, purchaser violates law, 211
Johnson, E. D., defeated for speakership of House, 183
Johnson, Forney, 203
Johnson, Senator J. F., opposes amendment to state constitution, 142, 180
Johnson, W. Bert, editor, 267
Johnston, Mollie, wine served, 38
Joint resolution, Eighteenth Amendment ratified, 188
Jones, Reverend Bob, *Montgomery Advertiser* attacks, 207
Jones, Reverend Richard, license revoked, 17
Jones, Thomas G., 273
Julian, Frank N., 156
Julius Caesar, Comer as ambitious, 143
Juniper, liquor adulterated with, 95
Jurists, 33
Jury, 11, 151
Justices, 4
Juvenile, 54

Keener, Bishop J. C., 64
Kelley, Mrs. Prescott, member of W.O.N.P.R., 223
Kellog, J., 57
Kennedy, Samuel, 177
Kennemer, C. B., 208
Kentucky, 47
Kilby, Thomas E., prohibitionist, elected lieutenant governor, 180; favors Eighteenth Amendment, 187; supports enforcement, 210; dismisses Conrad W. Austin, 214; retraction on Eighteenth Amendment, 214, 215, 218
Killed, revenue officers, 42
Kimball, Lucie E. G., superintendent of Sunday school department of W.C.T.U., 55
Kindergarten, 56
King, Jere C., 107
Kirby, A. D., 107
Kitchen, 152
Klan, 202
Knell, death of Sons of Temperance, 37
Knights of Columbus, 208
Knot of White Ribbon, 54
Knownothingism, temperance confused with, 36
Knox, John B., opposes amendment to state constitution, 142
Knox, W. H., 214
Kolb, Reuben F., 176, 178
Labels, on whiskey bottles, 31
La Crade, Mrs. Thomas, W.C.T.U. president, 53

Lafayette, General, beverages to entertain, 25
LaFayette, dispensary profits, 91, 93
La Grange, first dry area in Alabama, 30
Lamar, the Reverend, house bespattered with eggs, 71
Landslide for drys, 114; victorious local optionists, 169
Lane, J. O., prohibition a failure, 170-171
Lang, Colonel John W., liquor a menace to Ft. McClellan, 265
Lauderdale County, dispensary profits, 93
Law Enforcement Division, came to Dothan, 271-272
Law and Order League, 127
Lawrence, Reverend Brooks, becomes superintendent of the Alabama Anti-Saloon League, 103; writes to legislators, 105, 113, 122; criticises state supreme court, 130; organization perfected, 136, 143, 157; resolution aimed, 160; lobbying, 163; legislature hand-picked by, 181; anticipate veto, 184; selects candidates for the legislature, 186; political boss in Alabama, 187; resigns from his office, ???
Leadership sought, 52
League, Anti-Saloon formed, purpose, officials, 102-103, 104, 105
Lee County, require candidates to make statement, 34, 72, 75
Leedy, Mrs. W. B., member of W.O.R.N.P.R., 223
Legalized liquor, drunkenness increases, 174
Leigh, Norville R., 254
Leighton News, 168
Leland, Ella M., 53
Leslie, Edward and Frank, co-editors, 65, 82, 102
Lewis, "Cousin" Charles, paid agent of the breweries, 156, 160; supports the Parks Bills, 163; his money bags, 166, 177, 178
Lewis, John, sold whiskey to soldiers, 10
Lewis, Oscar S., 183
Lewis, William, 25
Liability, A.B.C. store was, 273
Libel, campaign of villification, 147
Liberty, every man his own prohibitionist, 151
License, 4, 11, 30, 42, 69, 70, 98-99, 111, 172, 189, 288
Lieutenant, got fifty *pots* of brandy, 1
Limestone County, 67, 83; dispensary, 92, 156
Limestone Democrat, 66, 148, 150, 281
Lincoln, D. F., 57
Lindsay, R. B., 35
Lipscomb, A. A., editor, 25

Liquor, 114, 180; dealers, 288; trinity, 203
Literary Digest, 222
Literature, temperance, 54
Litigation, less, 187
Livres, 2
Lobbyist, 89, 92, 105, 110, 163, 186; investigation, 216
Local option, 32; law, 105, 114, 118, 149, 158, 159; ticket, 156-160; optionists, 160, 167, 176, 180
Locke, Judge Hugh, Smith repudiates the platform, 201; let us dare to fight, 202; attorney for drys, 274
Long, J. Lee, anti-amender, 136; on sanctity of the home, 148; no stopping place, 188
Long, William H., Jr., 134
Lord's Supper, 62, 64
Louisiana, 1, 2, 229
Louisville, Kentucky, 46, 52, 55
Lovelady Local Option Bill, 108
Lovelady, R. F., 107, 109, 110, 114
Lowndes County, 108, 123
Luina, 72
Luverne Journal, 96, 179
Lyons, A. S., 121
Lyons, LeBarrons, 120
Lyons, Major Pat, 120

Madison County Temperance Society, 21
Madison, President James, 1
Maidens of Temperance, contemporary of Sons of Temperance, 22
Majesty, in Council, 5
Majority, Underwood defeated Hobson, 180
Malfeasance, charged against managers, 96
Malt beverages, sale of, 244
Mallory, Hugh S. D., dry candidate for governor, 149; amendment a dead issue, 150, 151; campaign methods, 153; supports Alfred E. Smith, 205
Malone, George H., Hoover-Curtis elector, 202
Mammy, legislature the, 258
Maner, O. C., 108
Mansfield, Reverend C. H., vote for the best man, 199
Mantle, Brooks Lawrence's, 193
Manufacture, corn liquor, 27; government controls, 40; sale and keeping for sale, 130
Map, dry areas, 43
Marengo County, votes dry then wet, 278
Maring, Mrs. D. H., member of W.O.N.P.R., 223
Marion, 18, 75, 274
Marion County, 239
Martin, Judge H. K., 269

INDEX 317

Martin, John, 21
Mathew, Father Theobald, Apostle of Temperance, 15
Maurepas, Jean Frederic Phelippeaux, 1
Mayfield, James A., 213
Medical Faculty, get an expression from, 33
McAdory, Mrs. C. H., attends W.C.T.U. district conventions, 285
McBride, Dr. F. Scott, President of National Anti-Saloon League, 241
McCall, Charlie C., 214, 215
McCants, J. E., editor, 138
McClellan, Justice T. C., prohibition law valid, 126
Macon County, 38, 59, 183
Macon County Republican, 36
Macon County Temperance Society, on liquor license, 31
McCord, Judge Leon C., head of Safe and Sane League, opposes prohibition amendment, 132; joint debate, 143; remarkable campaign, 147, 156; a question of states rights, 226; telegram to, 227; James A. Farley wires, 228; candidate for governor, 232; never voted a prohibition ticket, 233, 257
McCoy, J. H., 102; trustee of Alabama Anti-Saloon League, 103; led parade, 117
McDermott, M. J., Mobile prepared to secede, 121
McDonald's opera house, 78
McDowell, Charlie, 215
McDuffie, John, 206
McGuffey's Readers, lessons on temperance, 24
McGuffey, W. H., 24
McMillan, Lee, 110
McMullen, J. R., trustee of Alabama Anti-Saloon League, 103
McWhorter, Senator G. T., 108
Madden, T., 17
Madeira, wine, 3
Madison, 45
Madison County, on retailing liquor, 11; led in production, 27, 107, 156, 183, 242, 259, 272, 273, 278, 279
Medicinal, whiskey for, 189
Mell, Mrs. J. B., her gold pen used, 122
Memphis, Tennessee, 19
Merchants, report amount of rum, 6
Memorials, presented to General Assembly, 32, 33
Merrill, Walter, 264
Merit, H. M., 163
Merritt, Senator H. P., 108; introduces bill for state-wide prohibition, 183
Message, inadequate of enforcement, 132; law can be enforced, 158

Methodist, 16, 103, 114, 228
Methodist Episcopal Church, South, renews opposition, 48
Methodist Episcopal Church, all out battle against liquor, 59; not to alter prohibition laws, 157
Methodist Protestant, 158
Middlebrooks, Action E., editor of *Alabama Christian Advocate*, 286
Miles, Myrtle, on modification, 239
Milford, Dr. John J., 274
Militant, campaign, 178
Miller, B. M., supports Alfred E. Smith, 205; endorses prohibition in campaign for governor, 215, 216; vetoes near-beer bill, 219, 224, 225, 232; opposes repealing state dry laws, 241; toured the state, 257
Miller, Judge John, 185
Miller, N. L., 137
Miller, Webb U., 269
Mills, Chester P., republican prohibition administrator, 197
Mills, J. Bibb., superintendent of Alabama Anti-Saloon League, 193; leads anti-Smith democrats, 200, 229
Milwaukee, Smith said prohibition a farce, 197
Mind, people of unsound, 43
Mines, dry area around, 43
Miracle, results of prohibition, 191
Mirth, 3
Missiles, eggs and bottles thrown, 209
Missions, Baptist State Board, 102
Mississippi, 8, 50, 53
Mitchell, Samuel, Indian agent, 10
Mitchell, William K., Washingtonian pledge, 22
Mobile, 2, 3; three license for, 4, 6, 8, 26, 53, 89; liquor dealers, 111; stubborn opposition, 120, 124, 161
Mobile County, 1; number of saloons in, 100, 168, 173, 169, 178, 203, 213; district chairman appointed for, 237; for modification, 242, 243, 244
Mobile Baptist Association, opposed Alfred E. Smith, 204
Mobile Bay, 5
Mobile Register, consistently wet, 67, 106, 109, 121, 131, 134, 138, 152, 159, 167, 176, 178, 198, 200, 210, 251
Monopoly, Governor Winston vetoes, 37
Molasses, not to be distilled, 40
Monroe County, 38; dry law working well, 77; votes dry, 278
Montague, Dr. A. P., 129
Montgomery, 15, 26, 35, 37, 43, 46, 52, 75, 104, 105; platform, 156, 203, 219, 232, 237, 243, 256

318 INDEX

Montgomery Advertiser, consistently wet, 66, 69, 71, 80, 106, 109, 112, 130, 132, 136, 138, 144, 146, 150, 153, 154, 161, 162, 167, 178, 185, 193, 199, 193, 202, 204, 205, 210, 224, 241, 251, 255, 259, 271
Montgomery County, 38, 154, 161, 164, 168, 169, 184, 244
Montgomery Journal, 109, 116, 139, 153, 176, 187, 196
Montgomery, Robert R., liquor owned, 11
Montgomery Station, 17
Montpelier, 12
Montrose, 98
Moody, Frank S., introduced dispensary into Alabama, 66; introduces bill, 88, 89; special act, 93; local option dispensary bill, 109, 114; opposes amendment to state constitution, 136; supports H. S. D. Mallory for governor, 164, 156, 161
Moody, Mary, 53
Mooers, W. A., was assaulted, 152
Moore, A. B., 1; elections improved, 101; on General Assembly during Republican rule, 206
Moore, Dr. Arthur J., opposed Alfred E. Smith, 199, 207
Moore, Reverend A. R., 114
Moore, Jones G., for saloons, 170, 171
Mooresville, 44
Morality, advanced by acceptance of people, 35
Moreland, Mrs. M. E., 258
Morgan County, written consent reuired, 39, 75; means disruption of Democratic Party, 134, 145, 256
Morgan, J. A., 267, 268
Morris, Reverend Sam, 273
Morrison, Bishop P. C., 140
Morrow, Hugh, president pro-tem of senate, 161
Moulton, 73
Mount Pleasant, 18
Mountain Eagle, 94
Mulkey, W. O., 163
Mulatto, restricted from retailing, 29
Mullin, Atticus, Pensacola doing good business, 237
Mullins, Senator Sanford, leader of wets, 225; elected state chairman of League for Prohibition Reform, 235; ask no quarters and give none, 237, 238, 242, 243
Murphy Club, total abstinence, 47, 48
Murphy, M., 262
Musgrove, L. B., 95, 194, 213

Napier Field, 275
Narcotics, 285
Narrell, A. S., 82

Nashville, 102
National Bulletin, 180
National Committee, 208
National Voice, 284
Near-beer Bill, 219, 232
Negro, 5; retailers forbidden to sell to, 11; freed negro a problem, 46; "True Reformers," 47, 50; urged to organize temperance alliance, 84; drunken, 96; saloons, 101, 206; not a factor in repeal, 259
Newark, 217
New England rum, 3
New Jersey, 222
New Spain, regulates liquor traffic among Indians, 7
Newville, 207
New York, 114, 195, 203, 223
New York World, 195
Nicks, A. Q., non-committal on liquor question, 24
Nihart, F. B., 196
Noah, got drunk, 276
Norman, James D., trustee, 103
Norment, James M., editor, 24
North, 60, 103
North Alabama, temperance vote light, 36; more dry territory, 38
North Alabama Conference, M. E. Church, South, banish rum, 60; opposed to local option, 181; drunkenness decreasing, 191; drive the "bushwhackers" out, 192; defend the Eighteenth Amendment, 218; oppose to return of liquor, 231, 235; temperance through education, 286
North Carolina, 53
Norwood, D. H., guilty of selling liquor, 17

Oates, William C., 142
Obituary, a good man when sober, 26
O'Donovan, Mrs. Lawrence, 223
Office-seeker, treats with liquor, 32
Offut, Mary, sold liquor through ignorance, 6
Ohio, 103, 180
Old South, drinking a social custom, 25
Old Town Creek Cemetery. *See* Alexander Bowling
Oliver, W. B., 205
Oliver, Reverend W. C., 82
O'Neal, Governor E. A., accused of drunkenness, 81
O'Neal, Emmet, candidate for Governor on local option ticket, 149; his strategy, 151; charged with bolting the party, 152; elected governor, 155; inaugural, 158; message, 159; for party loyalty, 160, 176; candidate for United States Senate, 213

INDEX 319

Oneonta, 108
Opera House, 78
Opinion, 71
Opium, 95
Option, local, 71-72, 104, 106
Operator, 21
Ordonnateur, 3
Orr, J. C., 82
Osborne, Dr., 12
Our Mountain Home, 66, 80, 93
Owenton, 115
Ozark, 91, 93

Parade, in Birmingham, 146
Parents, keep best brands of liquor, 37
Parker, E. B., 236
Parker, Mrs. Rosa, on unfermented wine for communion, 63
Parker, Z. S., 80
Parks, W. L., 162, 164; Parks Bill, 163-165
Parliament, 4
Party, bolted, 206
Pastors, against repeal, 256
Pastors, Negro, 75
Patronage, Republican party, 42; administration, 166
Patterson, A. G., 215
Patton, R. E., trustee, 103
Patterson, A. G., 215
Patton, R. E., trustee, 103
Patton, Reverend W. K., selling liquor, 19
Paul, admonition to Timothy, 26, 37
Payne, Jake R., 254
Payne, R. A., eggs thrown against his drug store, 71
Pearl Harbor, losses, 287
Peas, distilled, 40
Penalty, for free Negro, 29
Penitentiaries, 191
Penland, Reverend N. A., used ardent spirits, 19
Pensacola, Florida, 5-6, 236-237
Percer, Reverend D. L., prohibition party, 82
Perry County, 75, 107, 274
Petitions, 38, 167
Pettus, Senator E. W., 145
Pettus, E. W., Jr., 204-205
Phelps, Homer, shot while running away from still, 214
Philip, Uncle, on the story of Tom Smith—Be ware of the first drink, 24
Phister, A. B., 34
Physiology, effects of alcohol, 57
Pickens County, special act for, 72; votes wet, 73; votes dry, 113-114, 123
Pickenville Register, 21
Pickering, Timothy, Secretary of State, 9
Pickett, Dr. Edward, 21

Pike County, crime decreasing, 77, 136, 160, 177
Pilloried, Shortridge was, 36
Pine Belt News, 66
Pitchlyn, John, agent to the Choctaw Nation, 9
Pitts, Alexander D., 108
Pitts, W. L., 107
Plank, prohibition party, 193
Planters, carried their liquor well, 26
Platforms, 220-221
Pleasant Valley Presbyterian church, formed the first temperance society, 20
Pledge, 14, 43, 208, 284
Pliant tool, 180
Plight, 246
Polemic, 81
Policewoman, on drinking among women, 255
Politics, temperance enters, 28
Polls, 147
Pope, 203. *See* Senator J. T. Heflin
Pork, 12
Portuguese wine, 3
Postcards, 208
Pot, 2
Potatoes, distilled, 40
Pounds, sterling, 4-5
Powell, R. H., editor, 74, 78-79
Power, Tryone, 26
Pray, 117
Prayer meetings, 146
Presbyterian Church, on temperance, 15-16, 49, 56, 60, 89, 102, 104, 112, 114, 182
Presbyterian Church, U.S.A., on communion, 63
Presbyterian Societies, 18
Presbyteries, 61
Prescriptions, call for liquor, 110
President, society, 21; W.C.T.U., 53
Press, on temperance, 24
Price, Kyle B., temperance orator, 137, 143
Priests, 121
Prime-of-lifers, torch-light parade, 153
Primitive Baptists, never vote temperance ticket, 15, 23, 34, 36
Prisoners, violating dry laws, 289
Probate Judges, call elections, 44
Probation, discretion of the courts, 232
Proceeds, allocation of, 260
Procession, local optionists celebrate, 171
Proclamation, 119
Professors, protect them, 37
Program, local option, 36
Prohibition repeal, 235
Prohibitionist, 82
Prohibition party, formed, 80, 84
Promiscuous shooting, 214
Propaganda, 15, 25, 217

INDEX

Provincius, 7
Pro Tem, 105, 161, 183
Prostitutes, 275
Protestant, 115
Protestant Bigotry, 199
Protestantism, 209
Province, 4
Puchshannubbia, 9
Puerile, 147
Pugnacious, 206
Pulpit, 49, 115
Pulque shops, 7
Purify, John, 156, 187
Puritanical, 47
Pussy-cat, Hoover used such words, 222

Qualms, right or wrong, 13
Queries, answering, 31
Questionnaire, views on temperance, 34
Quitting, pulpit, 207
Quo warranto, test validity of law, 166

Rabb, C. S., 102
Racketeering, 197, 245
Radical, 155
Rage, 197
Randolph County, 27; votes dry, 72, 77, 114
Raskob, John J., Chairman of Democratic Party, Republican and wet, 197, 201, 203, 205; Vice-President of A.A.P.A., 208, 209, 217; would commit party to repeal, 219
Ratcliff, P. D., 103
Rates, license, 42
Rechab, Baptist church, 17
Records, not well kept, 15
Recommendation, for license, 4
Reconstruction, for temperance forces, 50
Reese, Senator H. F., 120
Referendum, 232, 271, 272
Reflector, 102
Reform, Baptist Church, 113, 192
Relaxation, 40
Relief, from abuses of prohibition, 161
Religion, 35
Religious, 199
Rencher, C. R., 75
Rendezvous, 101
Repeal, 208, 213, 231
Representatives, 13, 216
Republicans, 42, 80, 83, 84, 195, 197, 206, 209
Republican National Convention, adopts plank on prohibition, 220
Repudiated, State Democratic Convention, 156
Repudiation, religious freedom, 199; Raskob's, 208
Resign, see A. K. Callahan
Resolutions, 76

Restaurants. *See* liquor
Retail, 41, 173
Retail Liquor Dealers' Association of Mobile, license fee raised, 111
Return, to county local option, 149
Revenue, 29, 91
Reversed, 214
Rice, Fleetwood, 107; opposes dispensary, 114
Rice, Judge James, 262
Richardson, Judge J. C., 124
Richardson, Schuyler, 274
Richter *v.* State of Alabama, 125
Riddle, D. Hardy, candidate for governor on prohibition ticket, 279; defeated, 281
Rights, abridged, 151
Riley, Reverend B. F., 75; opposes prohibition party, 80
Ring, 195
Road, how financed, 5
Roadhouse, 267, 269
Roak, George, 238
Roanoke, 72; profits from dispensary, 93
Roberts, Alvin, on Safe and Sane League, 145
Roberts, Hugh W., 158
Robertsdale, liquor store, 260
Robinson, A. J., 75
Robinson, Senator Joe, telegram from Alfred E. Smtih, 197
Roche, Reverend Father, 53
Rock Mills, 72
Rockribbed, democrats, 228
Rogers, C. M. A., 244
Rogersville, Murphy Club, 48
Roman Catholic, Alfred E. Smith, 205, 208
Romans, Bernard, on drinking, 3
Roosevelt, Franklin D., conservative wet, 219; checkmates Raskob, 220; endears himself to drys, 221; favors the repeal plank, 222, 227-228
Round Island Baptist Church, expells minister for drunkenness, 15
Rowe, N. M., 107
Rudy, Captain, confiscated whiskey, 10
Rum, 5-6, 9, 59
Rushton, Ray, 154; candidate for United States Senate on Local Option ticket, 180, 213
Russell, E. P., 246

Sabbath, 49
Sabin, Charles H., 217
Sackcloth, get out of, 223
Saddle, prohibitionists in, 183
Saddle bags, ministers carry favorite brands in them, 26
Sailors, amount of credit, 5-6
Saloon, preferred to dispensary, 98, 112; number, 172

INDEX 321

Saloon opposition League, 169
Saloonkeepers, want license lowered, 42
Samford, T. D., 205
Sampson, J. B., 53
Sanders, A. C., on lobbying, 160
Sargent, Governor Winthrop, on selling liquor to Indians, 9
Savage, Reverend D., 53
Schools, in the temperance cause, 24, 246
Schoolhouse, whether liquor to be sold within prescribed distance of, 44
Schoolmaster, on temperance, 14
Schoolteachers, 233
Scotsboro, 202
Screws, W. W., 25
Sea Girt, New Jersey, 222
Searcy, A. R., 53
Searcy, M. S., 53
Seay, Thomas, candidate for governor, 81; a moral question, 84
Secede, Mobile prepared to, 121
Secrecy, Sons of Temperance, 23
Secretary, 47
Seed, Walter D., whiskey or no whiskey, 137; candidate for lieutenant-governor, 149; elected, 155-156; candidate for governor on prohibition ticket, 176, 178
Selective Draft Act, no liquor to be sold to men in uniform, 190
Selma, Maidens of Temperance, 22, 53, 106, 149, 205, 278
Selma Journal, 139
Selma Times, 66, 153, 155
Session, 4
Sessions, W. L., chairman of dry campaign committee, 115
Sheaves, bringing in, 117
Shehan, Will T., charges against B. B. Comer, 177
Sheffield, 91, 279
Sheffield Standard, 168
Shelby County, written consent of voters required to get license, 38
Shelby Sentinel, 66
Sheppard, Senator, attempts to get Congressional action against liquor, 186
Sheriff, sober, 26; to hold elections, 38
Sherlock, Cris, candidate for governor on wet ticket, 282
Shillings, credit in, 5
Shiloh church, expels minister for selling liquor, 17
Shipwright, could not get license to sell liquor, 5
Shortridge, George R., candidate for governor, 36
Shorter, Governor John G., 40
Shouse, Jouett, President of A.A.P.A., 217

Sibert, Mrs. Charles, on unfermented wine for communion, 63; bishop disapproves resolution to use unfermented wine for communion, 64
Signatures, 115
Silly, Prohibition party of Alabama, 85
Simmons, C. G., O'Neal the best lost fellow, 152
Simpson's decision, Richter v. the State, 126
Sin, a product of ignorance, 14, 49
Sinner, drinks, 26
Sipsey Valley Baptist Association, legislators committed to local option, 104
Skeggs, Judge W. E., denies mandamus, 124
Slaton, Mrs. S. T., lectures on temperance, 258; on educational fund program, 285
Slaves, 5; could not buy liquor, 29
Sloan, Dr. Leon, Superintendent of Anti-Saloon League, 229
Slogans, 117
Smashing, wet victories, 259
Smith, to get no license, 5
Smith, Alfred E., disapproves prohibition, 195; as wet as the ocean, 196; favors local government, 197; circulars attack him, 198; W.C.T.U. opposes Smith, 200, 203; not to vote for Smith, 204; Smith had not bolted, 206; daily papers endorse Smith, 207; prohibition and religion the main issues, 209
Smith, A. G., 136
Smith, Brooks, 156
Smith, Mrs. D. R., for modification, 239
Smith, Reverend E. P., 113
Smith, Major Emmet P., opposes the election of Alfred E. Smith, 203
Smith, John V., 161; opposition to his bill, 164, 166
Smith, Mrs. Lamar, President of W.C.T.U., 240
Sobriety, 151
Societies, temperance, 15
Sols, 2
Sommerville, Ormand, 156
Sons of Temperance, formed, purposes, features, membership, 22-23; oppose the license system, 30; sponsor local option law, 32; enter politics, 35; failure in politics, 37; efforts reorganize after the Civil War, 44-45
Sorrell, Mrs. N. F., on unfermented wine for communion, 64
South, teachers should be chosen from, 37; Methodist Episcopal Church, 48, 59, 106, 157; A. R. P. Synod of, 192, 287
South Alabama, Presbytery, 18

INDEX

South Alabamian, 198
South Carolina, 95
South Western Baptist, 30
Southern Advocate, 19, 25, 31, 37, 50
Southern Baptist Church, endorses instruction in Sunday schools, 55
Southern Democrat, 155
Southern Passenger Association, 102
Southern States, temperance society required to admit Negroes, 46
Southern Times, 25
Spain, 1; provision of treaty, 29
Spanish, 3, 7-8
Sparks, Chauncey, give State Liquor Store a chance, 280-281; favors state-wide referendum, 282; pledge renewed in his inaugural, 283
Speake, Judge D. W., 125
Spragins, Senator Robert E., opposes local option bill, 108; charges B. B. Comer, 141, 149, 156
Springville, local option election, 38
Spur, anti-saloon league, 102
Swann, Ensign, bought barrel of whiskey, 12
Square, whiskey displayed in, 31
Stagg, J. W., trustee of anti-saloon league, 103
Stallings, J. F., state committeeman, his blast, 136
Stanley, J. B. eggs thrown at his house, 71
State, Federation of Labor, 237
State-at-large, Hoover-Curtis electors, 202
State ABC Store, 251-254, 260, 266, 268
State Democratic Convention, requested to endorse local option, 80; favofs local option, 156
State Docket, mostly whiskey cases, 76
State Grand Divisions, Sons of Temperance, 23
State Highway Department, 271
State Temperance Convention, 35, 75
State *v.* Murphy, constitutionality of ABC Act upheld, 262
State-wide prohibition bill, vetoed by Governor Chas. Henderson, 184
Status quo, 157
Statutes, 35
Stayton, William H., President of A.A.P.A., 217
St. Clair County, local option election, 38; local option by precincts, 39; special act for, 72; many whiskey cases, 76; dry by special act, 114, 239
Steagall, Henry B., 206
Steam boats, cost of license, 30, 98
Steele, Reverend I. D., 102
Stephens, M. S., name on prohibition ticket, 83

Stewart, Oliver W., President of Flying Squadron and favors Eighteenth Amendment, 229
Stiles, J. P., Probate Judge of Jefferson County, 169
Stills, destroyed, 289
St. John, Prohibition candidate for President, 80
Stoddard, Lieutenant Colonel, 12
Street, Judge Oliver D., 202, 203; publicity, 208
Stripes, penalty of twenty-five, 29
Stuart, M., on communion, 62
Students, liquor not to be sold to them, 29
Sugar, forbidden to be distilled, 40, 203
Sugar of lead, 95
Sumter County, money leaving, 91
Sunday Schools, temperance material added to the curriculum, 55-57, 75, 110, 129
Sunday, 110, 269
Superintendent, 6
Supernumerary judge, issues injunction, 122
Supreme Court, 124, 130, 166
Sweat, M. M., secretary of prohibition convention, 75, 103
Sweden, 86
Sylocoga, 67
Symbols, temperance orders, 23
Synod of Alabama, endorses temperance, 18; intemperance declining or does not exist, 60; A.R.P. of the South, 175

Taft, President H., vetoed Webb-Kenyon Bill, 206
Talbot, Clayton, retailing, 11
Talladega, 223
Talladega County, special act for, 72; voted wet, 73; votes to retain saloons, 94, 113; votes dry, 114, 245
Tallapoosa County, votes dry, 161
Tammany Hall, 210, 217
Tammanyite, and Roman Catholic, 205
Tanner, not eligible for retail license, 5
Tanner, John T., temporary chairman of prohibition party convention, 78; elected secretary, 79, 82; candidate for governor, 83
Tanner, W. P., church lukewarm to temperance, 48; elected president temperance convention, 75
Tauton, Lee, killed while running away from still, 214
Taverns, 4, 10
Tavernkeepers, complain license too high, 11
Taylor, Edward F., reward to sustain veto, 250
Taylor, John M., 21

INDEX

Taylor, Mrs. M. D., charter member of W.O.N.P.R., 223
Taylor, W. C., 244
Teachers, keep them sober, 37
Teachers-in-service, 284
Teague, 2
Tears, women burst into, 189
Teasley, Charles B., 187
Teaspoon, put out hell, 79
Telegrams, 54
Temperance, state convention, 75
Temperance Alliance, 79, 84, 277
Temperance Banner, 61
Temperance Herald, 52, 65
Temperance Legions, 56
Temperance Times, 26
Templars of Temperance, for white people only, 47
Tennessee, 50, 221
Tennessee Conference, 20
Tenney, Dr. S. M., curator for Presbyterian Foundation, 56
Territory, Mississippi, 8
Terry, Hill, 245
Texas, 186
Textbooks, contain lessons on temperance, 14
Thanksgiving service, for dry victory in Jefferson County, 118
Thomas, Elias P., 108, 110
Thomas, General George L., on prohibition party ticket, 83
Thomasville, 108
Thompson, votes dry, 73
Thompson, J. F., 137
Thompson, W. W., 25
Thornton, H. L., 21
Thousands, turned out to parade, 117
Threadbare, prohibition issue is, 194
Tigers, complacency to, 91, 105, 115, 175
Tillman, Benjamin, introduced the dispensary into South Carolina, 86; on bad whiskey, 95
Timothy, Paul's admonition to, 26, 37
Tippling houses, where liquor only was sold, 4, 10
Tirade, leads to throwing eggs, 209
Tobacco, used to adulterate liquor, 29, 95
Tomkins, Oscar L., 269
Torchlight procession, in Birmingham to celebrate wet victory, 171
Toulman, Judge Harry, 9
Tourist camps, 269
Tracy, R. S., 57
Trader's Bank, 118
Treating, with liquor to get votes, 31
Trenton, votes dry, 73
Tri-Cities Daily, 139, 276
Troy, votes dry, 73, 91, 149, 177

Troy Messenger, 71, 76, 139
Trucks, confiscated, 289
Tunstall, A. M., campaign manager for repeal, 226-227
Tuscaloosa, to suppress election treating, 53, 79, 86, 93, 107, 113-114, 136, 149, 206, 239
Tuscaloosa Baptist Association, against treating to secure votes, 32
Tuscaloosa Blade, 50
Tuscaloosa County, greatest dry victory, 172; legislator punished, 219
Tuscaloosa Gazette, 89
Tuscaloosa Presbytery, 19
Tuscaloosa Temperance Society, pledge, 32
Tuscumbia, 19, 91, 149; votes wet, 168; unfortunate incident, 276
Tuskegee, 60, 108, 183
Tuskegee News, 67, 76
Twenty-first Amendment, repeals eighteenth, 225

Ugarte Y Loyola, 7
Underwood, Clarence, keeps lights on in church in Greenville for drys, 81
Underwood, Oscar W., local optionist, candidate for United States Senate, 179; accepts prohibition, 194; elected to Senate, 195
Unfair, plan to ratify twenty-first Amendment, 225
Unfermented wine, urged by W.C.T.U., 54; grape juice displaces wine for communion, 62-65
Uniforms, worn by temperance organization, 15
Union, Catholic Total Abstinence, 53
Union Signal, 54
Union Springs, 93
Union Springs Herald, 50, 66, 78
Union Springs Journal, 52
Union Temperance Society of North Alabama, formed and purposes set forth, 20
United States, 29, 214
United States Congress, 41
United States Internal Revenue Reports, 99
University of Alabama, retailers forbidden to sell to students of, 29, 229

Vagrants, drunks as, 268
Valley, counties in the Tennessee, 259
Valley Creek Presbyterian Church, 15
Vestry, official body of an Episcopal church, 4
Veto, passed over President Wilson's, 190; near-beer bill passed over Governor Miller's, 232

Vetoed, bill to prevent selling liquor within three miles of Athens Female Institute, 37; bill for State-Wide Prohibition, 184
Veterans, in temperance cause, 46
Viceroys issue ordinances on drink, 7
Victory, wets flushed with, 149
Villification, flood gates of, 147
Violation, 6
Violators, 29
Virginia, religious freedom, 199, 206
Voice of Temperance, 277
Volstead Act, 190, 208, 212, 228
Walker, Mayor A. E., defends Emmet O'Neal, 153
Walker, Harry, Speaker of the House, 246
Walker County, tax payers recommend, 39, 72, 83; votes for dispensary, 84, 262
Walker County Tribune, 267
Wall Street, F. D. Roosevelt too dry for, 220
Wallace, J. R., prohibitionists and bootleggers, 250
Wardens of the church, have charge of liquor tax, 4
Warren, John F., editor of temperance paper, 25, 30
Walsh, David L., 221
Walsh, Thomas J., staunch dry and permanent chairman, 221
Washington, George, owned and operated a private distillery, 242
Washington County, reverts to dry column, 278
Washingtonians, society of reformed drunkards, 14, 22
Wasson, Reverend S. E., organizer of Anti-Saloon League of Alabama, 102; vice-president, 103; trustee, 137
Waters, Private John, deprived of whiskey rations, 12
Waverley, 202
Weakley, Judge S. D., attorney for drys, 127; author of statutory prohibition, 129; supports amendment, 141; firm of, 143; author of bone-dry bill, 188, 213
Webb, Atticus, Anti-Saloon League official, 289
Webb, J. O., Hoover-Curtis elector, 202
Webb-Kenyon Anti-Shipping Act, 179
Weiss, Major Jake, Senator from Mobile and liquor dealer, 111; liquor lobbyist, 110
Wellborn, Senator M. B., 264-265; on results of election in Calhoun County, 268
West Alabamian, 50
West Indian Rum, 8

Western Company of Louisiana, 2
Westerville, Ohio, Anti-Saloon League Headquarters, 229
Wet, John J. Raskob, 197; vote dry and drink wet, 206
Wetumpka, 24
Wheat, under ban, 40
Whigs, against Sons of Temperance, 34
Whip, party coerces, 168
Whipping, twenty-five stripes, 29
Whiskey, election treating with, 31; extreme man, 176
White Ribbon, official organ of W.C.T.U., 54, 193
Whitten, L. F., delegate to National Anti-Saloon League, 60; prohibition party, 83
Whitten, M. L., Grand Worthy Christian Templar, 45
Wholeheartedly, drys claim legislature, 178
Wideman, Mrs. James H., 225
Wiggens Hotel, Emmet O'Neal lost, 152
Wilcox Banner, 96
Wilcox County, distillery erected in, 41; dry law working well, 77; local option election, 114, 156
Wilkinson, Horace C., tests validity of ABC Act, 262
Wilkinson, General James, 1
Willard, Frances, President of National W.C.T.U., 62
Williams, Mrs. Claudia, drinking by women and arrests, 255
Williams, Welder, possessed liquor in dry county, 262
Williams, Dr. W. H., 138
Williams, Travis, 196
Wilson, John F., 108
Wilson, Reverend R. A., organizer of I.O.G.T., 45
Wilson, President Woodrow, 187
Wine, 1, 5, 37, 194
Wine a Mocker, Sunday School lesson, 56
Winston, John A., 34; elected Governor, 36; vetoes special dry acts, 38
Wisconsin Malters' Club, appeals for funds, 216
Witherspoon, W. B., candidate for governor, 85
Wizard of Temperance, Reverend Sam Morris, 273
Woman's Christian Temperance Union, formed, purposes, incorporators, 53; number of students reached, 55-56; hygiene in public schools, 56-57, 60, 61; on communion, 62-65, 75, 82, 84; endorses dispensary, 87, 94, 103, 113, 122, 129, 135, 140; pinned on badges,

INDEX

162; publicity, 182, 186, 192; urge law enforcement, 193; oppose Alfred E. Smith, 200; grieved at his nomination, 200; Judge Hugh Locke defends, 201, 202, 208; oppose repeal of state dry laws; schisism in ranks over referendum, 237; parade in Montgomery, 241; scholarship fund, 284; temperance through education, 285

Woman suffrage, prohibition for, 65

Women's Organization for National Prohibition Reform, 223, 225, 239

Women, 288
Woodcliffe, Mrs. L. C., 53
Woodruff, George T., 256
Woodlawn, 115
Workers, 77
Wounded, revenue officers, 42

Yankee, meddling, 28
Young, Dr. G. W., assistant superintendent of National Anti-Saloon League, 102; lobbyist, 105, 106
Young, Wayne, 26

THE JAMES SPRUNT STUDIES IN HISTORY AND POLITICAL SCIENCE

No. 1. PERSONNEL OF THE CONVENTION OF 1861. By John Gilchrist McCormick } (Out of print.)
LEGISLATION OF THE CONVENTION OF 1861. By Kemp P. Battle.

No. 2. THE CONGRESSIONAL CAREER OF NATHANIEL MACON. By Edwin Mood Wilson. (Out of print.)

No. 3. THE LETTERS OF NATHANIEL MACON, JOHN STEELE, AND WILLIAM BARRY GROVE, WITH NOTES. By Kemp P. Battle. (Out of print.)

No. 4. LETTERS AND DOCUMENTS RELATING TO THE EARLY HISTORY OF THE LOWER CAPE FEAR, WITH INTRODUCTION AND NOTES. By Kemp P. Battle. (Out of print.)

No. 5. MINUTES OF THE KEHUKEY ASSOCIATION, WITH INTRODUCTION AND NOTES. By Kemp P. Battle. (Out of print.)

No. 6. DIARY OF A GEOLOGICAL TOUR BY ELISHA MITCHELL IN 1827 AND 1828, WITH INTRODUCTION AND NOTES. By Kemp P. Battle.

No. 7. WILLIAM RICHARDSON DAVIE: A MEMOIR. By J. G. de Roulhac Hamilton.
LETTERS OF WILLIAM RICHARDSON DAVIE, WITH NOTES. By Kemp P. Battle.

No. 8. THE PROVINCIAL COUNCIL AND COMMITTEES OF SAFETY IN NORTH CAROLINA. By Bessie Lewis Whitaker.

VOL. 9, No. 1. THE SOCIETY FOR THE PROPAGATION OF THE GOSPEL IN THE PROVINCE OF NORTH CAROLINA. By D. D. Oliver.
CORRESPONDENCE OF JOHN RUST EATON. Edited by J. G. de Roulhac Hamilton.

VOL. 9, No. 2. FEDERALISM IN NORTH CAROLINA. By Henry M. Wagstaff.
LETTERS OF WILLIAM BARRY GROVE. Edited by Henry M. Wagstaff.

VOL. 10, No. 1. BENJAMIN SHERWOOD HEDRICK. By J. G. de Roulhac Hamilton.

VOL. 10, No. 2. BARTLETT YANCEY. By George A. Anderson.
THE POLITICAL AND PROFESSIONAL CAREER OF BARTLETT YANCEY. By J. G. de Roulhac Hamilton.
LETTERS TO BARTLETT YANCEY.

VOL. 11, No. 1. COUNTY GOVERNMENT IN COLONIAL NORTH CAROLINA. By W. C. Guess.

VOL. 11, No. 2. THE NORTH CAROLINA CONSTITUTION OF 1776, AND ITS MAKERS. By Frank Nash.
THE GERMAN SETTLERS OF LINCOLN COUNTY AND WESTERN NORTH CAROLINA. By Joseph R. Nixon.

VOL. 12, No. 1. THE GOVERNOR, COUNCIL, AND ASSEMBLY IN ROYAL NORTH CAROLINA. By C. S. Cooke.
LAND TENURE IN PROPRIETARY NORTH CAROLINA. By L. N. Morgan.

VOL. 12, No. 2. THE NORTH CAROLINA INDIANS. By James Hall Rand.

VOL. 13, No. 1. THE GRANVILLE DISTRICT. By E. Merton Coulter.
THE NORTH CAROLINA COLONIAL BAR. By E. H. Alderman.

VOL. 13, No. 2. THE HARRINGTON LETTERS. Edited by H. M. Wagstaff.

VOL. 14, No. 1. THE HARRIS LETTERS. Edited by H. M. Wagstaff.

VOL. 14, No. 2. SOME COLONIAL HISTORY OF BEAUFORT COUNTY. By F. H. Cooper.

VOL. 15, Nos. 1 and 2. PARTY POLITICS IN NORTH CAROLINA, 1835-1860. By J. G. de Roulhac Hamilton.

VOL. 16, No. 1. A COLONIAL HISTORY OF ROWAN COUNTY, NORTH CAROLINA. By S. J. Ervin. (Out of print.)

VOL. 16, No. 2. THE DIARY OF BARTLETT YANCEY MALONE. Edited by Wm. Whatley Pierson, Jr.
THE PROVINCIAL AGENTS OF NORTH CAROLINA. By Samuel James Ervin, Jr.

VOL. 17, No. 1. THE FREE NEGRO IN NORTH CAROLINA. By R. H. Taylor.
SOME COLONIAL HISTORY OF CRAVEN COUNTY, NORTH CAROLINA. By Francis H. Cooper.

VOL. 17, No. 2. JOURNAL OF A TOUR OF NORTH CAROLINA BY WILLIAM ATTMORE, 1787. Edited by Lida Tunstall Rodman.

VOL. 18, Nos. 1 and 2. SLAVEHOLDING IN NORTH CAROLINA: AN ECONOMIC VIEW. By Rosser Howard Taylor.

VOL. 19, No. 1. PRESENT STATUS OF MODERN EUROPEAN HISTORY IN THE UNITED STATES. By Chester Penn Higby.

VOL. 19, No. 2. STUDIES IN HISPANIC-AMERICAN HISTORY. Edited by W. W. Pierson, Jr.

VOL. 20, No. 1. NORTH CAROLINA NEWSPAPERS BEFORE 1790. By Charles Christopher Crittenden.

VOL. 20, No. 2. THE JAMES A. GRAHAM PAPERS, 1861-1884. Edited by H. M. Wagstaff.

VOL. 21, Nos. 1 and 2. THE DEMOCRATIC PARTY IN ANTE-BELLUM NORTH CAROLINA, 1835-1861. By Clarence Clifford Norton.

VOL. 22, Nos. 1 and 2. MINUTES OF THE NORTH CAROLINA MANUMISSION SOCIETY, 1816-1834. Edited by H. M. Wagstaff.

VOL. 23, No. 1. THE PRESIDENTIAL ELECTION OF 1824 IN NORTH CAROLINA. By Albert Ray Newsome.

VOL. 23, No. 2. THE SECESSION MOVEMENT IN NORTH CAROLINA. By Joseph Carlyle Sitterson.

VOL. 24, No. 1. JEFFERSONIAN DEMOCRACY IN SOUTH CAROLINA. By John Harold Wolfe.

VOL. 24, No. 2. GUIDE TO THE MANUSCRIPTS IN THE SOUTHERN HISTORICAL COLLECTION OF THE UNIVERSITY OF NORTH CAROLINA.

VOL. 25, No. 1. NORTH CAROLINA BOUNDARY DISPUTES INVOLVING HER SOUTHERN LINE. By Marvin L. Skaggs.

VOL. 25, No. 2. ANTE-BELLUM SOUTH CAROLINA: A SOCIAL AND CULTURAL HISTORY. By Rosser H. Taylor.

VOL. 26, No. 1. THE PROHIBITION MOVEMENT IN ALABAMA, 1702 TO 1943. By James Benson Sellers, Ph. D.

www.ingramcontent.com/pod-product-compliance
Lightning Source LLC
Chambersburg PA
CBHW021353290426
44108CB00010B/225